Understanding Kids, Play, and Interactive Design

Endorsements for *Understanding Kids, Play, and Interactive Design*

"Fortunately for us, Mark Schlichting has created this marvelous book. By understanding and thoughtfully explaining what children do in the Kingdom of Play, and how and why they do it, Mark has provided a wonderful resource to those of us who would create fresh, invigorating playthings."

—**Jesse Schell,** CEO, Schell Games; Distinguished Professor of the Practice of Entertainment Technology, Carnegie Mellon University; author of *The Art of Game Design: A Book of Lenses*

"Mark Schlichting's book, *Understanding Kids, Play, and Interactive Design*, combines deep wisdom about kids at play; comprehensive, clear (rare) understanding of play and "play science;" and the manifold practical routes to interactive game design. It is the magnum opus of a creative lifetime, full of usable details framed in engaging and visually captivating formats. As one steeped in the biology of play and its necessity for overall human well-being, Mark's book pioneers the blend of ever present technology with culture-enhancing guidance for the next generation of play-savvy designers. Belongs on every kids' play/game designer's bedside table."

—**Stuart Brown, M.D.,** Founder and President, The National Institute for Play; author of *Play: How it Shapes the Brain, Opens the Imagination, and Invigorates the Soul*

"Children play in order to have fun, not to learn; but learning is the side effect that, from an evolutionary perspective, is play's purpose. In this book, Mark Schlichting reveals a remarkably sophisticated and accessible understanding of play, learning, and children, including differences among children related to age, gender, culture, and personality. This book will go a long way toward connecting game designers to the minds of children."

—**Peter Gray,** Ph.D., Research Professor of Developmental Psychology, Boston College; author of *Free to Learn: Why Releasing the Instinct to Play Will Make Our Children Happier, More Self-Reliant, and Better Students for Life.*

"For over 25 years, Mark Schlichting has been an indispensable voice in children's media. To those of us who've had the pleasure to know him, he has been a voice of wisdom and reason. To those lucky children who have discovered the products he's created, his voice has been one of playfulness, surprise, and supreme silliness. In *Understanding Kids, Play, and Interactive Design*, Mark sets out the principles that have animated his work, starting with the deepest respect for the power and passion children bring to their play, and following up with a fierce determination to create digital spaces where that play flourishes. We will all benefit from the clear, well-argued, and generous way he shares his wisdom with the next generation of designers."

—**Scot Osterweil,** game designer, Creative Director, the Education Arcade, MIT

"This book must be in every children's interactive designer's library. In fact, *every* interactive designer should read it. . . a few times."

— **Warren Buckleitner, Ph.D.,** Editor, *Children's Technology Review*

"TeachersWithApps has had the honor and privilege of working directly with Mark Schlichting on several projects. He brings a wealth of knowledge, insight, and passion to everything he touches. Every page of Mark's new book brings another 'aha moment,' and I thought I knew a bit about children's digital space. This book is the bible and a *must read* for anyone involved in any area related to children, education, and technology."

— **Jayne Clare,** special education teacher, Co-Founder, TeachersWithApps

"Mark Schlichting's new book, *Understanding Kids, Play, and Interactive Design,* is a fantastic resource—the best I've ever seen—for interactive designers and others who want to understand play and learning. Mark is a master creator of great interactive experiences. He's dazzled us for decades with his really funny, endearing products. Now we can learn how he does it. Mark is thorough, precise, and incredibly generous to share his secrets of success. Reading Mark's book, I want to go create new apps, better than any I've created before. Hats off to Mark! Don't miss this book if you want to create great games children will love. It's a classic that teachers and others should have."

— **Ann H. McCormick,** Founder of The Learning Company and
Co-Founder of Learning Circle Kids

"*Understanding Kids, Play, and Interactive Design* is a much needed reference book in a space which previously has had little focused attention. Mark has created a very thorough and comprehensive guide which is both great for beginners and for more established developers in the field looking to further develop. I especially commend him on bringing gender and diversity issues to the forefront, since this is an important matter for our industry which is too often overlooked."

— **Björn Jeffery,** former CEO and Co-Founder, Toca Boca

"Despite what the rest of the world believes, developing successful and engaging interactive products for children is anything but easy. I've worked in the children's industry all of my adult life, and with every passing year have asked why a singular guiding source on how to make engaging interactive products for children does not exist. Finally the industry has a great new book, rich with professional best practices, case studies, and helpful advice from seasoned professionals. With Mark's new book, the children's industry takes one giant step forward, and end users around the world can't wait for the results!"

— **Scott Traylor,** CEO, 360Kid and VP of Software Design, Wonder Workshop

Understanding Kids, Play, and Interactive Design

How to Create Games Children Love

Mark Schlichting

CRC Press
Taylor & Francis Group
Boca Raton London New York

CRC Press is an imprint of the
Taylor & Francis Group, an informa business

CRC Press
Taylor & Francis Group
6000 Broken Sound Parkway NW, Suite 300
Boca Raton, FL 33487-2742

© 2016 Mark Schlichting
CRC Press is an imprint of Taylor & Francis Group, an Informa business

No claim to original U.S. Government works

Printed on acid-free paper

International Standard Book Number-13: 978-0-367-07525-5 (Hardback)

Visit the Taylor & Francis Web site at
http://www.taylorandfrancis.com

and the CRC Press Web site at
http://www.crcpress.com

This book is dedicated to all the children who may someday
be directly or indirectly touched by it.

To my children, Jerome, Jesse, and Aaron;
my grandchildren, Roman, Ryven, Cayden, and Theo;
and my stepdaughter, Nicole.
What they have taught me is immeasurable.

And to my beloved partner, Barbara Chase,
without whose love, dedication, and amazing skill set
this book might have never seen the light of day.

Table of Contents

Foreword

This is a book about a secret place.

A secret place called the Kingdom of Play.

The Kingdom of Play is vast, and only children are allowed to live there. Of course, we were all children once, and so naturally we were all once citizens of the Kingdom. Unfortunately, we can never fully remember it, probably because we are different people now than we were then. Adults tend to remember the Kingdom of Play as a place of rest, and while parts of it are gloriously restful and relaxing, in reality, it is far more often a place of challenge and risk-taking. The Kingdom challenges children physically, mentally, socially, emotionally, and spiritually. Play takes enormous energy, and well it should, for we are most alive when we play: play is how we explore the world, and how we learn best. This is why great educators must understand play. But how can we understand it, if we are forbidden to enter the Kingdom? Perhaps "forbidden" is too strong a word. After all, adults may visit, for a few minutes now and then, but with our adult minds we think adult thoughts, and awkwardly stumble, fumble, and tumble back into the adult world.

But we need entry, desperately! The Kingdom is full of what children love best: toys, games, and stories. Ironically, these are mostly created by adults. While adults are not welcome in the Kingdom, the toys, games, and stories adults create are very welcome there indeed. Children visit the adult world, peruse the things we make for them, and take the ones they like into the Kingdom. The very best ones take root in the Kingdom's culture, and become part of the landscape of Play for years, decades, or even centuries. If only we could get in to see it happen!

Fortunately for us, Mark Schlichting has created this marvelous book. By understanding and thoughtfully explaining what children do in the Kingdom of Play, and how and why they do it, Mark has provided a wonderful resource to those of us who would like to create fresh, invigorating playthings. This book is a map to the Kingdom and an almanac of the goings on there, but most importantly, it is a passport, once again permitting you entry (*Finally! At last! It has been so long!*) to the Kingdom of Play. It will let you stay long enough for Mark to give you a thorough tour of the major landmarks, and to remind you (for you were once a citizen yourself) of the local customs and practices.

What gives Mark the credentials to serve as tour guide to this magical place? Mark is a digital pioneer who has devoted his life to shaping new media to improve the lives of children. I first encountered his work when I was at Disney, where his Living Books were considered exemplars of how best to create engaging, enriching digital story experiences for children. Later, I got to know Mark personally at the annual Dust or Magic conference, the best gathering for people who care about creating top quality digital media for kids. As much as I learned from studying his Living Books, I learned even more talking to Mark. He always had such wise things to say because he knew so much about how children think and what they care about. Naturally, when I heard he was planning to put his lifetime of wisdom into a book, I was excited, and now that the book is a reality, I am pleased to say that it has exceeded my expectations in every way.

There are many books that study play academically, from a great distance. There are other books that give tips for making great games. But if you would like to understand the practical realities of play, so as to design the most powerful and transformative play experiences, I know no better way than *Understanding Kids*. Because Mark's career has spanned decades, his guidance isn't rooted just in today's fleeting technology but instead is presented in a timeless way, making it good advice for the technologies of yesterday, today, and tomorrow, covering crucial topics such as:

The etiquette of play: There are rituals and etiquette to play that most adults have forgotten about. Mark carefully reminds us of these – for in any kingdom, even the Kingdom of Play, if you gauchely ignore manners and customs, you yourself will be ignored. Mark reminds us of the importance of designing an invitation to play, not wasting a child's time, and always remembering that the child is in charge of the play experience. Adults have the embarrassing tendency to ignorantly violate the manners of the Kingdom of Play, causing children to respond (appropriately) with eye rolls, frustration, and a quick tap of the "home" button.

Sorcery: Mark reminds us of what computers really are: magic boxes. Whether hiding in TVs, phones, or virtual reality systems, computers are magic boxes with rich powers that fascinate children, and this makes them quite welcome in the Kingdom of Play. These magic boxes can tell stories, have conversations, make things appear and disappear, solve problems, even create and destroy whole worlds. Using these powers to the utmost effect is the central purpose of this book.

Temporary parenthood: Mark is well aware that the best digital experiences are treated by the child as a surrogate parent, and he thoughtfully reminds us that our experiences should do what good parents do: encourage, allow flexibility, communicate clearly, set a good example, be patient, and treat children with love and respect.

Children change: The Kingdom of Play is a multidimensional space, and one of those dimensions is time. A child's time in the Kingdom of Play is not static – far from it. The very point of the Kingdom is to allow children to change and grow. As such, what children do there changes drastically during their time there. How and why they play, who they play with, and what they play advances and changes, and Mark gives careful accounting and examples of how and why play changes with age and how you as a designer can create experiences that help children to master the challenges of growing older.

The truth about education: Mark understands that for children, there is no difference between learning and fun, only a difference between interesting and not interesting. Learning and growing is the very point of the Kingdom, and Mark gives excellent tips on engaging a child's curiosity.

Gender: Another dimension, fraught with peril for designers, is that of gender. This can be a minefield where one wrong step leads to designs rejected by kids, or worse, play patterns that make kids feel rejected, when something in a toy or game implies that it isn't "normal" for boys or for girls to engage in certain kinds of play. Mark handles this sensitive issue deftly, with due care and consideration, illustrating each potential pitfall with good and bad examples from the real world of toy and game design.

Special needs: Some children have special needs, and as a result, their experience in the Kingdom of Play can be different. Through touching examples and stories, Mark shows how it is not enough to think about how to "accommodate" special needs, but rather, how to help kids with special needs use play patterns to heal and grow in ways that happen best in the Kingdom of Play.

And there is so much more in this wonderful volume. We, as adults, can never again live in the magical place that is the Kingdom of Play. But by following Mark's wise advice, we can help give children what they need to make the most of their short time in the Kingdom. And this is important work, for how they spend their time in this magical place will determine what kind of adults they become, and the very shape of our society.

So, turn the page already—your tour begins now!

—Jesse Schell, CEO, Schell Games, Distinguished Professor of the Practice of Entertainment Technology, Carnegie Mellon University

Introduction

As a child I was totally captivated by the magic of animation and the fantasy worlds of children's picture books. I imagined going inside storybooks, such as Dr. Seuss's *Horton Hears a Who!*, to play with all the weird musical instruments and contraptions in Whoville. I followed my artistic passion as I grew, received a degree in Fine Art from California State University, East Bay, worked as a book publishing art director, and then went back to school to study traditional animation at San Francisco State University.

By 1986 I was a parent with Nintendo guilt. As the father of three boys, I watched their passion for *Mario Bros.* and dedication to achieving "level" mastery, but couldn't find a single program that was educational *and* fun enough to hold their attention in the same way. My boys, and their friends, would cooperate and work diligently for hours to get to the next level, but getting them to do 20 minutes of homework was an entirely different story. That was a big *aha* moment for me. My children inspired me to create programs that combined the attention-grabbing play aspects of great games with meaningful content. I wanted to develop titles my kids would love and learn from, and to inspire all children to follow their innate desire for play and learning through self-directed exploration and discovery.

My software career began as a freelance digital artist and animator for early floppy disc PC games like *Where in The World is Carmen San Diego?* But I already had a vision of highly interactive animated picture books for children, which was my inspiration for creating Living Books. Brøderbund Software, where I had taken a job to try and sell the concept of interactive storybooks, believed in my vision enough to allow me to create a small prototype in-house. Philips, the Dutch electronics hardware manufacturer, happened to come through on a tour and, based on my prototype, gave Brøderbund $500,000 to make a title that would run on a new television set-top box player they were developing. All of a sudden, my little demo concept became a development group, and we dived into the problem of turning the single-speed CD-ROM drives of the day into responsive multimedia players.

As the first full-featured prototype of Living Books began to take shape, I immediately tested it with kids to see what tickled them, and I talked with teachers to hear what they wanted for their classrooms. There were a lot of technical issues to work through, but when we shipped our first title two years later, we created the first cross-platform authoring system that delivered a full-color animated multimedia experience. Our first title, based on Mercer Mayer's book *Just Grandma and Me* (1991), was an instant hit. The software came with three languages on one disc (English, Spanish and Japanese) and shipped with a copy of the original paper book.

Microsoft bought 300 disc copies and sent them to their hardware manufacturers, with instructions that this software was the standard for multimedia, and it needed to run on their equipment.

Just Grandma and Me, along with the eighteen other Living Books titles, went on to sell tens of millions of copies in multiple languages. One of the original Living Books stories is from my own children's book *Harry and the Haunted House.* Many of these titles have been rereleased for computers, tablets, and mobile devices by Wanderful interactive storybooks..

As the CD-ROM market declined in 1997, I went on to oversee creative development at JuniorNet, an early online children's network, and in 2000 I founded

NoodleWorks Interactive, a children's interactive design consulting and production company. Over the years, it has been my pleasure and joy to bring many well-known and beloved children's properties to the world of interactive digital content. I was the first designer to bring to digital life the works of Dr. Seuss, Marc Brown (*Arthur),* Stan and Jan Berenstain (Berenstain Bears), Mercer Mayer (Little Critter and Little Monster), Jack Prelutsky (*New Kid on the Block),* and other children's favorites. I also had the pleasure of creating digital content with *Ranger Rick, Highlights for Children, Weekly Reader, Zillions* (Consumer Reports for Children), *Sports Illustrated for Kids,* and Jim Henson's *Bear in the Big Blue House,* among others. In 2012 NoodleWorks published our own first smartphone/tablet app, *Noodle Words.* It was featured by Apple and won numerous awards, including a KAPi Award for Best Educational Product—something my team and I are very proud of.

My life for the last 30 years has revolved and evolved around the practice of understanding kids and creating award-winning software for them. I've consulted and lectured at LeapFrog, Fisher-Price, Stanford University's Professional Publishing Courses, Game Developers Conference, the Smithsonian, Pearson, Consumer

Electronics Show, Dust or Magic Design Institute, Digital Kids, California Governor's Conference on Technology, and many more.

Designers' responsibility. To be a creator of interactive content for children is an important responsibility. Today's children are tomorrow's leaders, and to offer them engaging developmentally and emotionally appropriate content is a worthy investment in all of our futures.

Children are the living messages we send to a time we will not see.[1]
—**Neil Postman, author**

Children are drawn like magnets to technology, and this book is dedicated to supporting designers of children's technology in creating ever more wonderful and appropriate software activities. Many of the best children's interactive designers came into this line of work because of the sheer joy of creating lively content and because of the opportunity to make a difference for children. The pleasure of creating something fun each day (thinking like a kid) is a joy unto itself and helps sustain designers and producers through the sometimes grueling process of bringing products to launch.

Over the years, I have met and heard from many kids who have enjoyed my titles. Some were learning a second language; others benefitted from the sense of surprise and joy they got from playing. One autistic child learned to speak; many have learned to read; and all, I hope, felt empowered, gained a sense of control and confidence, and became agents of their own change even in their lives off the computer. To a designer there, is no greater satisfaction than to have one of your end users come back and tell you, often years later, what a difference your creation made to them.

Interactive software is no substitute for love and human touch, or the modeling of a great teacher or caring parent. Interactive media is, however, an opportunity for kids to explore subjects at their own pace in a learning process that interests and delights them. This book is offered as a toolkit for making emotionally satisfying digital toys. It is a gift to future designers and to all the children who may eventually touch something influenced by its contents. I hope it will help inspire new designers to see the world as kids see it, and to feel as kids feel.

Why read a book about interactive design? Especially if you've already had success in creating games or apps for kids, reading a book might not seem necessary. But where do you go to learn what you need to know—or to get new ideas to take your designs to the next level of child engagement? When I started out creating products for kids, there were no books on the subject. Interactive media was still in its infancy, and we made things up as we went along, paying attention to what worked and what didn't work. Many designers have an intuitive sense about what will tickle kids' funny bones or keep them playing a game for hours, but understanding why those choices work well, and learning other tips and techniques, can help you to take your design to the next level of engagement, or explain your choices to decision makers.

This book came about as a way of sharing insights empirically gathered, over decades of interactive media development, by myself and other children's designers. I have included as much emerging theory as possible in order to provide background for practical and technical aspects of design while still keeping the information accessible. My intent for this book is not to create an academic treatise but to furnish an insightful and practical manual for the next generation of children's interactive designers.

Play patterns are device independent. Even though I love to talk about new media technology and the wild possibilities of what we can do with it creatively, I have stayed away from tech talk in this book because technologies change way too fast. More importantly, technologies come and go, but the timeless nature of human interaction, childhood play, and innate learning are constant. In this book, you won't find code or recommendations about the best graphics program to use. What you will find is in-depth, usable knowledge about the art of creating great multi-media products that appeal to and delight children. You will learn what speaks to children at different ages, and how to apply that knowledge creatively. The intent is to inspire and inform you to become a greater designer and producer.

This book is meant as a resource both for designers who are just starting out and those who want a better understanding of their craft. It is a result of over 30 years of designing for kids and figuring out the science and psychology behind that magic moment when a child playing a game starts laughing out loud or shouting with excitement.

What I mean by *kids*. For the purposes of this book, I define *kids* as children between the ages of three and twelve. Below three they are toddlers and, at thirteen, they are officially teenagers, and by their own account, wish to not be considered "kids." The three-to-twelve age group is fun, lively, and full of rapid developmental changes, growth, and evolving social, intellectual, and physical skills. This book serves as a road map to help connect with the needs, wants, passions, and desires of children everywhere.

All play is educational. There is no one large section of this book that exclusively addresses "educational" content as a separate category, but examples of great educational content and how to create it are peppered throughout. When children are engaged in true play, they are learning, and the goal of this book is to help designers develop interactive experiences that tap into that natural desire to explore, no matter what the subject.

The term *interactive design* means different things to different people. What I consider most important in what I do is the philosophy behind the technology. This can be summarized in one sentence: *Connect with children's natural play instincts to empower their learning.* From the smallest detail of an interface to the largest concepts in a game, this idea informs everything I do. Even when designing a program specific to learning, natural play patterns are tremendously important. Why?

We all learn differently. If you go to a typical classroom, you'll see that some kids take to sitting at a desk with a book in front of them. Others wiggle around, look at anything but their books, make noise, cause distraction, and are generally unhappy or bored. They're not bad kids. They just don't learn best by sitting at a desk. The traditional institutional model of learning is not for everyone — it wasn't for me. Today, teachers are adding diverse approaches to educational content to reach kids who need something more than lectures and workbooks.

A huge component of helping kids learn is engagement. When a child is engaged, learning happens because the process has become like play. It's easy to make a flashcard for a kid to memorize, but it's better to foster a deeper kind of learning. When kids are happily engaged in playful learning games, they are not only spending time on task but also driving their own learning and creating a love of learning that will serve them throughout their lives. True play is part of emotional well-being. But, as a designer, how do you make that happen?

Play is universal. It transcends different kinds of learning modalities, meaning that kids learn more easily through play than through traditional classroom instruction. When kids play, they may not be learning spelling words or fractions, but they're learning. The point of an interactive game is to offer learning through play because play is the single most important thing kids do. It's what they want and what they are instinctively drawn to do. A lot of us understand play intuitively, but when we are faced with creating a play activity, we can't always duplicate the conditions for a spontaneous play experience. We can't always explain what makes something fun, but I have done my best in this book to share those little secret moments that set the conditions for play to happen spontaneously.

The stakes are high when it comes to inspiring children to learn. A child's instinct is to learn about the world. It is the designer's job to understand this instinct and to facilitate the process of learning. Play, passion, and purpose are the foundations of innovation. Part of why I wrote this book is to get designers thinking differently about the products they create, so they'll develop games and interfaces that offer opportunities to get kids excited about learning, thinking, and innovating.

Self-directed play is especially important. Over the years, modern kids have lost opportunities for self-directed play and exploration because these opportunities used to occur in the physical, external world outside of the home. One hundred years ago, kids may have had a ten-mile roaming radius. Even a few decades ago, kids wandered their neighborhoods, played in vacant lots, explored old buildings, collected bugs, you name it. They did dangerous stunts on their bikes or built secret forts. Their parent-free radius might have been a couple of miles. Now it is more common for all children's activities to have parental supervision. Play is often adult-controlled, or at least adult-sanctioned and -refereed. Free time to play outdoors, exploring with their peers, is a thing of the past for many children. The parent-free radius may be as limited as the backyard or the apartment when no adults are home, and play companions may be only siblings.

The situation doesn't need to be so grim. There are ways for children to explore, play, invent, and interact in digital worlds without the (adult-presumed) dangers associated with unsupervised real-world exploration. I'm not advocating digital worlds over real-world exploration, but in the absence of real-world possibilities, digital worlds can be—and are—a venue for children's creative impulses and self-directed endeavors. Design should support the kind of freedom kids had when they could wander their neighborhoods alone. Self-directed play experiences create adults who have the innovative and creative thinking to change the world. If you are not creating products that speak to kids and their natural desire to play, you are failing them.

Self-directed play allows development of a child's relationship with the world. Without self-directed play, it is very difficult to form that relationship. If kids can't have physical territory for self-directed play, let them have digital territory for wonder and exploration. Play is the starting point of this book because it is the starting point of learning. Leading developmental psychologists like Peter Gray emphasize this idea. The growth of the homeschooling and unschooling movements are evidence that traditional educational models or methods of instruction are failing many of our kids. It is our job to step up and provide ways for all kids to learn the skills they need to succeed.

Giving kids self-direction does something else: it creates intrinsic value in your product instead of external or imposed value. An imposed value could be to master fractions in order to pass a test. Intrinsic value offers inner motivation, engaged learning, real retention, growth, joy, and the desire to do and learn more. A great fractions program will offer that.

What you'll know by the end. Within these pages are hundreds of examples of effective interactive designs for children gathered over thousands of iterative cycles of user research and experimentation. With highlights gleaned from a wide history of products, this book contains the best and most usable design tricks and techniques for creating winning, child-focused experiences.

You will learn the best uses of color, animation, sound, character development, and interface design to get attention, support accessibility and usability, and generally empower kids' interactions. Most importantly, you'll learn how to understand and use play patterns to make great products that kids will love.

Our children are humanity's future. How we empower them and what we teach them will affect who they are as adults in the world. A child's job is to learn about the world they have been born into, and they are naturally voracious consumers of experiences and information. The quality, safety, age-appropriateness, and general joy of what we offer those open minds and hearts is very important. As designers of children's content, we have a responsibility to support and nurture their growing developmental process in the best ways possible. I hope by the end of this book you'll become an advocate of engaged **play**, and a master of the magic that comes with understanding the art of interactive design for children.

The great man is he who does not lose his child's heart.[2]
—Mencius, Confucian philosopher (372–289 B.C.)

PART 1

Sparking Interactive Magic

What makes an interactive experience compelling for children? What turns a simple click or tap into a magical interchange? Truly engaging interactive content for children is a blend of psychology and technology that listens and responds to kids' interests. To create great products for children, designers need to understand the nature and value of intrinsic play, dynamics of attention, and strategies for continued engagement. Knowing what delights and excites a child's imagination allows you to deliver a satisfying experience that brings kids back again and again.

Play is the only way the highest intelligence of humankind can unfold.[1]

Children are our real teachers.
Listen carefully and they will teach you
about the lost world
of carefree being in the present moment.

—Tibetan wisdom

CHAPTER 1

The Power of Play

Why start a book on design by talking about play? Because play is what children do, how they learn, and *what* they are doing while in a designer's program. For both the user and the designer, play is the primary component and the goal in good design. The bulk of this book is about how to create dynamic, engaging play experiences. It's important to begin by knowing more about play itself. Children often use the word play to describe activities they don't *have* to do. Kids consider play to be pleasurable, and, for them, tasks that aren't fun aren't play.[2]

For great children's design, play is not *an* essential ingredient, it is *the* essential ingredient. Play is instinctive for kids, and it is how they are wired to learn naturally. To recognize and comprehend different patterns of play is paramount in creating interactive experiences that invite and support continued involvement and exploration. This chapter covers various aspects of play, how to recognize it, and what it means to kids.

Play is often talked about as if it were a relief from serious learning. But for children, play is serious learning. . . . Play is the real work of childhood.[3]

—Mister Rogers

The Importance of Play

Play is not frivolous or trivial in its impact on humans. It is a basic biological and psychological function that supports our health and well-being in countless ways each day, lowering our stress, helping us learn new skills, or facilitating congenial relationships. When we play, we open ourselves to new possibilities, insight, and creativity. Playfulness helps us view life with optimism, create new options by testing alternatives, and develop social coping skills for a happier life.[4]

We have all seen the joy on children's shining faces when they are deeply engrossed and engaged in play. Play is what kids do best. It is essential to a joyful life, and it is an instrumental partner in learning.

What We Learn Through Play

In addition to social skills, children develop motor skills, spatial sense, creativity, organizational and classification skills, observational skills, abstract thinking, and hand–eye coordination through play. This applies to digital play as well as real-world physical play. For example, a game like *Tetris* involves many of the same spatial and pattern recognition skills as building with wooden blocks.[5] A good digital product will leave room for creativity, open-ended play, and self-direction, the same qualities that make more traditional types of play so important to growth and development.[6]

What else does play do? It may surprise you to know that pretend play improves language acquisition and facility with numbers.[7] Social play and collaboration also contribute to literacy.[8] Classification and observation skills employed in many digital games and activities are the same skills useful in learning science.[9]

Play is central even to games or products whose primary function is to teach, rather than to entertain. Children master new tasks and abilities through practice and repetition, and we are all more likely to repeat something when we enjoy doing it.

When children are playing and having fun, they are also more absorbed and more likely to spend extended time on task. This depth of concentration is important in all aspects of life, from childhood to adulthood. Not only that, but in a state of play, kids learn in a different—and often more effective—way than they do when they're working or studying in a traditional classroom setting.[10]

Play in the classroom. Play doesn't just help kids have better concentration and focus. It also reaches out to many kinds of learning styles, something traditional classroom methods can't always do. For example, a school system invested in the phonics method may have trouble reaching students who see things from a whole language approach, or a student with delayed motor skills may struggle to master early writing. Learning delays, ADHD, and autism-spectrum issues may compound the difficulty. Play distinguishes itself from traditional approaches because it engages innate learning patterns and methods.

A key characteristic of many kinds of play is the use of multiple senses (not just vision, but hearing, touch, and physical movement). When all the senses are engaged, it also happens that learning is improved.[11] Schools are catching onto this idea, and they're beginning to use methods like kinesthetic learning (e.g., learning reading through movement) to motivate nontraditional learners.[12]

Too much instruction impedes involvement. Although many children learn a great deal from direct instruction, research has shown that some pathways of discovery are closed off when too much direction is given.[13] Young children *decrease* exploratory play with a toy when its use is first demonstrated by an adult.[14] Similarly, the amount learned by playing a video game, which allows creativity and self-direction, can be drastically higher than the same content learned through a lecture.[15] Yet traditional styles of teaching in early primary school rely on this kind of direct pedagogy: students imitating teachers or teachers directly instructing students. Minimal or no instruction, on the other hand, leads to exploration, experimentation, and discovery, which means more time spent with the toy or game.[16] Regardless of whether you want a child to learn from your product, these principles apply. Understanding basic phenomena like these allows designers to make decisions that maximize the time a child wants to spend with a product.

> *Anyone who tries to make a distinction between education and entertainment doesn't know the first thing about either.*[17]
> —**Marshall McLuhan, philosopher of media theory**

Good design is important. Parents and teachers appreciate when a game or toy fulfills the dual purpose of entertaining as well as teaching. There are many products for children that are described as "educational" for parents' or teachers' sake, but many of these products fail to inspire the child. When an interactive title is designed correctly, children want to get their hands on it. Tapping into innate childhood play patterns and interests transforms a dull subject into a delightful experience. All of this means that what you do as a designer is incredibly important.

Respected psychologist Peter Gray draws two connections between play and learning that are useful for interactive designers to consider: First, that curiosity is complementary to play, motivating exploration and learning; second, that an exploration process often precedes play—a child will explore a new item or device, then, gaining confidence, will begin to play with it. The key takeaway for a designer is that a toy or game must offer opportunities for exploration and rewards for curiosity. These qualities will encourage play. A desire to play means a desire to repeat processes and practice skills, the foundation of mastery. Further, Gray writes that play is the primary component of what education specialist Sugata Mitra calls "minimally invasive education." The desire to learn comes from the desire to play, not from a promised external reward like a good grade.[18]

© Reana | Dreamstime.com

Kids are naturally curious. Young children in particular are naturally entranced by the magic of life. They love to explore and experiment. You can see this while watching children at the beach as they let grains of sand run slowly through their fingers. They are learning about relative size, granularity, gravity, texture, heat absorption, and more, but what they are doing is playing. They explore something until they have learned what they can about it at that moment. No one has to tell kids to do these things. They do it because it is in their DNA to interact with the world and uncover how things work. Curiosity drives them to experiment, and the consequent insight impels them into further research and experimentation. Curiosity is not something to be afraid of, as in the old admonition "Curiosity killed the cat," but a quality to be embraced, supported, and developed.

Play is a child's favorite way to learn. It's how they are wired. Through play, children can pretend, explore, and rehearse. They can creatively experiment with real-world problems, but in a safe environment. They can try things out without endangering themselves. After all, they are "just playing." Play is how we all best learn something new, and ultimately how we learn about learning. Ben Franklin was one of many philosophers to express the notion, "Tell me, and I forget. Teach me, and I remember. Involve me, and I learn." Interactive design is at its best when it creates inviting and supportive environments that replicate the involved, self-directed exploration and discovery that kids have been exhibiting for millennia.

Kids need self-directed play and independence. As mentioned in the introduction, today's children often have more limited opportunities for self-directed and independent play than children of the past. At the same time, some schools, constrained

by budgets and resources, are doing away with recess. Yet studies show that children who don't have time to play are less able to sit still in a classroom. Without recess, they also miss out on valuable socializing that helps them to learn interpersonal skills and conflict resolution.[19]

Play is an increasingly important aspect of school curricula because of its universality, its contributions to information retention, and its appeal to different learning modalities.

Stacy Barnett/Shutterstock.com

Game-based learning is gaining traction in school curricula[20] because educators recognize that children learn in many different ways, and play is one of the most effective. Educational games provide flexibility to teachers and offer students practice and learning via multiple methods and approaches, as well as a refreshing change from traditional instruction. Children often play on their tablets, phones, or computers, and this can happen in the classroom as well as at home. Increasingly, mainstream classrooms can access newly developed educational games released on the Apple and Android platforms, due to school district investment in mobile devices—as well as the Bring Your Own Device movement, which addresses the need for inclusive access to devices for students. In response, games for kids have experienced a flush of development in recent years, but they too often employ the "flashcard" mode of learning, where children are expected to watch, listen, and repeat, rather than engage with the content in an interactive, playful way.

You can't really fail at play.[21]
—J.C. Herz, author

Some students shut themselves off from learning due to frustration with early experiences, becoming "reading averse" for example, and even students who respond well to traditional pedagogy may become bored with it over time. In addition, being observed and monitored (i.e. graded, tested, evaluated) can decrease success in learning for those who are struggling.[22] Performance is improved when an activity is done for intrinsic reward.[23] Grades and test scores are an *extrinsic* reward. Play is something we do for ourselves (for intrinsic reward), not for a measurable result by others, even when we're competing on a sports team.

Educational games and toys, especially the short-form games that are most accessible to the classroom model,[24] can address this need for compelling, interactive learning that appeals to both traditional and nontraditional learners.

The Biological Roots of Play

Play, in all its forms, is not just a human trait but a mammalian trait. You can witness it with your pets and with mammals in the wild. In fact, we are drawn to, entertained by, and love watching animals at play. There is something so charming about it that it has spawned countless YouTube channels.

marchello/Shutterstock.com

Psychologist and play researcher Peter Gray discusses the seminal idea that "play in animals … is essentially an instinct to practice other instincts."[25] Young monkeys play at swinging between tree branches, lion cubs practice stalking and pouncing, and young zebras play at fleeing and dodging. While some survival abilities are innate (fight or flight, for instance), many of the skills we use in life are acquired through experience. Play is the way we (and other animals) practice and perfect these skills. The larger the brain size (in proportion to the body size), the more playful the animal.[26]

The desire for play comes from something instinctual and deep inside; it is a powerful motivating force that drives us to interact with the world. For designers of kids' content, true play is the essence of the kind of engagement we aspire to ignite.

iStock.com/Bobbi Gathings

Categories of Play Patterns

Children intuitively create learning experiences for themselves through a variety of creative play inventions that tend to fall into a few simple categories: **Active Body Play**, **Mastery Play**, **Social Play**, **Object Play**, **Creative Play**, and **Make-Believe Play**.[27] These classifications are for the purposes of discussion and to facilitate recognition of play patterns in interactive design. Children don't create these categories or label their play in these terms. For them, all types of learning are woven together and happen at the same time.

Recognizing and understanding play patterns is essential to children's content creation because every program you create as a designer will, intentionally or not, offer opportunities for one or more of these patterns. Enhance designs to support pure play, and you will create titles that delight as well as enlighten.

Active Body Play

Children love to use their bodies. Active Body Play is primarily physical exploration and movement done for the sheer joy of doing it. This could also be called **Sensory Play** because it stimulates the five senses: sight, sound, touch, taste, and smell. Swinging on a rope, climbing a tree, chasing each other around, jumping crazily on the bed—there doesn't need to be a reason; all there needs to be is the opportunity. Much of what babies and toddlers *do* is pure active play because it stimulates brain development, develops motor skills, naturally builds growing bodies, and teaches them about the material world.

Physicality is crucial for optimum growth both in the body and the brain, and it feels good. Testing the limits of their developing abilities, kids invent impromptu games wherever they go. They will make a game of jumping between rocks, standing on one foot at a time, or taking off running for no reason. They will invite anyone nearby to participate, thereby also turning the game into Social Play.

We explore the world through movement; it's a crucial ingredient for learning. As Maria Montessori pointed out in her 1936 book *The Secret of Childhood*, "Through movement we come in contact with external reality, and it is through these contacts that we eventually acquire even abstract ideas."[28] Active use of the body during play is also how children begin to create context for language. Through movement, they experience concepts of space (here or there), time (now or later), and speed (fast or slow). Experience becomes a way of knowing and learning.

All kids need physical playtime. More and more designers are taking this into consideration as they try to find a balance between the amount of time children

spend being physically active and the time they spend playing on digital devices. Games like the foot-controlled *Dance Dance Revolution* were a start, but Nintendo took it to the next level with the Wii and its sports and fitness games. The Kinect for Xbox uses game hardware to recognize the outline of the user's body. This allows movements to affect gameplay by putting the player on the screen. We can look forward to seeing even more sophisticated interfaces in the future, interfaces that allow Active Body Play as the key interface control.

Mastery Play

Mastery Play takes several different forms: exploration, repetition, and problem solving. As children grow, they are constantly learning new skills. (In fact, all through life, we continually master new skills just to keep up with technology.) For the youngest children, Mastery Play is the dominant pastime since everything is still new to them, including their bodies. They are still mastering the basics of standing, walking, and getting their bodies wired to do what they want. In older children, mastery learning takes on more and more levels of refinement, from acquiring intricate dance moves to honing the finer points of a sport or a game (like any Mario game) where progressive "controller" skills are required in order to move forward. All play involves skill

development, whether physical, intellectual, or emotional. Once a skill is gained, the next impulse is to play with it. Mastery leads to *exploration* and *experimentation*.

For example, the first time children go down the playground slide, they hesitate at the top; it seems really high up, and they will have to give up control to go down (somewhat scary and outside their comfort zone). They don't know what it will feel like or what will happen. There are a lot of unknowns despite the fact that they have seen lots of other kids do it. At some point, they throw caution to the wind, try sliding, land, integrate the experience, and *do it again*. **Repetition** is a big part of mastery. It builds confidence and adds to a child's database of experiences. (Q: How do you get to Carnegie Hall? A: Practice.)

Over time, children gain even more mastery of the "slide" experience, and begin to play with it. The next thing you know, they are going down the slide upside-down-and-backwards, head first! A few years later the tween child wonders, "What happens if I ride my skateboard down the slide?"

Mastery Play takes many forms for a child. Consider **Language Play**. We are linguistic animals, and children instinctually engage in Language Play while learning to talk. No one has to teach Language Play to them; they do it on their own by playing with sounds and listening to people around them. They begin with cooing sounds, then progress to a kind of babble as they put vowels and consonants together to resemble words in their native language. First words will be repeated over and over in a playful way. Babies only do this when they are happy.[29] They do it not to achieve something but because they can, and it's a pleasurable exploration, which is, by definition, play.

The main form of Mastery Play could be called **Exploratory Play**. In order to understand how things work (both inside and outside of themselves), children need, and like, to explore and experiment. This becomes a **Strategy Play** activity that deals with the discovery of properties and rules through trial and error, sometimes called **What-If Play**. Experimentation leads to insights, hypotheses, and new exploration. There is such an inherently satisfying pleasure in solving *pieces* of puzzles that the completion can be anticlimactic. Solving one problem inspires children to try solving another one.

Again, mastery leads to exploration, experimentation, *and engaged learning*. Later chapters will talk more about *level* mastery and how it is used in gameplay, but, for now, consider how learning is an aggregate of all things mastered and learned previously. Mastery Play is an element in every human activity.

Social Play

From games with a few friends, to organized gatherings and sports, humans enjoy doing things with others. If we didn't care about connecting, communicating, and playing with others, social networks and game sites would wither on the vine.

This social connection to others begins at infancy with **Attunement Play**, the intimate interactions between parents and their babies that are crucial to development. Attunement Play sets a foundation for complex versions of play later in life.

When an infant makes eye contact with her mother, each experiences a spontaneous surge of emotion (joy). The baby responds with a radiant smile, the mother with her own smile and rhythmic vocalizations (baby talk). This is the grounding base of the state-of-play. It is known, through EEG and other imaging technologies, that the right cerebral cortex, which organizes emotional control, is 'attuned' in both infant and mother.[30]
—**National Institute for Play**

iStock.com/Christopher Futcher

Children are naturally social, especially with other children. Children of about the same age and size are drawn to one another. You can see this most often with younger children who share a pint-sized view of the world and have a common wish to relate to someone like themselves. Young children who have never met before will connect and play together through self-initiated games. These impromptu games are easy to engage in and enjoy since the participants are often at the same developmental stage and skill level. They "get" each other. The dynamic is no different in electronic or online games: the mere visual presence of other kids in virtual worlds adds a level of excitement for potential interaction.

In his book, *The Power of Play: Learning What Comes Naturally,* psychologist and author Dr. David Elkind writes that kids live in a world that adults have made and that is made for adults. Therefore, when kids meet other kids, they have common ground and feel they're meeting people like them. They don't need a common culture or language to connect. **Kinship Play** embodies this connection.[31]

When children are engaged in Social Play, which is *any* play done with someone else, they are exploring and experimenting with everything from humor to social justice. Children are busy trying to understand the world and explore how it works. Social Play teaches us lessons about ourselves and how to live with others.

Adults don't always perceive exactly what it is kids are learning at any given moment. Will Wright, creator of *SimCity*, *The Sims*, *Spore*, and many other great programs, tells a story about himself and friends as kids playing with "army men" figures in the dirt. He realizes now that, when they would argue about the rules of play and what was fair, they were actually learning about the law and what was right.[32] It's a great observation because, as adults, we might just see two boys playing in the dirt without considering what the boys are learning as they play.

Cooperative Play and **Competitive Play** are forms of organized Social Play that often happen at the same time in team activities. Cooperative Play is characterized by teamwork and a sense of shared purpose toward a common goal. Competitive Play is characterized by setting goals with two or more opposing sides, each attempting to reach the goal first. (Competitive Play is not always social because kids will also create spontaneous self-competitions as part of skill building to see how many times, or how long, they can do something like keep a hula-hoop going or jump on a pogo stick.)

stockbroker © 123RF.com

Some play has no obvious goals or rules; this is often referred to as "unstructured" or "open" play, whereas play that has clearly defined goals and a structure based on rules gets called "a game."

Object Play

Touch is primal, and there is inherent joy in playing with objects, physical or digital: this is a deep-rooted, innate play pattern. Manipulating, experimenting with, collecting, sorting, organizing, and making things with objects comes naturally to our species, and kids invent this kind of play with whatever is at hand. The objects chosen influence and inform the direction and state of playfulness. For older babies and toddlers, banging on pots and pans with a wooden spoon is one way they learn about the physical world around them. As children develop, playing with objects becomes more personalized because toys are often imbued with human qualities and become the vehicles for imaginative **Storytelling Play** and **Fantasy Play**. Different objects lead to different explorations, connections, and expressions. Play with toy cars is going to offer different opportunities for exploration than a coloring book or action figures and dolls.

One form of Object Play is collecting, sorting, and categorizing objects. Games naturally arise out of manipulating sets of objects. Object Play can take the form of creative **Expressive** or **Maker-Builder-Creator Play**, where something new is made from the pieces available. It can also consist of **Sorting Play**, which can be about finding relationships between the objects just for the joy of it. Look at the popularity of games like *Tetris* (fitting shapes together), *Bejeweled* (finding three in a row), *Solitaire* (finding a sequence of numbers), or word games like *Wurdle* and *Words with Friends* (finding words in a jumble of letters). They're all based on the challenge of finding and organizing objects into patterns, often with the added motivator of a time limit.

Subsets of Object Play, **Collecting Play and Classification Play**, involve the assembling, sorting, organizing, classifying, and displaying of objects. Younger kids seem to be collectors because they like accumulating lots of stuff, but at around seven or eight years of age, collecting becomes more earnest, and kids become more discriminating accumulators.[33] They become very focused on discerning all the various and different properties of their collection pieces (and they are happy to tell you all about them if you ask). Baseball cards were popular collectibles for decades, but these days Pokémon cards speak to this same desire to collect along with the added bonus of being usable in gameplay as well.

While collecting and organizing are more intellectual than physical, the physical manipulation of objects has an important impact on the development of the brain. As children's skills in manipulating objects (through play) develop, the related circuitry of the brain becomes richer in ways that go beyond motor skills. Neural connections used regularly become stronger and more complex. Dr. Stuart Brown (founder of the National Institute for Play, a nonprofit dedicated to the science of play) and renowned neurologist Dr. Frank Wilson have noted this relationship in their research, and it is a crucial connection to keep in mind when designing games for children: involving the body and motor skills means developing the mind.[34] One way this idea of kinesthetic learning is being used successfully in the classroom is with Body Phonics, a way of teaching spelling with hand gestures and other motions.[35]

Creative Play

Calling a category "creative play" is somewhat redundant because *all* play is creative in its own way, but in Creative Play, something new is being made during the process of playing (the explorative and expressive *process* being the important

part). Creative Play happens spontaneously and effortlessly wherever and whenever kids are given the opportunity. Examples include arranging shells on a freshly built sandcastle, painting digital pictures in apps like GIMP, Tux Paint, or Kid Pix, or building anything in *Minecraft*. But creativity happens best in an environment without pressure to be creative. High incentives, deadlines, evaluations, and other pressure to perform well all interfere with creativity. What's important is to let kids focus on what is being created, and to create for its own sake.[36]

Creativity is an outcome of curiosity and playful exploration. Creative Play opens the door for improvisation, serendipity, and innovation by recombining elements of the known in new ways. It allows the mixing together of different ideas, fields of knowledge, points of view, techniques, and technologies into new, imaginative expressions. Because kids love this kind of play, designers should include opportunities for creative exploration and play in every program and game they design.

In learning, it is more powerful to make a playful and engaged connection to content than to have it presented as predigested fact or equation. One method is inviting and stimulating; the other is just memorization without personal ownership.[37]

Play, by definition, is self-controlled and self-directed. It is the self-directed aspect of play that gives it its educative power.[38]
—Peter Gray, author and psychologist

Part of Creative Play is **Transformative Play**, play that involves customizing, personalizing, reorganizing, and constructing—basically changing the state of something to make it one's own. For kids this sometimes means just signing their name, but, more often, it includes decorating, enhancing, and otherwise modifying something (like a game avatar or a toy) to make it uniquely theirs.

The important thing for designers to remember is that Transformative Play, like Creative Play, creates *ownership*. Ownership, in turn, fosters player retention and continued participation. Everyone likes feeling creative, and everyone is creative in their own way. Part of the role of a designer is to help children be prepared for a world that thrives on innovation and change, where creativity is currency. Therefore, we need to create programs that foster the opportunity and mindset for creative exploration and discovery to help kids prepare for the world they will inherit. (For more on player retention through Creative Play and Transformative Play, see Ch. 3, pp. 42–44 and Ch. 16, pp. 265–270.)

I think it's possible that human imagination shines brightest in childhood. When I create games, I've always tried to think of ways for kids who play to think on their own and be as imaginative as possible.[39]
—Shigeru Miyamoto, game designer and producer at Nintendo

Make-Believe Play

Whether by playing with dolls or action figures or by dressing up as a favorite superhero, animal, or animated TV personality, role-playing happens spontaneously as children use their imaginations to explore social interactions or to "try-on" archetypes and roles to see how they feel. **Pretend Play** is an important and natural expression of kids trying to make sense of the world around them. From pouring out pretend tea for stuffed animals to battling make-believe bad-guys in the bedroom, **Imaginative Play** allows kids to explore things from different emotional viewpoints. This ability to see from different perspectives helps children to develop empathy and connection with others, as well as to give themselves coping skills.

alkir © 123RF.com

Designer's Note

Whether we realize it or not, when we are designing games for kids, we often imagine them playing with the games, and, as I write this book, I am imagining you reading it and what you might like to know. We use this imaginative and creative mechanism easily and seamlessly in our thought processes each day. Often, it is virtually invisible except when we imagine things that scare, excite, or tickle us, and get our bodies to react as if the imagined scenario was real. Our imaginations are very powerful—imagine good things!

Make-Believe Play, also called Imaginative Play or Pretend Play, allows for the creation of "What if?" situations like being a pirate, a superhero who can fly, a beauty queen, a fairy princess, or a mash-up of beautiful-pirate-fairy-princess-who-flies. Anything imaginable in the mind of a child (or adult) is fair game for make-believe adventures. *Imagination* is something humans excel at; we can imagine things and times beyond the here and now.

Children have a huge appetite for explorative excursions and adventures into the fantasy world of make-believe, with themselves playing leading roles. They easily jump back and forth between reality and fantasy play, existing in both worlds at once. Make-Believe Play is always accompanied by some form of running narrative and story, usually broadcast live in monologue as it occurs. These stories help children make sense of their lives and sort through their feelings and experiences.

It's not just children who do this: everyone everyday uses a pretend-real combination to replay old stories, re-examine current situations with different outcomes, and envision possible future events. It is a daily component of our human stream of consciousness.

Make-Believe Play is often therapeutic on its own, but there is a specific form of **Therapeutic Play** used by child therapists to get kids to communicate about what is happening in their lives. Children who are reticent to talk will often, while talking *through* puppets, dolls, and figurines, express themselves in ways they might never do when asked directly.

Designer's Note

Game and toy designer Cynthia Woll, who has worked for Mattel Media (as well as Disney, Electronic Arts, and others), related a story about testing a new idea for a Barbie that could "talk" with the girls. It turned out that the girls had no interest in what Barbie had to say; they just wanted to use Barbie as a "talking stick" for themselves. They used Barbie to express their feelings and tell stories about their lives. The girls acted out their hopes, dreams, and aspirations through the medium of the doll. Cynthia saw that it was all about the story. Girls acting out stories is the predominant play pattern for the Barbie line of toys.[40]

Kids are looking for opportunities to express themselves, and Make-Believe Play gives them the opportunity to do so. Pretending to be a tiger, hero, or ninja allows exploration of strength, ability, and power. Pretending to be a doctor, nurse, zoo-keeper, or mother allows exploration of nurturing. **Power Play** and **Nurture Play** patterns seem to be universal, and are great components to consider in product design. The main thing is that kids crave opportunities to become someone else and to tell a story through that character's eyes. Give them opportunities to do so, and remember these may be private explorations where insight comes from telling the story, not from the end result. Kids may or *may not* care about sharing these stories with others, at least until they reach the upper end of the "kids" age range, when their storytelling is considered art as much as personal play.

Properties of Play

To create engaging interactivity for children, designers need to have an awareness of what real play looks like so they know it when they see it. They also need a good understanding of the different patterns of play before they can build some-thing that truly delights a child's spirit and ignites the imagination. True play is the magic that turns ordinary products into award-winners that kids will love and come back to.

Dr. Stuart Brown has identified and described the key properties of play. Brown's principles apply to interactive learning and game design because, to design for play, we first need to understand what the experience of play looks and feels like. Below are the key properties of play (as defined by Brown) followed by descriptions of how these properties are important to designing games and learning experiences for children.[41]

Apparently purposeless. "Play activities don't seem to have any survival value. . . . Play is done for its own sake. That's why some people think of it as a waste of time."[42]

Parents often don't understand a child's fascination with a game or toy; they only see the time "wasted playing games" without connecting to what the child gets from that play. In all gameplay, there is much more going on than is apparent in the minds of most adults. Games designed with more of an open-ended structure help facilitate a child's natural drive to find their own purpose for the play involved. This is when games become toys, and let the child follow their own imagination and curiosity.

> *It should be noted that children at play are not playing about; their games should be seen as their most serious-minded activity.*[43]
> —**Michel de Montaigne, philosopher**

Voluntary. "[Play] is not obligatory or required by duty."[44]

We play because we want to, and because we are called to do so. This idea is paramount in terms of interactive design because kids vote with their attention. A program has to engage their interest so they don't walk away. What value is an "educational" game that kids won't play without coercion? The idea of play as a voluntary act can be frustratingly clear to designers when they first hand a tablet to a child to test a new app. After a few minutes, the child may just hit the home/escape button and be out of there. The designers may say, "Wait, wait, there is more to do," but the child has already authentically given some great feedback.

> *Play is, first and foremost, an expression of freedom. It is what one wants to do as opposed to what one is obliged to do.*[45]
> —Peter Gray, author and psychologist

Inherent attraction. "[Play is] fun. It makes you feel good. It provides psychological arousal (that's how behavioral scientists say something is exciting). It is a cure for boredom."[46]

What is it that gets a child's attention? What do they expect is going to happen? What do they want to see more of? Later chapters examine this more extensively, but asking yourself—and your kid users—these questions is very helpful in building content that meets a child's needs, wants, desires, and expectations.

Freedom from time. "When we are fully engaged in play, we lose a sense of the passage of time."[47]

Play is how we learn something new. Children need the time and space for creative exploration. Learning is about making connections between things, and that kind of process takes time. When children are absorbed in play, they step out of "adult time" and into what is speaking to them at the moment. Children deeply engaged in play won't notice time passing. As Einstein said, "An hour sitting with a pretty girl on a park bench passes like a minute; but a minute sitting on a hot stove seems like an hour."[48]

Unstructured play is so important to children that the American Academy of Pediatrics (AAP) states, "Free and unstructured play is healthy and—in fact—essential for helping children reach important social, emotional, and cognitive developmental milestones as well as helping them manage stress and become resilient."[49]

Diminished consciousness of self. "We stop worrying about whether we look good or awkward, smart or stupid. We stop thinking about the fact that we are thinking. . . . We are fully in the moment, in the zone."[50]

This is what psychologist Mihaly Csikszentmihalyi calls *flow*.[51] When a child is in this state of pure engagement, it's a sign of great design, and it's something to look for when testing prototypes with kids. When they become so engrossed in play that they forget anyone is watching, it's a magical moment to be appreciated. It is also an important interactive design element to understand. In an engrossed play state, kids will often imagine your design doing something you didn't imagine it doing, and that can lead to valuable design enhancements and new features.

Improvisational potential. "We are open to serendipity, to chance. We are willing to include seemingly irrelevant elements into our play.... The result is that we stumble upon new behaviors, thoughts, strategies, movements, or ways of being."[52]

Kids want to feel they have control, and it's important to give them opportunities to experiment, to do things "wrong," to break the rules, and generally to muck-about inside a game. In design, it's an asset when you can allow for the recombining of elements, the making of a mess, or the solving of problems backwards or in surprising ways. Insight and creativity flow from seeing things from new perspectives. Play opens up the opportunity for unexpected things to happen.

Provides a continuation desire. "We desire to keep doing it, and the pleasure of the experience drives that desire. We find ways to keep it going.... And when it is over, we want to do it again."[53]

As the saying goes, "The journey is the reward." When play meets all our needs for curiosity, challenge, and engagement, we can be disappointed when it's over. In fact, if something in the rules jeopardizes our enjoyment or signals an end to the fun, we invent new conditions to let us continue. Building in the potential for unexpected surprises and connections in a product allows children to, as Warren Buckleitner, Editor of *Children's Technology Review*, says, "Accidentally succeed."[54] The freedom to experiment and the delight of responsive results feed curiosity, insight, and the desire for further explorative play.

Children do a good job of looking as if they're wasting time, but secretly they are in the business of educating themselves about how the world works.[55]
—Tzvi Freeman, author and philosopher

CHAPTER 2

Creating Invitations to Play

Great interactive design invites children to participate, and it quickly allows them to become engaged in exploration. But first you have to get their attention. This chapter continues to explore play patterns and what works when designing inviting experiences for kids. It also looks at the lure of animated characters as agents in children's products and how social etiquette affects interface design.

You can discover more about a person in an hour of play than in a year of conversation.[1]

—unattributed adage

Creating Invitations

Designers of children's content need to create environments that intuitively invite and allow for engagement in the natural play patterns described in the last chapter (Active Play, Object Play, Mastery Play, Social Play, Make-Believe Play, Creative Play, etc.). *All kids instinctively know how to engage in play*, and they are drawn to do so. But how do you create an invitation?

Invitations to play come in several forms, from outright attention grabbers to subtler summons that draw the user in. Can you remember what it was like for you to be invited to a party, game, or event? Consider how to make that invitation without using words. In order for children to say "yes," the interactive environment should be interesting enough to pique their curiosity, feel safe enough for them to risk an action, and be visually stimulating enough that they want to see what happens.

Kids are wired to pay attention to the world and instinctively respond to certain environmental cues. Additionally, what makes something attractive to a child varies by age, stage, and gender (discussed further later), but some basics are universal: movement, sound, color, and interesting visuals. It's no wonder kids are drawn like magnets to animated characters, who usually possess and exhibit all four of these attention-getting qualities—interest-worthy images, color, sound, and movement—at once! Of the four, movement is the most important. (For more on the nature of attention, see Ch. 3, pp. 35–39 and Ch. 5, pp. 65–70.)

Movement as invitation. If it wiggles, it's alive. When something moves in our visual field, especially in our peripheral vision, it is hard not to look at it. That autonomic response is a hard-wired survival gift from our mammal ancestors for whom a moving object was immediately regarded as alive and something to pay attention to. Modern brains react similarly to movement: if it moves, people look, and designers who animate something literally *bring it to life*.

© Olga Galushko – stock.adobe.com

When children, especially young children, see an object move on a computer screen, they are immediately attentive, engaged, and drawn to the movement, just as they would be to bugs and butterflies in the natural world. To children, when something is animated it not only seems alive, it also immediately becomes imbued with a sense of *agency*. The object is perceived as an unknown. It's unpredictable, and kids are curious to know more. They immediately want to play with it just to see what it'll do. These digital sprites are alive to children, and *alive* implies opportunity for interaction. Kids want to inspect the mystery that this independently moving object possesses. They don't know what to expect. They hope to be astonished and surprised by what they find. Our job as designers is not to disappoint them.

"Hello! Welcome!"—Direct audio and agent invitation. Audio space is omni-directional. As part of early human survival warning systems, people can hear things from quite a distance in all directions. Abrupt and loud noises make us turn our heads involuntarily to see what's there. Sounds of all kinds can let a child know a program is "awake" and ready for action. Even if a program is dark, a snoring sound will lead a child to intuit that tapping will wake the scene up. Sounds evoke images of things, and it's best practice if the attractor sound relates directly to what kids expect to find when they engage. Any interesting sound can attract a child's attention, but voice is especially effective because it says, "Someone is here and ready to play." (For more on creating and using agents and agent animation, see Ch. 14, pp. 233–241.)

An audio invitation, especially if it's from an animated agent/character, is a great way to encourage participation. Although you can have text-only and audio-only invitations, the strongest by far is that of an animated character. Keep in mind that agents only need to give simple instructions because kids are anxious to start *doing*, and they tend to remember only the last thing said. A good example is later in this chapter: Example #7—Social Interaction.

Bright colors grab attention. Bright colors, especially in contrast to more subdued backgrounds, stand out and can grab a child's attention even from across a room. Colors can highlight a character or set a mood. This fact is not lost on toy makers, who have been using color to call to children from toy aisles everywhere. Well-chosen colors reflect the target demographic's interest and identity profiles. (For more discussion on using color, contrast, tones and shades, see Ch. 6, pp. 79–83.)

Create interesting visuals that provoke examination. This is about creating a **"What *is* that?"** effect. Design something that makes kids curious enough to want to look further and interact to learn more. This can be anything from cute to gross, depending on your audience. It can also be a mystery, like a heavy wooden door with a sign that says, "Do Not Enter," or a button that says, "Do Not Push" (especially irresistible to tweens and teens).

Offer visuals that provide an empowering call to action. As with any other invitation, a game invitation is asking kids a question (often non-verbally). In digital media, the invitational question is, "Do want to want to *do* something?" Children answer with their actions, not their words. A good design needs to give them something to do immediately to deliver on the provocation to play. If the game offers the invitation of control, it must deliver it. Some examples are driving, feeding hungry animals, shooting a bow-and-arrow, popping balloons, and knocking down or blowing something up. Any weird contraption that has an arrow pointing to a switch or lever that can set it in motion will provoke an action.

The goal is to invite interaction, and then give a cool reward for participation. Kids want to be empowered to take the driver's seat and steer where they want. Show them the possibilities of what they can do, and they will be there in a heartbeat to give it a try.

Tap into instinctual play patterns. One wonderful thing about digital media is that designers can work with children's natural play patterns to explore new material or to delve into old content in new ways. Play patterns are a child's innate approach to experimenting with new experiences and learning. When a designer taps into a play pattern, kids instinctively figure out what to do.

Deliver immediate opportunities for interactivity. Don't create hurdles to begin. Don't make kids wait through a long list of instructions or a long intro before they can do something. Create an invitation for empowering interaction as soon as possible. Kids are just waiting to interact, and they will start tapping or clicking immediately without waiting for instructions. This is especially true for younger children for whom delayed gratification is a much harder concept to grasp.

Examples of Play Pattern Invitations

The most basic invitation is non-verbal and is simply a situation that is ripe for interaction. Play patterns are instinctual behaviors and often only need the right situation to support their blossoming. When you find a pattern working in your design, you know you are on the right path to a good play experience. Here are a few samples.

Example #1—Visual Invitation

Where does this go? *Busy Shapes* by Edoki Academy offers a puzzle game for two- to five-year-olds that uses progressively more challenging shape, color, size, and operational actions to solve visual problems. The basic premise is very easy to grasp: "Put this in there." No outright instructions are given; children instinctively understand how to begin. The invitation is as simple and clear as could be. Upon putting the purple disc in the purple outlined hole, another puzzle presents itself and visually asks the question, "Now, where does *this* go?"

Busy Shapes app by Edoki Academy.

Example #2—Visual Invitation

Kids with blocks. If you have ever watched kids (or been a kid) playing with blocks, it looks kind of like creative Object Play, either alone or with friends. It involves lots of pieces stacked, balanced, and arranged in patterns or as buildings, usually done with a narrative. It may include cars and action figures.

What happens next?

grafvision © 123RF.com

All the blocks get knocked over to great effect! I witnessed this with my own boys; I've seen it in kindergartens and day care centers, and I've done it myself. This is an intrinsic Object Play sequence: build it, knock it down, build it, knock it down. You can see this exact play pattern driving the game *Angry Birds* by Rovio Entertainment.

Angry Birds is a classic example of this intrinsic play pattern being used with new technology tools. The user controls a slingshot that shoots birds toward the snarky pig's house in order to knock it down. A "physics engine" is used to simulate gravity and object collision, while sound effects complete the experience.

Angry Birds has a sling shot, a score board, a variety of ammo (different birds create different kinds of destruction), and many levels of mastery (with hundreds of structures to knock down). It's a kid's dream product.

This is an invitation to play. *Angry Birds* is a digital version of carefully stacked and balanced blocks *waiting* for something to happen to them. With both the blocks and the birds, it's the kid's *job* to knock things down. It doesn't take kids more than a nanosecond to get the goal of the game, and they are at it. They are motivated to play again and again. Cause and effect, cause and effect, cause and effect. This is a digital version of a real-world play pattern that supports intrinsic learning through play. But, while the play value is

Angry Birds app by Rovio Entertainment.

Designer's Note

To take the edge off of what some might think of as violence, the game designers at Rovio added a story to make it okay to wreck the piggies' houses. The pigs stole the birds' eggs! They took the birds' children! To add insult to injury, the pigs are also unrepentant, and they chuckle at the user who doesn't get them, further inviting (taunting and challenging) players to try again. It wouldn't feel the same if the pigs writhed in anguish, crying and squealing, or sincerely begged for mercy and forgiveness.

very high, the educational content is relatively low beyond exploring some critical thinking and strategy skills. (The trick for designers of educational products is to generate this level of engagement and gameplay in an environment with more rigorous content.)

Example #3—Visual Invitation

The tea party. A "tea party," whether tea is involved or not, is another well-known play pattern in younger children. The party may be more about gathering various "families" of stuffed animals and dolls together for Social Play and Fantasy Play than about a meal, but, since meals are a common family reason for gathering, they are a real-world event that shows up regularly in play.

Toca Boca used this play pattern to create *Toca Tea Party*, a simple iPad app in which the screen becomes the tea party table. Without any instructions (other than exploration learning through the interface and a few highlighted spots suggesting item placement), children three and up can choose a tablecloth, plates, drinks, and desserts.

Toca Tea Party is also social, and it works well for up to three children at once. They easily shift into the pretend party with yummy digital desserts. The concept of gathering to eat is a familiar experience to kids, and they already know what to do. Toca offers the place and objects, and kids bring their imaginations. When it's all finished, kids can clean up, which the app allows them to do by tilting the screen until all the plates and cups slide into the sink full of hot soapy water.

Toca Boca has successfully followed the same model in other digital and fanciful versions of real-life situations, such as *Toca Hair Salon*, *Toca Kitchen*, *Toca House*, and more.

Toca Tea Party app by Toca Boca.

Designer's Note

When I am testing tablet prototypes with three- to five-year-olds, I often have *Toca Tea Party* available to keep kids engaged between testing sets. They happily play and explore for about ten or fifteen minutes, then hand back the device with a proud smile, saying, "I washed the dishes."

Example #4—Visual Invitation

A scene from *The Tortoise and The Hare*, republished by Wanderful. There are 51 active hotspots on this page, including individual words.

Turning over rocks. Kids are naturally curious. It doesn't matter if they're turning over rocks to see what is living underneath, yelling loudly just to hear their own voices, or tapping on an app in ways the designers never considered. Kids want to know "What's that?" and "What's it do?"

When I created Living Books, I was inspired by my own childhood fantasy of wishing to go inside the pages of a picture book to play with the objects in the scene. I chose existing picture books or designed books full of scenes that allowed tons of exploration via clicking (or tapping now) on everything in the page. If it looked like a button, I tried to make it one. All the objects, characters, and individual words were "alive" and triggered by contact.

What I see now is that this play pattern is not that different from turning over rocks or touching a bug with a stick to make it jump. The questions being asked are, "What is hiding here that I can't see?" and "Is it ALIVE?" The interactive pages allow for child-controlled experimentation in an environment that is very alive, hence the original product line name, Living Books.

Example #5—Visual Invitation

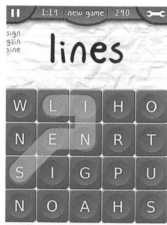

Wurdle app by Lucky Star Software.

Sorting stuff. In **Object Play**, it is natural for humans to look for relationships between objects. Just seeing collections of numbers, letters, shapes, or colors starts the human mind sorting, grouping, and looking for relationships. This is also a form of **Puzzle Play**. Children and adults are collectors, and with collecting comes categorizing objects into some order or pattern—this is a form of Classification Play.

People love the challenge and joy of finding the relationships between objects and organizing them into patterns. When looking at a screen like this one from *Wurdle*, people

Designer's Note

Wurdle is good game for new word acquisition. While exploring letter links during gameplay, if the user accidentally finds real words they are given audio clues to acknowledge it and the words are added to their list of words founds. It works well for emerging readers up through tweens.

immediately start to look for relationships between the letters to make sense of the jumble. With three-in-a-row games like *Bejeweled*, it doesn't take long to figure out that getting three in a row moves the game forward. Seeing pieces and open spaces in a puzzle draws people to find relationships with the shapes and put the piece where it belongs. This is a play pattern of the human mind, and the interface utilizes that fact to entice us and invite us to play.

Example #6—Audio Invitation

An audio invitation may be an interesting sound that piques a child's curiosity. It might also be a familiar sound (like a puppy barking) coming from an unusual place (a mobile phone). Again, the child wants to know more. But the most inviting sound is a human (or human-like) voice. Children expect to see who is talking, and they will tolerate a disembodied voice only as long as the designer can keep some mystery and implied promise of seeing who it is *or* give them something else to interact with immediately. The real draw of an audio invitation comes when it is coupled with an animating agent (character, object, vegetable, or *something* with a mouth and eyes).

Designer's Note

In MarcoPolo Learning's *Ocean*, every time a child begins a new construction, the voice-over invites them to participate by saying, "Let's build a submarine," or "Let's build an orca."[2] When I was testing *Ocean* with young kids, I was surprised by how many answered cheerfully aloud, "Okay!"

Example #7—Social Invitation

Character invitation. Kids like to be greeted, welcomed, and invited to participate. This technique of direct address invitation from a character has been used since the earliest programs for kids. It was used to great effect in Disney's original *Mickey Mouse Club* in the 1950s, where Mickey would say hi to everybody watching, welcome them to the day's show, and ask if they were ready (of course kids were). For younger children, having a character invite them to play through direct address is just as charming today as it was back then. It feels so real to them that sometimes they answer back!

Little Monster at School app by Wanderful.

Designer's Note

When I was first designing Living Books, I went into different computer stores to see how software was being shown and sold. I noticed that stores needed something to show the (then) new multimedia machines' capabilities. So I designed an "attract mode" beginning to the storybooks before kids started the story. The main character introduced itself, welcomed kids to Living Books, and told them simply how to begin playing, then waited a bit. But instead of repeating that talk loop, which could get boring really fast, we created a dance loop with good music that was okay for adults, too. That way, when kids or parents were in the store, there was our character dancing away, getting attention. It turned out to be so popular that many parents wrote us, telling us how their child had learned all the moves and would dance along. Many of the original Living Books have been updated as apps by Wanderful, and now allow touch control interactivity.

Creating Relationships

Humans are social beings, and it is only natural that a good interface invites users in a friendly and compelling way to come and play. As Byron Reeves and Clifford Nass explain in *The Media Equation*, what we look for in a human–computer interaction is a polite and responsive version of human–human interaction.[3] Being invited and welcomed is a great way to start.

In a best-case scenario, a designer doesn't just create a good interaction but develops an ongoing and deeper *relationship* with the user. When you design a game, you are building a social interaction and an overall emotional connection that kids experience as they play. These interactions will affect how kids feel while playing and how they feel about themselves after they leave the program. They are developing a relationship with *your* content and expectations about what they will get from it. This relationship is key to product acceptance and creating a long-term connection with future titles you create. It matters that a child likes what you have built.

Children are gathering knowledge about how the world works, and they are deeply fascinated by living things and the things those critters do. Interfaces that come alive are irresistible to their curiosity, and it's important not to disappoint them. Offer experiences that actively invite children to explore. Movement, sound, and reaction invite and support the illusion of life and generate a desire for more.

Maintaining Engagement

Getting children's attention is easy. Keeping them engaged is another story. Once you have their attention, you have to honor it and know what things they do and don't like.

This chapter includes basic practices for children's interface design, common mistakes, and, most importantly, tips on how to create and maintain deeply involved engagement that will keep kids charmed, delighted, and coming back for more.

Too often we give children answers to remember
rather than problems to solve.[1]
> —Roger Lewin, anthropologist and science writer

Interface Basics

When a child is in a state of true play, the pleasure of the experience drives a continuation desire. This is what makes any activity successful and worthy of their attention. The key to good design is to include elements that support magical interactions and eliminate interactions that detract from the experience.

© Mactrunk/Depositphotos.com

When interactive media is easy to use and respectful of children, they are more likely to dive in and use it. Here are some basic features of good interface—design specifics will come later in the book.

Easy to understand and use. Children are more likely to engage when they understand what to do and how to do it. Clear and intuitive opportunities for navigation and interaction at the beginning (and throughout) will make participation easy and support continued play. Ideally, kids will feel successful and in control as soon as possible. Intuitive design of function buttons allows kids to navigate easily, and it supports their desire for exploration and control. In general, the simplest designs are the most elegant.

Limit instructions. Children *do* first and listen second. Limiting audio or text instructions supports their desire to start doing. Any sign-in screens or other hurdles to reach activities should be intuitive and kept to a minimum or eliminated altogether. Give instructions only as needed. As an added bonus, programs where kids can get started with minimal instructions are easier to take out into the world market because they need little translation.

Responsive interface. Nothing kills play more than waiting for a response to a tap or click. Kids expect an *immediate* reaction to their action—just like touching something in the real world—and when they don't get it, they tap again and again, assuming the program is slow, dumb, broken, or not listening to them. They can feel very frustrated if a game makes them sit through long instructions before they can begin. Responsive interfaces, on the other hand, are satisfying. Every action a child makes should immediately result in something happening on the screen, or an audio cue should register their action. Keep responses snappy and crisp.

Good interface encourages curiosity.

Kid controlled. Children avoid activities in which they are given little or no control. In real-world play, children expect their actions to have an effect, and they have those same expectations of their digital interactions. Good interactive content increases children's feelings of control, allowing them to "drive" as much as possible. It also offers choices with abundant opportunities for their input.

In interactivity, control trumps looks—always.[2]
—Warren Buckleitner, Editor,
Children's Technology Review

Children want to be successful. Let them be. When a child is drawn to a screen, it is often because they begin to *imagine* what they can do, and they imagine being successful at it. Allow them to have an effect, to have agency in the environment. If you do this early on, they will feel empowered and come back for more. Success is less about praise (as in "Good job!") and more about the ability to have an impact and to influence the play environment.

Get to the good stuff quickly. Allow children (especially the younger ones) to be successful within the first twenty seconds, and they will stick around for more. Make it hard for them to get started, and they are gone. If your best stuff is buried deep in the game, many players may never see it. Helping children be successful early on gives them confidence that they will be successful again.

Know your target age/audience. One size does not fit all. Products designed for four- to five-year-olds are going to be very different than ones created for ten- to eleven-year-olds. *Respect where children are developmentally, and meet them there.* Give kids something worthy of their time, and they will reward you with their attention. Canned animated responses to tap or click interactions can be engaging and frequently repeated with a three- to six-year-old audience, but older kids want to do more than just click/tap. They want tools and interesting places to use them. They want challenges, such as quests, and that might include having friends along for the adventure. If they come back, you know you are speaking to their interests. (For more on children's ages and stages, see Ch. 10.)

Activity Basics

Children choose activities they enjoy doing. To support a child's engagement means to understand what interests them.

Focus on fun. If you want to connect with kids, give them something intrinsically fun to play with. Fun is subjective to each child, but when you understand exactly whom you are designing for, it is easier to match play patterns and players. Get to know what each demographic group likes, and offer them activities that match their desires.

Often, especially in learning products, it is easy to get too focused on the educational goal. When this happens, designers can forget what's important to the kids.

If you deliver something intrinsically fun to play with, children will go further and learn more than expected. Almost every subject can be framed in a way that allows kids to have plenty of explorative entertainment value.

Offer variety. Kids are voracious consumers of content, and they will quickly go from hot to cold once they think they have exhausted the novelty and learning they can get from a product. This is especially true for older kids, whose interactive media tastes are more sophisticated and advanced. Strategies to counteract this appear later in this chapter.

Leave opportunities for open-ended play. Most games have a goal, and most activities have a specific purpose. In terms of user retention, it is also important to leave open-ended play opportunities in which kids can use their imaginations to be creative. A dollhouse is a perfect example: there are lots of component pieces and characters, and the child creates a scene and a story in the process of their own **Narrative Play**. Kids do this when dressing and outfitting their avatars and decorating their online rooms. Open-ended play is where some of the most creative

Inventioneers app by Filimundus.

exploration takes place because it allows the recombining of elements to create new meaning.

I have watched kids play games (like the old *Incredible Machine* from Sierra Entertainment or current *Inventioneers* by Filimundus) where they have to assemble a lot of animated pieces to solve a problem. There is a point, after several rounds of structured play, where kids stop following the rules and begin to create their own wacky Rube Goldberg-like machines. In both cases the designers were smart enough to give kids a *free play* mode where children could experiment and invent. This free play feature added hours of playtime to the product.

Two other great examples of open-ended exploration apps include Game Collage's *Bobo Explores Light,* in which kids get to play with different aspects of light, and *Off the Rails* by Dan Russell-Pinson. In *Bobo*, the designers (Dean MacAdam, Bob Tedeschi, and Juraj Hlaváč) created an interactive science title that is truly explorative. Kids can swipe tabs across the screen to examine sunrise, sunset, and night with the moon. They can also learn cool facts about blue skies and day and night. Each section allows kids to experiment with new aspects of light.

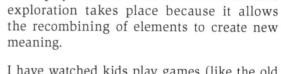

Bobo Explores Light app by Game Collage.

In *Off the Rails*, the entire nature of the game is to build a roller coaster moment by moment as the tablet screen is tilted to direct the building process. Each coaster built is replayable from several viewpoints. The free play is dynamic, spontaneous, and invites further experimentation.

As Joyce Hakansson, a pioneer children's game designer, once mused: "In all of the programs that I have ever created I have tried really hard to think about leaving them open-ended. Not closing the child off. Trying to give them room to do things that I never imagined could be done and not to put a cap on their imagination or their creativity."[3]

Off the Rails app by Freecloud Design.

Provide ample doses of humor. Kids love to laugh, and they do so easily. Humor is a hook that keeps them coming back. Younger children will replay their favorite humorous interactions over and over, and get giggles out of them each time. Humor, especially when delivered by characters, adds emotional color and life.

Let kids improve your design. One of the best techniques for improving interactions that meet the needs and imaginations of kids is to watch them play with your prototype. Notice when they begin trying to do things you didn't think of. Ask what they are trying to do, or what they expect your program to do. Because of budgets and schedules, designers can't include every idea a child has, but leaving room for some of their imagination will almost always improve the product by better meeting their needs and expectations for quality play.

Designer's Note

I had a fish-feeding game prototype where the cursor could be turned into a piece of fish food. The food, when held above a pond, would be eaten by a jumping fish. Kids testing it would invariably begin experimenting to see how high or where they could make the fish jump. The kids had elaborate ideas of what they thought was possible, such as the fish jumping higher each time to reach food being held at the top of the page. What they imagined wasn't really happening in that prototype because the fish always went to the same height. In the final product, we allowed the fish to go higher each time and eventually get the food on the third or fourth jump, just as the kids had imagined. On later testing, it proved very satisfying to other children who imagined the same outcome.

Intrinsic vs. extrinsic motivation. Motivation is the psychological purpose for an action. **Extrinsic motivation** comes from outside of a person and **intrinsic motivation** comes from within. Common extrinsic motivators in games are rewards (including praise), threat of penalty, and competition. An activity is considered intrinsic if the person is engaged in it "for its own sake" without concern for reward.

After years of watching children play, I believe the best learning games are primarily intrinsic because they tap into natural curiosity-driven play patterns, and there is a fair amount of evidence that this quality provides the best and deepest way to learn. Studies have shown that children who are intrinsically involved stay interested longer and spend more time on task than when they are regularly praised. Praise (as in "Good job!" and "You are doing terrific!") is an external motivator.[4]

External motivation can add a lot to gameplay in terms of engagement. The best games and activities often have some elements of both internal and external motivation, but games based solely on external motivations tend to fall flat because the joy of play itself is often missing.

Keeping Kids' Interest— The Magic of Surprise

Computers are like magic. They can make things disappear and appear. They can talk and respond even though no one is there. This "magic" experience makes them feel alive. After years of watching kids play, one question has continued to drive my design: "What are the factors that support truly magical interactive moments?" You can see answers in hundreds of little interchanges, including the pieces we just discussed—a sense of self-directed control, responsiveness, and interesting content. But when things are especially magical, they often include something more mysterious, unknown, and unexpected—surprise!

Surprise!

Surprise is defined as:

- An unexpected or astonishing event, fact, or thing.

- A feeling of mild astonishment or shock caused by something unexpected.[5]

The key word is "unexpected" because it has the wonderful power to engage children in several ways.

iStock.com/EricVega

Surprise, in all its incarnations, can be found throughout the best award-winning interactive titles and entertainment for children, and it is frequently connected to the most magical and engaging moments. A good magical experience also happens when content is very reactive, or even proactive.

We all like surprises. Well, we all like *good surprises*. In software design, as in life, there can be bad surprises—surprises so unrelated to the content that kids consider them just plain dumb. For the purposes of making great interactive magic, let's talk about the good kinds of surprise, and why we like them.

What makes a surprise? Through the repetition of experience, the brain begins to make assumptions. It develops expectations about how things work, and how they should or will work in the future. Surprise occurs when something unexpected happens, creating a mismatch with previous knowledge or prediction.

Surprise can be as extreme as something suddenly lurching nearby with a loud noise that startles the whole body to attention, as subtle as an "aha!" insight about how things work, or as humorous as the best joke ever heard. The crucial part of surprise is that, if it's done well, kids will want more, and that leads to a great interactive experience and deeper engagement.

Surprise gets our attention. We humans come hardwired to react automatically to surprise stimulus. Research has shown that the brain is activated more by unexpected events.[6] *We can't not look* when something surprising happens near us. Surprise triggers a jump in psychological and physiological arousal. It's automatic for our primitive brains to respond, and suddenly we are paying attention.

Surprise creates a mental–emotional state called **disequilibrium**, a state of being thrown off balance. Child psychologist Jean Piaget talked a lot about **disequilibration** and **equilibration** as essential components of a child's learning process.[7] Surprise generates a spike in curiosity. When people are surprised and thrown off balance by something, it inspires them to focus their attention, to examine and explore what has just happened. (For more on Jean Piaget and his theories of child development, see Ch. 9, pp 135–136 and Ch. 10, pp. 143–146.)

Children are delighted by surprise. From early childhood, our attention is captured by surprise. Peekaboo is a quintessential example. In a baby's early developmental mind, if they can't see something, *it's not there*.[8] When you cover your face you literally disappear for them, even though they sense your presence, and when you peek out...Wow! It's as if you appeared from nowhere. Now that's interactive magic!

Surprise suggests there is more to explore. Kids naturally love to explore and experiment. It's part of their instinctive learning-through-play process. They explore something until they have learned what they can about it at that moment. Once they have satisfied their curiosity, and they have a basic understanding of how they think something works through cause and effect, they are ready to move on.

If an object only has one reaction, kids will quickly learn that. Single-reaction objects can work if the reaction is entertaining, or if the children are five or under (because their world experiences are more limited, and getting a basic reaction is still a magical experience for them). A seven-year-old, however, will tap once, learn the reaction, and get out of there. This is where inserting surprise through unexpected variations can add value and interest in extended gameplay. Surprise suggests there is more to be seen.

Surprise adds renewed interest. When something interesting and unexpected happens, children are drawn to explore further to see if they missed something. Surprise reminds kids that they don't know how everything works yet. It implies a larger world of unknown events and mystery. *Surprise promises the possibility of more surprises.* Psychologist B. F. Skinner developed the theory of intermittent reinforcement, where certain behaviors are only reinforced intermittently.[9] If something special or unusual happens without warning, the current play or learning patterns will be reinforced more strongly. Intermittent reinforcement is an attention getter. Because it isn't easily repeatable, it generates more play, exploration, and experimentation via attempts to cause a repetition of the reinforcing event.

Designer's Note

Some years ago, I was working on an interactive version of the Jim Henson/Disney property the *Bear in the Big Blue House*. In one app, we had created a card game that kids could play against the highly excitable Muppet character Tutter

the mouse. Tutter had hilarious reactions whenever players drew a card he wanted. In one of the funniest moves, he made a big noise and passed out, falling off the screen, under the table.

It was such a surprising and funny move that kids would play the game over and over just to get that response. Intermittent reinforcement can also be used to reinforce FUN! Even though the game was designed for three- to five-year-olds, we noticed children as old as ten coming to play against Tutter.

Puppeteer Peter Linz brought Tutter to life in a hilarious way.

Categories of Surprise

One might think that surprises are just that. There are big ones and small ones, and that's it. In fact, there are several categories of surprise, each with its own instinctual response and circumstances for eliciting it. The four categories are: Startle, Amaze, Insight, and Humorous Surprise.

Startle Surprise

Sometimes associated with fear or caution, startle surprise is the one that makes you jump. It's part of ancient survival hardwiring, and it has been used in almost every scary movie as a way to get you to react. (Just when you think the bad guy is finally dead, and you've relaxed, letting your guard down, he lunges out one more time, making you jump!) There are smaller, subtler startle surprises that give just a little charge, and people tend to find them entertaining in a different way.

iStock.com/boyfriend

Think about the appeal of a jack-in-the-box. You know Jack's in there—you just pushed him back down—but when you turn the crank to make Jack pop back up, he still surprises you. Because most kids like being surprised *and* are in some control of this surprise, they will do it again and again until it no longer surprises them or holds their attention.

Amaze Surprise

In children's interactive design, the amaze surprise effect is one in which *the child's action* creates a *much larger* or different effect than expected. For this reason, it is often associated with a sense of empowerment because the child's effort has an amplified and surprising outcome. The involvement of the child in creating the effect or outcome distinguishes this kind of surprise from startle surprise.

© David Notowitz

Because amaze surprise is associated with a more dramatic and radical result than anticipated, it is sometimes also called the OMG, or "Oh, my God" effect. Amaze surprise can include states of wonder, astonishment, and disbelief that are not about the game itself but about the player's ability to affect the game's outcome.

iStock.com/Jason Lugo

Designer's Note

The amaze surprise effect was one of the main interactions inside the pages of Living Books, where clicking around the screen on anything that looked clickable or interesting would launch a lively animation with silly sound effects. Young children immediately took ownership of what happened when they clicked, amazed that they could create delightful audio and animation effects. The phrase "Look what I did, Mom!" (or "Dad") has a direct relationship to the child's amazement at the program's response to their exploration.

StartupStockPhotos / Pixabay.com

A great example of amaze surprise in gameplay is the scenario of an **epic win**. The photo to the left shows kids in the midst of an epic win during a computer game. In the TED talk she gave in 2010, Jane McGonigal, game designer and author, described the experience this way, "An epic win is an outcome that is so extraordinarily positive you had no idea it was possible until you achieved it.... And when you get there you are shocked to discover what you are truly capable of."[10] This is a great definition for that moment of ultimate amaze surprise. Jane defines an epic win not by a score or technical effect, but by the player's *reaction* to their own efforts. An epic win gives the player more belief in what he or she can accomplish. They will believe in themselves at a deeper level, inside and outside of the game. Any game where a designer can do this for a child will have players excited about further exploration and discovery.

Insight Surprise

Insight surprise is an awakened understanding of *how things work together*—that flash of comprehension when, all of a sudden, something makes sense. It is the "Aha!" moment when the brain makes direct cognitive connections. This abrupt understanding of a specific cause and effect is often referred to as an epiphany.

© Design Pics Inc / Alamy Stock Photo

Insight surprise is related to puzzle solving, glimpsing the interactive relationships between things, and sometimes the social behaviors between people. It may be that moment for kids when they see how fractions work for the first time, such as after playing a game with pizza slices. "Oh, I get it. One eighth is one of eight pieces of the whole pizza!" Insight surprise is empowering. It makes kids feel smarter because now they *get it*.

© Catriona Bass / Alamy Stock Photo

Humorous Surprise

Humorous surprise is the kind of cognitive mismatch that is a major component in all good storytelling, and it is a critical part of most jokes. The surprise factor plays itself out as the storyteller weaves a perception of specific events and places that are somewhat familiar and relevant to the audience, gaining their involvement through imagination and their scrutiny of the facts. The audience unconsciously anticipates the arc of the story, makes a leap to the end, and believes they know what the natural conclusion will be. The surprise and delight come when the end of the story takes an unexpected turn and winds up being completely different from the audience's assumption. This classic surprise by *plot twist* is what the storyteller has been skillfully leading you to all along.

Designer's Note

I heard a story of someone watching a clown at the circus talking to kids about their favorite part of the show. One child confessed that the elephants where his favorite, to which the clown smiled and replied, "Yeah, the elephants are my favorite, too." Then he added, "They are the best kissers in the whole circus!" The look of surprise and bewilderment on the kid's face was priceless as he tried to integrate the information and imagine the clown, and then himself, trying to kiss an elephant. A definite surprise change in perspective.

With joke telling, the surprise twist that makes the joke work is called the *punch line*. The less expected the punch line, the bigger the surprise, and the funnier the joke is. We all know kids love the mental surprise that comes with corny jokes, which are often based on words having more than one meaning or sounding like other words that mean something different. What tickles kids changes as they become older and more sophisticated, but this basic function of surprise in all jokes is universal, and it can be easily seen in jokes and stories kids love.

Consider the classic knock-knock joke: "Knock, knock. Who's there? Doris. Doris Who? Doris open, come on in!" We imagine a person named Doris, but then the name is pronounced to be "door is," giving the image of a large wooden object instead of a person. The punch line furnishes a completely different meaning than what the listener expected. Corny as it is, kids get a giggle from this, and they can't wait to try out the cleverness of it on all their friends and family. Humor Surprise frequently contains an unexpected, sudden shift in perspective, a good thing to remember whenever you are trying to make a joke.

Haikus are easy
But sometimes they don't make sense
Refrigerator[11]
—Rolf Nelson, designer

Humor

Adding even a little humor and silliness to a program can go a long way toward getting kids to love it and come back to it. Kids love humor. It's a great way to connect with them, and it's much easier to tickle a kid's funny bone than an adult's. Humor is entertaining, lifts spirits, adds life to products, and makes kids feel better. But remember that kids' humor is usually not the same as adult humor.

© Dan Piraro.

Humor is in the eye of the beholder. Humor comes in various flavors, and it shifts depending on age. Younger kids love more slapstick, physical humor like the old pie-in-the-face or slip-on-a-banana-peel kind. Boys may have more interest than girls in aggressive humor, but this could very well be cultural.[12]

Many kids these days love to pass around favorite YouTube videos of cats, dogs, and people doing silly things. As kids get older, various levels of social humor begin to make them laugh. There is an age—after more logical thinking functions become available—when, all of sudden, the old *Mad Magazine* style of humor, sarcasm, and parody just tickles them. The humor of some jokes unfolds more slowly, as in the *Bizarro* cartoon on the left.

Multilevel humor. Jim Henson (of *Muppets* fame) and his team were famous for mixing kid silliness with adult-level parody and illogic. Longtime children's designer Joyce Hakansson (her first products were in the late 1970s!) commented,

I think part of what really made Jim's work so effective was that it worked at two levels. There's a level that appeals to the child because it's quirky and silly and full of great characters, and kids just kind of go with it, and there is the part that appeals to adults. And the two are not at all in conflict. I remember watching *Sesame Street* one day, just to keep up with it, and they were doing the *Guy Smiley Show*, which is really funny and kids like it and they don't realize that it is a parody of TV. He was introducing the "next

"On Vacation with Guy Smiley," *Sesame Street*.

contestant" and his name was Bill Jones and he came from Oceanview, Kansas—which just cracked me up, you know, because it was so illogical, irrational, and silly, and a kid wouldn't think that was funny. And yet, it didn't disturb their enjoyment of the show. There were other parts for them. So I think that if you can get that double layer of humor, that really does address both populations—doesn't have to be adults per se, but different age groups. I think then you have something that will work extraordinarily well for a large audience.[13]

Humor isn't necessarily sweet. Conflict, rivalry, jealousy, fear, and difficult situations are at the heart of good drama and humor, *and* are emotions kids can relate to. Donald Duck wasn't funny because he had a sweet and patient personality. Younger children prefer less conflict and violence, but the drama of emotional situations, especially when tied to humor, holds kids' attention because they want to know what happens next.

Characters are funny. Well-designed characters with plucky or quirky personalities are naturally funny and appealing to kids, and they can get away with all

kinds of wacky shenanigans that are harder to pull off in text or with real people. Characters are often outside the social norm and can act out and have larger-than-life reactions to situations. Kids love that. Characters can allow themselves to be more playful, to follow their feelings, to be characters, with a kind of freedom that entrances and delights kids of all ages. (For more on character development and design, see Ch. 14.)

Get silly yourself. In the midst of deadlines and long workdays, it is easy to take life too seriously. It is difficult to be playful when you're focused on the mountain of work in front of you. As part of the practice of connecting with kids, it is important to take time to connect with your own internal kid. Take some time to play and open yourself to inspiration, joy, and laughter. When the production teams have had a great time and are excited about what they are building, it *shows* in the final product. As Annie Fox, an author, teen-advisor, and designer of children's CD-ROMs, says, "I enjoy being in an environment that looks like the people who designed it had *fun* designing it."[14]

Designer's Note

One thing I like to do when I am feeling too adult is to go see the latest big animated movie for kids and listen to when all the kids laugh. Besides it being wonderfully contagious for me, I get to tune in to what makes them laugh. Often, different gags and scenes will make different age groups in the audience laugh. I like to practice taking off my adult viewpoint and open up to let the film entertain me in all the ways it can, just like the kids.

Deepening Involvement

Engagement Through Personalization and Ownership

User retention is key to success for any kids' game, site, or service, especially in a subscription environment. Consistent retention is directly linked to kids feeling successful in their actions, being heard and seen, and having some creative ownership in the games and worlds they inhabit. Here are some of the main attributes that affect kid-user retention.

Ownership

Children stay involved in sites and products that allow, promote, value, and *recognize* their participation. Participation gives kids a sense of membership and ownership in a game or site. A sense of ownership can be achieved through a variety of means:

rmarmion © 123RF.com

© pressmaster/Depositphotos.com

Personalization and customization. Personalization is one of the easiest ways for kids to express a sense of themselves. With personalization, kids get to make their own whatever from available variables. In a digital world, they get to name their avatar, pick aspects of its looks, and choose what combination of clothes will make a great outfit. Within their personal room, they may get to pick wallpaper, arrange furniture, accessorize, and decorate just as they like. It is their creative expression of themselves, one that they also like to show and share with others. This simple ability to customize their world fosters a strong sense of ownership and supports kids' desire to return.

Ability to post/share personal creative output. Kids are proud of what they create, and they like to save, share, or post their creations online for all to see.

We love what we create.
—**Sophocles**

Collecting. Kids are natural collectors, and allowing them to earn and gather digital items can be a strategy to keep them coming back to your game or site. In virtual worlds, items are usually kept in a child's personal "room" or inventory box. The items may reflect a child's level of attainment or just be an extensive set of furnishings for the space, accessories for an avatar, or items to barter. The desire for ever better items is a popular reason for returning to a site, especially if the items are tools and powers needed to proceed with the larger meta-theme of a world. Collecting for collecting's sake holds some interest, but receiving badges, for instance, is not enough of a reward in and of itself. The activities employed to get the badges must also be interesting.

Pets. Children love having animals as pets. Digital pets are popular, and you seldom have to clean up after them! Kids have an intuitive inclination for caretaking, and they often have digital pets on several sites and programs. Children will often return to a site again and again to collect items for their pets or simply to check on them. Finding a balance of caretaking responsibilities and having pets that are "independent" is important. Too much regular caretaking becomes tedious and boring, but making a digital pet "happy" by petting, feeding (especially treats), and playing with them can be a fun activity. New activities and pet reactions need to be added over time to keep the sense of freshness and discovery alive.

Opinion polls and voting. Kids have opinions, and they appreciate the opportunity to express them. Opinion polls give them a voice and may allow them to see what other kids are feeling as well. Occasionally, kids can be asked to vote on what they would like to see happen next, how things should work, or what to name a new character. In a "What's Hot, What's Not?" poll, kids might get to see trends in other parts of the country or the world—a great way to learn geography without calling it that.

Communication. Kids like to talk to other kids, especially when they reach the tween years (9–12) and their communication skills improve. They connect in every way possible: through email, text, instant message, chat, video chat, and more. Sites and tools that support and enhance communication will create loyalty, retention, and community.

A host of safety issues can arise from games and services offering direct communication. Consequently, many children's sites have limited communication in order to maintain safety. Kids, however, want to connect with each other and are always inventing new strategies to do so. They are very creative. One of the best solutions I have seen many kids use is to adopt a third party web communication tool like Skype, so they can talk and be connected with friends while their avatars play games together in a virtual world. (For more on different solutions for kids communication tools, see Ch. 16, pp. 260–264.)

Personal empowerment. Kids want something interesting and empowering to do. Give them a good hook by building a compelling mission, goal, or challenge they can take on (like saving the world or finding the treasure). It should be clear-cut, easily understandable, and highly desirable. Empower them with the tools and directions and set them loose. Consider *World of Warcraft*: no matter who you are, or how old you are, there is always a quest where YOU are needed to save the world. That's empowering.

Challenges, Leveling, and Pacing

For younger children, there is so much to explore and experiment with that finding challenging new things to do is easy. As their knowledge base gets larger, and motor skills get better, kids look for greater challenges. With their emerging identities and senses of self, they also enjoy ways of establishing, recording, and showing the results of their achievements.

Challenge

The human brain likes solving problems, and we spend much of each day doing so. Interactive media is a perfect venue for delivering a flow of challenges that can captivate attention and engage players young and old. As children develop, they look for incrementally greater levels of challenges through **Problem Solving Play.** They are deeply involved in the process of Mastery Play, and they enjoy interacting near the limit of their skill level. A challenge should be doable, but not too easy; it should push the boundaries of knowledge and experience. The challenge should come from the gameplay itself and *not* from interface hurdles, such as non-intuitive icons, lengthy instructions, or required reading in preschooler titles.

Success. All children develop feelings of competence as their skill levels increase, and those feelings of competence inspire them to take on new challenges, especially when they believe they have a reasonable chance of success. It is our responsibility as designers to provide activities with solvable problems that are at or near a child's developmental level.

An appropriate challenge is naturally interesting to a child. The key to making a problem interesting is to design the task to be just hard enough to require work, but not so hard that the player gets stuck. If it's too easy, kids get bored, and if it's too hard, they get frustrated. In either case, their attention and engagement will wane, and their motivation will suffer.

Leveling. Leveling is the most common method of offering challenging activities that build incrementally on previous success. Difficulty increases as levels are mastered. Children like the feeling of mastery, and a great game maintains just the right level of challenge to keep them involved and moving forward. A leveled design needs to support the building and inclusion of skills and elements previously mastered. The goal is to build a history of competence in the player.

Designer's Note

Shigeru Miyamoto, designer of Nintendo's *Mario*, *Donkey Kong*, *Legend of Zelda*, Wii series, and more, is a master of level design, pacing, and building on previous skills. As a player progresses in a game like *Super Mario Bros.*, each new challenge teaches the player skills and tricks needed to move forward. I was inspired to become a designer, in part, because I saw how engaged my own children were when playing Miyamoto's games. My kids and their friends were captivated for hours while riding that sharp edge of challenge that spurred them on. I used to joke that I was a parent with Nintendo guilt because my children spent so much time playing, but I knew that those same design principles could be used in environments that included more educational content as well.

Pacing. In designing for younger children, pacing is not an issue. Younger kids prefer a sandbox environment where they can play at their chosen speed. Older children like the challenge of more complex games in which pacing is a greater factor. Pacing is the throttle that sets the rate at which new material is delivered to the player; it controls progress. Pacing balances ability and level of difficulty to keep games interesting. It is a factor in all good storytelling, and it works much the same way in interactive content. If pacing is too fast, children can be overwhelmed, and if it's too slow, they become bored. As Harry Gottlieb, founder of Jellyvision, so perfectly describes in *The Jack Principles*,[15] it helps to follow these tips to keep a good flow in paced activities:

- **Give only one goal/task to accomplish at a time.** This allows children to make a series of brief decisions that quickly propel them forward and hold their attention. Being asked to react moment by moment creates momentum and engagement.

- **Make sure kids know what to do at any given moment.** If children have to pause because they don't know what to do, that is a hiccup in the pacing, and flow is compromised.

- **Provide only meaningful choices.** Kids love the sense of "steering" and being in control that comes in a fast-paced and challenging game. Any choices that don't support getting to their goal are distracting, annoying, and a hindrance to engagement. Agency is also important—kids should feel that what they do makes a difference and has an effect on the final outcome.

- **Keep the number of available choices low.** Limiting the number of choices available at a given moment means that less time will be used to make a decision, and pacing will be sustained. As the consequences of decisions are understood, children learn the answers and, because gameplay is repeatable, they get to explore choices again with more information.

- **Focus attention on the task at hand.** What's important to kids is what they need to do next in order to continue interacting. Keep distracting elements to a minimum, and keep information relevant to decisions they will need to make.

- **Give direct and efficient input control.** Kids want to drive and have control of the action. Make sure the game's input controls work well for the device and for the developmental level of your players. The better the input, the more empowering the play.

- **Set clear time limits or consequences for inaction.** Gameplay (for older kids) is not very exciting if there is no pressure to act or move forward. Consequences give kids a reason to take action. Learning to avoid undesirable outcomes adds to the thrill of the game, as does a ticking clock.

- **Have choices ready.** Pacing is about movement and action. Make sure to keep players sufficiently occupied until they reach their goal. A new group of choices should always be coming up.

Meaningful tension. Injecting plot tension into gameplay adds excitement and immediacy. It is a classic dramatic technique that children understand easily. Tension is meaningful when it has consequences (like certain disaster) for not completing the task in a timely fashion. Tension can take the form of:

- **Challenges and quests.** Action challenges and quests are overarching story lines with an ultimate goal, a challenge that the player must overcome. The goal needs to be clearly defined. It can be as simple and short as helping a sad character find something they lost, or it can be something larger like getting into the treasure room of a mountain castle, or as epic as battling the Dark Lord to save the world. If a challenge seems doable and worthwhile, kids are quick to take up the task. Having a story line helps kids connect emotionally to the activity.

- **Conflict and competition.** Dramatic conflict, such as having opposing characters vying for the same goal, can heighten the need to complete the game or level. Competition adds excitement to most games but works less well in learning activities where repetition is part of the learning process.

- **Time pressure.** A time constraint forces a player to react quickly, take action, and try things without overthinking. The ticking time bomb is a classic storytelling trick to enhance tension, and it works the same way in games. The challenge and pressure to make decisions and move forward in an expedient way adds excitement and enhances the need to act. Time elements aren't always clocks. They may be monsters or other critters that catch a player who doesn't proceed quickly enough.

Rewards. Rewards can act as incentives to keep kids involved, especially if the rewards are ones kids care about. Some games have elaborate reward systems and in-game economies based on the game's "coin-of-the-realm," be it money, power chips, power-ups, or jelly beans. The potential loss of rewards is also used to motivate action. In general, it is a good idea to be liberal when giving rewards and light on imposing penalties. Reward systems can be helpful as ways of:

- **Demonstrating progress.** Games often reward players' progress with new (game-themed) titles, badges, and increases in status. These things may not be money, but they are levels of attainment that come with bragging rights.

- **Sharing skill/attainment levels with peers.** Getting their names on a leader board or registering an achievement level in a way that other players can see can be a great motivator for kids to strive for a higher score. This is especially true for kids who love multiplayer competitive games where a player's skill status is visible to all.

- **Gaining *power-ups*.** Power-ups are instant in-game rewards that a player's avatar receives during play, often extending a player's "life" and performance at that level. Power-ups usually have a short life and must be used quickly. They reinforce the need for greater immediate action.

- **Acquiring points/currency.** Many games use point systems as currency. Players can use their points to open new areas or buy special items for their characters or later gameplay. Acquiring a large bank account of coins-of-the-realm is most valuable when there are things kids are interested in spending them on. Coin for coin's sake has less value, and coins too easily earned have little value. It is important to keep the value and prestige of currency high in order to make the effort worth it.

Rewards come in all shapes and forms. The most basic form of reward is acknowledging the actions of the child. Acknowledgment can be as simple as a crisp audio or animated interface response to a child's actions, or it might take the form of praise. As kids get older, things like status, higher rankings, access to special earned areas, or just plain old points become more important. Either way, rewards support engagement by adding additional goals as payoff for continued play. When added to an intrinsically fun environment (without interfering with intrinsic play), they can enhance and extend playtime and bring kids back for more. (For more on play patterns, see Ch. 15.)

While the aisles of a toy superstore can make kids jump up and down with longing, what is more important than grabbing kids' desire is to feed and sustain their interests by making smart products that connect with their inner motivations. Think of your design as a way to honor a child's play integrity.

So far, this book has focused on understanding the nature of play, how to create invitations, and tips on sustaining play. The next few chapters will talk further about how to connect with built-in wiring for interactivity, how to work with vision and sound, and what all this means for the nuts and bolts of design.

anatols / 123RF Stock Photo

PART 2

Engaging the Senses

Digital games or computer-driven devices might seem light years removed from the primitive world of our ancient ancestors, but in many ways, how we interact with modern media evolved from their experiences. This section will first explore the relationship between survival hardwiring and modern media, then look more deeply at how our brains interpret visual and audio information, and finally discuss how to use that knowledge to create engaging interactive visual and audio experiences for children.

The broader one's understanding of the human experience, the better design we will have.[1]

Old Brains in a Modern World:
How Inherited Hardwiring Affects Our Perception of Media

Every human comes into this world with a body, and that body is designed to experience the world by receiving information through the senses. The brain learns to interpret the body's sensory experiences. That brain also possesses a large array of preprogrammed responses developed by our ancestors over millennia and encoded with reactions designed to help *us* survive. Why does this matter to interactive media design? The brain has amazing potential to translate sensory information into complex thoughts and emotions. By understanding some of the brain's hardwiring, and how to trigger certain reactions, designers can intentionally tap into the most primitive aspects of human experience and perception to create more immersive and powerful media, whether for children or adults. This chapter offers a perspective on why the survival patterns of our ancestors affect how we relate to modern media.

The eye—it cannot choose but see; we cannot bid the ear be still; our bodies feel, where'er they be, against or with our will.
—William Wordsworth, poet

We Are the Survivors

Where did you get your body? You are the son or daughter of a son and daughter, going back thousands of generations. Even as you read this book, the hands that hold it open are connected back through those generations; only because they survived are you here today and reading this book. We humans today, all of us walking around our planet in these breathing bodies, we are *the survivors*.

Our Ancestors' Media

The "media" of our ancient ancestors was the world around them… and the game they played was survival.

Except for perhaps a good story around an open fire (if they had fire), or a painting on a cave wall, the media of our ancestors was the living world they existed in, where they spent a lot of effort trying to stay alive. Those who reacted quickly to danger survived; those who didn't were eaten. Over successive generations, natural selection preserved these reactions and instincts of our ancestors. Survival instincts are hardwired into our brains.

What does that mean for you? It means that how your eyes automatically track movement in your peripheral vision; why you startle at loud noises; and how you are able to hear, even in your sleep, all are relevant to how you take in the media of our modern world. *You relate to media with the same instincts your ancestors used to relate to a more primitive world.* Part of you relates to media *as if* it was real. (Why else would we care about moving images on a screen?) Your primitive instincts are alive and well, operating at a preconscious level, continuing to serve you, and continuing to respond automatically to stimuli in your life, including entertainment.

We are sensing beings. Smelling, tasting, hearing, seeing, and touching. People are walking, talking, feeling beings who continuously absorb vast amounts of information from this amazing world around us. People take in so much information that in any given moment we unknowingly prioritize what to notice, and much of the rest of what we sense falls quietly into the background, often below conscious awareness. Your body is listening to things your conscious mind doesn't hear. How often are you aware of your breathing? Mostly, your body breathes unconsciously, and only when there is a significant change, or when someone calls attention to it, do you notice.

(Did you just take a deeper breath?)

We process media on multiple levels at once. All good interactive design and media already speaks to our body's ancestral wiring; that's why we like it. Let's take a look at some of that wiring, and how we perceive information on more levels than expected.

Ancient Brains in a Modern World

In the 1960s, evolutionary neurologist Dr. Paul MacLean put forth a model of the triune brain, which suggests that three separate structures of the human brain developed during the course of evolutionary history.[2] This theory provides an interesting lens through which to consider how modern media interacts with our older instinctual wiring. Current neurological theory has moved to considerably more complicated models that allow for more intricate interconnection between all parts of the brain and body than Dr. MacLean originally proposed, but MacLean's ideas are still useful for designers who are thinking about the ways certain design elements create responses in the kids (or adults) who are using their interfaces. What follows is a very simplified version of MacLean's theory.

The Triune Brain Model

As life developed on this planet, it took on many wondrous, diverse forms, from jellyfish to giraffes, from ants to elephants. Life is a branching tree with new forms building upon older ones. We can think of our brains in the same way. The oldest brain component, which operates at the lowest levels, is often referred to as the reptilian brain. Over time, a new layer, which MacLean called the mammalian brain, was added, with new features and functions, such as emotions and nurturing. The more recently developed third layer, the neocortex, is home to language and abstract thought.[3] The brain takes in all media as sensory information, integrates it in microseconds, and then has a reaction. In the triune model, each area of the brain interprets and responds to input differently, depending on its function. You will have a different reaction to a wasp landing on you than to the same wasp landing on a friend. Your reaction to the wasp landing on *you* comes from an older part of the brain.

According to MacLean's theory, the three brains operate like "three interconnected biological computers, with each having its own special intelligence, its own subjectivity, its own sense of time and space, and its own memory, motor, and other functions."[4] The three brains are intricately and deeply interconnected, but in many ways, they seem to operate independently, interpreting the same information differently. These evolutionary "brains" are really one brain that works as our human operating system. They are part of the wiring that comes with the body, and they influence how we react to external stimuli.

In order to create really great games, it's important to consider how the brain works; to know, for example, that received sensory data from the world comes to the reptilian and mammalian brains before the neocortex can act on it. Good design balances different types of effects to purposefully engage a specific part (or parts) of the brain.[5] For instance, flashy movements on the side of the screen will trigger the reptilian brain to go on alert and cause the user to focus there. This is great if the goal is to get the user to explore more of the screen. Otherwise, it's not.

The Reptilian Brain

A bulbous enlargement at the top of the spinal cord, in the center of the physical brain, is the oldest brain in evolutionary terms: what MacLean called the reptilian brain or R-complex. It includes the brain stem and the cerebellum, and it is much like the brain of present-day reptiles. Its purpose is physical survival and maintenance of the body. It regulates breathing, heartbeat, digestion, blood pressure, temperature, startle reflexes, and other bodily functions. Though it has little to no emotional wiring, a reptile's brain has the capacity for instinctual behaviors such as courtship, mating, and territorial defense.[6] Through this brain, we share some ancient wiring with all reptiles on the planet.

Autonomic functions. Evolutionarily and physically, all parts of the brain are interconnected with the spinal cord. The brain stem is the lowest part of the brain because it is at the top of, and contiguous with, the spinal cord. Often called the **autonomic nervous system** (ANS), it functions automatically, like a thermostat regulates temperature. The ANS controls breathing, digestion, and heartbeat, and it prompts functions like swallowing, perspiration, and salivation.[7] It is active, even in deep sleep, and it regulates life functions even when a person is temporarily "brain dead" after an accident.

Basic survival instincts. The reptilian brain is primarily concerned with getting food and keeping you from becoming food. It is the body's most basic survival wiring. It automatically draws your eyes to small movements in your peripheral vision and wakes you even from a deep sleep if an unfamiliar noise occurs. Reacting to sound and movement is instinctual, and it often happens beyond conscious control. The brain's early warning system is supported by omnidirectional audio and the ability to hear things from quite a distance.

"Made you jump!"—the reactive brain. The reptilian brain is particularly good for making quick decisions *without* thinking. The reptilian brain focuses on survival. It takes over when you are in danger and don't have time to think. It reacts to stimulus from the world with or without any conscious effort or input. It is why you may instinctively jump out of the way of a falling object or duck when a ball flies by your head.

Sensory-driven media. You can see the reptilian brain at work in a lot of teen and adult media, especially horror, action, and adventure movies and games. In these games and movies, you are watching colored images and synchronized sound representing things that are not really happening. You logically (with your modern brain) know these events are not real, yet you *feel* fear and apprehension. The media is stimulating your older brain to manipulate responses for the purposes of entertainment. This is modern media talking directly to the ancestral body/brain to get a reaction and your attention. Your older brain says, "Better look at this movement. Better listen to that sound. Might be something important." This is why animated banner ads can be so annoying; they are hard *not* to look at. And all media is about getting your attention because *attention is energy*. Engaging someone's attention in a compelling way brings energy to your site, game, or product.

Designer's Note

Throughout this book there are a variety of examples describing how to trigger the reptilian portion of the brain for entertainment, attention, and engagement. For instance, Chapter 7 discusses how making an object progressively larger, especially quickly, signals the brain that something is getting closer. This technique was used at the beginning of every *Bear in the Big Blue House* episode, and it is also used in interactive media to gets kids' attention and ultimately draw them in.

The Mammalian Brain

As air-breathing life forms became more complex, the brain evolved beyond the functionality of its reptilian instincts. Wrapped around brain one, the reptilian brain, is brain two, often referred to as the limbic system, the paleomammalian system, or just the mammalian brain. The limbic system is the seat of human emotions and instincts that influence nurturing and caretaking interactions with our young and with each other.[8] Some simply refer to it as the "feeling" brain. Like the reptilian brain, the mammalian brain is concerned with feeding, fighting, fleeing, and reproduction. However, for mammals, these behaviors are more than just an auto-response to a stimulus. This system helps people determine whether they feel negatively or positively toward something, as in a "gut" reaction.

What MacLean calls the mammalian brain includes the hippocampus, hypothalamus, and amygdala.[9] It is the "feeling" brain, which is pre-language, but has the ability to play.[10] Other mammals' brains share this physiology, from mice to monkeys, deer to dolphins, and our favorite friends, cats and dogs.

The mammalian/limbic brain is where you begin processing and remembering somatic (body-oriented) information—what you see, hear, feel, taste, and smell. It is the home of

memories. The limbic brain learns to *act on* that information, rather than just *react* to it as the reptilian brain might do. The mammalian brain has extensive interconnections with the neocortex, the modern brain, so conscious function is never purely limbic or cortical, but an interwoven mixture of both.

The "feeling" brain, home of emotions. The mammalian brain is called the "feeling brain," not just because of our senses, but because it is at the core of our emotional being. It is the home of our ancient emotional architecture, and a big part of why we care about others. The limbic system includes the physical heart and related systems. When someone "thinks with their heart and not their head," it means they employ limbic body reactions rather than purely logical ones.

> *Emotions reach back 100 million years, while cognition is a few hundred thousand years old at best.*[11]
> —from *A General Theory of Love*

Mammals are nurturers. To care for our young and each other is a mammalian trait (in contrast to reptiles whose parental responsibilities mostly end with laying eggs). In humans, nurturing is imperative for the survival of our young. Human babies come into the world needing a lot more care than any other mammals, and caretaking and nurturing is critical to their survival. In order to thrive, babies need not only food and warmth, but also attention and touch.[12] Humans have elaborate and involved child rearing instincts to nurture and protect our children, and since our children take *so long* to mature, we develop strong social bonds during the nurturing process. These bonds last throughout our lives and extend beyond our immediate family.[13] We live our lives in limbic relationship to others.

Mammals are social. Along with all the bonding and emotional connection mentioned above, survival rates favor small groups and bands over individuals.[14] This is evident in how mammals tend to form herds, packs, and pods. Banding together was a survival strategy of our ancestors as well. No matter the culture or the country, people tend to build houses close to one another. In addition to providing safety, being together in social groups allows for other enjoyable activities like grooming, playing, and sharing resources. Even before humans developed enough to have true language, we lived together in small social bands. We are social beings at our core.

The traits often considered most "human" are our mammalian traits, and since almost all media is about interaction with and between other humans, understanding more about how to speak directly to this part of ourselves is fundamental in creating satisfying interactive content.

Body language was our first language. Even before language, the mammalian/limbic brain communicated through emotions and an intuitive understanding of body language. All animals use posture and facial expression to communicate.

Just looking at a dog's tail (or teeth) can tell you a lot about how he is feeling. Body language was our first language, and people can still read information about others' state of being based solely on how they hold themselves and move. Effective body language is the stock and trade of all great actors and animators because it allows them to express the mental and emotional state of a character through gesture and movement.

Why is all this important to interactive design? Because even though people seldom consciously recognize the extent to which this older, preverbal mammalian brain is at play in daily life, it informs and affects everything they do. There is no interaction that is not influenced by its ongoing operational presence. Great interactive design for children must create opportunities that speak directly to and connect with the deep-seated, emotional patterns of social relationships and play.

This brain can play. One unique quality in animals possessing limbic brains is that they can *play*. A dog wants to engage you in a tug-of-war with an old rope not because he wants the rope; he wants the interaction with you. The same thing occurs when he joyously chases a ball thrown for no purpose. In contrast, you probably won't ever get your lizard or snake to play fetch or any other game. Play in humans, and especially children, is important to supporting health, happiness, and intelligence.[15] It is as important as good nutrition or getting enough sleep. According to MacLean's and other models, the limbic system is evolutionarily much older than the acquisition of language. In other words, we knew how to play before we knew how to talk.

iStock.com/Charles Mann

© Ksuksann/Depositphotos.com

For a mute mammal, play is physical poetry: it provides the permissible way, as Robert Frost said poems do, of saying one thing and meaning another.[16]
—from *A General Theory of Love*

The Modern Brain

The neocortex (also known as the cerebral cortex or neomammalian brain) is our thinking brain. It is also our largest and most evolutionarily modern brain, physically covering the first two brains. The human neocortex is made of two symmetrical sheets; each about as thick as six business cards and then wrinkled up to allow more of it to fit into the cranium.[17] In humans, the neocortex makes up about 80% of the brain, the largest percentage in any animal.[18] It is what people generally mean when they refer to "the brain," and it is, in fact, what they think *with* when they do so. The higher cognitive functions found in the neocortex also distinguish humans from other animals.

Awareness and self-awareness. What MacLean calls the modern brain is our consciously aware brain, the one reading this now. It is the brain that allows us to use a mental mirror and to see ourselves, to be "self-conscious," and to contemplate what we are experiencing. It is the command post for conscious motor control, what we think of as will, like being able to tell the index finger on your left hand to scratch your nose. It is what directs our bodies when we are doing something on purpose. We just will it, and our body follows. (Think "blink eyes," and they probably just did.)

The thinking brain. The neocortex controls our higher-order thinking skills, such as reason and speech. Speaking, writing, reading, planning, reasoning, strategizing, and all abstract thought happen in the neocortex.[19] Our ability to think abstractly is part of what makes us the powerful (or terrible, from the POV of other species) predators that we are. Abstraction allows us to contemplate the future and to think in terms of time. It also allows us to use symbols to create systems of writing, reading, and mathematics.

The logical brain. The neocortex is the logical brain that Spock of *Star Trek* so appreciated. It can analyze all the reasons why something should, could, might, or did happen. It also performs rational, unemotional evaluations of events and delivers judgments. It is why this brain is good at games of logic and strategy like chess. It is all about logical sequences and conceptual problem solving.

Highly creative. Another side of this same ability to think abstractly, holding several concepts and ideas at once, allows for the recombination of information we call *creativity*. It is one of the ways the modern brain plays, and it's directly related to our ability to learn.

Media and the Three Brains

When designers construct an interactive experience, it's helpful for them to consider how the different parts of the brain will react to particular sensory input and to more abstract concepts and problems. By including interactions that communicate with more than one area of the brain, a designer can improve the overall level of interest, engagement, and satisfaction for the user. This section will cover the ways each part of the brain responds to media.

The Reptilian Brain

As mentioned earlier, much of the reptilian brain works in an autonomic fashion, instinctively reacting to stimuli. Since the reptilian brain is about survival, it is immediately active in frightening situations. It takes over when people feel threatened or endangered. Two of the most reactive instincts of the reptilian brain are the *fight or flight* mechanism and the startle reflex. The fight or flight reaction gets your adrenaline pumping and powers escape or defensive actions in the body. The startle reflex triggers an ancient hardwired response to abrupt movement and/or noise that makes you jump involuntarily.

Scc.comics/Shutterstock.com; beatriagj © 123RF.com

You will probably never find a scary movie that doesn't try to startle the audience at least once by invoking these basic responses. How many times have you seen that, just when everything finally seems safe, and you peer over the edge into where the supposedly dead monster went, it lunges out one more time to get the audience to jump in their seats. The mock danger triggers ancient auto-reactive areas in the reptilian area of your brain, pumps your body up with response hormones and gets your heart beating, and you are entertained (if you want to call it that). Media often uses this ability to scare people because it gets attention and a big reaction. This strategy is also used by some politicians seeking followers, because when people are scared, they act from the reactive mind, not the logical mind. In other words, that which scares us steers us.[20]

As talked about in the last chapter, an autonomic response doesn't have to be scary to entertain us. Some of the fun in interactive content for children comes from smaller "surprise!" moments activated by a child's action. The child touches something, and it responds by making a noise, animating, or triggering a disproportionately large event. It is empowering and stimulating at the same time. A classic surprise response occurs with a jack-in-the-box. Even though they know what's going to happen, kids still get a little jolt to their autonomic system each time Jack pops out.

I think, therefore I am.
—**René Descartes**

The Limbic and Neocortex Brains

The neocortex and our limbic systems are deeply interconnected, with neither being purely limbic or purely neocortical. Despite their connection, they deal with the same information differently, operating in many ways as if separate. This is why you can have the incongruent experience of knowing intellectually that something is true, while simultaneously feeling emotionally that it is not true. For instance, you might find yourself attracted to someone you don't even like. Or, as anyone who has tried to diet knows, you can tell yourself (a direction from the neocortex) that you are going to eat less and lose weight, but the next time you are stressed, you find yourself with an open ice cream container, feeding your body. Who is in charge here, the conscious brain (neocortex) or the (limbic) body?

The neocortex thinks it is in charge. Because of its superior intellect, the thinking brain thinks it is *the boss*, while emotions are secondary. To the thinking brain, emotions, although sometimes nice, are messy and unpredictable. The modern brain likes to think it is in control, and in many ways it does not acknowledge the power of concurrent emotions until those emotions take over and explosively express themselves. Emotions create the pathos of drama, and they are an essential element that brings passion to life.

Media content and the caretaking trait. Caretaking, a limbic brain trait, includes sharing the basics needed to sustain life: food, water, warmth, and touch. It also includes creating a sense of safety and protecting ourselves from potentially dangerous things. The relationships formed and expressed during all these levels of caretaking are the life dramas from which almost all media draw their stories.

> *Scientific evidence suggests that we have been caregivers since the outset of our existence.*[21]
>
> —Shelley E. Taylor, psychologist and author

How well or how poorly a character takes care of others is seen as the highest form of being human, the territory of heroes. It is universal in media. Usually, heroes are battling threatening forces outside of their social unit, be it family, tribe, community, culture, country, or planet. The person who jumps in the freezing water, not thinking of their own safety, to pull others out of the plane crash is someone to honor. Taking care of people in need (even strangers) resonates in real life and in media.

Another example of the limbic system's role in play patterns comes from mammals' instinct to care for babies. This instinct carries over to connecting with and caring for other animals. Younger children, especially, are drawn to baby animals, cartoon or otherwise, and instinctively want to nurture and take

iStock.com/nautilus_shell_studios

care of them. This inherent behavior is driven not by logic but by deeper mammalian hardwiring. Having virtual pets is very common in online kids' worlds, and it is popular in part because of the natural desire to care for the young. Kids don't need words or logic to know how to respond to a pet or baby animal. They intuitively connect.

Designer's Note

The popularity of social networks has a lot to do with communicating with others through language, but I see kids populate virtual worlds even when they seldom use the communication tools to connect. They appear to enjoy being in a space where there is a lot of action and where there are other kids playing. Interest in language-based communication increases with age, but all kids seem to enjoy the presence of others interacting (nicely) and being active. They don't necessarily need to talk to others, especially when younger, but they appreciate the experience of being with others.

Emotions and speech. Speaking and language are considered part of the function of the neocortex, but emotions carry the real content behind words, making them believable or not believable. The emotional nuance applied to a word can make it mean many different things, including its opposite. A good actor can make the word "Welcome" sound like "Go away!" Even though the words themselves are processed by the logical part of the brain, it is emotion that makes us care about what characters are saying because *we are interested in what they are feeling*. Emotions draw us more deeply into a story.

Limbic resonance. One of the interesting aspects of the limbic system comes from its ability to sense the feelings of, connect with, and non-verbally communicate with other limbic systems in close proximity. This phenomenon is called limbic resonance.[22] It is comparable to the way you can make two similarly tuned guitar strings vibrate by just plucking one of them. The second string resonates sympathetically. Limbic resonance is a way of accounting for animals' ability to empathize with each other and with us. It is also a foundation for our own deep social connectedness.[23] It is a big part of what is at play in our ability to share and understand the feelings of other people. In media design, good character development is judged by how it makes you *feel*, how strongly your body experience resonates with the feelings of the characters. You feel the emotional content by way of limbic resonance.

Feelings affect thinking, thinking affects feelings. In reality, the logical and emotional are parts of one system, and neither operates without affecting the other. Strong emotional experiences and conditioning during childhood (a time when you are most vulnerable) can influence how you think about certain situations for the rest of your life. *Imagined* threats in the future can make your body feel scared or stressed even if there is no danger in the present moment. Such is the reciprocal ongoing interaction between thinking and feeling. Both have a big influence on the other, and both need to be considered when designing content for children who are more susceptible to manipulation than adults are.

Thoughts, loaded with emotional content, flow through the body's limbic system and create a vibrational frequency of what you are feeling at any given moment. Like the plucked guitar string, others who are close enough to us can feel this frequency or vibration. (This is commonly referred to as "the vibes.") You are able to sense some level of what others are feeling. This is huge in terms of media because people love to feel *along with* characters in stories.

"Vibes" are contagious. Limbic resonance is also at play in a group experience. Connecting with other humans is why going to a movie with an engaged audience is more fun than watching at home alone. The authors of *A General Theory of Love* put it this way, "Because limbic states can leap between minds, feelings are contagious, while notions are not."[24]

This energetic phenomenon also accounts for how panic spreads through crowds or how laughter can be so incredibly contagious.[25] The latter phenomenon is why many games (and TV shows) add prerecorded group responses to the audio tracks to support what they want the audience to feel. Prerecorded responses include not only laugh tracks, but also "Ahhhhh..." for sadness and cheers for passing a level or making a great move.

Anthropomorphism and media. Humans are so immersed and practiced in the art of limbic resonance that we look for it everywhere. We instinctively relate to anything that displays a moderate ability to communicate in ways that mimic human communication. For example, even the youngest kids understand the communication between characters in the first twenty minutes of Pixar's *Wall-E* even though no words are spoken. Wall-E's gestures and behavior are human-like, and therefore the audience connects.

We talk to our cats and dogs, we talk to our cars when we are driving, and we may curse at our computers when a program crashes unexpectedly. We know machines are not people, but we yell, curse, plead, and talk to them anyway. Maybe it's a piece of our ancient tribal culture emerging as we try to talk to the spirits in the machine: "Please don't crash, please don't crash."

We project our emotional communication abilities onto anything and everything. We give objects human-like personalities just by adding eyes and a mouth. In the children's world it's absolutely everywhere: in books, games, movies, toys, and more. Anything can come to life, especially when we are younger. This is an important point to remember: humans unconsciously relate to modern media as if it were a person, and are pleased when the computer responds back.[26]

Practically all our stories are about *human relationships* in one form or another. (Can you think of any that aren't?) We even anthropomorphize animal and robot stories to be about human relationships. This is particularly true in the realm of children's stories, which are concerned with teaching lessons about building and understanding aspects of character.

Logical arguments rarely change emotional beliefs. Logical arguments come from the neocortex, but emotions can easily override logic, motivate us to action, or change how we feel about something. Because this emotional part of us influences decisions, advertising and media talk around the thinking brain, going directly to this emotional/feeling part.[27] Automobile commercials, for example, are all about creating an experience through visual and audio storytelling, not a list of features. Product features are what advertisers say to the neocortex to keep it occupied while they sell people emotionally on the sizzle of the experience. Children's advertising is all about how cool and fun it would be to have the latest gadget or doll. In play, it is how a toy or game makes you feel, not how it makes you think, that is enjoyable. The appeal is almost always emotional in nature, supporting a child's desires and potential experiences.[28]

> *What matters is not what is written on the page. What matters is what is written in the heart.*[29]
>
> —Gregory Colbert, photographer

Good design talks to our emotions. When you think of a favorite game, movie, or book, what you remember is how it made you feel. Creating an engaging interactive experience is about deliberately talking to all the brains at once, offering something for each, and then offering the opportunity for ongoing communication. In essence, the goal is to create the opportunity for the user to have a *relationship* with the program through the computer's interface. Great children's content comes from communicating with a child's emotional brain as well as the more logical brain. If media is not talking to the emotions, it will not hold a child's attention.

> *When I was 5 years old, my mother always told me that happiness was the key to life. When I went to school, they asked me what I wanted to be when I grew up. I wrote down "happy." They told me I didn't understand the assignment, and I told them they didn't understand life.*[30]
>
> —attributed to John Lennon

Seeing is Believing: Visual Perception

When you look at the world, you take in information in the form of light, but what you see is a function of how your brain understands and interprets that input. As humans, we have a predilection for visual information; it is the sense we use most for navigation, interaction, survival, and entertainment. This chapter covers how the eyes and brain work together, and what that means in terms of getting attention, creating engaging images, and using visual information to hold a game together.

The real voyage of discovery consists not in seeking new landscapes but in having new eyes.[1]

—Marcel Proust, novelist

Look

Vision and the Brain

How humans perceive and process visual information has a huge impact on how to design programs for children. The more you understand visual perception, what you take for granted every day, the better you can intentionally make visually enchanting products for children.

Vision Is Our Predominant Sense

The old saying, "A picture is worth a thousand words" is an accurate adage in terms of data input to the human brain. Compared to the rest of our human senses, we take in huge amounts of visual data every second just by looking around. As John Medina, Director of the Brain Center for Applied Learning Research at Seattle Pacific University writes, "Vision is by far our most dominant sense, taking up half of our brain's resources."[2] Media that uses good visual strategies, especially anything with motion, easily gets attention and draws us in.

Vision as Metaphor

Of all the senses, terms related to vision are used the most to identify and express a state of mind. Moods can be *sunny* or *dark*, minds can be *brilliant* or *dull*. People can be *reflective, transparent, blind, bright,* or *dim-witted*. Someone can be *radiant, luminous, glowing,* or *colorful* if they are a character. Positive attributes are often expressed in terms of light. People can have *clarity* when they see things *clearly,* have *vision,* or become *enlightened*. *Seeing* is equated with understanding, *visibility* with truth. All these metaphors indicate how important vision is.

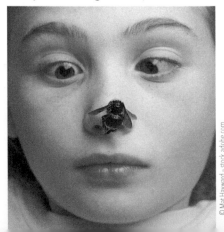

Focus

Humans are lucky enough to have forward facing binocular vision that allows them to direct their attention in a very focused manner. We all know what peripheral vision is, but what is it when it's not peripheral? It's foveal.

As you use your eyes, you are continually scanning the environment, moving your attention from place to place. Even though you think everything you see is in focus, the only area of your vision with truly sharp resolution is a small central point exactly where your eyes are focused. This is called foveal vision. Since this focused point has such a small diameter, the much larger area of our visual field, as taken in through our peripheral vision, is at a lower focal resolution.

Visual experience is really a series of separate focused snapshots stitched together by the brain to create an informational gestalt, and since any time you *look* at something, it is in focus, you just assume everything is.

You can check this out yourself right now by focusing on the word LOOK in the left hand margin. With your attention fully on LOOK, notice how quickly other words on the page lose their resolution. In the right margin, the word HERE is more of a dark shape than a word. Believe it or not, most of what you perceive visually at any given moment is fuzzy and unfocused.

Here

Foveal focus, along with *fixation*, the ability to quickly and accurately locate and inspect a series of stationary objects one after another, allows us to focus attention on small details.[3] Foveal focus is the essence of most puzzles, such as the *Where's Waldo?* books and games, *Highlights Hidden Pictures*, and the *I Spy* series, which all require the reader (or viewer, in this case) to find and identify objects in a deliberately busy scene. You are fixating with your foveal vision right now. Fixation is what allows us to move quickly from word to word while reading.

Online *Hidden Pictures Puzzle* by Highlights for Children.

Understanding and Getting Attention

Attention Is Energy

Attention is the focus of your mind (primarily through your eyes and ears) on something specific and the exclusion of other items in your awareness. People want your attention because *attention is energy*, and it is how we communicate with each other. Television networks gauge success by the number of viewers, and website hosts speak in terms of how many eyeballs they have each day. We all have attention to give, and we all want attention (at least a little).

Attention is like a garden hose of energy that we point around us as we look. What you put your attention on, you get more of. If you regularly put attention into improving your relationships, or your business, or your art form, whatever you put your attention on gets better. In interactive design, getting the user's attention is the paramount task. Then, if we don't want to lose it, we need to offer something enchanting. Part of the art of interactivity is *keeping* attention. The best ways to get attention through visual content are surprise, size, and movement.

Surprise!

Surprise, as discussed earlier, gets attention. In interactive software, surprise can cause a disproportionately large reaction to a mouse click or something spontaneous that catches the user off-guard. Humans are wired to respond to surprise. Surprise grabs attention and creates a sudden jump in arousal levels. It is also a valuable design tool for rekindling interest in the midst of gameplay.

SherryAnn_Elliott/Bigstock.com

Size Matters

When something is approaching us, it gets bigger. Size is one of our most primitive clues to proximity. Our brains evolved in a world where images could not be made arbitrarily larger or smaller. If something appeared large, it either was close, or large, or both! Something close to us still holds psychological significance whether enjoyable or frightening. We instinctively feel that a large image means an object is close, even when it's only on a two-dimensional surface like a TV or computer screen. Size is also is used in media to let us know what is important. Bigger things stand out. Like this:

Very Important Text   Less Important Text   Not Very Important Text

Close means more visual detail. When something is close, it feels more intimate, and we can see more detail. Look at your hand and the all the fine lines and creases of the skin. Now stand six feet back from a mirror and look at it again. What you notice most now is the shape of your hand and the possible movement of the fingers. Artists and animators often copy this real-world perception shift when developing characters. The closer characters are, the more detail we are able to see of them, and the more we know about them. When characters move farther away, the details become less significant, but their movements and gestures become increasingly important. As characters get smaller, or seemingly move farther away, we see less and less detail until all we are reading is a silhouette.

We remember big what we see big. This is a memory trick sometimes called the *binocular effect.*[4] Once we have seen something large and up close, it's easy to imagine the detail when it is seen small and far away. At large events, binoculars let us see things up close, but we never watch the whole event that way. We take the binoculars out, watch the players or performers in action until we've processed the close-up, then we put the binoculars down. Even after returning to a wider view of events, we continue to map the detail of the enlarged image onto the smaller characters.

Animation is much more expensive than still images, and animating small characters is cheaper than animating large ones. As a result, in many children's virtual worlds, the bulk of the animation shows avatars and characters at a distance. The downside is that it's hard to have a "personal" relationship with characters if they are always perceived as far away. Animators and children's designers frequently use a combination of less active large images of a character and active smaller animations to tie the two together in the child's mind. This technique is often used with avatars. Kids get to dress and personalize their avatars with accessories in the large view, where they can see the detail of everything they do. Later, when the characters are more active and animated, and that red hat the child added is now only a red dot, it doesn't matter because in the mind of the child, it still is that big red hat they put on earlier.

Designer's Note

© Disney

See it big.

In the children's online world *Club Penguin*, the designers needed to have dozens of independently controlled penguins (kid users) on the screen at once. They also needed to have them animate on a wide range of computer speeds. Their solution was to use very small and very simple penguin animations for the main navigational and gathering place scenes. There were larger versions of the penguins in their own rooms (igloos) where the number of moving objects on the screen was considerably fewer, leaving more processing power available. The larger versions let kids connect to their avatars by dressing and accessorizing them. Then, when the penguins get very small, kids can still imagine them in full detail.

© Disney

Remember it small.

When something gets bigger, it is coming toward you. When something moves *toward us*, it gets our attention, and our rate of arousal jumps dramatically. Our ancestors needed to know immediately if something was charging at them. Being alert and ready to respond was a matter of life and death. The speed of movement (How fast is it getting bigger?) determines how much attention we allot it, and how tense it will make us. Just like any critter in the wild, we instinctually want to know if a movement is something we need to worry about, fight, or take flight from.

This hardwired response to something big and close is nothing new, but if it is used well, it is engaging and entertaining. One good example showed up in the opening of a TV show (and was then repeated in software versions) for young children called *Bear in the Big Blue House*, a Jim Henson program created by Mitchell Kriegman for the Disney Channel:

The show opens, zooming in on the front door of Bear's house. The door opens. Bear comes out and starts to greet you, but before he completely invites you in, he sniffs around. He smells something. It's YOU. To your surprise, that big, sniffing schnoz quickly comes forward, filling the screen. He gives you a good sniffing up close (as the size would imply). Bear then pulls back and says something positive like, "Were you just eating cookies and milk, or do you always smell that good?"

Whether on TV or in the software version, the initial response from the young target audience is to lean back or back-up a little to get out of the way of that nose. Sometimes kids even stiffen up with raised shoulders when being sniffed. It almost tickles them, it feels so close. This big bear up in their faces gets the kids' attention, and then, when Bear says something nice, they are totally engaged. It's a memorable experience and a great way to start each show. When Bear gets larger, he is getting closer, even though the TV or computer has not moved. We easily suspend belief in what we know logically, and instead believe what our older natural instincts tell us. Media feels like real life.

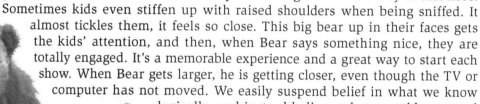
©Disney

Designer's Note

A simpler version of this response can be done with babies. When my first grandson was four months old, we were playing games with him. One of my other boys, his uncle, made different smiley faces, and then came toward the baby from about three feet away. Each time, my grandson blinked in surprise as this big face stopped about a foot from his head, and then he just totally cracked up. He thought it was so funny. That proximity arousal button was pushed each time, and each time, it made him laugh.

Movement

In the wilder, more dangerous world of our distant relatives, staying alert meant staying alive. Our brains are hardwired to be attentive to movement. Motion of any kind in our peripheral vision sends a small warning signal to our brains, telling our eyes to pay attention and scan in the direction of the motion. To our ancestors, it might have been something that they were looking for, or worse, it might have been something that was looking for them! Anytime anything moves in our field of vision, especially if it's coming at us, we are unconsciously compelled to look at it.

We Follow the Action

The instinctual reaction to look at movement is still alive in how we visually interact with the world and how media interacts with us. Advertisers in particular have long used this behavior to grab our attention by using many rapid cuts and plenty of movement in their commercials. To our old brains, they are basically saying: "Look, **Look**, *look*, *look*, **LOOK!**, Look, Look, £ooK, *Look*, Look, LooK, **LOOK!**, *Look*, Look, Look, look, *look*…. **LOOK!**" If you think this is not true, try having a long conversation with someone while sitting in front of the TV. The TV ends up with your attention even when you try to avoid it.

Some banner-ad designers use movement because it works well to get attention, even though they know it annoys you. The creators of *Sesame Street* used quick cuts to enhance the pace, and therefore kids' attention. They also used perennial kid favorites: lively animation, cute characters, and direct address, which later chapters cover in more detail.

Most kids don't like the evening news because the "talking heads" are not interesting enough to hold their attention. Public speakers know that if the audience is getting a little sleepy, moving around the stage and "talking" with their hands makes their presentation much more interesting. Magicians also use this natural visual reflex to intentionally misdirect attention with a larger movement while the card, coin, or rabbit goes the other way. **Movement steals our attention away from what is not moving.**

Seeing Is Active

All of the factors above are ways of getting attention by taking advantage of how humans see and how they process what they see. Seeing is an active function compared to hearing, which is generally more passive. You actively use your eyes to continually scan the world. When your attention lands on something, you inspect it, and your brain makes comparisons and conclusions as to what you are seeing. Sight is also the perceptual vehicle we most commonly use to interact with abstract and symbolic languages like the text on this page.

Designer's Note

The biggest motion gets the attention. In the early days of multimedia (circa 1990) we spent a lot of time trying to create a sense of living immersive environments by adding small random and natural animated effects like waterfalls, moving clouds, passing cars, character eye blinks, etc., and we were subsequently always pushing up against what those early wimpy CPUs could handle. When we needed to run a large animation in a scene, we could easily get into latency problems. (Latency is generally used to mean any delay in perceived response time beyond the response time desired; a slow response.) Interestingly enough, through kid testing we found that, since the children's attention always followed the biggest motion in front of them, we could turn off all the other animations during the main one, and no one ever noticed.

Shapes to Symbols, Icons, and Text

We see shapes and symbols in graphic design all the time. We're so used to them that we don't think much about why they're effective. Breaking down the way the most basic visual elements work can help you to use them more powerfully. Shape recognition is a skill that goes back to the most primitive humans, which means that deft use of shape and symbol has the potential to invoke visceral emotion. The simplicity of stripped-down images also forces the brain to fill in the gaps with imagination.

Communicating in Signs

Humans are really good at shape recognition and can easily guess most objects just from their shape. When early humans saw something coming at them, even a distant object that was only a silhouette, they need-ed to know immediately if it was dangerous or not. Their brains immediately went to work interpreting what they saw, creating meaning. Today, humans experience the same reactions in how we interact with and interpret media.

Nachaliti/Shutterstock.com

Neither of the adjacent images *are* tigers, but our brains respond with our knowledge about tigers. Tigers are dangerous, and our ancestors got a good adrenaline jolt from recognizing the tiger shape. Having grown up sur-rounded by millions of images, we don't have the same primal response they did. But we still immediately identify the image, even if it is just a silhouette.

Designer's Note

Our strong natural ability for shape recognition is part of why people like tradition-al jigsaw-style puzzles and shape–pattern games like *Tetris*. Despite how modern these games are, the skills they employ are primitive.

> *Pictures are received information. . . .*
> *Writing is perceived information.*[5]
> —Scott McCloud, illustrator, cartoonist, and author

Silhouettes are an old storytelling art form, and we can get a lot of story details from looking at them. Learning to recognize, categorize, and respond to shapes of real things *as images* is at the heart of the beginning of written language. Why is this important? When you're designing for kids, you're often designing for non-readers. Some symbols and icons are easy for kids to understand, while others take more exploration. The ability to recognize more complex icons expands as children's brains and cognitive skills develop.

© adrenalina; onjoe; awng; Cundrawan703; art-l@i.ua; niklson101; pablonis; slaviana; Bestgreenscreen; abrakadabra; nexusby; BigAlBaloo; Aliaksei7799; adrenalina; Dazdraperma, pakmor /Depositphotos.com

Why Kids Like Icons

Icon design is about the creation and assignment of a graphic element to a com-puter function. Ideally, icons will express the potential function in a clear way because they serve as the trigger to launch that function.

Kids decode images before they decode words. This happens in the very first stages of life, but it's easy to observe during the toddler years when kids begin to "read" books not by deciphering the letters on the page but by putting images together into sequences and stories. Because of this developmental pattern, kids take to icons more easily than they take to words when they're playing games. Icons are a strong design element in kids' games because:

- **They are accessible to kids who can't read.** Younger kids or those with learning disabilities can participate. They don't need to read in order to play.

- **They are immediate.** Kids hate to wait. An icon is like a shortcut, a quick jump in digital space to where kids want to go.

- **They convey information quickly.** A picture is worth a thousand words. With icons, kids can scan through a pile of activities and get a quick sense of what they might be interested in.

- **They support exploration.** For some, icons are like entrées on a menu where all the options can be seen at once. When one option is explored, curiosity about the next icon motivates further exploration. Interaction is the name of the game, and if the icons look interesting and empowering, kids will try them out just to see what's there.

- **They can be cute.** Well-drawn children's icons are appealing and friendly. Their simplicity and openness invite kids in. Occasionally, icons for very young children will be simple cartoon characters that may have a one-frame animated reaction when clicked or rolled over.

Imagine This

Imagination, one of the most human and creative processes, comes from the word *image*; it is what you *see* inside your head when you think about things. Often it is the result of combining parts of things you know, and then filling in the holes between them to create a new whole, or gestalt. This interpretive filling in phenomenon of observing one thing but perceiving/seeing something else is sometimes referred to as *closure*, closing the gap between the known and unknown.[6]

Our Brains Like to Fill in the "Holes" in Perception

Your brain is always working to interpret what it is seeing, and it tries to make some sense of it for you. Thousands of tiny colored dots on a page merge to become a picture (like every photo in this book); fast-moving still images create "flicker fusion," producing the experience of movies; cartoon drawings of inanimate objects come alive with human-like personas. Your brain fills in the holes in your perception to create whole answers and stories.

> *We do not see with our eyes. We see with our brains.*[7]
> —Dr. John Medina, author and developmental molecular biologist

Imagination Is Closure in Action

You can't see everything at once, but your mind uses closure to reassure you that unseen things are still there. Comic book artist Scott McCloud writes that "Perception of reality is an act of faith, based on mere fragments"[8] of what you know. In everyday life, you mentally create closure by completing things based on your previous experiences. Closure is such a part of who you are, it is like the

air you breathe; you take it for granted, even though it affects everything you do. With art, you use closure to make sense of an image and imagine what it means or what it is trying to tell you. You do the same with *all* media. *Closure is how you actively participate in media, filling in the blanks between scenes of a story with your imagination.* You only need to see a piece of something, and your brain triggers closure to imagine what happens next. It is also at play when you see something other than what is there. Do you see faces in the light socket? That's closure at work.

You can read this. What we see and comprehend is a function of our brain's experience and its desire to help us. Here is a marvelous example, popularly circulated on the Internet, showing how the brain uses closure to help us make sense of things.

I cdnuolt blveiee taht I cluod aulaclty uesdnatnrd waht I was rdanieg. The phaonmneal pweor of the hmuan mnid! Aoccdrnig to rscheearch at Cmabrigde Uinervtisy, it deosn't mttaer in waht oredr the ltteers in a wrod are, the olny iprmoatnt tihng is taht the frist and lsat ltteer be in the rghit pclae. The rset can be a taotl mses and you can sitll raed it wouthit a problem. Tihs is bcuseae the huamn mnid deos not raed ervey lteter by istlef, but the wrod as a wlohe. Amzanig, huh? Yaeh, and you awlyas thought slpeling was ipmorantt![9]

Optical Art Plays with the Brain's Assumptions

Our wonderful brains are always trying to help us make sense of what we think we see. Optical Art, or Op Art, is art that deliberately plays with our brains to create experiences that are outside of learned assumptions. Below are a few classic examples.

Do you see a musician or a girl's face?

How many legs does this elephant have?

People only see what they are prepared to see.
—Ralph Waldo Emerson, poet

In this next optical illusion, the lines appear to curve, as if the drawing represents a convex object, but in fact all of the lines are straight and parallel to one another.

Our brains are always interpreting visual information, but we seldom notice until we are confronted by interesting graphic anomalies like these; they remind us that our brains actively interpret what we see. To facilitate closure, our brains look for connections between things and then group them together to become something else, especially if they create familiar shapes and images.

How many triangles and circles are in this image?

The answer is none. The mind ignores the fact that the lines do not connect. It connects them for us. All of these examples show the power and desire of the mind to make **closure**. Using the illusions created by visual closure, we can *imply* a lot visual information about story without having to draw it, letting the mind do the work. The triangle image is an example of creating negative space, the space around and in-between the subject of an image. You have seen this used in cartoons where a character has run through a shut door, leaving an exact (negative) image of them as a hole in the door.

Why is closure important? It allows designers to imply reality (realistic or fantastical) and then let the user fill in the blanks mentally. By animating simple illustrations and adding a few sound effects, whole worlds can be implied. Animation is illusion. It is all about fooling the brain. When you're watching a movie or playing a video game, your brain first joins still images to create movement, and then imagines life because of that movement. That means your brain is doing several levels of work at once, but you're not aware of most of that work. Closure happens naturally, but by understanding how it works, you can understand a lot of the tricks of animation.

Animism as a Principle of Animation

When you watch an animated film or have interchanges with talking agents in a game, you seldom consider how easily you suspend rational knowledge that these characters are neither people nor alive. You are simply engaged in the interaction at hand and think nothing of the fact that these digital beings are not really there.

Animism and the Illusion of Life

Animism can be defined as "the attribution of a soul to plants, inanimate objects, and natural phenomena. The belief in a supernatural power that organizes and animates the material universe."[10] In cultures throughout the world, anthropologists have recorded the existence of a distinction between animism (objects are alive and have their own agency) and artificialism (objects are acted upon by a conscious agency).[11] Child psychologist Jean Piaget notes that both animistic and artificialist thinking are also part of how young children attempt to make sense of the bewildering world they have been born into. When you consider that children under seven tend to think more holistically, and are mostly prelogical about how they view the world, this makes perfect sense. They don't know why the sky is blue or where the lights go when you turn them off. They just know that things happen, and they often construct elaborate invented hypotheses to help solve these mysteries for themselves. These solutions often include magic forces and beings that create what they see in the world. When something moves on a computer screen, they don't reason that it's an artificial illusion of quickly moving sequential images, they simply take the animistic viewpoint that it's alive. And "alive" for a child is an invitation for interaction.

Alive means interesting and worthy of attention. A chair, a ball, a doodle... if it moves, kids are willing to imagine that it's alive. Add eyes, and it's conscious, add a mouth and it immediately becomes a character with personality traits.

BLOB   BLOB AWAKE

BLOB WITH PERSONALITY

Dan Russell-Pinson, the designer of the popular app *Stack the States*, used this trick to turn the puzzle piece shapes of various states into personalities, thereby making them more interesting.

"Alive" implies living, but what does it mean to bring something to life? What was it before? What changes to make it appear alive? Here are the main characteristics of something that is "alive" on a screen:

Stack the States by Freecloud Design.

- **Movement.** An object or character is able to express its physical agency.

- **Sound.** Audio effects and voice expand and complete the illusion of life.

- **Reaction.** Everybody wants a reaction to their action, and getting an immediate reaction from touching something is further proof this "thing" is alive.

Designer's Note

It is no mistake that when long time Disney animators Ollie Johnston and Frank Thomas wrote their classic book on the art of animation, they called it *The Illusion of Life: Disney Animation*.

When you put all of the above illusions of life together into a character, the result is something even more profound than a game element, you have someone to play with, someone children feel may listen to them, respond to them, play games, talk, or just act as a companion. Characters (also called agents in many games because they help facilitate the gameplay) come in many models, from talking cardboard cut outs (not much movement) to "smart" agents who remember children's names, when they last played the game, and what they like to do.

When something is alive, it has its own set of behaviors for its own reasons, and the puzzle for kids is figuring out the what and why. You can get a child's attention with a wiggle, but you need more than that to keep it. What's important here is to remember that if something seems alive, it should offer more than just the wiggle used to get attention: there should be some mystery, illusion of latent magic, potential surprise, or more available. A great example is StoryToys' *My Very Hungry Caterpillar* app. In their adaptation of Eric Carle's work, the subtlety of the animation truly brings the caterpillar to life.

My Very Hungry Caterpillar by StoryToys. Art by Eric Carle.

Anthropomorphism

Animistic belief is one reason why anthropomorphism is so prevalent and powerful a storytelling medium in all cultures. Anthropomorphism is the appointment of human characteristics to animals, objects, non-living things, phenomena, and even concepts, such as organizations or spirits.

Scene from *The Tortoise and the Hare.* Art by Michael Dashow (characters) and Barbara Lawrence (background).

Humans have been attributing their qualities to things non-human for thousands of years. Dating back to sixth century B.C. Greece, Aesop's Fables are a wonderful example of using animals to illustrate well-known human behaviors. Today, we still actively look for and assign those qualities to our pets, plants, cars, and more. When we see talking animals in contemporary games and cartoons, we are seeing an ancient storytelling device in action. Children in particular are enchanted by the magic of talking animals or objects, which makes anthropomorphism very effective as a method of communicating with them.

Animism and Anthropomorphism in Children's Design

Animism and anthropomorphism are elements in all Imaginative Play, where dolls and cars become alive with personalities and gain the ability to interact. Both are pervasive in children's interactive media. In fact, they are often the essence of what makes content engaging and entertaining.

For a child, it is magical when non-living objects and mythical creatures come to life, or when living things, especially animals, exhibit human-like behavior. From talking teacups and candlesticks (Disney's *Beauty and the Beast*), ogres with dorky donkey sidekicks (*Shrek*), to fish fathers (*Finding Nemo*), caring cars (*Cars*), and talking toys going on rescue missions (*Toy Story*), children's movies, television, and digital entertainment are dominated by non-human things acting like people. No matter which medium, whenever characteristics that support animistic and anthropomorphic projection are added into children's products, they're almost always (not too scary, please) well received, and they add life and personality to otherwise more static content.

Today, we think nothing of animation—it's everywhere—but consider that, to our ancestors, seeing modern animation would be nothing less than a supernatural phenomenon. Later chapters cover character design and development more deeply, but first the upcoming chapter will dive into animation tricks and how color can affect mood in children's products.

Michellangelus/Shutterstock.com

Seeing is Believing: Art and Animation

People like to *look*, and we are naturally drawn to colorful scenes and interesting images, especially if they move. Art and animation together create a visual invitation and mental hook that are the first tools in a designer's palette. They anchor our attention and give us something to explore and play with. This chapter delves into using color, background, and animation tricks to engage and delight children of all ages.

We become what we behold. We shape our tools and afterwards our tools shape us.[1]

—attributed to Marshall McLuhan, author

© Carole Daly Photography

Using Color

Color plays a big role in our lives; it can irritate or calm, tell us which food to get, or motivate and move us in a variety of ways. Color has a huge influence on package and branding design, and children learn about color with the safety message "red means *stop* and green means *go*." Images without color, although descriptive, don't deliver the same emotional content or attract our attention in the same way.

Typically, a lot of color (and multiple colors) gives a sense of energy, light, and life in a scene, while gray and diminished colors reflect an absence of light, life, and vitality. For instance, graveyards and spooky backgrounds tend to be grayish with black tones and flat, washed-out colors to set a lifeless tone.

Andrew Park/Shutterstock.com

Identical black and white and color photos. How do you feel about these two images?

Designer's Note

When I was studying art in school, I had one teacher who dragged us through many explorative assignments of color theory, styles of image balancing, and how to direct the eye on the page. At the time, it seemed a bit tedious, but over the years I have found it to be some of the best practical training I had in school, and I've used it throughout my career.

Basic Color Theory— The Color Wheel

Though, as designers, we don't often consult the color wheel, understanding the relationships between colors is helpful in creating visual experiences that work. Here is a brief review of the theory:

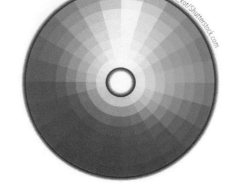

3d_kot/Shutterstock.com

- The three **primary colors** are red, yellow, and blue.

- The **secondary colors**, green, orange, and purple are made by combining two primary colors (e.g., yellow and blue make green.)

elenabo/Shutterstock.com

- The **tertiary colors** are combinations of the first two sets. Further combinations will take you into finer gradations of the spectrum. Adding white or black lightens or darkens the color accordingly.

Two tertiary colors in saturated hues of relatively equal value were used in Op Art and late 1960s rock posters to create a jumping or movement effect.

williammpark/Shutterstock.com

- **Complementary colors** are opposite each other on the color wheel. They tend to evoke a sense of excitement.

hugolacasse/Shutterstock.com

- **Monochromatic colors** are all of the tones, tints, and shades of a single color hue. Photographs in black and white are sometimes referred to as monochrome. More often, a monochromatic illustration will include all the tones of a single color from white to black (so white or so dark you no longer see any color). Monochromatic colors are often used in backgrounds to set a particular tone such as cool (bluish) for underwater or arctic scenes, or warm (yellow-oranges) for desert or sunny beach scenes. They also work well to add interest to silhouettes.

- **Analogous colors** sit next to each other on the color wheel. They have a harmonious relationship, are often found in nature, and support a particular feeling, whether warm and friendly or dark and mysterious. Analogous colors allow for more variation and range than a monochromatic scheme might, while maintaining a sense of sameness. Analogous colors with similar tints, shades, and tones are used to create camouflage and help a soldier disappear into the background. To keep your analogous background from being overly flat or bland, make sure there is enough contrast to help bring some areas forward and others backward.

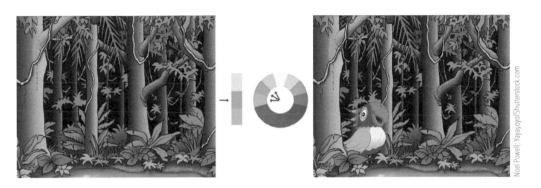

One of the benefits of using analogous colors for a background is that when you add a character with complementary colors, that character stands out and is easy to follow in a scene.

Designer's Note

Color blindness is, in most cases, the inability to easily distinguish red from green. It is estimated that 8% of boys and 0.5% of girls are color-blind.[2] I hear from game players and designers (a small but relevant sampling of people) that it usually doesn't cause them too much trouble in gameplay. But if you are creating a children's product that is based solely on color recognition, be aware that some kids will have problems with it. If possible, make sure there is enough contrast (lightness and darkness) between adjacent reds and greens to allow for differentiation. To someone with color blindness, these two images look identical.

Tones, tints, and shades are terms that describe similar color concepts, they are regularly used incorrectly.

- A **tone** is what you get when you add gray to a pure hue/color.

- A **tint** is a color made lighter by adding white.

- A **shade** is a color made darker by adding black.

Kids and Color

sam74100 © 123RF.com

Kids love color, and they love playing with it. It attracts them just like a bee to a flower. A child's interest and response to a color may be influenced by level of maturity, culture, personal experience, interests, and even (some believe) physical makeup. There are no hard and fast rules for applying color in kids' products, but some guidelines show up again and again.

Toddlers like bright primary and rainbow colors. Walk through the toddler aisle in any toy store, and you'll see touchable toys in bright primary and rainbow colors on white or light-colored backgrounds. Big companies like Fisher-Price, who have been creating great toddler toys for decades, have done their research, and they know that those simple bright colors are what toddlers naturally reach for.

Blue and pink. *Blue for boys, pink for girls* may be a cultural artifact from older generations, but there are still echoes of it today. This pattern starts with baby clothes and room attire, and continues through early development. Therefore, it is hard to separate from cultural bias and conditioning. Toy designers, manufacturers, and stores have certainly promoted color preferences for girls and boys. All you have to do is walk through a toy store, and you will know the girls' area is separate from the boys.

This is beginning to change, and because color preferences do have trends, it's worth looking at them. (For more info on color preferences, see Ch. 11.)

Mega Bloks First Builders by Fisher-Price.

Designer's Note

Just making something pink **does not** make it a girl's product. In fact, when designing products for girls, because of basic differences in viewpoint, I always make sure there are women designers on the team who can more easily connect with what works for girls on social and emotional levels.

On a related note, designer Brenda Laurel spent years researching girls' interactions and interests while at Interval Research. As she and her team were ready to name their girls' company, they enlisted tween girls in the process. The name they chose was *Purple Moon*, because it was a name all the girls liked, and partially because it was the name the boys disliked the most.[3]

When girls are first old enough to care about their clothing and toy choices, they tend to pick colors from the full rainbow spectrum, with a focus on pinks, purples, pastels, and floral prints. In contrast, boys lean toward colors that are *not* associated with girls. Instead, they often go for more subdued and neutral choices, and/or bold, strong, "power" colors.

Toy designers and manufacturers have learned that many young girls seem to like pink. Yes, girls like other colors, and yes, many girls are very un-pink. But even Barbie™ has her own trademarked shade of pink. Pink may be over-used in girls' products, but pink is a color that young girls seems to enjoy, appreciate, and gravitate toward, even though parents may do their best to avoid the cultural stereotype.

If you are building a website or game to attract both boys and girls, picking neutral or non-gendered color schemes seems to work best. There are no absolute rules. Color likes and dislikes change with age, culture, and other factors. Testing with your target audience is the best way to know if your choices are working. Let kids decide color preferences themselves through product testing.

Understanding Backgrounds

In visual design, the background supports the foreground and the overall experience by filling in space around the main active elements. Backgrounds hold the pieces of an experience together by being the canvas upon which everything else takes place. They are the context for the main content.

Background establishes the foreground. *Backgrounds should be in the back*. You might think this is obvious, but this simple rule is sometimes forgotten. In relation to the foreground, you can dial a background forward or backward based on the intensity of the contrast, level of focus (blurry in the background), and color saturation between the two. The background of this page is white, and the text is black. That is about the highest contrast possible, and it makes the text really easy to read. The background established the foreground by contrast.

Simple backgrounds let you focus on what's important. As mentioned earlier, busy icons and characters on a busy background become invisible. This makes them annoying to find and use. Kids are looking for something to do, and they want to do it now. Visual noise is distracting, and it obscures what is important.

Camp Bewajee virtual world prototype. Art by Michael Dashow.

Keeping the foreground in front makes the target items obvious and easy for kids to get at.

Backgrounds promote a sense of place. Beyond a simple canvas, the background is the stage or world that provides context for gameplay and exploration. It is where the characters and avatars live and interact.

We take in and understand a scene in moments. That quick impression gives us an imagined logic about the world portrayed and the type of actions that are likely to happen within it. It gives the characters a frame of reference and reasons for their actions. Backgrounds can also imply a larger world and set up expectations for what might happen there. When you see a background, you imagine what else might be in that world, and where that doorway or road might lead.

Window or box? How the edges of the screen are treated by the characters affects whether the user sees the screen as a window to a larger world or a box that contains only what is seen. If the characters can't go beyond the edge, then it's a box. If they can peek into the scene or run offstage, that supports the illusion of a larger environment. Both approaches have value. The box supports focus and clear communication while the window implies there is more to explore.

Scenic backgrounds support story and mood. Backgrounds are part of the storytelling process, and they affect how people feel, even if it's only a subtle mood. In children's media, backgrounds are sometimes pushed further to reflect the emotional/mental state of the main character. One of the first great examples of this was in Disney's *Snow White and the Seven Dwarfs*. When Snow White first escapes the evil queen, she runs through the forest at night. Snow White imagines scary creatures all around her in the background, and turns a tree stump into a threatening open-mouthed alligator. Understanding the mood needs of a scene helps the artist and animators create backgrounds that come alive in support of the mood.

Staging. Staging is about decorating and filling a background scene to support the mood and context of a story or place. In software, it is also about designing environments to support the interactive exploration goals of the program. Staging helps the viewer understand what is going on in a scene, and if important, what it might *feel like* to the character.

Staging creates potential for interaction. In children's software, it is also about designing environments to support the interactive exploration goals of the program.

This is a page from the *Harry and the Haunted House* storybook, which was created with the knowledge that it would become an interactive animated title as well. The colors affect the mood, and every item in the room supports the story theme and potential for interactive animations. In this case, every item in the room is also interactive. Below is another example of a scene that is bigger than the stage. The

Harry and the Haunted House storybook by Mark Schlichting.

stage moves to follow the child-directed character through the scene. The lighter area is the visible screen inside the app.

Little Red Riding Hood interactive storybook app by Nosy Crow. Artwork by Ed Bryan.

With staging, designers construct unique models of the world for users to interact with. Making these models function like the real world creates experiences that everyone will intuitively understand and enjoy.

Keeping Your Eye on the Page

One of the tricks of staging is to position things on the page in a way that they direct the users' eyes where you want them to look. Understanding where the eye goes in a scene can make all the difference in creating a successful layout. If done correctly, a layout feels aesthetically pleasing, balanced, and focused. The idea is to create a spatial order that supports the purpose of the scene and visual storytelling.

The graphic design principle of **continuity** suggests that the eye follows the direction of lines as if they continue, even after they have ended. These lines can then be aligned with other lines and shapes to create a more coherent composition. Additionally, when the eye can easily follow multiple shapes along a continuous line, those pieces are often perceived as a unit. This is a trick well used by painters and sculptors of old to bring a solidness to their scenes.

Your eyes are drawn
HERE

For instance, all the lines in the illustration to the left direct the eyes to the center bottom. Your eyes tend to go down, then back up, and then follow the curve from one side to the other, before focusing on the details.

One trick that brochure, magazine, and book designers use to keep the eye on the page is to have diagonal lines in images and photos lead toward the center of the layout rather than toward the edges of the page. This may mean flipping photos horizontally or moving some text blocks around to properly place images that can't be flipped. We followed this practice (as much as possible) throughout the pages of this book.

Of course, this all happens in seconds, and often unconsciously, but knowing where the eye goes in a layout can help set up the action you may want to have happen.

Not only does human vision unconsciously follow lines, it also follows the body language and eye direction of characters. Keep your characters facing and looking in, toward where you want the kids to look. The kids will follow your layout.

All these considerations are for static backgrounds and tableaux with characters (such as in a puzzle), but when you really want to keep children's attention on the page, animation is the way to go.

Basics of Animation

Animation is powerful in children's design because it gets attention and can bring *anything* to life. Creating believable character animation is a well-developed art form, but there is more to animation than creating characters. Here are a few basic thoughts and tips on successful animation in children's interactive products.

Use Animation to Direct Attention

Since the eye naturally follows movement, use movement to direct attention. It's common in children's programs to focus attention by highlighting, or adding a special glow or color around the object you want kids to tap. This can also be done by making the object wiggle or blink. Chasing a tappable, blinking, or moving object can be a game in itself. Attention always goes to what is moving, or to the biggest movement if there are many.

Designer's Note

In one of my first prototypes, I tested highlighted text. The main character (the storyteller) entered stage left, stood, and "talked" (mouth moving in sync with the voice). The text was highlighted as the words were spoken. In product testing, we immediately saw that every kid was watching the character's mouth instead of the text. In the next version, we kept the character offscreen and highlighted the text in sync with voice-over only. When the voice-over finished, the character bounded into the scene, screeched to a stop, bounced into the air, and landed in his chair with a "plop" sound. That way, we used animation to direct attention where it was needed. The kids watched the highlighted text and then the character's entrance. We gave them one thing at a time to focus attention on, while also creating a character entrance that was much more dynamic, entertaining, and silly.

Learn Animation Basics

You may be in a big company with lots of animation talent, but if you are a small developer, it's possible there's only an artist on staff, not a trained animator. There are many great books on animation (like Frank Thomas and Ollie Johnston's classic *The Illusion of Life: Disney Animation*). Getting a basic understanding and time to play with animation techniques can take your characters a long way toward coming alive. Here are a few basic, but powerful, concepts to get you started:

- **Squash and stretch.** This basic trick can be used to enhance any animation. Squash is the illusion of an object being compressed when it is stopped by another (unmovable) object (like when a ball hits the floor). Stretch is the illusion of dynamic release when that same object recoils.

- **Anticipation.** The easiest way to describe anticipation is to consider how you shoot with a bow and arrow. You have to pull the bow back before the arrow can go anywhere. Anticipation is like that. The character often leans back  a little in the opposite direction before they are going to take off. Baseball pitchers do this naturally at the beginning of each pitch.

- **Follow through.** When a character in motion comes to a stop, even though the feet may stay in place, the inertia of the upper body will take the top of the body a little past where the feet are before it stops and sways backward and forward in smaller movements until it come to rest centered over the feet. The largest movement happens farthest away from the stationary point—in the above example, the head. Below is an example of character anticipation before a run, and follow-through after the stop (not all frames are shown).

ANTICIPATION   FOLLOW THROUGH   AMBIENT

- **Slow-in, slow-out.** When an object or character in motion comes to a stop in the real world, it doesn't stop all at once and freeze. The same is true for an object beginning to move. There is a natural slowing to a stop, and then a slow start again as the object overcomes inertia. Using slow-ins and slow-outs gives many movements a sense of real weight and presence.

Designer's Note

When these tricks are used properly, the technique becomes invisible because the movement feels natural. We are used to seeing real movement, so good animation doesn't catch our attention. It's when animation is jerky that we notice something is wrong, and we are pulled out of the illusion of the experience. Remember, your animations don't need to be perfect or long. Just using some of these tricks will help. Kids are very forgiving, especially if they feel empowered by the rest of the interactive experience.

- **Exaggeration.** Animation allows us to push character expressions and reactions way beyond what we think of as normal, but in doing so, it allows the essence of the emotion or action to be clearly understood and felt. In interactive software, exaggeration works well to intensify big reactions in characters or objects after a child triggers an event. A big payoff, even if it is very quick, adds a lot to the experience due to the surprise factor and the sense of empowerment it gives the child.

Tricks and Tips for Character Animation

Character animation is vast subject with a long history that could easily fill this book all by itself, but it's helpful to learn about practical insights and simple tips that have proven useful in keeping production costs down while at the same time enhancing the user experience. (For a tip on using audio as animation, see Ch. 8, p. 110.)

Speed it up with motion blur. On movie film or video, when something is moving fast enough, it creates a blur against the (in-focus) background. This is commonly referred to as a *motion blur*. Motion blurs leave blur streaks in the direction of the motion. Digital animation has come a long way in perfecting this technique since traditional cell animators began using it in the 1930s, but since much of children's animation is still done with replacement frames, those old techniques (i.e., squash and stretch, anticipation, follow-through, etc.) work really well. In children's products, adding just a frame or two of motion blur can be used to inexpensively create the illusion of speed or quick action with your characters. In the *spin* image shown here, just two alternating frames of this blurred spinning bug give the illusion of him rotating extremely fast. Sound effects complete the illusion.

In the image below there are three different kinds of running motion blurs. The fastest looking character of the fully blurred image on the right only requires one frame of animation because no extra arm or feet positions are needed. Adding a good *zip* sound effect helps to complete the illusion of speed. Zip animations like this are sometimes valuable, but are only used occasionally because much of the humor and cuteness of the character's run (including their expression) is lost in the blurring process.

Designer's Note

When frame rate speeds were still quite slow, we were in production on an interactive animated storybook of *The Tortoise and the Hare*. Tortoise was easy to animate because everything already ran at his speed, but Hare was more problematic. Nothing we did seemed to show his quickness. Finally, we went back and studied old cartoons with motion blur from Warner Bros. film libraries, and we implemented their technique with Hare. Instead of using sets of frames of animation, we used only one or two frames, and that made him look like he was just a flash.

AMBIENT POSE

RUN MOTION BLUR   STOPPING BLUR   FOLLOW THROUGH POSES   ANTICIPATION   SIDE RUN BLUR1   SIDE RUN BLUR2

Selected frames from *The Tortoise and the Hare* by Wanderful.

Animation is (generally) very expensive, and it eats a hole in the lining of your budget's wallet. But because the combination of movement and character is so compelling for children, it is difficult for products with little or no animation to compete. Some of the most expensive animation is character animation, because creating a smooth-looking walk cycle requires so many different character positions. New cycles have to be created if your character runs, hops, jumps, dances, climbs, or performs any major physical movement. Separately drawn cycles are needed for each character, and the cost can add up quickly. A sample walk cycle gives a sense of how many frames it can take.

© Dermot O'Connor

CONTACT   RECOIL   PASSING   HIGH-POINT   CONTACT   RECOIL   PASSING   HIGH-POINT   CONTACT

Children's titles generally don't have big budgets. Therefore, animators, designers, producers, and programmers are always trying creative tricks and new technologies to get the most animation bang for the buck. Here are a few favorite tricks and tips to help keep your animation as inexpensive as possible.

Reuse as much as possible. Animation is expensive to create. A good rule of thumb is to reuse as much of it as possible. Walk, run, and talk cycles are some of the most repeated sequences. Keeping a character in the same outfit or giving them a trademark "look" helps also. Animation production software varies widely, but, regardless, it's always smart to have an idea of how your animation might be used and reused before you begin production.

Create simple characters. One trick that can save on animation expenses is to use or create characters that have few or no appendages. Fewer body parts means less animation. For instance, a cute fish, a robot with wheels, or a fat hedgehog with tiny feet are far less budget intensive than long-legged spiders, giraffes, or octopuses because their movements are simple. Adding appendages or long arms and legs increases the amount you have to draw to make something feel right when animating. Aim for something you can easily move around in an environment without a lot of illustration, and be sure to pay attention to believability of movement. (For more on creating characters and avatars, see Ch. 14.)

Designer's Note

The designers of the virtual world *Club Penguin* went for uniformity as a cost-saving measure, among other reasons. When you have multiple characters, you have to create movement cycles for each of them, but in *Club Penguin* everyone uses the same penguin, therefore every penguin requires the same animation. Creating a uniform animation allowed the *Club Penguin* team to reuse a single penguin animation across millions of users. Instead of having different penguins, kids collect clothing, wigs, and props to personalize their penguins, but every character in the world reuses those same props. The penguins have flippers that serve as hands, and they have no legs, just feet, so a walk cycle is little more than a two- or three-frame waddle.

© Disney

Use objects, not legs, for mobility. A similar classic trick is to use modes of transportation other than walking for your characters. Put your character in a flying saucer, in a car, or on a magic carpet, and it allows them to move about without a ton of replacement animation. Some games just have characters "beam-out" and "beam-in" to new scenes. Another classic trick, often used by Monty Python animator Terri Gilliam, is to avoid legs altogether by having your character walk behind a bush or a brick wall, or with legs off the bottom of the screen. An alternative to this is to have the legs covered completely by a dress, gown, robe, or other prop. Or, as is done with *Disney Fairies*, give all your characters wings and let them fly everywhere. These are all very believable and infinitely less expensive.

In the virtual world *Fantage*, avatars move around via themed flying boards.

Designer's Note

Children's game designer Ron Gilbert is well known for creating characters that don't need a lot of replacement animation. In his award-winning *Putt-Putt* series, the main character is a car. All the car needed was some facial expressions and a few wheel-spin highlight animations. Gilbert also created the popular *Freddi Fish* series where, once again, there were no arm and leg cycles to create, just fin wiggles and reusable bubble animations. This was very clever and economical. Gilbert took this concept to its simplest extreme in *Ollo in the Sunny Valley Fair*, in which the main character is basically a ball with a face on it, and movement action was primarily some squash-and-stretch animation.

Putt-Putt Joins the Circus app by Tommo.

Eadweard Muybridge was a pioneer of early photography. In the 1870s, Muybridge invented a system for taking a rapid series of photographs. The resulting photos displayed human and animal motion in a new light, answering questions such as, "Do all four of a horse's hooves leave the ground while it is trotting?" Muybridge's innovation became the basis for motion picture film, which is simply twenty-four images flashed each second, giving the impression of continuous movement. By looking at the thousands of images in Muybridge's work, animators can get a sense of all the stages in a movement. *The Human Figure in Motion* and *Animals in Motion* are great reference materials for anyone trying to break movement down into its components.

By Eadweard Muybridge. *Man in pelvis cloth running and jumping,* plate 160. (1887).

Keep Characters and Scenes Alive with Ambient Animation

In real life, people and places are seldom completely still, and it can feel strange and stiff when games don't reflect the ongoing life of the real world. Designers can go a long way toward creating the illusion of life in characters and scenes by simply adding ambient and random events to environments.

- **Ambient character movements.** When people are standing around, they aren't frozen statues. To keep characters alive, some of the most economical animation tricks a designer can add are eye blinks, head turns, toe taps, nose wipes, and other minor movements. Remember: if it's moving, it's alive.

- **Ambient background environments.** Adding *occasional* ambient cars passing, birds flying, tree leaves rustling, flags waving, bugs crawling, bees buzzing, etc. gives a scene a deeper illusion of being real. Adding extra people moving in the distance helps cityscapes feel more natural. Remember that ambient animations are triggered on a random cycle and should follow whatever would be natural in the real world. Ambient animation should not be predictable (unless it is something with a constant state like waterfalls or clouds), but it should support the illusion of life inside an environment—whatever fits the scene.

- **Random events.** Life is unpredictable. Adding random elements to a game increases the illusion of life. Random elements may include characters or other events *that don't affect gameplay* but add spice to the experience by implying a larger and more lively world. The events or characters should be consistent with the world they are in. Kids (and adults) will then go beyond seeing them as random, and they will associate the random elements with actions they have taken. The response is often to try to repeat an action to produce the same random event.

A truly magical interaction is one in which an object has the potential for many different kinds of responses, and through its unpredictable nature, it invites further interaction. It's alive, and the child doesn't know what it is going to do. It's the unexpected that tickles and piques kids' interest.

Designer's Note

When users see random animations and events, their minds often try to connect the events to some action they have taken because our minds want to find cause-and-effect relationships as part of the process of learning to play. Game players (kid and adult) are more than willing to assume that random events are related to a more complex, programmed logic engine than is actually there. I have heard this feedback from other designers and experienced it myself. In a design I created for very young children, kids could tap on objects in a scene and have them react. In some cases, there were multiple tapping locations on one object, just offset from one another. The kids could tap different areas on the object to get different animated responses. Many people told me they loved how smart our software was because it watched how they tapped, and it gave them a new response each time. Of course, I always just said, "Thanks, glad you liked it," but in actuality, the kids were creating the varied responses themselves by not tapping consistently in the same place.

Tricks to Help Avoid Lip-Sync

Lip-synching voice and animation really helps characters feel real. It adds a level of believability to character interactions, but matching mouth movements and dialogue can be very time consuming. This is especially true if your product goes into multiple languages. Some games and environments deliberately have characters that don't speak directly to the user or other characters because of the production time and expense. Instead, they use body language, a narrator's voice offscreen, and text boxes (which are easily changed or converted to other languages) as the means to communicate what's going on. (Of course, using text means users need to be able to read.) Lip-sync is more engaging, so one solution is to mix these tricks with lip-sync to keep the overall animation cost down.

- **Simplify lip-sync.** There are various methods to simplify lip-sync, here are a few of the favorite tricks animators have employed to keep lip-synching to a minimum.

- **Obscure the mouth.** Hide the mouth behind a prop, such as a big mustache, large beard, microphone, bandanna, or space helmet. Or have the characters far enough away that any mouth movement at all will work. Use a robot character whose mouth is a kind of oscilloscope; when he talks you see wavy lines. For complete simplicity, you can put the characters in a dark room for a few scenes with only their eyes visible. Action in the room can be denoted by sound effects. It saves on lip-synching and animation. Over the years, all of these techniques have been employed in children's games.

©antonbrand/Depositphotos.com

- **The disembodied voice.** Sometimes it's convenient to have the character think out loud. That way, users get to hear the internal dialogue in the character's voice. A disembodied voice can also be a storyteller commenting on the character and progress of events.

- **The mumble mouth.** Instead of having mouth movements that simulate vowels, as is traditionally done in animation, the mumble technique uses a few open and closed mouth positions that cycle randomly every time a character talks. It isn't as satisfying as good lip-sync, since people naturally look at mouths and have some idea of what they should look like when talking. But it does let the viewer know which character is talking, and that is better than nothing. This technique is sometimes referred to as "lip-flap," and it has a similar effect to old martial arts movies that were loosely dubbed into English. It works some of the time, but not all the time. Again, the closer you are to the mouth, the more in sync it needs to be.

- **The emoticon bubble.** Sometimes it is helpful to show what a character is thinking simply by using an emoticon or object image inside a thought bubble. This can work for giving hints to users about what a character is trying to do, or to communicate between avatars in a virtual world. Here is a scene from the adventure game *Machinarium* where clues are given in the form of images. This saves on voice recording, and makes a product understandable in multiple languages and countries at once.

Machinarium app by Amanita Design.

All of this background might seem like a lot to keep in mind when you're chomping at the bit to create something magical and bring your idea to life, but planning ahead and allocating your resources wisely will end up saving time, money, and frustration. More importantly, understanding why certain techniques are effective is the foundation of creating a magical interactive media experience. While, to you, animation might be about technical specs and platform limitations, kids see wonder and possibility, which makes all the hard work worth it.

The Magic of Audio: How We Hear

From the moment we are born (and, in fact, even before that), we are immersed in a world that constantly bathes us in the vibrations of sound waves. Through those terminals of perception we call our ears, these waves are transported to our brains, where we process them into what we call "sound." Our inborn reactions to audio input have evolved over millennia to aid us in survival and socialization. These reactions are also incredibly important to understand when you are attempting to create engaging interactive media.

Look behind you without turning around. Now you are in acoustic space.[1]

—W. Terrence Gordon, author

iStock.com/OJO_Images

Hearing: Our Ears and Our Brains

You've learned how your eyes work and how you react to and process visual information. The next step is to understand how your ears work, how you process aural information, and how hearing has evolved to aid in survival, socialization, communication, and for our purposes, entertainment.

Hearing

We often take our ears for granted, but they're more than something to hang glasses on. They work with the brain to form an audio recognition system called hearing. In terms of cognitive perception, hearing has taken a back seat to our preference for seeing, but in terms of media and survival, it is equal in its influence on the human psyche and emotional involvement.

Sound is created when an object vibrates. Those vibrations disturb the air and create pressure waves that travel out in all directions from the source of the sound. When sound waves reach our eardrums, the eardrums transfer the vibrations to the inner ears, which in turn send electrical signals to the brain. The brain interprets the signals as sound. This basic system is the means by which all sounds are created and perceived. An object causes air to vibrate, and another object captures that vibration. Sound is one of the first sensations an unborn child perceives with the beating of its mother's heart.

Our Ears

Ears don't blink, and they don't shut (you don't have earlids). Even when you are asleep, your ears are always "on," monitoring. They operate as an early warning unit wired to our instinctive survival system in the oldest part of our brain. Our ears are special data gathering devices that have a large field of awareness, can easily distinguish between thousands of sounds, and can locate information multi-directionally in space.

Since you can't close your ears the way you close your eyes, you are always receiving ambient audio information from spatially diverse sources. Most of this information is tuned out until a particular sound gets a reaction from the brain and grabs your attention. Even as you're reading this book, your attention is mostly on translating these little black and white letters into spoken language in your head, a process which causes any audio input to move into the relative background of your awareness as you read. The audio track you hear loudest is the words being said in your head.

Meanwhile, you are surrounded by the ongoing ambient audio track of your life. If you stop reading for a moment and listen, your awareness will shift from visual to audio, especially if you close your eyes. All of a sudden, you'll be aware of a clock ticking, a car driving by, an electric motor humming, a dog barking, an airplane passing by miles overhead, etc. The longer you shut your eyes, the more you hear. Ambient audio is always there, we just tune it down in our awareness in order not to go into a state of information overload. We are so bombarded by man-made noise that we have become especially good at tuning it out.

Why is this important? Because understanding how humans process auditory information is the key to creating emotionally effective audio experiences and immersive, believable environments in any medium.

Our Brains

Side Doors to the Brain

For the most part, our ears are passive. In contrast to the constantly directed use of our eyes, which are very active, we only occasionally focus our ears on something. While our attention is occupied with a good visual, the bulk of the information received by our open ears slips in only partially noticed. Our brains sort and prioritize that information. Ears are like the side doors to our brains—the sounds we take in are processed, mostly unconsciously, just below our level of awareness. This has huge implications for software and entertainment design.

How is the unconscious processing of sound used in media? A classic example appears in *Star Wars*: viewers knew that Darth Vader was in that spaceship before they ever saw him because of his distinctive musical cue. (Dum, dum, dum, dumm, de dum, dumm, de dumm.) That sound design technique is called foreshadowing, and you tend to experience it peripherally before you consciously notice it. Foreshadowing is often used to set you up emotionally for what is coming next.

Sound designers in the movies often use cellos to create a heightened sense of tension in a scary scene. The sustained, slow, "bow" sound of a cello, often in a minor key, is followed by a loud, sharp noise as something jumps out at you on-screen, hopefully getting you to jump out of your seat. This anticipation that something is going to happen is heightened by the musically unresolved note from the cello, which creates the mood of a scene. Try watching any really scary scene without the audio on. Do you notice the difference in the emotional impact in your body?

The impact of audio on media is so profound a part of the experience that, while designing, it's important to remember:

Good audio makes poor pictures look better.

Good audio production is as important as the visual production (if not more so) in creating a complete and engaging entertainment experience in our minds. Though we may feel more captivated by and fixated on the visual flow of movement and color in front of us, it is the audio information that confirms to our brains that what we see is real. High quality audio fills in the blanks in our *experience* of the visual and makes it believable by making it seem more like the real world. But the reverse is not true; hot graphics won't make clunky audio sound any better. In fact, poor audio can make great graphics seem flat, fake, and phony.

" It's a painting. There is no sound. "

The profound effect of audio has been demonstrated by many research labs. At Stanford University, media researchers Byron Reeves and Clifford Nass ran tests to determine the effects of both visual and audio fidelity. They found that the quality of the audio made a big difference in their test results, and concluded, "Audio fidelity matters. When it is poor, presentations sound *un*natural, and people consciously monitor the content. When it's good, people are immersed."[2]

What this tells us, and what can be seen in countless software products, is that designers need to pay close attention to the quality of their audio.

Audio information is less in the foreground of our brains than the visual. Therefore, it is more absorbed than noticed. Because we are surrounded by sound, we tend to focus on it only as the by-product of an action taking place in the world. We hear tires screech—and then turn to see what happened.

Great Audio Enhances the Experience of Immersion

The better the audio fidelity, the more realistic and lifelike the sounds. The more realistic the sounds, the less people focus on them. Like any well-designed technology, good sound design becomes invisible in the overall experience. It feels so natural that we don't think about it. This is why sound designers and audio engineers work so hard to preserve the natural quality of sounds, sometimes under incredible platform constraints. They want the listener to experience the game or other media like the real world, feeling it intuitively rather than perceiving it consciously. Visuals usually convey information, while audio often conveys emotion.

This is especially true for children, who often respond more to the feelings of things than the content, and who have grown up surrounded by media full of motion and sound.

iStock.com/KatarzynaBialasiewicz, Tuned_In

Virtual Reality via Audio

Designer's Note

Of all the games I have played, software I have tested, and movies I have seen, one of the most immersive virtual experiences I ever had was an audio-only experience. It helped to teach me about the power of audio imaging.

It was at a conference on virtual reality in the early 1990s. I attended a demonstration of new equipment for designing enhanced spatial audio mixing. The company was trying to better simulate the effect that real sound has when emanating from specific places in an environment, trying to make canned audio feel spatially real to the brain.

We were led, in groups of four, into a little space that had two sets of chairs facing each other with an aisle between us. We sat and were given blindfolds and a pair of standard, high quality earphones.

Once we were blindfolded and had our earphones on, the woman who had led us in explained that the spokesman from their company was coming in to talk to us about their new sound system. In a minute he came in and walked between us and began his rap about their new technology. He took out a little box with paper clips in it and walked around shaking it near our ears and talking about audio quality. He had a pair of scissors and did the same thing. At one point, he accidentally dropped a small toolbox and just missed the fellow next to me, who jumped.

Then he said goodbye and left. A group of people came in and stood around above us, talking as if it was a party. They wondered why we were sitting down like we were. "Vut are de doing? Is dis some kindt of an experiment?" said someone with a German accent to my right. At that point, I couldn't stand it anymore, and I lifted my blindfold. To my surprise, there was no one there but the four of us sitting quietly! I put the blindfold back down over my eyes, and once again experienced a room full of people! A woman leaned close to me from behind me on my left side and whispered in my ear, "Isn't this cool?" I had to agree it was. No one had been in the room since the first woman had left—no spokesperson, no paper clips, no scissors, no toolbox, no partygoers. It was all done with audio. Smart audio. In fact, these designers considered this to be such a new field that they called themselves "spatial acousticians." (This is an example of new gigs developing out of new technologies.)

What they had done was to simulate the way sound enters the human ear by using models of the ear with a cluster of little microphones built throughout them. They could record directionally make something sound above or below, close or far, left or right, and it really worked. Those party folks really seemed to be standing while I was sitting, and the woman talking in my ear was close enough to bite it.

One other cool thing they did was to put every chair on a sonic low vibration pad, which produced sound recorded in sync with the actors. So when someone walked past or near you, you felt the subtle vibration of their weight up through your feet and chair. Again, this was below our awareness level, but it registered in the brain and body as authentic. That added dramatically to the overall immersive experience.

This experience profoundly changed my perception of the power of audio to create images and shape reality without any graphic input. If audio alone can be so dramatic, it must play a much larger role in our experience than many game designers say it does. It also helped me to understand how much we use our imaginations to fill in images corresponding to what we hear.

Square Peg in a Round Hole—Brain-Based Audio Jokes

Peter van Dam/Shutterstock.com

Using the concept of audio information slipping in through the side door of our awareness, designers can create a kind of audio joke that is particularly popular with kids. In psychology-speak, it is called a "categorical mistake." It is created by replacing a logical sound with a similar but different sound, or an illogical one. The disjunction between what you see and what you hear creates humor. The best way to illustrate this is with an example.

On the first page of the original 1992 interactive storybook, *Just Grandma and Me*, there was a simple gag with a bird hidden in a tree. When readers clicked on that spot, the bird flew into the scene, dived, turned, and swooped back toward its nest, sort of "buzzing" past a cow, who ducked and mooed as the bird returned to its perch. The audio joke was that the designer had used the sound of an airplane flying and swooping down and zooming back up past the cow.

When the book's prototype was demoed at trade shows, the design team had the opportunity to see repeated audience reaction, a tremendously useful learning experience. The gag was shown hundreds of times, and there was always a place about three-quarters of the way through where a third of the audience (adults and children) would give a little chuckle or laugh.

As this kept happening, the design team realized that it was an almost unconscious joke, like a square peg in a round hole. Birds fly, and airplanes fly, but the sight of the little bird didn't quite match up with sound of the airplane. Because the audience's audio awareness was lower than their visual awareness of the animation, the sound effect sneaked in the side door of cognition, and the discrepancy went all but unnoticed, except it did make a little brain hiccup. That discrepancy between sound and picture tickled people's funny bones, even though they weren't always aware of why it seemed cute.

Music is what feelings sound like.
—author unknown

Music

Every known culture has some form of music. Archaeologists have discovered 40,000-year-old vulture bone flutes in southern Germany,[3] denoting humanity's long relationship with music. Acoustic experts believe that the areas of the caves where many of the famous cave sketches are drawn were specifically chosen for their naturally resonant sound, which helped focus, amplify, and transform the sounds of musical instruments and human voices.[4]

People often hear a song and cry, or feel great joy or sorrow. All of those kinds of emotions help bond people together.[5]
—**Nicholas Conard, archaeologist**

Music's influence on humans (and society) can be seen throughout history. Music can change a person's mood and elicit responses in groups of people simultaneously; it has direct effects on human physiology. It can affect heart rate, blood pressure, emotions, and ability to focus and learn. Our brains react to happy and sad music. We may even perceive a neutral expression differently depending on what kind of music we're listening to.[6] This phenomenon, called "musical priming," has not been lost on movie and app designers, who use music to create emotional landscapes for their projects, influencing, directing, and sometimes misdirecting how people feel about a character in order to heighten the experience.

Music is so naturally united with us that we cannot be free from it even if we so desired.[7]
—**Boethius, 6th-century Roman philosopher**

Music is all about mood. Built on melody and rhythm, it has the amazing ability to transport people emotionally. It can be fast or slow, hot or cold, smooth or sharp, scary or friendly, primitive or celestial, and everything in-between. Music can enhance sadness, joy, fear, love, apprehension, anger, and much more. Musical compositions create, support, and underscore the changing moods of a media experience, be it game, movie, or television.

What Evokes What?

For most of our lives, we've heard the generic musical refrains that connote certain feelings. The majority of people can easily describe their feelings about a piece of music even if they don't know why. Here are some *very* generalized and simplified examples of musical types and the common emotional responses they evoke.

©val_th/Depositphotos.com

- **Happy, lively, positive, busy:** Quick music in major keys.

- **Sad, reflective, depressed, negative:** Slow music in minor keys.

- **Confident, regal, dignified:** Slow music in major chords.

- **Suspenseful, nervous, driving, anxious:** Fast music in minor keys.

- **Mysterious, scary, demonic:** Slow music in altered keys such as diminished chords.

Even though these are broad, stereotypical reactions to chords and tempo, they are a good starting point for understanding the effects of music. As mentioned earlier, minor—and especially diminished—keys are used for scary and shadowy effects. The diminished fifth, or triton, was once called the "devil's interval," which is why Gregorian monks were not allowed to use them for chants. The monks most often wrote their spiritual music in major keys and avoided the diminished keys at all cost.[8] While there are no hard rules about this, some harmonics do have more of a physical effect upon our emotions.

Rhythm and harmony permeate the innermost element of the soul.[9]

—**Plato**

To Resolve or Not to Resolve, That is the Question

Music that resolves sounds right, like a finished sentence. Music that does not resolve creates tension because we keep waiting for it to complete. Unresolved music is great for creating uncomfortable environments that are a little scary, or that have suspenseful action, like a car chase. Keeping music unresolved sustains suspense.

Imagine the classic door knock, "Shave and a hair cut. . . two bits." Now imagine leaving out the two beats on "two bits." "Shave and a hair cut, _____ _____." The folk singer Arlo Guthrie used to occasionally end (or not end) a musical set that way. Because the musical sequence wasn't quite finished, the whole audience would do the last beats in their heads for the next five minutes, trying to make the sequence resolve. (This was also a major plot point in the movie *Who Framed Roger Rabbit*.)

The pitches in musical scales are likely derived from language. Turns out, aspects of spoken English and Mandarin correlate to the intervals between notes in a chromatic scale (the black and white piano keys in an octave). Is it music we love or the sound of our own voices?[10]

—**Marian Bantjes, designer and artist**

We like things to resolve, to feel right. In fact, the impulse is so powerful that there is an apocryphal story that Mozart's father used to get him out of bed in the morning by playing an unresolved piece on the piano. It would drive the young Mozart so crazy that he would have to get up, come down to the piano, and hit that resolving chord.

Voice

Laures © 123RF.com

Of all sounds, the human voice is probably the most absorbing for us. A disproportionately large section of the brain is devoted to the recognition and processing of other human voices, and it can quickly and easily distinguish them from all other sounds. This makes a very compelling argument for the use of voice as a design element in any media. Just hearing voices coming from a game can attract kids from across a room. Of the three amigos of audio (sound effects, music, and voice), by far the most important is voice. Because almost all media is about storytelling and communication, voice is usually given priority in the foreground. Music and sound effects are subservient to voice in almost every case. If you cannot hear or understand the voice, you might as well not have a voice there (unless your goal is to irritate and confuse the user, but this is seldom the case in kids' software).

We are subtly conditioned from birth to pay attention to the sound of voices. We are so attuned to the nuances of voice that we can easily detect an incredible range of real (emotional) communication just from a simple conversation. We can often feel what is *not* being said as much as what *is* being said because communication is emotional as well as cognitive.

> *Words mean more than what is set down on paper. It takes the human voice to infuse them with the shades of deeper meaning.*[11]
>
> —Maya Angelou, poet

Contrasting Text and Voice

With text, we take information in with our eyes and decipher the meaning of a word in the context of the sentence. We do this in our heads with voice as our internal reader. We process quickly as we read, and it takes a good writer to get text to come alive with more than the immediately apparent meaning. Voice, on the other hand, is processed through our ears and interpreted with our emotions. It can therefore communicate an amazingly vast continuum of subtle meaning, including easily changing the meaning of the words to imply the exact opposite of what is being said.

A familiar exercise for actors is to play with expressing the same phrase over and over to explore alternative meanings and a range of character inter-pretations. "I'm so happy to see you" could be pitched, paced, and accented in many different ways to project different emotions. You can say it in a way that implies romance, ego, joy, humor, anger, sarcasm, a question, and more. This becomes an incredibly important tool in the design of interactive media because it adds dimen-sion to what was previously just text. Think of the difference in experience between the written text of a children's story and the sound of a real voice reading it.

Text is wonderful at letting us experience the internal thoughts of a character in a story. This is one of the reasons that movies of good novels seldom seem as good as the books: we miss all that is going on in the character's head—and the changes they go through. But when it comes to dialogue and person-to-person communication, voice is king. Particularly in media for children, voice is a pow-erful communicator. It's well known that young children, especially those under five years of age, can easily absorb multiple languages in a way that is much more difficult for adults. Designers can take advantage of this fact and use voice for a broad range of purposes, including exposure to multiple languages.

Voices Mean People Are Present

We tend to see computers as social actors,[12] but with the addition of real voice, our relationship with them gets even more personal. Logically, we know it is just a computer, but our older brain takes it in on a more visceral level. Voice basically tells us that someone is present, which triggers our social response awareness system, and we interpret communication from the computer as if it were a person talking to us. For children, this is especially true, and it happens at a subconscious level.

As a behavior, our intuitive desire to participate in social groups is some-thing that has evolved from millennia of living together in families, tribes, and clans, and it is important to understand because aspects of it show up in different areas of media production

Encourage Participation via Voice and Sound

Television producers have known for years that we care what others think, and that we get many of our social cues from others, which is why they often add laugh tracks, applause, and other emotional cues to television sound tracks. These sounds enhance our feelings of social acceptance and emotional enjoyment while watching the show. If others think the show is funny, then we should too. (Can you think of a show that adds "Boo" and "Hiss" tracks?)

Fred Rogers with the Neighborhood Trolley,
© Family Communications, Inc.

Children's television has taken the social aspects of sound a step farther by directly addressing kids at home, breaking the "fourth wall." This works very effectively with young children, especially six and under. Captain Kangaroo, Mister Rogers, Barney, and others have talked directly to kids for decades. Mister Rogers took great care not to give the impression that he could hear the home viewers, but still spoke directly to them. Television characters who speak directly to their viewers are friendly, and they can help kids feel good about themselves.

Sesame Street, *Blue's Clues*, and other TV shows have been using a similar—and popular—technique to help kids feel that they are solving puzzles and problems with the characters on screen. They do it by having prerecorded versions of other kid voices (peer age range) responding to questions the host is asking kids watching at home. The viewers know the answer (like the other kids do), and the host doesn't seem to know until you help him. Young children at home answer aloud, addressing the TV, because they feel as though the host is talking to them, which he is. It's a fun game, and the presence of other kids, even if only by voice, makes the watchers at home feel more involved.

> *Anyone who does anything to help a child in his life is a hero to me.*[13]
> —**Mister Rogers**

The same sound principles work in non-linear interactive media. We use group cheers and applause in some games to give positive feedback when a child completes a level or wins a game. We all like positive feedback, and when those cheers follow something we've done, it feels great (even when we know it is a canned response). Younger kids especially like it because they are looking for acceptance and positive feedback for their actions.

iStock.com/DSGpro

When you create products for children, you regularly need some kind of payoff to communicate how players are doing. The social cues of group sound effects (cheers and applause) can be very helpful *if not overused*, and they are an inexpensive solution that children's sound designers have been using for years. Remember, however, that this can be easily overdone. Sound effects become monotonous and predictable if the kind of approval given is always the same or if it is too easily given. Again, this kind of praise reward is most effective with younger children. The effects are much smaller for children eight and over.

Another form of breaking the fourth wall occurs in games where you play against a digital character (as opposed to an avatar representing a friend of yours). What makes this experience so powerful is the sense that the character is paying attention to you, talking to you, and interacting *directly with you* through the game interface.

Scene from *Blue's Clues* TV show by Nickelodeon.

Designer's Note

When TV programs use this technique with younger children, the person addressing the kids leaves a pause of at least four seconds after asking a question. *Blue's Clues* is well known for doing this; both Blue and Steve (the host) look directly at the viewer and wait. Four seconds is very long and almost annoying to adults and older kids, but perfect for the young ones because it gives them a chance to process the request and respond.

Let's move onto how this insight about our deep connection with sound effects, music, and voice can be used to create engaging and entertaining titles for children.

The Magic of Audio: Designing Soundscapes for Kids

Audio is indispensable in creating engaging and immersive environments. It adds reality and presence that visuals on their own cannot come close to. Well-designed audio accesses game players' or viewers' imaginations and emotions to enhance their experience. This chapter covers the basics of sound design's role in the larger design process and includes some favorite tricks to create effective and fun audio environments for kids.

Sound design is the art of getting the right sound in the right place at the right time.[1]

—Tomlinson Holman, audio engineer and inventor

Audio Economics

If you want to design successful interactive products and services for kids, audio is a great place to invest your time and money. You can't beat its bang for the buck. It enhances all aspects of the experience and glues everything together. In most cases, sound effects and music can create a quality experience more quickly and with less expense than complicated animation or 3-D.

Drawing with Sound Effects: Audio as Animation

Audio enhances the visual experience to such a degree that you can use sound effects to *imply* action instead of drawing it. Your imagination responds to sounds by creating images. This is similar to the way you "see" pictures when you read. It's incredibly economical, and it's a favorite trick of animators because they don't have to draw *everything* a character does. We have all seen it: characters run off screen; we hear crashes, bangs, pots and pans, a cat howling, and/or an explosion; and then the characters stagger back into view with stars orbiting their heads. The sound effects create the comic/tragic situation in viewers' minds. We *imagine* the animation, and then we see the results when the character reenters the scene. It's extremely efficient compared to animating everything.

Designer's Note

Supporting the user's ability to see with sound has been a favorite shortcut technique in animation for years. In one title, we created several easy gags by simply having the main character run behind his home in a tree, where we could hear him brush his teeth, make a funny gargle-and-spit sound, or flush the toilet before he returned. All of it was done with sound effects, just a little reused "running" animation, and, of course, the imagination of our users. It was great fun to watch the little kids run the gags over and over, giggling each time. This same technique is used frequently today in some mobile device games where memory constraints can be an issue.

Creating Audio Experiences

As mentioned earlier, good audio makes poor graphics look better by enhancing and completing the believability of a graphic interaction. Audio tracks are a key component of any great interactive experience.

In terms of sound design, audio is traditionally broken up into the three amigos of audio production: **sound effects**, **music**, and **voice**. Even though these elements are usually experienced acoustically as a unified sound track, they are built separately with the others in mind, and then combined near the end of the sound design process. Each element brings something special to the gestalt of the emotional and cognitive experience, and each in turn moves in and out of the foreground of the audio score. In this section, we will take a look at how these audio components work together and see some examples of how each has been used in children's interactive products.

Sound Effects

Sound effects are sounds added to punctuate and flavor specific events. Sound effects, even more than music, are driven by events on screen. Their primary purpose is to add realism; their secondary purpose is to add color (and occasionally humor, as mentioned in the previous chapter). They enhance the impact of a visual, and can even change its meaning. In animation especially, sound effects make visuals believable. A silent explosion or door slam just doesn't have the same effect. Media users need sound effects to help their brains accept the visual illusions as reality.

> *One of the things that the average viewer of films doesn't understand is that almost none of the audio, except perhaps for some of the voice, was recorded live. It has all been constructed after the shoot from libraries of sound effects and originally composed music.*[2]
>
> —Jeff Essex, sound designer and author

The World as Your Palette

Sound design offers an amazingly diverse palette to work from. First, there are a variety of sound effects libraries available with multiple versions of almost any noise you can think of. And then, of course, you have infinite source material from the world around you. But the best part of digital sound design is the magical suite of new editing tools available. They offer endless opportunities to take any sound and twist it, tweak it, pitch it, slice it, or dice it. You can make anything from a sweetened version of the original to something completely bizarre where none of the original material can be recognized. This is definitely part of the fun of sound design, turning the sound of a tapped power tower support cable into a laser sword (or whatever).

WGY Noisemakers: A live radio play with sound effects at WGY, Schenectady, New York, 1925.

Most of the sound effects we create today follow in the footsteps of Jack Foley, the first sound person credited with adding live sound effects to movies after they were already shot. He used many of the tricks of radio soundmen, such as crushing cellophane or paper to sound like flames, or shaking a large sheet of metal to get a sound like thunder. The only limit to creating sound effects is your imagination.

Designer's Note

In an early prototype I built (and continually demoed for months on end), I used a simple door opening sound from a sound effects library when an animated character came into a room. I got to know that door squeak intimately over the next several months as I repeatedly ran the demo or tweaked it. To my surprise, I began hearing the exact same door sound in movies, on TV shows, and in commercials. It was everywhere! It was a classic door squeak effect, and all these others designers working from the same library were using it. I had never noticed before because the designers had done their jobs well, and the door sound was perfectly integrated into the scenes. Only my repeated use of it made it noticeable. The experience brought home to me how much the audio experience of a game, movie, or TV show is painstakingly constructed, piece by piece, and tweaked extensively so it is seamless with the visual scene. When we do our work well, the sound is unnoticeable, and it seems natural to us.

Ambient Audio Effects

Ambient audio and effects create the sensation of being somewhere other than in front of a digital device; they feed the ears and help to fill any environment with life.

Ambient sound can either be constant or occasional. The constant sounds are ones that run continually in the background of a scene. If you are outside, it might be crickets at night, waves crashing on the beach, or crowd/city noise for a busy street. Indoors, ambient low-volume music might be used to create mood. Occasional ambient effects are generally used to mirror the randomness of sounds in real life, increasing the believability of the sound track. Chirping birds, an airplane flying, or a car driving nearby are examples of random sounds that imply a larger living environment.

Ambient audio is background sound. Its role is not to punctuate but to immerse the user in the illusion of the environment and to create the experience of being there.

Creating User Focus

Too many sounds can be distracting; they become audio mud. When overloaded with audio stimulus, our brains tend to block out competing noises in order to help us focus our attention on the more important sounds. Good audio design always knows which sounds need to be in the foreground and which in the background.

In an interactive game, particularly an arcade-style game, our minds can get very confused because the pace is so quick. This is where judicious sound design comes in. We need to direct the focus of the game player's brain, just as a director does in a movie sound track. We can do this by prioritizing particular sounds at particular times. The predominant sound will always be shifting from voice to music to sound effects and back again as activity demands.

The Sounds of Silence

It is never absolutely quiet in real life. The total absence of any sound is a very strange experience. We are so used to being bathed in ambient sound that when it disappears it seems very unnatural. Complete silence sounds just as strange in media, so much so that all sound effects libraries offer ambient "room tones" with no frequency modulation. Room tones can be used as background when no other effect or music is happening in the audio channel.

Because true silence is so unusual, it can be used as a (non)-sound effect. The absence of audio can create a negative space that wants to be filled. Often, it is used as a kind of foreshadowing effect because you are waiting to hear something.
You can use silence to crank up the effect of any sound that follows, because of the contrast it creates. For instance, the best way to make something seem really loud, like a big explosion, is to have total silence just before it. The juxtaposition of nothing to something makes that something sound even bigger.

We might also make the distinction between silence and quiet. Where true silence is the absence of any audio vibration, quiet is often thought of as a place where we are not interrupted by any man-made sounds. We go to the beach or the mountains for quiet, hopefully to hear only the natural world as our ancestors did.

Pull My Finger—Kids and Sound Effects

Laughter is contagious. In adults and in kids, there is something about laughter that makes us want to join in. It goes beyond social response, accessing something more primitive about our natures. We are hardwired to respond to laughter. Laughing makes us feel good, and finding a way to use real laughter in a natural way will enhance the joy of any children's activity. (Yawning is also very contagious, although putting your audience to sleep is not usually a goal!)

Kids like physical humor. They have a love of funny sound effects, anything that sounds like farts, burps, splats, or plops. Slapstick and cartoon-style action and the accompanying sounds always get their attention. The three- to seven-year-old is trying to understand how the world works, and the seven- to eleven-year-old is trying to fit in with his or her peer group and deal with the larger rules of society. Both age groups enjoy physical humor sound effects, which lie just outside the boundaries of how they are supposed to behave. Kids like being able to trigger those sounds themselves. (For more on humor, see Ch. 3, pp. 39–41.)

Kids like to be grossed out. That is part of why farts and burps are popular, but kids also have a love/hate relationship with snot, slugs, barf, insects, and anything slimy. Sound effects to go along with any of those images are likely to be a hit.

Kids like to be scared—a little. This does not apply to kids below about seven, but it is certainly true of older kids, both boys and girls. Since sound is about emotion, it's quite easy to use just a few effects to create a texture of foreboding, unexplained mystery, and scariness.

Sound Effects as Interface Feedback

Good interface is part of any enjoyable computing experience, especially for kids. One of the main things that helped catapult Kid Pix, the kids' painting program, to the forefront of children's software sales in the mid-1990s was that not only did it use cute sounds for the main interface, it used them in all the drawing and painting tools *while* kids were creating. Kids weren't just painting; they were making funny noises and music. The sound effects added an element of power to their actions. What Kid Pix did has become standard in kids' paint programs, but when Kid Pix premiered it, it was something no one had thought about doing before.

Interface effects are usually set at a mid- to low-volume level. Because you will hear them over and over again, the last thing you want to do is create a feedback sound so annoying and/or loud that the user wants to turn all the audio off. You have failed your sound design class if that happens. (For more on interface design, see Ch. 12.)

Designer's Note

For me, the sounds associated with losing a game can affect how I feel about playing it again. In the app *Solitaire City*, a generally well-designed card game app, the losing sound is a group of people going "Aaaawwww," as if you had just fallen flat on your face in front of a crowd. In the rest of the game experience, I am just playing by myself solving the current puzzle, but when I lose, all of sudden it feels like all these others were watching. At first, I thought it was cool, but after playing the harder levels, where you lose more often, I found myself turning the audio off because I didn't like the "crowd" feeling sorry for my loss, even though I knew there was no crowd.

Some ways you can use sound effects in interface are:

- **To acknowledge user actions.** Yes, a mouse makes a little click sound in the real world, and fingers make no sound on a touch screen, but try to make the *effect* of our kids' actions bigger. When they are clicking a button, give that button its own special sound, something very short, pleasant, or fun.

- **To mask transitions.** Whether a player is waiting for a download, page load, or scene change, you can maintain continuity and interest with an audio transition. Especially in a story or adventure game, theme-related sound effects or music help to carry players though transitions by keeping the mood alive. Sounds can also divert attention from lulls in activity, keeping players' interest piqued until action begins again.

- **As payoff.** Payoff sounds tend to be in the foreground. They are an audio reward for winning, passing a level, or getting everything right. It's very positive feedback. Classic kid program examples include sound effects like a crowd of people cheering, applause, a trumpet or other instrumental fanfare, or a combination of all three. What is most important is to have an immediate audio acknowledgment of the users' actions. It doesn't need to be long—nothing more than a few seconds at most—and shorter is often better.

- **As warning.** Sounds in the interface can alert users of problems or opportunities. Usually, these are also foreground sounds since they are WARNINGS! Sometimes, in games that use time limits to create pacing, a warning sound will let the user know things on screen are about to change. Sound effects can also let the user know they can't do something they just tried—they may have misplaced a piece in a puzzle or incorrectly answered a question. These sounds should not be annoying, loud, or long. Simple audio feedback is usually the best.

Designer's Note

Something we hear over and over from parents and teachers is that they appreciate an easy way to turn down audio, particularly the repetitive interface sounds. Making specialty settings for audio and other features teachers want is a great way to get your app sold into schools.

Remember to create interface effects that are tonally or musically related across an entire program. Consistent feedback is important, especially with kids. Navigation is different than interactivity because it's about ease of getting around and doing what you want to do more than it is about entertainment.

Sound effects support, enhance, and create interactive experiences to a greater degree than most users are aware. Deliberately study the audio tracks of your favorite films and apps to enhance your understanding of what works and what doesn't.

Music

Music brings magic to a media experience. Like water, it moves fluidly from foreground to background, from leisurely to speedy, and from gloomy to joyful, all in direct support of the characters and action on the screen. Music has the power to affect mood, suspense, and pacing, and it works as emotional glue to tie a story together.

Foreshadowing

Foreshadowing, as mentioned before with the Darth Vader signature musical refrain, is another good audio trick to imply something offscreen before the viewer even sees it. The music sets the mood for the scene to come. This helps the viewer to have an unconscious emotional opinion about what's going on as it happens or is about to happen.

A variation is called a prelap, a common film trick for creating transitions between scenes. Sounds from the upcoming scene begin while, visually, the viewer is still in the current one. The juxtaposition of image and sound creates a short, unresolved situation that resolves when the image finally matches the sound. The sound creates an expectation that is rewarded when the next scene begins.

Foreground Music

Foreground music is just what it sounds like; the music is "in front," or louder (remember louder or bigger means closer) than other audio components at that moment. Foreground music is used to heighten the intensity of emotional content because it indicates where emotion takes precedence in the story line. Most easily noticed in film scores, it is the place in the story where the action is non-verbal. It

New Super Mario Bros. Wii by Nintendo.

can be anything from car chases, fights, or battles, to romance, forgiveness, or the stunning effect of tragedy. Basically, it is used in any place where the story is being moved forward by emotion.

Foreground music is also used a lot in console and handheld gaming devices since there is little dialogue. The lively music, punctuated by sound effects, directly follows the action of the game's characters as they navigate and interact with the game's world. The Mario games are a perfect example of this. They combine simple background music with a wide variety of sound effects, such as an electronic gliss each time Mario jumps, a bling when he catches gold stars, and chord progressions when an obstacle has been defeated.

Background Music

Background music is in the back layers of the overall score, beneath the dominant foreground sounds. It continues to set the mood, supporting and underscoring the emotional content of the dialogue. It enhances the other content and provides continuity to tie all the elements together. The background is the foundation upon which everything else rests, even if it was created last. Background music is used to draw the audience in.

When people or characters are talking, we want to know what they are saying. Voices attract us because they are how almost all stories are told. Therefore, the music layer, or channel, is constantly shifting between the foreground and the background as it drops *behind* the dialogue or moves back to the foreground as the story progresses with more action and emotion.

Voice

Children are naturally drawn to voices, especially those of other children. Getting a good performance is the key to a character's believability. Here are some tips on finding and working with voice talent.

Voice Talent: The Actors

With your main characters, and especially with narration, it's good to use professional voice talent. Even though it is fun to do some of the voices and vocal sound effects yourself, it may not be the best choice for your product. People new to the industry often think, "Hey, Jenny, the new receptionist, has a nice voice, let's use her." Even though it seems like a great idea, it can be frustrating, time-consuming, and even demoralizing to the inexperienced talent. It's not easy to get a strong performance from someone who has little to no training or experience as a voice actor.

Before hiring voice actors, you will need to know a number of things. Does the actor need to sing? How realistic or cartoonish a performance are you looking for? What is the character's relationship to the user? How does one character relate to the other characters you are creating? If you have a lot of different characters to keep track of, be sure the voices all work well together and are easily distinguished from one another. Usually, it's best to cast the main characters first and then build the ensemble of other voices in relation to them.

Actors are specialists at emotional communication. They can make us laugh or cry, sympathize with or dislike a character. With pitch, pacing, punctuation, and personality, actors use their voices as instruments.

They can take us on flights of fancy or teach us to tie our shoes. Whether the actor is singing, acting, or narrating, a good voice performance is pleasing. The human voice is such an expressive instrument that when it is used correctly in kids' media, kids naturally respond positively.

An important consideration is how long you will need your voice talent. Kids really like hearing other kids' voices, especially for characters who are supposed to be kids. There is something guileless about a kid's voice that you can't capture with an adult playing a kid's part. Kids bring an authenticity that is almost always missing in an adult performance. The only problem with using kids is that their voices tend to change quickly, and after a while, no level of pitching up is going to make changed voices sound right. Have a sense of how long you might need your kid actor or actress before you begin production. An actor may work well once or twice with the same product line, but if his or her voice changes, the shift in sound will affect the material produced later on.

Designer's Note

When we were building our first Arthur title, *Arthur's Teacher Trouble*, we cast a boy who was several years younger than Arthur's supposed age, and pitched his voice down to make him sound a little older. We did another Arthur title in the series a year and half later and his voice was just perfect as it was, but when we created a third title a year after that, we had to pitch his voice up in order for him not to sound too old. By the fourth title, we had to audition a new kid to play the part. This is why, on a show like *The Simpsons*, where the kids are the same age over decades of production, it's much easier to use adult voices for continuity. It all depends on the experience that you as the designer are trying to create.

Nancy Cartwright, the voice
of Bart Simpson.

In general, it's a good idea to use kids who have had acting experience, especially if they are lead characters in large project. You will save time in the long run by getting what you want sooner, and you'll probably get a more consistent performance over several recording sessions. A good voice coach can also be used to help get great performances from the voice talent.

Directing Kids

Kids have so much spontaneous energy, and sometimes their performances are so charmingly natural that even good adult actors can't pull off the same level of performance. (It is just too long since they were kids.) As a result, being a voice director for kids can be one of the most gratifying and entertaining experiences in audio design. It can also be one of the most frustrating, so remember:

Get help if you need it. If you or your sound designer have little experience with acting or are not comfortable with directing children yourself, hire a professional voice director who works with kids regularly. They are specialists at getting the best performances from kids and will often know talented kids in your area.

Be positive. The voice coach sets the emotional tone for the recording session. If the coach is not positive and upbeat it's hard for the kid actors to give a positive performance.

Longtime sound designer and voice talent Michael Barrett, owner of Barrett Tone Audio Productions, says:

> The biggest personal rule that I always try to follow in directing kids in the studio is to never let them hear the word "no." It's just been a principle I've always followed. When they do a take, even if it sucked, you say "Good job. Now, let's try it this way." If you always give them positive feedback, you'll get so much more from them in the long run.

> Once, we were doing a math title, *James Makes a Salad* (a Brøderbund title), with a company in Australia. I had gone over and recorded all the kids with the team there, and brought the tapes back. As often happens, we needed a few pick-up lines with the boy who was James, and so they recorded him there doing those lines. But when they sent the tapes back, it sounded like a different kid altogether, nothing like the character that we had already. We wondered what was going on, until we heard how he was being directed. After each take the director would say, "No, now I want you to try it this way." The kid had no positive motivation, and was getting tighter and smaller, and projecting less with each take. You could tell he was feeling as though he was really doing it wrong, even though he wanted to please the director. It was so obvious, listening to the tape, that it just really reinforced me to never tell a kid "no" or "wrong."[3]

A voice can convey so much more meaning than the words alone. Use of tone, timing, and volume in particular play a powerful role in how we interpret meaning from a performance. Getting great performances from your voice talent can make or break the overall experience of playing with a product.

Designer's Note

Finding the right narrator sets the tone for your product. We were working on a science app for preschoolers, and we were looking for a voice that would offer expertise in a way that wasn't off-putting to our young audience. We decided on a young actress who was able to make it feel like it she was your favorite big sister, and wasn't all this science information really cool. She was a nice balance of informally informative, sweet (but not overly so), and supportive.

Other Tips for Voice Production

- **Have the script finished before the talent shows up.** Talent and studio time cost money, so don't waste anybody's time by improvising a lot of the script after they show up. The script should have been revised several times before you send a copy for review, and especially before the studio clock starts ticking. Remember to include some of the basics of communication: "Hello," "Goodbye," "Okay," giggles, laughter, or other positive reactions such as "Wow" or the classic "Cool."

Mark Schlichting and his grandson, Ryven, recording voice and sound effects for the *Noodle Words* app.
Photo by Angie Dean-Schlichting.

- **Keep good notes.** Often during a recording session, it's good to have someone besides the engineer there to keep track of time code, dialogue, and which take was the "keeper." It will save you hours of time—and lots of money—later to be able to cut just the takes you know worked well, without having to listen to the whole session again.

- **Save everything.** You never know when you might want additional material or something unscripted that just happened off the cuff. It's a kind of safety net.

- **Avoid Frankensteining.** One of the blessings of digital editing is that you can easily cut and paste dialogue together. Sometimes you don't get all the right takes for a line or scene, and you have to build them from lots of little pieces that do or don't match. Stitching and gluing all these weird takes together has lovingly been called Frankensteining. Occasionally, you are missing one line of dialogue that was never in the script, but everybody needs it, and the kid talent is in France, visiting relatives, so you have to Frankenstein it together from hundreds of lines and different takes. This is far from efficient because it takes a long time to edit the pieces together, and the performance is seldom what you really want. It's another important reason to have a thorough script and keep everything in case of emergency.

- **Technological constraints can affect directing style.** Actors have to be louder and more extreme in their movements when acting on stage rather than on video or film, and, similarly, certain technological limitations may affect the kind of performance needed from a voice actor. Consider the constraints of your compression and destination delivery platform before recording. Environments with less data information (where the highs and lows of the bandwidth are restricted to keep the overall audio data smaller, as with 8-bit audio) have a tendency to flatten performances considerably.

In the early days of interactive software, we often had a great performance from the actors, but when we listened to it through smaller speakers, in 8-bit audio, it sounded flatter and less interesting than it had in the studio. To compensate, when we know we are going to lose data from formatting or compression, we try to push the actors to get a more highly modulated or exaggerated performance. It may sound a bit over-the-top at the time, but after compression and when played through tiny speakers, it sounds just right.

The Language of Sound Design

Here is some of the basic sound design vocabulary. Even if you aren't planning to do the sound design yourself, it helps to know the terms in order to communicate your vision to the sound designer.

Amplitude is directly related to volume. The greater the distance between the top and the bottom of the sound wave, the greater the amplitude. Amplitude, or loudness, is described in decibels (dB). Amplifiers make sound louder. Volume determines whether a sound is in the foreground or the background of your soundscape.

Audio proximity, like visual proximity, describes where things are in relation to the user. With visual proximity, objects that are large are perceived as being close; those that are small are perceived as being far away. Volume, or amplitude, is how we measure audio proximity. If it's loud, it's either very close or it is a big sound, like an explosion. When you hear a train coming, it gets louder and louder as it gets closer, and quieter and quieter as it recedes. Loud means close or big; faint means distant or small. We assign these real-world attributes to sounds we hear even if they are from a computer.

Background sound supports foreground sound and the emotional experience by filling in around the main dialogue or action. It tends to hold the pieces of an experience together by being the background upon which everything else takes place.

Ducking is the technique of adjusting volume so that foreground sound becomes background sound in order to be subservient to voice. Dialogue and spoken words almost always take priority over music and sound effects. Everyone has heard ducking: in a movie with a night club scene, the music will be loud until characters speak; then the volume of the music is lowered, moving to the background while the characters are talking. When the dialogue is over, the volume of the music goes up again, returning to the foreground.

Fade-in and **fade-out** are exactly what they sound like. Each sound has a beginning and an end, and the amount of fade-in or fade-out applied to the sound affects how sharp or gentle the auditory experience is. Most natural sounds have a short fade-in and a longer fade-out (or decay).

Foreground sound is the top layer of audio volume and presence. It is what you cognitively hear first. When dialogue is occurring, that is usually the foreground. Sound effects and music tend to be foregrounded only when no one is talking, usually during action-heavy sequences.

Frequency corresponds to the pitch of the sound. High-pitched sounds, such as the piercing squeal of a whistle, are the result of rapid vibrations. Low-pitched sounds, such as the rumble of a train passing nearby, are caused by slower vibrations. Frequency of sound is measured in terms of vibrations per second, and it is described in Hertz (Hz), or cycles per second.

Looping is a big part of many styles of music right now, but interactive media sound designers have been using it for a long time. Loops are especially good at reducing data size because they play the same data over and over again. This is especially useful when you need to shove the most content over the skinniest pipeline possible. The main trick to looping is to make it sound right. Be sure to cut on the beat! If you have a 4x4 loop, cut on a one so it repeats smoothly; otherwise it sounds like a three-legged dog running.

Panning is the stereo placement of specific sounds. Where does a sound fall in the stereo field? All left, all right, or in the middle? An example might be footsteps panning from left to right as a character walks from left to right. Some computers and most theaters are now using 5–1 systems. Front left and right, back left and right, and the woofer which, as bass, is generally omnidirectional.

Soundscapes: Putting It All Together

A soundscape is an emotional landscape made of sound. It contains sounds that reflect objects in the foreground, sounds that behave like scenery in the background, and sounds that are like interesting textures in-between. The word *soundscape* also implies a continuous environment that surrounds an experience. In interactive media, a soundscape is designed to enhance and punctuate the choices and actions of the user. Here are some of the things to think about when building a good audio score.

Creating Audio Glue

Layers of Sound

Even though final playback of the audio track may only happen in a one- or two-channel environment, the construction of the soundscape, or score, can involve ten or more channels. All of them will get compressed at the end of the process. You may have a channel for voice, music, character sound effects (walking, clothes moving, scratching, sneezing), scene sound effects (cars, airplanes, dogs barking, explosions, doors closing), and ambient natural sounds (birds, crickets, waterfalls).

These sounds are layered to form the user's experience. The top layer is the most important sound at a given point, and the bottom layer is the least important in that moment. Priorities in the action or interface push one sound or another to the forefront of awareness. A sound in the forefront of the user's experience is meant to focus the player's attention on what's important. It can be the voice of an agent explaining a particular activity, or a knock at a door inviting the player to open it. Audio cues usually work with video cues to focus the player's attention.

Continuity of Experience

We use our ears to maintain continuity in the real world, and good audio design is about creating continuity of experience in the digital world of your title. Something should always be going on to keep the experience alive. The sound track is the spackle that smooths over the gaps in the experience and glues it all together, making it one continuous soundscape.

Designer's Note

Children's sound designer Jeff Essex thinks of the sound track as the frosting on a layer cake. It sweetens and improves the entire experience while also filling in the spaces between the layers, connecting them to make one delicious experience.[4]

The soundscape needs to effectively communicate what you want the player to experience, supporting the focus and mood of the content. In order to do this well, always approach the sound experience from the user's viewpoint.

Balancing the Frequency

Another thing to think about in the larger design realm is that you have a frequency spectrum to work within, and there's only a certain amount of sound you can put in before individual sounds begin masking each other. You want to have some sounds in the low frequency range and others in the high range to prevent layers of muddy sound.

For example, if you have a low rumble as background ambiance for a spaceship, and then you want to add a loud, giant explosion, you have to figure out how to get that background spaceship noise out of the way, or you need to put in another frequency band. Somehow, you have to leave some low-frequency space available to punctuate the explosion. Otherwise, what was supposed to be a jarring explosion just becomes a layer of mud, and it doesn't have the impact it could have.

The same goes for high frequency sounds. If you've got something with a lot of birds in it, and you put your button clicks up in a high, chirpy range, people may not notice the button sounds. In soundscapes, it's important to have a balance of contrasting frequencies in order to support audio clarity for the different elements.

Don't Get Attached to One Style of Music

Because of kids' lifelong exposure to quick video cuts and the ability to jump between environments in software, we are constantly pushed to step rapidly through styles, especially in children's software. Variety is the spice of life, and key to keeping things fresh. Often, nothing lasts for more than 10 seconds before you have to go on to something else. Going from nursery rhymes to rap or rock is not uncommon. Don't get stuck in one style unless it's on purpose.

Orchestrate for the Whole Mix

Go for the gestalt. The whole is greater than the sum of the parts. Remember to listen to the whole experience of what you are creating. Does your attention go where you want it? Are your sounds all volume-balanced, so the wrong things don't jump out in your face? Does the music support the feeling you were trying to create? Do others experience what you were trying for? Remember that your audio track is what holds the entire experience together.

As expert sound designer Michael Barrett emphasizes: Don't overdo it. A little goes a long way with sound because it works in harmony with the visuals, strengthening them without dominating or obscuring them. Sound, able to operate on a more emotional and subtle level, complements the visuals, which tend to appeal to our cognitive side. As with many other things, the partnership between sound and visuals creates something far stronger than either could ever be on its own.

> *Sound provides the vibrational atmosphere that completes the immersive experience.*[5]
>
> —**Michael Barrett, audio engineer**

Designing Sound for Asynchronous Media

The joy and the pain of interactive media is that, at almost any point, the user can go somewhere else. Your job in designing sound in this asynchronous environment is to give the illusion that no matter where the user goes, their experience feels linear. Here are some design tips to help in the process.

Create a map or flowchart. You have to know the possible places a click might take a user. Creating a complete design flowchart or map helps to give you a list of the variables you need to consider. Some products are simple enough that this is not necessary, but it never hurts to try to identify problems before users do.

Understand your delivery technology. The last thing you want is to have the experience come to a halt while new content is loading. Understanding the limitations and strengths of the delivery medium can make the difference between a continuous groove or a deadly silence. You need to know how much time and what system resources are available. For instance, does your software allow or not allow for contiguous sound during loads? For smaller pipelines, you might need to have music loops preloaded to cover download transitions.

Design music to be interrupted. The more interactive a project, the more challenging its sound design because you have to be prepared for all the possible choices a user might make.

When the music changes,
so does the dance.
—**African proverb**

Most often, you are dealing with many looping fragments, and the trick is to arrange the loops for nonlinear but synchronized composition. Design the acoustic flow based on the possible paths a user may take and the emotional/environmental needs of the situation. Continuity is the key to creating a cohesive experience.

Create loops that work. Looped sounds are used to keep a melody, rhythm, or ambient sound effect (like birds in a forest, or street noises in a city environment) playing during gameplay. They have a defined length, and they *repeat* smoothly when they reach the end. Loops that resolve, like drum beats, play well continuously, but can be very monotonous after a while. The trick is to embellish loops with additional musical or sound elements (perhaps through a second channel when available) so that they don't become stale and repetitive. The longer the loop, the less noticeable (and less boring), but long loops can take up a lot of RAM in some systems. That's why they are often kept short.

Think about reusability. One of the difficult things to integrate into the gaming medium (particularly if low bandwidth is an issue) is the need to reuse as many pieces of content as possible. Whether it's graphic or sound data, designers must constantly create ways to optimize delivery to get the strongest experience with what will go through the pipeline, fit in a scene, or match a budget. One strategy is to invent new ways to use the same piece of content over and over. The trick is to do that without making it feel overly repetitive. One method that works well is to break sounds into smaller pieces that can be called up in different orders.

Use MIDI when you can. MIDI, software synthesis and algorithmic composition, and music playback tools offer a workable solution for non-linear sound. The major challenge becomes designing modular musical scores that can skip from section to section and still sound compelling.

Run audio tests on the target platform before the final mix. This may seem like a no-brainer, but we have seen a lot of time wasted doing the final mix for a game before it was tested on the target platform/device. It sounds great on your own system, but may get tinny, unbalanced, or muddy on something with little speakers. Blending the creative talent and the technical know-how is an important common thread that runs through every successful kid service or product. You must know how things will play and sound before you can do your final build.

File size is a factor. The higher the fidelity, or resemblance to real-world sound, the more storage space and/or bandwidth the audio data will require. For instance, an app's download size can balloon exponentially if there is a lot of dialogue. The goal is always to work in the highest quality format available, then apply lots of data compression just prior to delivery. Trying to get the best sound on limited bandwidth is one of the more technologically creative aspects of audio production. Voice almost always needs to be high quality or it doesn't come across as real. It's best to figure out how much bandwidth voice will require, then fill in the blank audio space. For years, sound design has been a balancing act of sampled loops, MIDI, reused sound effects, and lots of compression to make it work.

Good audio production is powerful in its ability to bring products to life. It can imply reality, affect emotions, and deepen engagement. Never underestimate the power of audio to bring your product to life and make it magical.

PART 3

Knowing Your Audience

A common problem in children's interactive media is that products are often created without knowing target audiences' likes and dislikes or the developmental appropriateness of content. How can you engage and entertain someone if you don't understand their point of view, interests, preferences, and what delights them? This section offers a brief overview of learning theories, a summary of ages and stages of development, and some thoughts on the ways gender affects what kids like and how they relate to the world. This information is essential to designing successful and truly engaging games for children.

We worry about what a child will become tomorrow, yet we forget that he is someone today.[1]

—Stacia Demler (Tauscher), originally quoted in *Reader's Digest*

How Kids Learn

Whether you are creating educational activities or games meant purely for entertainment, understanding learning processes and how children perceive and assimilate information will help you to connect with them and make truly engaging products. This chapter covers several of the main theories about learning, how perceptual skills change as children grow, and how learning theories relate to and affect the design of interactive media.

Man is by nature a learning animal. Birds fly, fish swim; man thinks and learns. Therefore, we do not need to "motivate" children into learning. . . . We do not need to keep picking away at their minds to make sure they are learning. . . . Give children as much help and guidance as they need and ask for; listen respectfully when they feel like talking; and then get out of the way. We can trust them to do the rest.[2]

—John Holt, author

Learning Theories: Four Main Perspectives

Researchers and educators are still figuring out how children learn, so much so that all discussion of learning is framed theoretically. Although there are still many unknowns, there are a variety of interlocking theories, each with their own viewpoint, that serve as guideposts. It is a bit like the story of the five blind men and the elephant. Each had touched an elephant and described the part they had touched, thinking that was the whole elephant. Each description was accurate, but it was not the whole picture. All five descriptions taken together, how-

ever, conveyed a broader sense of the elephant. Similarly, over time, new learning theories develop when earlier theories don't explain all observed behavior. The new theories don't replace the old ones. Instead, they are typically viewed as different perspectives on the same thing, and all the theories together deepen our understanding of the complex subject of learning.

Designer's Note

Trying to explain the larger universe of learning theories is complicated. For the purposes of this book, I am going to share just a few of the principles and describe how I have found them useful in children's interactive design.

Behaviorism

American psychologist John B. Watson, influenced by the conditioning and reflex experiments of Ivan Pavlov, advanced the concept of behaviorism in 1913. Another American psychologist, B. F. Skinner, took the concept further with his studies on operant conditioning. Behaviorists believe that animals (and humans) are motivated through a system of observable responses to environmental stimuli and rewards, rather than any internal mental processes. Learning occurs when an external stimulus (in the form of a reward or punishment) causes a change in behavior.[3] Some key points of behaviorism are:

- A child's behavior can be shaped through incentives.

- The learner is a passive participant who responds to stimuli.

- Rewards and punishments motivate the learner.

- Learning usually follows a teacher's predefined (often linear) path.

- The teacher can observe and measure the child's learning progress.

- The teacher sets up the learning activities so the child will properly respond to the stimulus.

Behaviorist ideas constantly pop up in software and other media designed for kids. Positive reinforcement motivates and provides incentives. Something as simple as a positive sound effect or some sparkles can boost a child's feelings of empowerment and desire to continue. The same goes for point systems, "power-ups," "unlocks," bonuses, and other similar features of learning apps and video games.

According to behaviorists, negative reinforcement also motivates, pushing the learner to improve. We've all experienced the desire to play a game again, this time

avoiding traps and penalties or even the simple buzzer sound that tells us we've done something wrong. Hasbro's board game *Operation* is one such example; the whole purpose of the game is to avoid the buzzer. Common forms of negative reinforcement in games include negative audio/visual feedback, decline in game character's strength or abilities, inability to proceed to the next playing level, and sometimes even a game character's death.

Designer's Note

Generally, game design is high in positive feedback compared to negative. If players get too much negative feedback, they are more likely to quit due to feelings of discouragement or frustration.

Cognitivism

Cognitivism became a dominant learning model in the 1960s, primarily in response to the limitations of behaviorism. Unlike behaviorists, cognitivists believe that the way people think affects their behavior. People don't merely respond to stimuli; they also have mental processes that contribute to learning. Cognitivists see learning as the mental activity of storage and retrieval that takes place in order to build a mental construct of the world. The focus is on mental processes—thought, problem solving, and motivation—that lead to a behavior. For a cognitivist, learning occurs when a change in knowledge and understanding occurs.

Like behaviorists, cognitivists believe that learning occurs when new information is linked to prior knowledge, and that learning is best accomplished when information is passed from a knowledgeable expert to a novice.[4] Some key points of cognitivism are:

- Learners acquire strategies to process information for learning.

- Knowledge can be broken up into simple building blocks.

- Organization of information presented to learners is important.

- Practice and repetition help connect new information to prior knowledge.

- Teachers must be aware of the student's thought process during the learning activity.

- The role of the teacher is to organize and transfer information to the learner.

Many games that challenge students with problem-solving tasks incorporate cognitive theories. However, games that use strict progressions that require rote answers to canned questions don't foster deeper learning and engagement because they don't hold the child's attention. Cognitivism emphasizes the need to engage thought processes beyond memorization. It is about creating "Aha!" moments of true comprehension. For an example of this type of design used to good effect, check out the sorting games in Little Bit Studio's *Bugs and Buttons* app, which help young children develop the mental construct of attributes.

Bugs and Buttons app by Little Bit Studio.

Constructivism

Constructivism extends cognitive theory to include more child-centric and collaborative approaches. Jean Piaget, Lev Vygotsky, and others helped to develop the constructivist learning theory. Constructivism asserts that children actively build their own knowledge via a cycle of repeated and expanded interactions with their environment, constructing meaning as they go. Children actively integrate new experiences with old to create a new reality. The idea that a child is an autonomous and active learner is central to this theory.[5] Some key points of constructivism are:

- Children are active participants in their learning.

- Learners collaborate with others to construct their knowledge.

- Children can direct their own learning, rather than following a predetermined linear path.

- Manipulation and experimentation are encouraged.

- Prior understanding, combined with new experiences, plays a role in learning.

- The learning environment is open-ended rather than controlled and predictable.

- Scaffolding (gameplay with levels designed to help students progressively understand the material) is used to support a child's exploration.

- The role of the teacher is that of a mentor, collaborating with and guiding the child.

Book Creator app by Red Jumper Limited.

Any interactive game that offers open-ended play opportunities or uses virtual manipulatives to build new creations is drawing from constructivism. Examples include *SimCity*, *Minecraft*, and *Age of Empires*. Another good example is *Book Creator* by Red Jumper Limited. This app lets kids create stories in powerful ways, mixing together video, audio, and drawings. What these games have in common is that they provide basic information, components, and tools, but they give users or players a lot of freedom to determine the course of the game. Players can combine and recombine elements in any way they wish, experiment with building different concepts, and create something unique. This is a contrast to other kinds of games with a set number of options, possible paths, and outcomes.

Humanism

Humanistic education grew during the 1960s, and is primarily based on the work of psychologists Carl Rogers and Abraham Maslow. Humanistic learning focuses on the learner as a whole person with choice and control. Learning is student-centered and emphasizes the development of self-esteem, goal-setting abilities, and cooperative and supportive environments.[6] Some key points of humanism are:

- A child's behavior is influenced by intrinsic motivation.

- The approach is student-centered and learning is self-directed.

- Learning is experiential, focusing on the process rather than the facts.

- Children are active agents of inquiry rather than passive recipients of facts and procedures.

- Personal growth of the learner is encouraged.

- Both the teacher and the students have a facilitating role.

Many games incorporate a humanistic approach, with designs that consider multiple learning modalities and offer learning experiences that work for varied individuals. Ultimately, the goal of the humanistic approach is to engage the child.

> *The only man who is educated is the man who has learned how to learn; the man who has learned how to adapt and change.*[7]
> —Carl Rogers, psychologist

Designer's Note

In my years of product testing with kids, I developed my own insights about how children learn. Later I was delighted to find out there are names and theories for the things I had observed, and I enjoyed reading the deep body of research available. It really is worthwhile to understand more about learning theories so that you can improve your own designs.

Key Principles of Learning Theories

All learning theories provide some insights into optimal learning conditions, and many are closely related. For instance, the work of Jean Piaget and Jerome Bruner is considered both cognitivist and constructivist. Each of the above theories contributes principles of learning that have practical applications in children's software design. Below are some particularly relevant principles and examples of how they can be used effectively.

Operant Conditioning

Edward Thorndike (1874–1949) was an important pioneer and proponent of behaviorism in learning. Among other things, he studied the role of rewards and consequences and a technique of breaking tasks into small parts for easier learning. He developed a theory that learning is incremental and automatic. Thorndike's *law of effect* states what might seem like common sense: if you're rewarded for a behavior, you're likely to repeat it. He was considered an early advocate of *active learning*, which gives kids the power to steer and control their learning instead of simply absorbing facts handed to them by teachers.[8]

Designer's Note

Interface design is about making something easy for humans to use. In interactive learning, that often means breaking new information up into small pieces that can be easily absorbed. Thorndike's research elucidated effective ways of doing that, and his ideas are still relevant today. In terms of interface, consider how the makers of Oreo cookies invented a whole new market opportunity for themselves—and the cookie industry—by selling Oreo Minis, "bite-size" cookies that people could just pop into their mouths. A more convenient interface (or "into face") size made it easier for people to snack on the cookies. Small chunks of information also are easier for learners to digest.

B. F. Skinner (1904–1990), a radical behaviorist who studied non-reflexive behaviors, extended Thorndike's laws of effect and developed the operant conditioning theory. Unlike Pavlovian classical conditioning, in which a behavior is triggered by a specific stimulus, in operant conditioning, a natural action occurs and is then reinforced in order to shape a desired behavior.

B.F. Skinner

Skinner was opposed to the use of punishment. Although he observed that punishment did reduce unwanted behavior, he also noted that it might not be permanent. In the long run, it's more effective to use positive reinforcement to bring about a *desired* behavior. He also believed that schools' use of punishment actually "taught students to dislike and avoid learning."[9]

In the 1950s, using his operant conditioning principles, Skinner developed "teaching machines" to improve the learning process in schools. These machines were mechanical devices whose purpose was to administer a curriculum of sequential, programmed instruction. The machines displayed a series of questions one "frame" at a time, and they offered a location where the learner could respond to each question. Then, the learner was provided with immediate feedback, whether they were right or wrong. The quick response is important because, in Skinner's own words, it "generates a high level of interest and enthusiasm."[10]

Though operant conditioning is not considered a complete explanation of the learning process, it is still important to consider when creating products for children. Some key points of operant conditioning are:

- Provide instant feedback.

- Offer positive reinforcement.

- Offer the possibility of random rewards (called *intermittent reinforcement*).

- Offer incremental levels of difficulty and individualized pacing.

Skinner's work shows that software incorporating some of these principles can be a powerful teaching tool. For example, *The Foos Coding 5+* app by codeSpark breaks the steps of creating computer programs into small and fun activities for young children. Their design utilizes most of these principles in simple and appropriate ways. In a larger sense, most software design uses aspects of behaviorism in the interface. People's behavior is modified by their interactions with the computer, generally not the other way around (we adapt to the quirks of different interface designs; the programs do not adjust to us).

The Foos Coding 5+ app by codeSpark.

Designer's Note

Skinner's *intermittent reinforcement* is a type of reward that is only given once in a while. In the adult world, it is part of the draw of slot machines and many games that are designed to reward players just often enough to keep them interested. Intermittent reinforcement can be used to great effect in computer-based learning to keep students engaged. My favorite implementation is to add random surprises that children trigger through their play. These unexpected delights create a desire to explore further.

Disequilibration

© 2016 Jean Piaget Foundation

Jean Piaget in his garden Pinchat. Photograph by Yves Meylan.

Swiss psychologist Jean Piaget (1896–1980), one of the pioneers in constructivist theory, described the dual nature of constructing meaning when encountering something new. One mode entails assimilation, which integrates new experiences or information using existing mental structures, or schemas. Learning to ride a bike with training wheels after already knowing how to ride a tricycle is a good example because the process is so similar. Accommodation, on the other hand, requires that you adjust your brain or mental structures in response to the new experience. This can create a feeling of being off balance, what Piaget called *disequilibration*. To return to our example, when you take the training wheels off, the experience changes; the child requires a whole new set of physical and mental rules to figure it out. Children constantly seek to regain equilibration by mastering the new challenge and modifying their internal schemas to accommodate the new information. According to Piaget, children move back and forth between assimilation and accommodation as they learn more about the world.[11]

Designer's Note

You might think humans really like balance, but we enjoy being off balance because it stimulates us and causes us to grow. Learning any new activity (like bike riding) or mastering a new level of a game takes everyone through moments of disequilibration, assimilation, accommodation, and equilibration. I try to reproduce this process when creating new programs. I want to surprise kids, thereby gently nudging them from equilibration to disequilibration. Exposure to almost anything new can create a sense of disequilibration, but encountering new information in smaller pieces makes it easier for kids to integrate the new material and bounce back to equilibrium. Nintendo's Mario games are designed to teach a different interface skill at each new level, continually pushing players out of their comfort zone. Each game level builds on and combines elements of the last, making players construct their own knowledge and skill base for the game. Learning in this way can be very engaging for kids and adults.

Hands-On Experiences

Italian physician and educator Maria Montessori (1870–1952) is best known for her philosophy of childhood education. The Montessori method is a child-centered approach structured around a child's natural desire to learn. Montessori's advice

Courtesy of Maria Montessori Archives held at AMI, Amsterdam.

was always to follow the child. Montessori teachers are trained to provide students with a stimulating environment (and the tools needed to explore and learn about that environment) and to offer open-ended outcomes. The Montessori method is constructivist because it promotes a discovery model rather than direct instruction.

Montessori teachers encourage a great deal of exploration, and they design curriculum based on the child's level of development, or "sensitive periods." Lessons engage students and allow them to apply what they have been taught. The idea is that learning something hands-on, as a multisensory experience, is superior to simply listening to a lecture. Offering subject-specific activities, moving from concrete to abstract with enough time for exploration, supports the goal of student mastery. All subjects are interwoven, not isolated from each other. Children study them in any order they choose. The proposed benefit of this method is that it allows students to become self-confident, independent learners.[12]

Child-directed learning is a perfect fit with many forms of software. Although software does not always allow for the tactile experience of physical objects, it can support deeper child-directed exploration on subjects of their interest. When

© Oahu Homeschooling Mom

programs offer carefully designed levels, are open-ended (allowing the child to self-correct), provide feedback that's directly related to the child's actions, and in general stay out of the way of the child's exploration, they become powerful learning tools for children. One such example is L'Escapadou's *Cursive Writing Wizard* app, designed by Pierre Abel. As the name implies, this app allows children to practice and explore cursive writing.

> *One test of the correctness of educational procedure is the happiness of the child.*[13]
>
> —Maria Montessori

Lately more products are being developed with manipulatives, such as Osmo by Tangible Play show to the right. Their apps are designed to interact with physical objects, helping to bridge the digital/tactile gap. The app shown here, *Newton*, uses any physical object or drawn lines on a page to create an obstacle course to catch and redirect falling balls onto targets.

Designer's Note

Because Montessori schools are commonplace today, it is difficult to fully comprehend how revolutionary Dr. Maria Montessori's work was in her time. To give you an idea, Montessori was invited to the U.S. by Alexander Graham Bell, Thomas Edison, and others, and she made a sold out appearance at Carnegie Hall in New York in 1915. She was a celebrity! The impact of her educational philosophy might be difficult to quantify with hard data, but *Sims* designer Will Wright, Amazon.com founder Jeff Bezos, Jimmy Wales of Wikipedia, and Google founders Sergey Brin and Larry Page (to name just a few) all attended Montessori schools. That is definitely persuasive evidence of the power of a Montessori education.

Zone of Proximal Development

Russian psychologist Lev Vygotsky (1896–1934), who did much of his work in the 1920s, is most often associated with the theory of social constructivism, or sociocultural theory. He believed that learning does not take place in a vacuum, but that social interaction and collaboration are integral to understanding new information. Teachers or mentors work *with* students to facilitate the learning process. Vygotsky also supported a discovery model of learning, where children learn by exploration.

Lev Vygotsky

Vygotsky is known for his concept of the zone of proximal development, which defines the level of task or problem solving a child can accomplish with collaboration and guidance from others. It is the space between the activities children can do on their own and those they cannot do at all. According to Vygotsky, the zone of proximal development is a measure of a child's

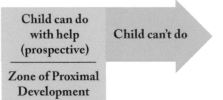

potential; he considered the zone to be the optimum situation for learning—a place just slightly beyond what learners can do by themselves. Children should be challenged (but not overwhelmed) and given enough support to succeed.[14]

Utilizing the concepts from this theory, it's possible to add suggestive gestures or hints to help the child solve a problem. A simple example occurs in these two images of *Motion Math* by Motion Math Games. This is a fractions game. If the player misses the mark the first time, a directional arrow appears on the number line, nudging them toward the proper mark. If the player misses again, an arrow shows them exactly where to place the ball. Other implementations of the zone of proximal development occur in products that support collaboration, allowing the child to learn from a more knowledgeable other, as well as those apps that track the player's *ability* to solve problems and adjust the gameplay accordingly so the child continues to be appropriately challenged.

Motion Math app by Motion Math Games.

In play a child always behaves beyond his average age, above his daily behavior; in play it is as though he were a head taller than himself.[15]
—Lev Vygotsky

Designer's Note

Vygotsky's zone of proximal development is the place where I believe almost all learning in interactive media takes place. Smart designers know where a child is developmentally and what's possible for them to accomplish. The zone of proximal development is where designers can support children in their efforts to go beyond what they can do and construct on their own. Any program that tracks past performance and follows up with a slightly more challenging activity is using the zone of proximal development concept.

Social Learning

Albert Bandura

The work of Albert Bandura (born 1925) expanded on behaviorist theories and led to the theory of *social learning*. This theory is similar to Vygotsky's. Bandura asserts that people learn within a social context, often by directly observing others, and that children especially learn from their environment and seek acceptance from society by emulating influential models. Bandura sees learning as a balance of watching and doing, a continual reciprocal interaction between cognition, behavior, and environmental influences.[16]

© Carole Daly Photography,

Designer's Note

The concept of "monkey see, monkey do," how kids are quick to copy each other in games and behaviors, is well known. But it is also true that kids learn behaviors from characters or people in the media. Especially when designing for young children, it is important to create animated characters with the awareness that children might learn from or imitate them. This does not mean characters should be perfect or one-dimensional; that would be boring. However, it is important to consider the implications of imitation. Bandura's research particularly pointed out that modeling aggression had a strong influence on young children.

The popular game *Minecraft* ties together constructivism, the zone of proximal development, and social learning. This is a great sandbox experience where users build with a sophisticated physics engine and create incredible imaginary worlds. Even though it can be played as a solo game, many children choose to play in an online community and cooperatively create, learn, and share the user-generated content with each other.

The Theory of Flow

Mihaly Csikszentmihalyi

Hungarian psychologist Mihaly Csikszentmihalyi (pronounced MEE-hye CHEEK-sent me-HYE-ee) is most often cited as the person who refined and expanded the study of flow. Csikszentmihalyi defines flow as "the state in which people are so involved in an activity that nothing else seems to matter; the experience itself is so enjoyable that people will do it even at great cost, for the sheer sake of doing it."[17] He is one of the major proponents of positive psychology and has devoted his professional life to the study of happiness and how people can attain it.

Flow is not a specific learning theory; it is a state that occurs when you get everything right. It is the mental state that athletes, artists, and musicians often call being in the "zone," where one is completely focused and engaged in the task at hand. Interactive design already benefits from the integration of flow principles because good gameplay draws a player in so deeply that long periods fly by without the person being aware of time. This optimum engagement state is a key factor in any award-winning interactive experience.

Design Components to Support Flow

A state of flow can arise during any activity, but it usually occurs when we are wholeheartedly involved in an activity or task we enjoy for its own sake. Flow can't be predicted, but some conditions support opportunities for flow. How can designers encourage flow in their games?[18]

1. **Set clear goals.** Clearly define attainable goals that are appropriate to a child's age, skill set, and abilities. Goals add structure and direction to an activity. Goals can be as simple as solving a puzzle or as involved as a quest. Quests or missions are popular ways to challenge players who are already familiar with an environment. As part of goal setting, any rules or other expectations should be clearly expressed in the beginning of the game.

2. **Support a sense of personal control.** Give kids the sense that they have control over the situation or activity. What constitutes control will change in relation to a child's developmental progress. For example, younger children will require simpler control interactions to match their motor and perception skills. A sense of control and self-directed exploration is a key component of intrinsic play, and it's something kids naturally gravitate toward.

3. **Give direct and immediate feedback.** Immediate feedback, whether for successes or failures, lets children know how they are doing and allows them to adjust their play strategies and performance to maintain a state of flow. Good feedback supports their sense of control and progress on their way to attaining the goal. Feedback can be as minimal as sound effects to acknowledge

actions or as full blown as "epic win" fanfare. Kids expect programs to respond in the same immediate way that the world around them responds. If they steer left in *Mario Kart*, they expect the kart to go left—immediately

4. **Balance ability level and level of challenge.** Choose challenging activities that require skill. Find a motivating balance between skill/ability and level of challenge so that the activity is neither too easy nor too difficult. Too difficult a challenge will produce anxiety; too easy an activity will produce boredom. It is important that kids *perceive* the challenges of the task at hand to be within the grasp of their skills. Children need confidence that they are capable of accomplishing the task at hand. The level of challenge will change as the child's skill/ability improves.

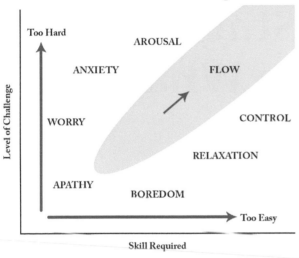

This graph depicts the relationship between the perceived challenges of a task and one's perceived skills. The area in the middle of the graph is your center, when you are doing what you really want to do. For instance, you may be in control during easy gameplay, but the experience may not be very interesting. To get toward flow, you would increase the level of challenge or skill, thereby increasing your level of engagement.

Csikszentmihalyi found similarities to creating flow states in the teaching philosophy of Maria Montessori, who said, "The greatest sign of success for a teacher... is to be able to say, 'The children are now working as if I did not exist.'"[19]

Designer's Note

The state of flow has been documented throughout history. It has been suggested that Michelangelo may have painted the ceiling of the Sistine Chapel while in a flow state. He supposedly painted for days at a time, so deeply absorbed in his work that he didn't stop for food or sleep until he passed out, later waking up refreshed to begin again and re-enter a state of total absorption.

Thinking about how kids learn is fundamental when designing a game for children. Unlike adults, who under some circumstances may persevere with a product that doesn't exactly meet their needs, children disengage. When an interactive experience is too complex for their learning stage, gives them insufficient control, or is too predictable, you've lost the chance for delight and immersion. However, when a team makes the effort to investigate its audience, design to the appropriate stage of development, adjust to gradually increasing skill levels, and give motivation and reward, children will respond.

Ages and Stages: Why Kids Do What They Do

The most important thing to know at the beginning of any interactive design is who is on the other end of the design. Adults perceive the world differently than kids do. The best interactive design connects with children by speaking directly to their evolving cognitive, emotional, social, and physical skills at the current stage. This chapter offers in-depth working knowledge and insight into children's inner lives. It looks at critical developmental moments that affect how kids learn, what they can do, what they are interested in, how they view the world, and how they react differently as they grow from toddlers to teens.

The path of development is a journey of discovery that is clear only in retrospect, and it's rarely a straight line.[1]

— **Eileen Kennedy-Moore and Mark Lowenthal,**
child and family psychologists

Ages and Stages

As children grow, they pass through well-documented stages of cognitive and social development that express their changing perceptions and evolving interactions with the world. There are no hard boundaries where one stage ends and the next begins. It is different for each child, and it is a gentle transition that happens over time, marked by noticeable shifts in abilities. As children develop, their actions and perceptions are shaped by the stage of development they are just entering or leaving. A quick look at these shifts in attitudes and interests will help you as a children's designer to better understand the motivating factors that drive your audience.

As a continuation of learning theories, and as a jumping-off point for discussion of developmental stages, let's look at two famous cognitive development specialists, Jean Piaget and Erik Erikson. Their ideas form an important base for thought about interactive design.

Cognitive Development

Jean Piaget's Theory of Cognitive Development

Jean Piaget in Ann Arbor.

One of the most influential early researchers and writers in the field of children's cognitive development is Jean Piaget. Piaget's observations and theories helped to show that children think very differently than adults, and actively build knowledge through exploration of their world. While educational psychologists have refuted some of Piaget's theory of stages, Piaget recognized that the transitions between the stages are very slow. Still, his theory helps create a basic organizational understanding of a child's perspective at different ages, and it can be used in the design of educational activities.

Designer's Note

Piaget proposed the idea that children are not capable of understanding and performing certain tasks until they arrive at a specific stage. When I begin a new project, especially for a new age group, I like to come back to this chapter's developmental material to remind myself who it is that I am designing for. Even with years of experience creating content for kids, I know how easy it is to slip into "adult mind" and lose the perspective of a child. I hope you will review this material from time to time to wake up your child awareness.

A basic understanding of child development will help you create more developmentally appropriate interactive media. Please note that a child may be in one stage regarding language and in another regarding mathematical concepts, and the transitions from stage to stage are gradual. What is important to children's media designers is recognizing that the stages follow a consistent sequence.[2]

A Quick Look at Piaget's Stages

Sensorimotor (Ages Birth to 2)

In the sensorimotor stage[3], a child is focused on sensory input and physical actions (motor skills development). Learning occurs with lots of exploration and manipulation of items in the environment. Children in this stage are very physical, using all of their senses to make meaning of the world. Warren Buckleitner, editor of *Children's Technology Review,* describes children in the sensorimotor stage as thinking like a flashlight beam:[4] they direct their attention in specific and limited ways, excluding what lies just outside their focus. Very young babies focus on and interact with objects that are within their sight, while those that are hidden no longer exist. As children grow and develop, they learn that those objects really are still there. As they transition from this stage to the next, children usually understand simple cause and effect and have acquired basic concepts of objects and space.[5]

Preoperational (Ages 2 to 7)

Children in the preoperational stage are mostly focused on themselves; they don't tend to consider another person's point of view. Even so, they can be quite empathetic. They are focused on language acquisition, and in the early portion of this period they tend to interpret figurative statements literally (e.g., "He kicked the bucket"). Preoperational children can now understand object permanence; they know an object exists even if they can't see it. However, their ability for logical, sequential thought hasn't completely developed. Therefore, though they can hold distinct thoughts in their mind, they lack the ability to reverse consequences, or connect ideas and understand how ideas relate to each other.

Preoperational children understand concepts based on the physical impression of objects, but not principles such as conservation. A classic example occurs when you pour the water from a tall, narrow glass into a short, wide glass; preoperational children will believe there is now less water. Children at this stage have strong imaginations, and they can use symbols to communicate and play. This allows them to engage in Pretend Play with available objects, for example turning a block of wood into a car or airplane.[6]

This is a great age for user-directed exploration and exposure to new concepts. Language acquisition and early reading begin now. An egocentric worldview limits conversational skills (or at least listening skills), and virtual world designs should focus on individual activities. This is a popular target age for many children's apps because programs can be relatively simple, but still a lot of fun.

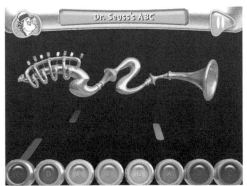

Dr. Seuss Band app by Oceanhouse Media.

Dr. Seuss Band, from Oceanhouse Media, is an example of user-directed exploration for this group. Kids can change instrument components, sounds, songs, and more. They can play along with songs (as seen in the image, with the song title listed at the top) or free-play with the instruments.

Concrete-Operational Stage (Ages 7 to 11)

During the concrete-operational stage, a child develops a deeper understanding of how things work in the world. They still depend on their own experiences, and their thinking is tied to experiments with concrete objects. But now they can follow and create strings of logical thought, although they may still struggle with jumping between or juggling ideas. This child understands conservation, so now they know that water poured from one jar into another does not change its nature. They can add and subtract, and distinguish fact from fiction.[7]

Designer's Note

My experience with seven- and eight-year-olds is that, due to their expanding reasoning abilities, they have a new perspective on the world and like to use that power. Sometimes they might turn to a five-year-old and immediately tell them that Santa Claus isn't real, much to the shock and dismay of the younger dreamer.

This age group loves to experiment, and it's a great time for science activities. Self-identity is on the rise, and concrete-operational kids can see themselves in relation to others. As a result, communication and games that show status become more important. Strategy Play, Challenge Play, and Competitive Play occupy a larger role in product design.

A good example for this age and stage is Nintendo's *Super Mario Galaxy 2*. Following in the footsteps of other Super Mario franchise titles, this Wii game delivers many of the challenges and features that this age has grown to love and expect. It is a planet-hopping game where you must steer Mario through multiple maze-puzzle levels, gathering Power Stars as you go.

Super Mario Galaxy 2 by Nintendo.

The game levels support increasing challenges and strategies to win, and two players can play the game. Unlike other similar games, the second player isn't just following the lead player but can have their own specific tasks and can do well regardless of how the main player is doing.

> *If you want to be creative, stay in part a child, with the creativity and invention that characterizes children before they are deformed by adult society.*[8]
>
> —Jean Piaget

The Formal-Operational Stage (Ages 11 to 17)

True operational thinking, the ability to consider several different solutions to a problem, starts around twelve years of age. These now adolescent children begin to use abstract thought and verbal reasoning—their thinking is no longer tied to concrete objects. They can now apply concepts learned in one context to different situations, and develop new hypotheses about why things happen the way they do. They have a growing ability to rely on and use abstract symbols to understand and learn. Fairness and equality are very important to these preteens and teens, a priority which at times brings them into conflict with adult authority.[9]

Designer's Note

The formal-operational stage is not the focus of this book, but this group teaches us about what the earlier concrete-operational group have yet to completely understand, including the fuller use of abstract thinking.

Erikson's Stages of Development Theory

Erik Erikson

Developmental psychologist Erik Erikson (1902–1994) is best known for his theory of psychosocial development. Erikson believed that society influences a human being's development, and that everyone goes through a number of stages to reach his or her full development. These stages cover an entire lifespan, not just childhood. He described each stage in terms of the emotional, physical, and developmental tasks that each person must master in order to develop a healthy personality. Each focuses on a major theme, with life's challenges pushing us to find a balance between the positive and negative views.

Erikson believed that children who don't master a task before proceeding to the next stage of development bring along a residue of that task. Toddlers who didn't fully experience "learning by doing" may doubt their own abilities, inhibiting later efforts at independence.

He also believed that a child's environment is key to healthy development, including growth, adjustment, self-awareness, and identity. Piaget and Erikson both stressed the importance of not rushing children's development but allowing each developmental phase to unfold naturally, with each stage building upon the successes of the previous stage.[10] Here are Erikson's first four stages:[11]

Trust Versus Mistrust (Ages Birth to 1)

From birth, infants are accomplishing the major developmental task of learning to trust or not trust other humans. Erikson believed that if an infant's parents or caregivers consistently provide for physical and emotional needs, the infant learns trust in others. Babies need consistent comfort with minimal uncertainty to trust themselves, others, and the environment. Another outcome of having trust is that it is directly connected with having a sense of hope.

Autonomy Versus Shame and Doubt (Ages 2 to 3)

As children gain control of motor functions, they begin to explore their surroundings. They begin to wonder, "Can I do this myself, or do I always have to rely on others?" At this stage, children are exploring *will*, and they work to master the physical environment while establishing and maintaining self-esteem. When caregivers are supportive and patient as children try doing new things like getting dressed or washing up for themselves, toddlers begin to establish a sense of confidence in their autonomy. But if caregivers are overly critical, restrictive, or ridicule preliminary attempts at performing new tasks, children may feel shame and doubt about what they are capable of.

> *Healthy children will not fear life if their elders have integrity enough not to fear death.*[12]
>
> —Erik Erikson

Initiative Versus Guilt (Ages 4 to 6)

At this stage, children show a greater sense of autonomy and begin to initiate, not imitate, activities. They are becoming *doers*. With this growing independence, children begin to complete their own actions toward a purpose. Adults who encourage and support this age group's efforts help children develop initiative-driven independence in planning and attempting new activities. A question that arises for this group is, "Am I good or am I bad?"

Industry Versus Inferiority (Ages 7 to 12)

Children at this stage have a growing awareness of themselves as individuals. It's important to them to be good, to be responsible, and to do things correctly, even in the midst of exploring some rebelliousness. They are exploring their own sense of competency as they begin to better see how the world works. For Erikson, the elementary school years were critical for development of self-confidence. If children are encouraged for their diligent efforts, they learn the enjoyment of applying themselves to tasks. If, on the other hand, children feel they are unable to perform tasks as successfully as their peers, or if they feel unable to meet parental expectations, they may feel inferior instead of competent.

You see a child play and it is so close to seeing an artist paint, for in play a child says things without uttering a word.[13]

—Erik Erikson

Ages Birth to 3: Infants, Toddlers, and the Beginner's Mind

Ask any parent or grandparent, and they will tell you that the rapid succession of cognitive, emotional, and physical growth that babies go through in their early years is nothing less than amazing. From helpless infant to mobile and confident toddler, a child is absorbing and integrating spectacular amounts of information. In fact, developmental growth is so profound that milestones for this age group are counted in months rather than years.

The Infant

The birth of a child into this world is a miraculous event. A new being has arrived, and in their new, sweet consciousness, they know very little about where they are. They are incapable of taking care of themselves, and their first lessons are all about the beings around them who feed, hold, protect, and, most of all, love them.

© Carole Daly Photography

Nurturing and Dependency

All through this period, children are the most vulnerable. They are helpless and dependent; everything must be taken care of for them. Both physical and emotional needs must be met in order for them to thrive. Meeting the emotional needs of a baby is as important to growth as meeting their physical needs. At the peak, babies generate two million new synapses in their brains every second. Positive experiences (such as being smiled at, hugged, kissed, and having their needs met) help babies feel secure and help them produce more neural connections that, in turn, help them grow up to have more secure relationships, and to experience success in their lives.[14]

Sensory Stimulus, Exploration, and Learning

The other defining characteristic of this age is the love of exploration. From the moment of birth, babies take *everything* in, and they begin to compile a log of experiences that are eventually used to make a map of how things work in their new world. Today's experiences are the basis for the perception of all future experiences. Kids at this stage are all about touch, smell, and taste. Almost everything babies can pick up goes into their mouths at one point or another. They are busy exploring the world of the senses and learning how their bodies work. Piaget called this the "sensorimotor" stage for a reason.

If little else, the brain is an educational toy.[15]

—Tom Robbins, author

Designer's Note

It's important to consider the appropriateness of tech toys for the zero- to two-year-old. Some children's toy and media companies create programs "for babies," but there is little research showing that these programs do much for this age group,[16] even though babies and toddlers can use tablets and computers as they get closer to two. As mentioned, ages zero to two are often referred to as the sensorimotor stage, in which most learning is done via physical exploration of the environment. Because of this, time during this age is best spent in free play, physical exploration, and discovery of immediate, real-world surroundings rather than in front of a media device.

This is not to say that children under two are not interested in media or handheld devices. They can be! Like older children and adults, babies are drawn to the moving colors, faces, and sounds of media. And babies in a family context are drawn to play with bigger kids' toys, even when the "bigger kid" is a parent. Babies are devoted to grabbing hold of items they see their parents or older siblings using. But even though I've known toddlers who could use a mouse at two (using two fingers in order to create a mouse click or navigate an iPad), children under age two are neither physically nor cognitively ready to spend much time in front of screen devices, whether large or small. There is, however, a strong marketplace for manipulatives with electronic components that create sound effects and flashing lights. These toys come from great early learning companies such as Fisher-Price, Playskool, LeapFrog, and others. When zero- to two-year-olds do play with tablets or smartphones, that time is best when it is lap time—something shared between parent and child. And, studies show that it's best to leave the TV off.[17]

Language Acquisition

Along with the exploration of their physical universe, babies begin the process of language integration. These early years—up to five or six—are the time when our brains are most elastic. A large portion of the human brain is devoted to language interpretation. That fact, coupled with the elastic state of young minds, makes infancy the easiest time in life to learn a language.

Early language and brain development researcher Patricia Kuhl, co-director of the Institute for Learning and Brain Sciences at the University of Washington, has studied how young children learn and how early exposure to language alters the brain's neural commitment to phonetic sounds. Her research indicates that the optimum time for multiple language acquisition occurs between a baby's eighth and tenth month. As Dr. Kuhl says, babies "take statistics" and develop a relationship with the sounds of language(s) they hear. It is interesting to note that in Kuhl's research, babies did not acquire the sounds of a language from exposure to audio or video, but *only* from direct social contact with humans speaking the language.[18]

> *Babies all over the world are what I like to describe as "citizens of the world." They can discriminate all the sounds of all the languages, no matter what country we're testing and what language we're using, and that's remarkable because you and I can't do that. We're culture-bound listeners. We can discriminate the sounds of our own language, but not those of foreign languages.*[19]
>
> —Patricia Kuhl

A toddler's first words often occur around twelve months (this is an average—each child is different), with baby babble happening much earlier. Communication skills take a big leap as babies begin to express their needs and interests, conversing by using both words and gestures. Young children will gradually add new vocabulary, about one word every three days, until around the age of sixteen months, and then language acquisition seems to increase rapidly. Between the ages of two and six they will learn at least six thousand words, including names of pets and people, places, and activities.[20]

Designer's Note

From a designer's point of view, it might seem like a great idea to create learning software in the form of flash cards and other picture–word combinations for this age group. But remember that picture and word representations are abstractions of the real objects that they represent. With very young children, showing them a picture + word representing "cat" does not substitute for saying the word in the presence of a real cat. For parents of very young children, I would suggest trying sign-language apps for babies so the parents themselves can improve communication with their preverbal children.

For a normally developing child, language integration never stops—it just becomes more sophisticated. Starting with the endearing first words celebrated by delighted parents, children progressively discover the power of other words, such as the famous two-year-old mantra, *No!* It may seem that they are getting quite bossy, but for the most part they are experimenting with how their communication affects the people around them. The toddler has discovered that words have power and can effect response. Some words, even those young kids don't know the meaning of, get bigger responses than others. As an example, a toddler might yell *Stop!* as a parent begins to sing a favorite song. It's not that they don't like your singing; it is more of an experiment to see how the adult responds to the order.

Toddlers

Learning to walk takes a lot of muscle development, coordination, and practice. Once children have progressed from sitting and rolling over to scooting and crawling, they are ready to try standing and walking. Most children take their first steps between eleven and fourteen months, but the range can be very broad—from nine to fifteen months.[21] Once babies stand up and take those first few steps, the world changes for them.

"I Can Go Where I Want."

With greater autonomy comes greater mobility. There is a noticeable shift once babies go mobile and become toddlers. Exploring the world on two legs greatly expands their universe. Depth perception has developed, so that they climb down from chairs and walk down stairs rather than just going over the edge. Mastery of this major movement skill leads not only to increased confidence but also to a struggle to become more independent.

"I Want to Do It Myself."

As children reach their thirty-sixth month, they desire and aspire to greater independence. Three-year-olds may all of a sudden insist on doing things for themselves. They do not want to feel babied, though they still want lots of love and attention. They might insist that they comb their own hair, brush their own teeth, or dress themselves (including choosing their clothing). Mealtime is another opportunity to push the independence boundary by requesting what and how much they want to eat. It's all part of growing up. Supporting children's growing initiative to do for themselves, whether in person or in software, provides them a base of security in their own abilities to handle new problems and situations.

Having a two-year-old is like having a blender that you don't have a top for.[22]

—Jerry Seinfeld, actor and comedian

"Look at Me!"

Look! or *Look at me!* is a frequent command, usually as a request for attention and approval. Toddlers crave attention for their newly developed skills. They may want a compliment on their scribbles and decorations, help building with their toys, or simple acknowledgment of the triumph of putting on socks unassisted. They want a lot of attention, and they are not in the least self-conscious about asking for it. In software for young users, it is common to offer lots of positive support and reinforcement to let kids know they are doing well and that the game is paying attention. (For more on positive audio feedback in games, see Ch. 7, pp. 107–108 and Ch. 8, pp. 114–115.)

At around 18 months, children also become self-aware. They begin to recognize themselves as separate physical beings with their own thoughts, interests, and actions. Prior to this time, young children may have enjoyed looking in a mirror, but now they have reached the moment of recognizing that the reflection in a mirror is, in fact, themselves.

Designer's Note

There is something captivating about seeing yourself in a mirror, and this is even more true of a video image of yourself. I have watched kids aged three to six be totally captivated by playing with their own image in the middle of a video chat, where making faces at themselves in the small window is more interesting than talking with others in the big window. This seems to change at around age seven, when communication becomes more interesting, but the desire to look at ourselves doesn't really ever go away. Several mobile apps—like Nosy Crow's *Cinderella* or JibJab Media's *StoryBots* apps and their *Starring You* books—use the built-in camera to include a child's image inside a story or game.

StoryBots app by JibJab Media.

"I Want to Do What I Want!"

The "terrible twos" are actually a sign of emerging independence and can begin as early as eighteen months or as late as thirty months. Toddlers at this stage may become very assertive and strong-willed and insist on doing exactly what they were told *not* to do. Or they may throw a temper tantrum if they don't get their way. During this stage, children discover that they are separate beings from their parents, and they begin to test boundaries and their own powers.

"I Like Pretend Play."

Toddlers are aware that they are growing bigger, and they understand they will someday be "big people." As a result, toddlers love to emulate their parents and caregivers. Piaget called this "representational play." Toddlers may try to walk in adult shoes or put on adult glasses, hats, or clothing. They are pretending to be big. Toddlers also pretend to parent their stuffed animals when they hold, feed (with pretend food like a block), and nurture the animal. To most preschoolers, Pretend Play is as natural as breathing.

"I Like Simple Songs."

Shortly before turning three, most children start to enjoy singing. Songs are therefore one of the best ways for toddlers to memorize things, such as the alphabet. Toddlers like to sing little songs to themselves, and they may spontaneously create them. When creating a song for this age group, make it simple and happy. Employ age-appropriate vocabulary, including descriptive words the child might use frequently. If children enjoy a song, they will make it their own, singing it joyously (and repetitively), even if they don't yet completely understand the meaning of it. This age group also likes to move along with the music. They will readily initiate marching, jumping, and dancing movements as they listen. This love of simple songs and movement continues for the next several years.

"Can I Watch It Again?"

Children younger than three are absorbing massive amounts of information, and they generally don't need fast-paced media to keep their attention. They tend to like a mellower pace with interactive media. This is partially why young children can watch the same movie over and over without tiring of it. They are getting something new each time they watch, and they love the familiarity of re-watching. Adults and older kids may find this slow pace very boring. The television show *Blue's Clues* is famous for having extra-long pauses when asking questions of the young audience. These pauses are so long that adults get jumpy, but the length is just right for young kids, who take longer to process the questions.

"What's That?!"

Everything is interesting to this age group—interactive toys and games have the same level of attraction as traditional pots and pans, rocks, flowers, and bugs. Walking with two-year-olds and seeing the world through their eyes can be very illuminating because they still have "beginner's mind." They may stop abruptly in order to squat and focus intently on a multi-colored leaf or a bug crawling on the ground in front of them. The miracle of creation is not lost on them.

iStock.com/MAEK123

Other Things Babies and Toddlers Like:

- **Lively colors and contrast.** Think of any preschool toy. It is seldom beige or gray. Visually bright or high contrast items stand out and more easily get attention. For a toy designer, getting kids to pick an item up is the goal, and happy, well-contrasted colors are the standard.

- **Animals.** Young children are fascinated by and attracted to animal characters in all shapes and sizes, but they especially love baby animals. They also seem to be drawn to non-threatening, nurturing cartoon animals or plush and cuddly toy versions of animals.

- **Faces.** Babies love to look at faces—it's part of their hardwiring. Faces speak their own language, a language babies are busy learning.

- **Cause and effect.** These little ones are explorers who desire to roam free in a safe environment and experience things for themselves. Pushing buttons, opening and closing things, turning lights on and off, and engaging in "busy box" types of activities allow them to experiment with how things work. They love to see that their actions can have an effect.

Ages 3 to 6: The Magic Years

This is a time of continued rapid growth and change for children. They are moving from toddlerhood to independent early childhood. In his book *What Kids Buy and Why*, Dan Acuff refers to this age as the emerging-autonomy stage.[23] Children at this age seem less logical (at least compared to adults!); they tend to view the world in a more magical and imaginative way.

It is this early period that grown-ups think of most often when they remember and define "childhood." It is that magical time when play, pretend, and fantasy are a big part of everyday life. Imagination reigns supreme, and anything is possible. This is a happy, lively, and enchanted time of exploration. But it is also a time of frustrations and of testing limits.

They See the World from Their Point of View

If you ask a four-year-old boy what his mother wants for her birthday, he might enthusiastically reply "Transformers!" or "Pokémon!" This is because he still operates with an egocentric view of the world, and he can't quite see things from another's point of view yet.

The differences in perception between children and adults should not be underestimated in terms of importance for anyone interested in creating engaging content for children. Of course, adults can fall prey to the same weakness of perspective. Take care to examine your assumptions about what you *think* will appeal to kids at a particular age. Younger children in particular do not look at the world through the same window as adults.

The Magic Years

Since the three- to six-year-old's ability to reason is still developing, they are unimpaired by adult-style logical thought processes. They can hold several ideas in their mind at once, but the ability to assemble them into a logical linear sequence, and, more importantly, reverse that process, is still to come.[24] They are imaginative and creative in their thoughts as they try to make sense of the world. This age group easily believes in reindeer on the roof, the tooth fairy, and magic in general.

Designers and storytellers have consistently entertained these children with magically gifted characters and enchanting, fantastical stories. For the three- to six-year-old, anything is possible, even in the real world.

One of the charming aspects of this age group is that they can see the world through the viewpoint of *animism*, the attribution of a soul and feelings to plants, inanimate objects, and natural phenomena. Basically, anything can be "alive,"

cajna'more © 123RF.com

and, if it moves, it probably is: a tree in the wind, sunlight's reflections making rainbows, or interactive sprites that come alive on a touch screen.

In children's media, and in almost all magical and mythical stories, animals and objects take on human attributes to interact with protagonists and advance the story line. Adding a human voice to inanimate objects often brings delightful surprise to an otherwise boring interaction. A rock that says *Ow!* when you bump into it, or a leaf that hollers as it falls from the tree, reinforces this sense of animism and creates interactions kids will want to repeat over and over again.

"They Are Talking to Me!"

Kids are also more than willing to believe that characters or people on the computer or television can see them and are talking directly to them. This has been used to great effect in age-appropriate television shows such as *Mister Rogers' Neighborhood*, *Sesame Street*, and *Blue's Clues*. Kid viewers are so engaged that when they are directly asked a question by a character on the screen, they shout their answer out loud. The effect is enhanced when the shows use the voices of other kids in the "audience" shouting out answers, too.

Season 46 of *Sesame Street* by Sesame Workshop.

Designer's Note

Apps and activity programs can support this age group's emerging desire for independence and interest in animals by creating opportunities for the child to be in charge and in control. For example, a program can allow a child to dress a character in different clothes or nurture a character by applying a Band-Aid or kisses to a "boo-boo." Providing immediate responses to kids' exploration empowers them and supports their yearning for independence and accomplishment. In a book I've just finished putting together, *If I Were a Zookeeper*, kids gets to assist Buzzy Bear and play nurse with all the animals who need help that day.

At our Zoo clinic we help anybody who needs it. Today the kangeroo fell down, and got an "ouchie". The hippo and others need attention too. I helped them feel better.

SOAPS　Good Spray　NEXT

If I Were a Zookeeper prototype by Mark Schlichting.

"I Love Animals."

Three- to six-year-olds have a fascination with real, stuffed, and/or animated animal characters. They easily attribute human qualities to objects and animals, making them active vehicles for emotional expression. The design of engaging animal characters will ensure instant fans among kids in this age group.

Animals react directly to situations without communication skills or conversational complexity. Therefore, kids may see animals as peers of a sort. Animals also seem to be unconsciously perceived as safe and can be abstract replacements for humans—they can sport all the good aspects of humans (e.g., a face, a personality, etc.) without actually being a scary stranger. Because they are still very tactile, young children are also in love with soft and fuzzy textures, which makes furriness a crowd pleaser.

Along with a fondness for animals comes a natural instinct to nurture them. Caring for digital pets, especially feeding them, is something this groups enjoys doing (as long as it's not too demanding or time-intensive).

"MOMMY!!!"

The three- to six-year-old is still very much in need of safety, affection, and encouragement. The bond between parent and child continues to evolve as the child becomes ever more independent. Good relationships during these years form a solid emotional foundation for children as they enter the sometimes not-so-safe worlds of school, playground, and peers. This age still needs to feel safe and in a protected environment that he/she can trust. Safety and appropriate content is of supreme importance to the parents of this age group.

Three- to six-year-olds need more praise and reassurance than older age groups do. They need to know they are doing well, and they like to be told so regularly. Designs for this age group often include lots of positive feedback and gentle redirecting feedback (never negative). Positive feedback doesn't necessarily need to be in the form of the often overused and repetitive "Good job!!" It can also be in the form of animation, audio, or other direct responses to their actions.

"Let's Play Together. Sort of..."

Before the age of six, kids have a tendency to play near other kids, often at the same activity with the same toys, but doing their own thing. It is similar to playing together because it involves awareness of what others are doing, but it is actually a kind of parallel play. Girls tend to play cooperatively sooner than boys.[25]

Design for this younger subset is best when it supports solo exploration and skill acquisition, rather than cooperation and turn-taking among playmates. Children respond best to cooperative games with rules that are easy to learn. Turns, if the game involves them, need to move quickly.

"I Love to Laugh and Giggle."

Life itself is entertaining to this age group. They love things that are silly and cute and happy, and they are ready to laugh if you give them half a reason. Even just empowering them with a charming surprise when they tap on something can bring delight to their eyes.

Three- to six-year-olds do not like a lot of conflict, violence, scariness, or unhappiness. They do like cooperation, silliness, friendliness, cuteness, and slapstick humor.

Designer's Note

At one point during the creation of an interactive version of *The Berenstain Bears Get in a Fight*, I thought it would be an great add-on to create a conflict-resolution game. We built a prototype that had Brother and Sister Bear's dialogue on either side of the screen, and kids could pick what each bear said to the other. If kids always picked the worst dialogue, the choices spiraled down until the bears had their backs to each other in a standoff/stalemate. To get out, kids had to pick dialogue that was less confrontational.

It was interesting to watch different groups play with the prototype. One big surprise for us was that the kids five and younger had little interest in fighting or being confrontational, whereas the older kids enjoyed experimenting with the more confrontational dialogue. The younger ones just wanted to have the characters talk to each other and be friends, so we had to add more conversation that allowed them to do that. They didn't have any interest in making the bear cubs fight.

"My Work Is Play."

For the three- to six-year-old, play is learning, and learning is play. Whether building forts out of sheets and couch cushions, or playing house and dress-up, it is a time filled with Expressive Play and Imaginative Play. Child psychologists have long promoted the idea that children learn critical lessons through play. Their "job" is to explore the world through their senses. Parents of three- to six-year-olds know this instinctively, and they are much more apt to support an activity (or product/service/app) that offers good play opportunities, including "soft learning" or "edutainment," with emphasis on fun rather than the need to achieve learning goals. Parents of this age group want their children to be engaged in something safe and enjoyable. If the activity promotes basic learning or skills, that's a bonus, not necessarily a prerequisite.

"Let's Do It Again."

One thing kids in this group have in common with younger ages is that everything is still relatively new to them. Like toddlers, they appreciate the familiarity and consistency of repetition because they need time to integrate new experiences. If children like an experience, whether a game, book, or movie, they will often play with it over and over and over again because they accumulate information through repeated viewing or playing. For example, mining what can happen from tapping on a bird's nest can provide many minutes of fascinated play. Not that many random animations are needed to keep a small interaction like this entertaining, but having them be visually different and surprising helps to keep kids wondering what will happen next.

Designer's Note

In an interactive environment, give young kids control over the pacing by letting them activate buttons or features. Give them opportunities to discover new things through their repetitions. While working on Living Books titles, we found that younger users would play with their favorite interactive hotspots over and over each time the story began. I believe they like the control of making things happen as much as they like the surprises themselves.

"I Like to Tap."

This young age group is particularly delighted by the sense of power and control they get from easily activating an interaction. They feel so empowered by it that they might claim ownership of what happens in an interaction. *Look what I did!* is a common exclamation and a great sign that the app or program is delivering the level of surprise and empowerment kids want. Good design supports their sense of doing something. Give kids meaningful things to tap on, and reward their actions through responsive interfaces.

"Don't Make Me Wait."

In a world where every sight and sound in the environment is competing to get attention, creating artificial barriers that delay getting to the good stuff of an activity is risky. In the early days of children's software design we used to do a "click test," which monitored how many times at the beginning of a game a child clicked the mouse to make something happen before they were actually given control. It was always informative to count the number of clicks that accomplished nothing, before they were allowed to have some effect. Children want a sense of control, and they want it now. They are still deeply exploratory and have little patience for a slow interface. Every designer needs to remember, "If it looks tappable, it should be." Taps should also produce real effects.

"I Can't Read Yet."

Giving three- to six-year-old children written instructions in a game is relatively useless and generally not age-appropriate, because emerging reading skills vary widely. All this age group really wants to do is to start interacting. If possible, design games and activities with little or no direction. Try to make everything discoverable through exploration. If you have to give game instructions to this group, it is best to give them verbally, and perhaps reinforce steps visually, but don't overdo it. All the kids want to do is dive in and explore.

Consider what a native English speaker would endure to learn a new language like Chinese, which is based on character shapes rather than letters, and you'll have some comprehension of what kids go through when learning to read. Kids of this age are going through a process called "mapping," a stage that connects the abstract black and white shapes of letters and numbers to the symbolic representation of something else, such as a sound or quantity of an object. During this stage, the child's ability to integrate more and more leads them from individual letters to words, and finally to meaning.

"I Get Bored Easily."

These kids are in active input mode, and the need for stimulation is strong. They have an insatiable desire to be busy, to be entertained, to be learning. They are naturally curious about life and are always ready to explore. Software and toys for this age have to meet their needs by being interactive, stimulating, and easy to play in order to foster the natural desire for exploration. Kids at this age vote on what they like with their attention. As soon as they've digested what they've learned, they are ready to do something else. This doesn't necessarily mean a different game. Even a game kids have already played many times can provide new opportunities, including building mastery.

Ages 7 to 9:
The Beginning of Reason

Ages seven through nine are a time of new personal and social awareness, along with group affiliations. These kids are moving from being little kids to big kids desiring greater independence as individuals. It is a stage largely defined by consciously leaving behind "baby things" from earlier years. This is what Dan Acuff calls the rule/role stage,[26] because kids focus on learning rules and trying to understand their role in the world. Both boys and girls experiment with role-playing

using dolls and action figures (Barbie and G.I. Joe) or virtual characters and objects.

"I Am More Logical."

A significant change between the previous group and the seven- to nine-year-olds is the increasing cognitive development and ability to more completely use logical thinking. Kids are better able to follow a mathematical or logical train of thought, retrace it, or reverse it.[27] Things that were magical before are now more transparent. This age better understands the difference between fantasy and reality. They have tasted the fruit of logic and reason and are now on the path to adulthood. They definitely want to separate themselves from anything "babyish," and they may reject toys that they played with the previous year as being "too young" for them. Designers can engage this age group cognitively by creating activities that stimulate logical thought and require problem-solving skills. Mystery stories and quest-like journeys, as well as classic board games like checkers and chess, are very popular with this age group. What's important is that games have a level of complexity, challenge, strategy, and variety that matches this group's abilities.

"Eww! That's Baby Stuff."

Because of a growing sense of identity and use of reasoning, kids at this age see through "magic," and instead are better able to understand the world of adults. They have a strong desire to cast off all things that identify them with little kids. They don't want to go anywhere near "baby stuff," and they will tease younger siblings about toys and shows they themselves may have enjoyed for years.

Kids above age seven want their own content. Younger kids will migrate up, but older ones *will not* migrate down. Nickelodeon network (and others), have solved this problem by creating "junior" versions of their services after first establishing their brands in the seven-and-up market.

"I Understand Jokes Better Now."

iStock.com/svetikd

Humor is important to all children, and it boosts their creative thinking capacity. The ability to understand humor changes with age, and the most dramatic shift happens around six or seven when kids discover that the same word can have multiple meanings. (What cake can you drink coffee from? A cupcake!) Humor for the seven- to nine-year-old becomes progressively more sophisticated as they are able to understand the nature of subtler levels of humor, including riddles, puns, sarcasm, irony, satire, wisecracks, and more. Slapstick and moderately gross humor, combined with a touch of irreverence, and perhaps a bit of violence, seem to be big attractors for this age group.

"The Dark Side Interests Me More."

The seven- to nine-year-old is now more interested in exploring the darker side of media, including scary movies; violent action games; and (for boys more so than girls) rude, inappropriate characters.[28] As mentioned at the beginning of this section, this is called the rule/role stage, and part of exploring rules is to try to better understand being a "good" or "bad" person. Attractive content can include things that are gross, irreverent, rebellious, or socially taboo, all as part of rule/role research. This exploration continues for some years beyond this age group.

The only way to know where the line is, is to cross it.[29]
—Dave Chappelle, actor and comedian

"Yuck, That's GROSS!" or "Cool, That's GROSS!"

The seven- to nine-year-old has a love/hate relationship with things that are gross. As interested as they are revolted, they will keep coming back for more. That is why this group is especially entertained by bodily function humor, such as farts and burps. This group's interest in gross things has not been lost on *Ranger Rick* magazine, which, as part of its ongoing appeal, commonly features close-up photographs of bat faces or hairy spiders. Designers need not shy away from disgusting (but kid-friendly) things, at least not for this age group!

Ranger Rick, Oct. 2011, National Wildlife Federation.

"I'm Discovering Who I Am."

The ability to see themselves as others see them has a major effect on this age group's sense of identity. Seven- to nine-year-olds begin to be aware of their physical attributes. Are they taller or shorter, thinner or stockier, lighter or darker compared to other kids? They are also more aware of their gender, and they tend to separate into groups of boys and girls. Designers have an opportunity to engage the seven- to nine-year-old by incorporating gender-related preferences in role-playing and fantasy activities. (More about this is in the following chapter on gender.)

"I Can Read."

The seven- to nine-year-old is an emerging reader, and this makes a big difference when creating content for them. Although they like verbal instructions, they have the ability to read simple directions and button labels. They can navigate by text alone, and this opens up a whole new world for them (and for designers). Reading levels vary, so limiting text instructions is still a good idea. This group will read on-screen text if it offers them a compelling story or something important to future action (like how to get power-ups or increase character attributes).

Text is a higher level of abstraction than an image, and it takes more effort to process. This means that kids (and adults) tend to go to images first for information before reading text.

Photo by Barbara Chase

Designer's Note

The incredible attraction of interactive media can motivate kids to learn to read and write. They want to communicate with friends, play "older" games, learn the special tricks and cheats of games, and follow their own interests. Being able to read and write empowers them, and they are inspired to learn for their own reasons and to meet their own goals.

I first saw this phenomenon with the original version of *Where in the World Is Carmen San Diego?* as my kids came running into the room asking "Where is Brazil?" The game was driven by geographical information, and because the gameplay was good, my kids needed to know the information. The game came with a real atlas, which was a big plus in parents' minds, but it turned out that most kids only used it to look up images (flags and maps), and then would ask adults the geographical questions they didn't know. Not a bad thing because that made it a family game, and eventually we showed them how to look up things in the book. Another good example of self-motivated learning is learning to read the guidebooks in order to figure out the maps and complexities of *Pokémon* or similar games.

"Let's Be Friends."

This age group begins to develop true friendships. This is especially true for girls,

who start to share secrets with close friends and to talk about other kids. Boys tend to form clubs and join teams. Words like "secret" and "club" are powerful concepts in design for this age group.

These kids have graduated from the "parallel play" stage and are now able to interact more fully when playing with other kids. Communication skills, especially with writing, are still fairly limited, and email, chat, and texting are just beginning to emerge as activities.

Designer's Note

At one of my family events, two kids (a girl and a boy) were going to meet for the first time and were going to spend the day together. We had some concern about whether there would be fun activities for these two to do together, but it turned out they both spoke Pokémon. They were immediately consumed in character attribute discussions. The adults watched in amazement as these two kids conversed (in what seemed like a foreign language) for hours.

"I'm into Collecting Things."

Before the age of seven, the act of collecting is more a matter of gathering lots of stuff. At around seven, a stage of more serious and discriminating collecting begins. Kids at this stage become immersed in the details and descriptions that differentiate one thing from another. They become more discerning collectors as their ability to discriminate between features and particular characteristics becomes apparent to them.[30]

He's so focused © Brooke Williams, Flickr CC.

Several decades ago, it was popular for boys to collect sports cards and the stats of various players. More recently, kids collect Pokémon characters, each with their own abilities. Girls used to collect accessories for Barbie and other dolls. Now they are more likely to collect virtual outfits for their avatars (and be fluent, for example, in Pokémon speak).

"Keep Me Challenged."

While younger groups desire it, repetition no longer holds the attention of this older group. Instead, they prefer faster-paced games and activities (especially true for boys). One key to keeping the action lively is to create *leveling*. Having lots of progressively difficult levels allows kids to keep playing at the edge of what they know and are capable of. Some apps, such as *Fruit Ninja* or *Dumb Ways to Die*, create challenge by simply demanding quick responses to succeed. No matter the game, keeping kids appropriately challenged is key to keeping them engaged. Specific group testing is crucial to identifying whether your target age really gets it and is challenged by your content. Don't skimp on testing!

Designer's Note

In the previous chapter, we talked about Mihaly Csikszentmihalyi's theory of *flow*, and how a key factor in creating flow is to find the balance between ability and challenge. It's important for the user to perceive the challenge at hand to be within the possibilities of their own skill. Kids are most engaged when they play at a level that they can almost always keep up with, but that also pushes their abilities to the next level as they practice. Piaget described this as moving from equilibrium to disequilibrium and back. Children are slightly off-balance when they encounter new things—this is what followers of Piaget call *disequilibration*. To recover equilibration (the balance between interacting factors), children ride the edge between control and challenge as they assimilate new information.

"I Want to Be Good at It"

The seven- to nine-year-old's desire for mastery is an extension of an evolving sense of self and the search for a unique place in the world. Kids in this age range love the challenge (if they think they can succeed) of attempting something and possibly excelling. Gender differences begin to arise because the expression of mastery tends to take slightly different paths.

Though we have for years been offering kids digital "sandboxes" for role-playing, designers of virtual worlds for kids are increasingly providing locations, such as cafés or rock band stages, with a variety of props and dress-up opportunities for their avatar that resemble the old tried and true costume chest.[31]

—**Gano Haine, game designer**

Ages 10 to 12: Tweens

The ten- to twelve-year-old is rapidly moving away from childhood on the journey toward adulthood. Kids of this age are aspiring teenagers, or, as they are called by marketers, "tweens," somewhere between kids and teens. These kids definitely do not want to be seen as or treated like children—they really want to be seen as older than they are.

"I Wanna Be a Teenager."

Tweens are aspirational. To understand them, designers need to look at the tween role model, the teenager. MTV, which for years successfully marketed directly to teens through music videos, sees "teen attitude" as those feelings associated with rebellion, independence, angst, sexuality, and an ongoing search for personal identity. Tweens live with one foot in childhood and one foot in teenhood. If you look at the bedrooms of typical tweens, you will see items from their younger years right beside new tools, tech toys, and posters that reflect where they are headed.

Teenagers are cool to tweens because teens get to do so much more stuff. They have jobs, car keys, money, and some autonomy about where and with whom they go out. Tweens know that they are headed toward being teens, and though they don't always understand all things that drive teens (for instance, talking about the opposite sex so much), the view of teen life still looks good to them. They look up to teens without seeing the teen angst or worry, and they're excited about having both more responsibility and more freedom. They aren't quite ready for teen responsibility, but they can see it from where they're standing, and they're looking forward to getting there.

Scary movies, books, and classic ghost stories appeal more to this group than to younger ages. Being able watch a horror movie with friends is a badge of honor to show how grown-up they are (emulating teen behavior), even if it comes with the consequence of imagining creepy stuff for weeks afterwards.

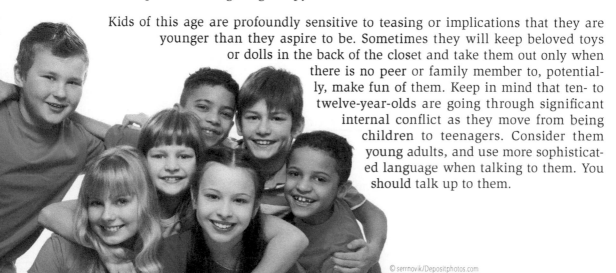

Kids of this age are profoundly sensitive to teasing or implications that they are younger than they aspire to be. Sometimes they will keep beloved toys or dolls in the back of the closet and take them out only when there is no peer or family member to, potentially, make fun of them. Keep in mind that ten- to twelve-year-olds are going through significant internal conflict as they move from being children to teenagers. Consider them young adults, and use more sophisticated language when talking to them. You should talk up to them.

© serrnovik/Depositphotos.com

"My Friends Are Important to Me."

Peer friendship is very important to tweens, and this is a value that carries over into the teen years. Tweens and teens are busy building their own identities, and this often includes some movement away from parents and toward the values of their friends.[32] At this stage, tweens are busy expanding their community. Friends share a tween's emerging interests, fears, and anxieties about identity. They are also sympathetic and understanding. Peer pressure seems to be strongest in these years, and an unconscious push to conform and fit in is expressed in how a group of friends dresses and uses tech accessories. Kids want not just any gadget or backpack or item of clothing but the one their group—or the group they'd like to join—has agreed is cool.

Most tweens maintain social lives online or via mobile devices. Texting, instant messaging, Skype, and other text/video/audio services are big because tweens can keep a running conversation going while exploring virtual spaces or playing games together. They can spend hours "together," doing all kinds of things while at home. It is their way of going out without car keys.

Designers can support tweens' need for friendship and peer connection by understanding that tweens aren't looking for a solo experience; they want something they can share in real life with their friends. Providing safe outlets for sharing and connecting while online will help meet tweens' needs for peer community.

Before this age, kids are learning to read. As tweens, they are reading to learn. They are busy taking in information from many sources and forming their own opinions. They are beginning to think more independently, outside of the orbit of parental beliefs. This is why, online, they like to participate in polls of their peers. They want to share their opinions on issues and see what other kids think, too.

"UGH! My Parents."

Since ten- to twelve-year-olds want to be older than they are, they are easily embarrassed by their parents, who still view them as children (imagine that!). Especially near the top of the age range, **tweens like to *pretend* they were immaculately conceived and are independently wealthy**. They suddenly want their own space and their privacy.

Marketers have exploited the evolving tween desire for independence and emerging rebellion against parents for years. The producers of the popular *Goosebumps* book series know their book covers have to be gross to make it with this age group because grossness is part of the appeal. The book could be fine, but the cover has to be something parents won't like.

Goosebumps book cover by R.L. Stine, Scholastic Corporation, 2011

"Who Makes This—and Is It Cool?"

Although awareness of brand-name products begins to emerge in the previous age group, it really begins to have more prominence with ten- to twelve-year-olds because it goes hand-in-hand with their peers' perception of what is cool. With their identity-building continuing to the next level, brand awareness begins to play a larger role in communicating who tweens are.

This is a good reason to make sure designs for seven- to twelve-year-olds really work for ten- to twelve-year-olds, because the seven- to nine-year-olds are watching. If your app is a hit with the older group, it will migrate to the younger. To be cool, a company has to reflect today's kid trends and interests, because this group is strongly influenced by popular culture. It is crucial to continually listen to the kids in the target audience.

Designing learning content for this age group has to be done carefully. Tweens can sniff out inauthenticity faster than Spiderman can scale a wall. You must speak directly to their interests and offer something creative and challenging. Tinybop's *The Human Body* is a good example of an app for this age group because it allows exploring everything from blood to poop, and the focus of the game is one of tweens' favorite subjects: themselves.

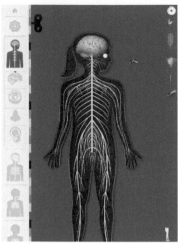

Human Body app by Tinybop.

"My Toys Are Technology."

This is an extremely tech-savvy group. Tweens have grown up with interconnected "smart" devices, and they use them as part of their normal world experience. They are often "power users" of some technologies (texting, tweeting), and they tend to be more technologically adept than their parents. These kids view tech gadgets as fashion accessories or entrée into groups of older or "more cool" friends.

Smartphones are an immediate hit with this age group because they allow kids to connect, communicate continually with their friends, share pictures of themselves, and play games *all* on the same device.

The social uses of the Internet are especially compelling to this group. Tweens have grown up with it, and they can't imagine life without instant access. Driven by an emerging desire to communicate, both sexes are developing their typing skills, sending text and instant messages (IMs) to their friends, and participating in online discussions—the possibilities are endless!

© Monkey Business Images | Dreamstime.com

Kids [today] are not just cable ready, they're tuned-in, tapped-in, and turned-on.[33]

—Esther Hicks, author

"I Still Love to Play."

Whether using computers, consoles, or handheld devices, ten- to twelve-year-olds are big game players, actively tracking what's new and hot. Since they grew up playing with emerging technologies, they are fearless and avid players of all kinds of games. They especially love multiplayer games where they can connect, compete, and share the experience with their best friends. Virtual world environments add a variety of social activities that are more cooperative and creative than those usually found on console devices. In order to power up their shared game experience, many kids use Skype or other online text/video/audio services to keep things more chatty and lively.

Ten- to twelve-year-olds are becoming more comfortable with their knowledge and abilities, and they wish to explore more real-world activities and interests as well. Even so, they want to do this exploration in a playful and fun way.

Popular apps for this age group often provide opportunities to build, make, and do, especially with friends. *Minecraft, Pokémon, League of Legends, World of Warcraft,* and other world-building games can inadvertently be quite educational in terms of teamwork, understanding commerce, working in social structures, creative problem solving, and more. However, it is possible to intentionally create educational products that kids really do love. One example is *Game Over Gopher*, one of the *Math Snacks* games by New Mexico State University's Learning Games Lab. The educational content—graphing of coordinate pairs—fits into the game as part of the tower defense strategy, and it's a crucial mathematics concept for middle school. Kids love playing the game, and they don't even realize it's teaching math.

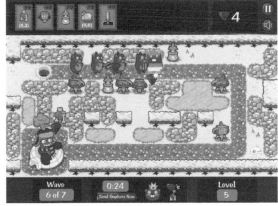
Game Over Gopher app by NMSU Learning Games Lab.

Designer's Note

Many times, I have had parents come to me asking why I didn't design more learning games for their twelve-year-old child. I tell them it is a tricky market. I might as well be designing for a sixteen-year-old or older, because that's who most twelve-year-olds are looking at. Also, even if the game or app is educational, kids (not parents) need to drive the purchase of it. For many older kids today, "educational" equals boring because years of schooling have drummed most of the curiosity, mystery, and excitement out of learning. Anything that feels too overtly educational is suspect to them. Design for this age can be done, but the designer needs to pay attention to intrinsic motivation and engaging interaction.

Ages 13 to 17: Teenagers

Teenagers are not children, at least not in their eyes. They want to be treated as if they were older already. This book is not about designing for teenagers, but it is important to discuss teenagers briefly because tweens often aspire to be like them. Teenagers are an important influence on the younger group's thinking and actions.

Turbulent Teens

Sometimes called the "turbulent" teens, the years between thirteen and seventeen have a growing desire for independence, a burgeoning interest in sex, and an increasing need to define identity, which often collides head first with familial and societal constraints. For the purposes of design, the teen years roughly encompass ages thirteen through seventeen because, by eighteen, kids are usually through high school, driving cars, sexually active, able to join the military, and are legally responsible for their actions.

"I Can So Do This!"

Risky behavior, coupled with a sense of invincibility, is an aspect of teen behavior that is sure to turn any parent's hair gray. Sometimes, teens have the egocentric view that, while others may be subject to the laws of nature, they themselves are immune and can therefore act as if they are invincible. In the context of exploration and self-discovery, some risk-taking is a normal part of pushing boundaries and testing themselves. Besides, it can be really exciting (something else teens like—*excitement!*).

Teen Attitude

Is it any wonder that taking good care of teens and protecting them for so many years may have the unintentional side effect of disempowering them and fostering the sense of identity angst and familial disassociation commonly joked about as teenage behavior and attitude? Teens in media are often portrayed as somewhat annoyed by and indifferent to their parents. Are we then surprised when life imitates art?

Teens commonly complain that parents interfere with their independence, but they may secretly appreciate parental concern and care. This confession may not occur until years later, and parents are old and gray before they receive appreciation!

Teens therefore may be more close-lipped with their parents than they

I CAN MAKE MY OWN DECISIONS I DON'T NEED HELP FROM YOU OR ANYBODY ELSE I'M CAPABLE OF TAKING CARE OF MYSELF SO JUST LEAVE ME ALONE WHAT'S FOR DINNER?

are with their friends. They want to experience their feelings and figure out what is right and wrong for themselves instead of being told ahead of time.

"My Friends Are Everything."

Friends are everything when you are a teenager. They are the ones who get you, who understand you, who you can talk to. Your friends are also trying to figure it all out, which supports a natural camaraderie. Your friends define you, advise you, and share much of your attitude. They are who you are in constant contact with. In days of old, the joke was always about the teenage girl tying up the family phone for hours on end. Today, teens have a vast arsenal of personal devices and methods to stay in constant contact with each other.

Constant communication with friends is the norm with teens. They can't imagine not being connected to their friends all the time. Cell phones are used for texting as much or more than they are for talking, and it is not uncommon for teens to have several modes of communication going on at once. Talk about being wired!

"I'm Not Moody. I'm FINE!"

Although they may not want to acknowledge or talk about it ("You wouldn't understand anyway!"), being in the throes of mood swings is part of the teenage experience. It isn't hard to imagine why, considering the expanding pressures many teens experience, such as developing bodies, new hormones, evolving mental capacity, growing responsibilities, body image, identity crises, increased parental expectations, peer pressure, and more.

Add in a few negative life events, such as not making a team you tried out for; doing poorly on a test; being turned down, snubbed, or rejected by someone you like; or experiencing a major shift like a parental divorce, and teenagers can feel easily overwhelmed. Many kids experience some form of depression during their teen years, and the compound effect of all the pressures could certainly make anyone moody. The common theme of much teen music speaks to this sense of angst, rebellion, and the desire to do what they want.

"Who Am I?"

The quest to understand their personal identity and their potential place in the world motivates many teen thoughts, feelings, and behaviors, whether they are aware of it or not. Questions like "What am I capable of?" or "Who will my friends be?" or "What am I going to do with my life?" tend to lurk in the unconscious, but they are nonetheless deeply felt as teens navigate their expanding lives and paths to adulthood. Teens tend to be idealistic, and they want to make a difference in the world, if they could only figure out how. Having even some small insight into what one is capable of is a powerful motivating guidepost for possibilities and action.

Online and console games are one way teenagers like to spend time and explore at least some of these issues. It is one of the places where they get to be in control and do something exciting (often with friends).

Appropriately understanding the interests, motivations, and behaviors of the children and young people who use and consume our content is fundamental to any successful interactive design. Beyond that, creative media content can also promote empowerment, self-esteem, a love of learning, and positive growth for all who use it.

Teenage Angst Has Paid Off Well © Jesse Millan, Flickr CC.

Gender: Understanding the Play Patterns of Girls and Boys

All people express a varying mix of what might be called male or female attributes. Sometimes, gender-based play patterns affect how kids approach interactive media. Girls and boys are the same in so many ways, and yet we often see differences in the importance they place on certain values, and what interests them when playing. Learning to understand these differences helps designers avoid unconscious gender-biased designs, lets them create activities that are gender inclusive, and allows them to be more aware when targeting a design to a particular gender. Ultimately, the goal is to create something beautiful and powerful for all kids.

How important it is for us to recognize and celebrate our heroes and she-roes![1]

—Maya Angelou, poet

Understanding Gendered Play Patterns

Designer's Note

It is nice to imagine a world with full gender equality, where all people are free to express individual gender identities without friction or expectation, but currently, in the U.S. and many other countries, we do not have this world. I offer these explorations into gender as a way to honor the varying approaches of feminine and masculine expression in play patterns and to encourage gender balance and equality when designing products for kids.

The information presented is gathered from research studies, direct observation over decades of gameplay and design, stories from other creators of children's material, and many discussions with kids themselves. I believe humans are individuals who approach life with a broad range of viewpoints. The goal is to work with these differences creatively, even though we may not understand all the reasons behind them. It is my desire to support gender equality and help all children reach their potential.

Limitations of Gender Nomenclature

Discussing masculine and feminine preferences and behavioral expressions can be tricky. The tendency is to polarize behaviors and create two large categories, one for masculine and one for feminine play patterns. But nothing about gender expression and play is that black and white. To better understand feminine and masculine play patterns we need to expand our thinking in how we, as designers, approach the subject.

Currently, culturally, we are beginning to better understand that a person's chromosomal or physical anatomy does not always determine their gender identity. The same is true of play interest, with the added complexity that what is thought of as being "for girls" or "for boys" is heavily influenced by culture. Activities and interests that are considered "male" at one time in history may be considered "female" in another place and time, and the tendency for girls and boys to cluster around certain topics or signifiers must therefore be understood to be influenced, even at an early age, by cultural pressures. In addition, although many young girls might like to play with traditionally female toys like dolls and stuffed animals, not all of them do. And though many young boys love to play with traditionally male toys like trucks and toys with wheels, not all of them do. No one wants to be stereotyped or told what they should do or should not do. Kids want to be free to follow their own interests, and to learn. In this chapter it is my goal to talk about known feminine and masculine play patterns, while keeping in mind that every person has their own blend of interests and attractions.

The best way to engage kids is to treat them as individuals.[2]
—Barbara Chase, Executive Producer, NoodleWorks Interactive

Looking Through Filters

Each one of us views the world through a slightly different filter. Our views of power, competition, cooperation, and human relationships, are shaped by multiple sources. How we perceive and react is formed from a tapestry of factors, including hormones, brain wiring, and cultural and familial influences and experiences.

The question is not what you look at, but what you see.[3]
—Henry David Thoreau, author

Statements about behavior must be seen as only generalizations because they give us a way of talking about play patterns and general interests, knowing full well that no statement includes all possibilities. Children view the world through various filters, which influences what they see and how they act, and having an understanding of resultant tendencies is important in creating meaningful products for everyone.

Going beyond stereotypes. No one wants to be stereotyped or told what they have to or should do. Kids want to be free to follow their interests. Stereotypes are convenient to describe a generalized phenomenon of behavior, but tend to divide children into two camps and therefore limit anyone who doesn't fit in the box

Factors of Gender Influence

Biological factors. There is a large body of research in biology regarding how changes in hormone balance alter behavior (in what can be called masculine or feminine directions). Male and female mammals, including humans, have a mix of both male and female hormones in differing amounts. We've all seen the effects of added steroids on athletes, and we have some sense that our biology can affect our choices at any given moment. Is it a coincidence that militaries worldwide tend to enlist young men at the early peak of their testosterone levels when they are naturally more prone to exhibitions of aggression and bravery?[4] Conversely, we know that higher levels of oxytocin increase a person's interest in tending and befriending; it has been called the "trust hormone."[5] Each person's individual hormone mix may affect what things they are interested in, regardless of their anatomy.

Cultural factors. We also know that nurturing influences and cultural indoctrination have a huge influence on how children see themselves in terms of gender. Proponents of biological determinism often cite the factors in the previous section as inescapable. Yet, if a child is told (by actions and words) from the moment of birth that they are supposed to act a certain way (in order to be loved and accepted), there is a similarly inescapable unconscious and conscious pressure to conform and act a particular way. Some cultures of the world are very fixed on the exact roles of men and women, and they frown on any deviation. Other cultures (like Sweden) are actively experimenting with new laws to make their culture gender equal. Most countries are somewhere in the middle, trying to climb out of the inherited patterns of their forebears.

Parents often swear they aren't trying to influence what their kids are drawn to, but, whether influenced or not, many girls gravitate to things pink, and many boys like toys with wheels. Some preferences appear over and over, and it's not always clear why. And yet, they are not necessarily innate. As recently as the early 20th century, some manufacturers in the United States promoted pink as the more appropriate color for boys, and blue for girls. It wasn't until the 1950s that the current preference of pink for girls and blue for boys became more widespread; and even then, it didn't become the dominant preference until the 1980s.[6] When we think, today, that a young girl has gravitated toward the color pink without cultural influence, it's useful to consider the historical changes in how colors are gendered.

> *When our daughter was born, we vowed to raise her with unisex toys so that she would have a better sense of herself as a whole person and not as a "pretty little girl." At last count, there are 17 Barbie dolls in her room and the only color she'll wear in public is pink.*[7]
> —Jerry Scott, co-author of *Baby Blues* and *Zits* cartoons

No matter where the preferences come from, as designers of children's content, we need to consider what works. Pink, for instance, may be a favorite color of some young girls, but coloring something pink doesn't automatically make it a girls' product. Some girls may prefer not to choose pink because they resist being pigeonholed. The content needs to support the play patterns that a majority of girls favor, while offering choices for outliers and leaving room for both genders to participate.

Designer's Note

I am a big fan of Lego, and I have a large Lego collection that I have accumulated over the years. I keep it inside a big sheet lining a laundry basket (for easy set-up and cleanup). When young, one of my grandsons always looked forward to building stuff with me when he came to visit. As birthdays and holidays rolled around, everyone began getting him the modern Lego sets, but something was wrong—he wasn't playing with them much. My daughter-in-law asked him why, and he said that all the new characters were unhappy and had grimaces and frowns. He wanted to play with my older sets, where the characters still smiled. With their more aggressive gender-targeting, The Lego Group had, in fact, created toys my grandson was less interested in.

Marketing influences. Toy and children's clothing companies often reinforce the cultural stereotype because they conveniently segregate the child market into smaller segments that are more easily targeted, and thereby increase profits. They also often superimpose, most commonly through packaging, an expectation about how a product is supposed to be played with and how that should look. A product may favor a boy/male pattern—but toy companies then tend to make it a strictly boy product in their marketing campaign and the available accessories. This tends to perpetuate the starkly demarcated gender aisles (pink and blue) in stores.

Marketing ad for LEGO, circa 1980s.

An interesting example of how product marketing can change the way a toy is viewed is Lego. Legos (interlocking blocks) were released in 1949[8] as a universal family building experience and were marketed as a toy for both genders. Their older campaigns show both girls and boys playing with the toy, and in 1963, the head of the company stated that their bricks should be sold to both boys and girls.[9] However, in the late-1980s, with the introduction of Zack the Lego Maniac, girls disappeared from the marketing materials for the traditional blocks, and Legos became a more segmented and boy-centric toy. The "for boys only" focus occurred not only in the marketing but also in the product design, as The Lego Group moved into more stereotypical male-centered theme sets and play patterns with an emphasis on conflict and combat.[10]

This is an interesting example of how a large company that marketed to all kids for over 30 years can fall into the trap of gendered branding. The Lego Group played into the cultural reality of the time, where girls more often crossed over to play with boys' toys than boys did with girls' toys. As a result, the company just focused on the stronger part of their market, a common marketing practice.

In 2012, The Lego Group launched Lego Friends, a girl-centered set of Lego pastel components with redesigned girl characters who are larger in scale with a more detailed look than traditional Lego minifigures. The new figures can share accessories and hair/hat styles, and even thought the feet are larger, they do fit on the standard 1x1 Lego block. After four years of research, The Lego Group learned that girls actually do like to build as much as boys, they just have a different sense of style and prefer storytelling as the foundation for what they build.[11]

Traditional Minifigure   Lego Friends Minifigure

Marketing is effective, and kids (and adults) can't help but internalize the sometimes limiting messages. Today, overall, there are few commercials for toys with boys and girls playing together; companies find it more profitable to create product segmentation, but it's kids who lose out with this marketing strategy. As designers, what can we learn from this story? I believe that gender inclusive design is always going to give you a larger market, and create products that stand the test of time.

Play Patterns Cross Gender Boundaries

We are who we are. As any parent with children will tell you, each child is unique. Children from the same family or nurturing environment often have highly individual personalities, abilities, and talents. People are who they are: part nature, part nurture, and part culture, with a mix of gender traits. While there are differences between men and women, boys and girls, it is also true that no one wants to be put in a box that requires them to behave in a particular way.

Diversity among individuals. One of the problems with gender labels is that we tend to make *assumptions about a child's interests* and activities based on stereotypes, rather than treating each child as an individual and supporting their personal interests. When products utilize play patterns that focus on just one gender, they often unintentionally exclude some who might naturally want to participate. On the other hand, if you ignore gender differences entirely and create something unisex or gender neutral, it runs the risk of being bland, less interesting and failing to meet the needs of a wider audience.

Products should appeal to both boys and girls who are intrinsically interested in the toy or play pattern. If you design a truck game, the important part is the trucks. Adding additional elements that create strict gender boundaries or imply that the game is only for boys does a disservice to girls who may be interested in the game. For instance, if all the avatars or characters have male names and identities, the play-space becomes exclusive. Likewise, if you are designing a game that uses dolls or dollhouse concepts, you want to make sure there are opportunities for male characters and players and that there are diverse design elements that allow a broad range of creative activities. That way, a kid who wants a pink, frilly house can have one, but a kid who prefers something entirely different (like launching cars off the dollhouse roof) will also have

iStock.com/ZargonDesign

RonGreer.Com/Shutterstock.com

appealing choices. *The Sims* games are a good example of a strong concept that appeals to diverse players because it gives them a lot of choice in what players can build and do.

Gender-inclusive design. Gender-inclusive design is often the goal of many children's developers today because it reaches the largest audience. This is not about avoiding gendered play, but rather creating something that allows opportunities for all kids to be engaged and to follow what speaks to them.

As Greg Beato noted almost 20 years ago in *Wired*, "there are girls and women who like to slaughter mutant humanoids as much as any man does." And not all boys or men automatically turn into "glassy-eyed alien snuff zombies" given the opportunity.[12] If we could chart gender behavior, a large bell curve would form in the middle representing how boys and girls *tend* to act. No statement about girls or boys means *all girls* or *all boys*, but rather points to general gender inclinations with lots of overlap.

> *Making toys gender inclusive doesn't prevent a girl from selecting a pink doll or a boy from picking a blue truck—it just stops such a selection from being obligatory.*[13]
>
> —Elizabeth Sweet, Ph.D., gender and toy researcher

The generalizations in this next section give us a way of talking about play patterns and general interests, knowing full well that they do not include **all**. The filter with which children view the world influences what they see and how they act, and having an understanding of tendencies is important in creating meaningful products for everyone.

> *Girls and boys tend to play differently as well as separately, and the differences are in some ways consistent from culture to culture.*[14]
>
> —Peter Gray and David F. Bjorklund, psychologists

Designer's Note

At a children's conference, a developer was demoing a new driving game. It was an exploration game, not a racing game. Children could navigate a car (seen from the side view) around an inventive world and interact with things they found along the way. At the end of the demo, a mother and game designer, Connie Bossert, said she had played the game with her daughter, who had asked why there were no cars for girls. The developer thought for a moment and said, "Yes, well, I guess we could have added some cars with flowers and patterns on them, or brighter colors." Connie asked her daughter if that was what she meant, and she said, "No, I mean cars with people in them."

Considering Masculine and Feminine Play Patterns

Although some natural gender differences are noticeable in younger children's play patterns, differences in game design are most important in children above five years of age. It is easy to create software that appeals to all preschool-aged kids because they mostly just see themselves as kids. They want to play, and everything is relatively new and interesting to them. This section focuses on the more obvious and significant gender patterns of older children. *Remember, no gender play pattern is black and white or includes all girls or all boys; rather, it's a continuum of preferences and mixed patterns.*

> *If you want to watch gender differences firsthand, just ask boys and girls to play the same game. Once, I was observing a group playing the touch pad version of the* Plants vs. Zombies *game. Girls leaned into each other and came up with a division of labor where each girl specialized in one feature—say, collecting the energy suns—while the other girl fended off the zombies. Boys, on the other hand, more often passed the device back and forth. After observing the girls, some of my young adult male players said, "Hey, let's play girl style," and enjoyed using the cooperative strategy.*[15]
>
> —Gano Haine, game designer

Social Structures and Relationships

Boys' social worlds tend toward relatively large, overt, and straightforward hierarchical peer structures with clear standings in group relationships. One might be the best at wrestling. Another beats everyone at Nintendo. Someone else is the best at soccer. Hierarchical standing is based on direct competition, is ongoing, and can always be challenged. You might think of it as a "king of the hill" play mentality. Whether as a coalition or individual, proving superiority is the main goal via games. Part of the process may include teasing and boasting. If used at all, intimidation, rather that exclusion, is utilized strategically to influence competition and completion during gameplay.

Each game/activity has rules, and that is how boys determine the identity of the winner. Playing by the rules is very important because rules set the standard for fairness and arbitration. Since being the best at something regularly changes by category and subject of competition, boys generally know their standing in the social/game hierarchy at any given time. They don't spend much time discussing personal issues. Their discussions are usually about things outside of themselves, such as sports, how to beat a game level, or what to do next. They are generally able to keep the different activities separate, each in its own box. One issue doesn't necessarily connect to others.

Boys, in general, play easily in small or large (loosely affiliated) groups and teams. They will play with almost any group, as long as everyone follows the rules. They play for fun, and, for the most part, it's not about who is playing or who is there.

Girls' social world structure is somewhat different; everything seems to connect with everything else. For girls, social order is not necessarily based on what score they get on a game or test, or how good they are at soccer. Sharing personal interests with their friends and playing cooperatively has the greater value. Competition, though still present, is subtler and not the reason for play. Girls establish social position with peers by affiliation and exclusion. Girls' relationships tend to be more non-hierarchical, with lines connecting in all different directions. The most significant girl in a larger group is often the one with the most interpersonal connections. Relationships are important and are all about social groupings. Girls' appetite for social and personal communication is much stronger than boys'. Game rules are welcome as long as the game continues to progress. Girls tend to prefer rules that are flexible and can be negotiated to fit the needs of the players. Everyone should have a good experience.

Girls, in general, tend to play in small, close-knit groups, often with friends they already know, mostly agree with, and can talk openly with, but group members can change from day to day. They enjoy challenging experiences, but they can be uncomfortable with changes in their support system.

The view of social worlds above is not a hard rule for girls and boys, but instead consists of generally recognized patterns of interaction within *segregated* groups. Play patterns seem to be more flexible in mixed-age play. In *Psychology*, the textbook by Peter Gray and David F. Bjorklund, they say "Age-mixed play generally centers less on winning and losing than does same-age play, so age mixing reduces the difference in competitiveness between boys' and girls' play. Moreover, several studies indicate that boys and girls play together more often in age-mixed groups than in age-segregated groups."[16]

Friendship Versus Winning

For many boys, but not all, winning is the goal. That's *why* they play a game—to beat the other players. Their friends won't think less of them for winning because they have been doing their best to win, too. The challenge of competition is a large factor in why boys enjoy playing. Any "table-flipping-turnarounds" or mock intimidation that occur during the course of the game are joked about afterwards, and quickly forgotten. It's usually understood that this is a part of the process and that games are a friendly way to test themselves.

Even though an alliance of players may try to keep whoever is winning from beating everyone else, most often boys play "each man for himself." Winning is how boys show mastery and help establish a social order. Scores are important because they show a clear ranking. Obtaining achievements is a game in itself. Level mastery may include encountering every conceivable scenario to obtain every single achievement, whether the game is set to easy, medium, or hard.

For many girls, but not all, friendship is more important than winning. Relationships are such an overriding value that, during social gameplay, girls may change the game's rules or negotiate changing the rules on the fly to ensure that no one wins or loses. Playing the game with friends isn't as much fun if someone is excluded or unhappy. Rules are only good as long as they are fun, and they need to be flexible to fit the needs of the players. If someone is really far behind, then it's okay with girls to give that person an extra turn or two to help them catch up. In a traditional board game like *Monopoly*, this may drive boys crazy. They are in disbelief when someone lands on Boardwalk with tons of hotels, and the girls want to change the rules so that person doesn't have to be out of the game.

This does not mean that girls are not competitive. They definitely are. If you have ever watched girls' soccer teams play, you know that they aren't afraid to mix it up. The comments above apply more to social gameplay with friends.

Action Versus Dialogue

Gender-conscious designers sometimes joke about different ways of creating games with something for everybody, such as an adventure game with multiple modes of achieving the goal. In one style, you might get into the secret castle by fighting with the demon at the door or smashing at the wall with a magic club. Or you can explore the perimeter of the castle, collecting magic gems and gain information about the story through conversations with the various characters you meet until they tell you how to get in. Good design offers opportunities for multiple ways to play and win, and children can choose what mode interests them that day. Here are some other things girls and boys lean toward in story lines and action adventures. Keep in mind that these are general tendencies and should by no means limit or confine you as a designer.

Girls

More girls than boys seem to be attracted to Narrative Play, and are engaged by good plots and complex characters that they can care about. They want to know the backstory and what motivates the characters. They favor familiar, real-world relationships between the characters, even if the scene is set on an alien planet or in a fantastical dream world. At least some of the characters should possess relatable personality traits and behave like people they actually know. They enjoy the process of making connections to the backstory during gameplay, even if it isn't by design.

Impromptu First Contact, watercolor by Michael Dashow.

Preferences girls have for the opportunity to engage and collaborate with each other can even overshadow considerations of age and look-and-feel that have been strong predictors of success in the toy industry. Barbie.com opened with an online world targeting girls four to seven years of age. To Mattel's surprise, however, in the site's first months, an overwhelming percentage of participants were in the eight to ten year-old age group, extending all the way up to twelve years of age. Not the age group Mattel had anticipated.

In Fantasy Play, the game *is* the ongoing story. Throughout the game girls may regularly negotiate the rules and what the characters are going to do, etc., letting the story evolve to match their creativity. Inventing the story and their roles is an important aspect of the play.

Girls appreciate personal relevance in content; they want something that is useful to them in their lives. Even in magical fantasies, kid characters should still act like real people who are just dealing with unusual situations. The *Sabrina the Teenage Witch* television shows are a good example: even though Sabrina has magical powers, she still has to go to school, deal with homework, work through issues of friendship, and cope with her aunt's parenting.

Girls, in general, like it when there is more than one right answer or way to complete a game. Being stuck with one puzzle that must be solved to move forward is less attractive than multiple options. In fact, they often prefer many ways to play, including writing their own endings.

Designer's Note

Designer Brenda Laurel did years of research on eight- to twelve-year-old girls at Interval Research before she co-founded the girl-focused company Purple Moon. She discovered that personal relevance was incredibly important to girls at that age. In an interview for the book *From Barbie to Mortal Kombat*, Laurel remarks, "It's so strong. And that was a surprise to me . . . because you traditionally think about fantasy as being off somewhere—you know, Cinderella, folk tales, fairy tales, superhero stuff. . . . So I was really struck by the demand for personal relevance and the way they'd take even a fantastical scenario and turn it around until it was, 'MY heart, MY life, MY values, the things I'm worried about, what comes up for me.' Those things just kept getting worked into the play."[17]

Laurel describes the eight- to twelve-year-old age range as "the time of self-construction. That's the project that's going on there, very explicitly so. It's one of the things that defines that break between seven and eight, where it's not about kings and queens and baby dolls anymore; it's now starting to be about my persona—'Who am I? What's going on with me?'—and acting out some of that [inner world] stuff in a much more relevant and close-to-home way."[18]

Girls often favor less aggressive stories.[19] This does not mean they aren't drawn to conflict. What would a good story be without some conflict? There would be nothing to resolve. But many girls consider the endless killing in first-person shooter games to be boring after a while. Some action game companies have added more extensive backstories just to engage women and girls more, giving them an emotional motivation to go to battle and kick some bad-guy ass. One example is the online game *Adventure Quest Worlds*, where they use cut scenes, cinematic shorts in between the gameplay, to convey more about the story as players progress through the game.

[In games], women need a reason to be aggressive. Men just need a place.[20]

—Jordan Weisman, co-creator of *BattleTech*

Adventure Quest Worlds by Artix Entertainment.

Girls have a passion for customizing and personalizing. Items that some male designers have formerly thought to be the frills of design, such as extensive avatar customization options and large varieties of props for accessorizing and decorating, are, for many girls, a very enjoyable piece of the gameplay experience. Rather than being trivial, these game features allow subtle character development, personalized worldbuilding, and scenario planning. They also support the formation of detailed narratives and allow players to situate themselves in relation to others through qualitative attributes (rather than quantitative comparisons like scoring).

Boys

More boys than girls are attracted to dramatic sports or fantasy stories, settings, and situations with lots of action.[21] They enjoy epic, larger-than-life struggles between good and evil. Their stories and fantasy play are filled with *power* characters: sports stars, superheroes, warriors, monsters, aliens, zombies, and bad-guy stereotypes. This does not mean that boys aren't attracted to other activities; it is rather that patterns for action and power continue to surface as a general preference.

Many boys are also attracted to the shadow side of characters. Usually, they have action figures of the bad guys as well as the good guys. In fact, over the years, some of the classic bad guys (Darth Vader, Skeletor, Cobra) have outsold the heroes.[22]

Boys, in general, don't mind violent games or stories, and they often enjoy them for the action. In first-person shooter games, they follow the rule "If it moves, shoot it." Unlike girls, they don't need a reason to shoot, just a target and the instructions to do so. This is the same logic behind the appeal of cars and trucks: they go fast and can smash into things to great effect.

Skeletor action figure by Mattel.

Designer's Note

Years ago, I knew several game designers at Atari Coin-Op Games. They told me that when they showed a new game to tweens, primarily boys, and asked what would make it better, the answer was often some version of "more blood." Who knows where this leaning comes from, or why, but its existence is empirical information from designers in the field.

A related phenomenon shows up around boys and toy guns. Guns are a symbol of power, a mobile unit of energy that can be shot at an opponent. Most American boys grow up playing with guns (toy, virtual, or real), and they use them in play battles with their buddies. Parents who advocate nonviolence have shared with me, more than once, that even when their boys were not allowed to have toy guns or watch any violent TV or movies, and were talked to about the reasons why, they still used sticks, or just their hands, as mock guns to shoot at each other in yard play. Something about the idea of a gun seems to touch an older protective, defensive, and/or offensive aspect of a male's psyche.

Very rarely do boys want personal relevance in their media choices. In fact, they may be embarrassed by material that's too close to their real lives. Like girls, boys are in the process of building identity, but because boys tend to operate somewhat differently, they are, at least at younger ages, less focused on their inner world. Characters and stories are secondary to action and gameplay. Boys may not notice the existence of a backstory, or they may not be interested in it until very far into a game. Even then, the story may only be a means to help them win the game or complete the level or quest.

Designer's Note

Opportunities for deeper shared experiences have made themselves available as technology advances. One trend I've noticed is that group communication over the Internet has become a bigger factor in how kids play games. Peer (or team) communication software has been around for a while in games like *World of Warcraft*. Now, younger and younger kids enhance their shared experience by using Skype and other similar programs to communicate while they play inside virtual worlds like *Club Penguin* and *Minecraft*. They may be at home, but they are having a somewhat traditional play date with kids and cousins all over the world.

Doll and Action Figure Play

Chapter 1 discussed briefly how play evolved in mammals as way to practice skills that will be necessary for their survival later. Mammals play at chasing, stalking, fighting, nurturing, and more. So do human children. (Today, children also play with computers!) You can easily name games and play patterns that fulfill these behaviors, such as chasing each other around the yard, stalking friends in hide-and-go-seek, or taking care of a family pet. Whether cultural, biological, or a combination of both, how children play with dolls and action figures tends to express slightly different values.

How girls—again, not all girls—play with their dolls and stuffed animals generally reflects an inclination for modeling relationships, and is a good example of Nurture Play. Historically, girls used dolls for social storytelling exploration and, some think, for aspirational role-playing. Barbie, for instance, has continued to change over the years, offering new role models to fit the times. She has been a nurse, a doctor, a paleontologist, a fashion model, an astronaut, and more. As mentioned in Chapter 1, dolls are also used as a "talking stick" for expressive **Role-Play**.

Marketers of boys' products call similar toys "action figures." Boys would never call them dolls because the term "doll" has long been stereotyped a girl toy. Action figure character models come from many media. Superheroes are the perennial favorites, science fiction characters come with cool accessories, and there is usually a character from a recent hit movie available. G.I. Joe is a classic, and, of course, famous sports figures are popular choices. All of these figures tend to reflect an inclination for action and expressions of power. Occasionally, dolls marketed to boys will commingle with dolls marketed to girls, but generally G.I. Joe does not play with Barbie.

Kids and Clothes

Designer's Note

A classic stereotype about females and clothing is the *Zits* cartoon below: that women (and girls) care more about clothes than men (and boys) do. It's a common legend that is pervasive in our culture. In fact, I was explaining to a young friend (age 11) that I was working on this book, and the part I was focused on was about how girls and boys look at things differently sometimes. Very interested, she asked me to share some of these insights. I said, "Well, girls tend to care more about clothes than boys." She looked at me incredulously and said, "Well, **duh!**" From that girl's point of view this is so obvious, but it's not always as obvious to boys (and male designers).

There is some truth to the interest girls have in accessorizing and decorating their avatars. (This is why offering a lot of clothes, wigs, and props is always a good thing to do in virtual worlds.) But boys are not without their interest in virtual clothing. Sometimes, in worlds for younger kids, it's just fun to dress the avatar in something silly or weird. It's a safe place for all to experiment with different "looks," but especially a safe place for boys whose clothing choices are more culturally constrained. As boys get older and move on to more intense adventure games, they may care more about what their avatar wears than what they wear themselves. "Skinning" your avatar correctly, adding virtual overlying outfits, and adding impressive armor and weapons, is an important part of preparing for a quest or battle. Boys tend to switch up their avatar frequently to cycle through items unlocked in gameplay to display status. There are times when a ninja outfit is a role-playing expression of power and competency, and it may have an effect on winning. Maybe, in a way, that's also what girls (and women) are doing with their attention to wardrobe.

Danilo Sanino/Shutterstock.com

Action and Competitive Games

In Competitive Play, girls tend to personalize other players' actions within the game. They see the world through their inner personal landscape, and thus may take the in-game action of others to heart. They can be very competitive, and with other girls it may be more about being the better girl than winning the game. Since most children's games aren't about battling to the death, this pattern is more prevalent in late tween and teen virtual worlds where competition is more intense.

Although research has not substantiated a difference between girls' and boys' styles of reconciliation, from years of observation and conversations with friends, it seems that when girls get in a physical fight with a friend, they may never speak to that person again. Trust boundaries have been seriously crossed, and the pain of being attacked is vividly remembered. In general, when boys are in a physical fight with a friend, they may end up closer afterward, having bonded in battle. They have stood up to each other, and may have a newfound respect for each other, and themselves (unless there was humiliation involved). Competitive in-game player actions for boys are more compartmentalized and considered isolated events. If they lose, it is just a game, and they consider that they may be likely to be successful later at something else.

This has echoes in gameplay with friends, where all-out competition may be considered less of a personal attack between boys, and more so, depending on the circumstances, for girls. On the other hand, boys may feel humiliated or defensive if attacked, successfully, by a girl. It's worth considering that, when boys and girls play games with each other, they may not fully understand the other's mode of play (many adults don't either.)

> *I have been gaming online for over 12 years, starting with* **Club Penguin** *when I was 5. These days I mostly play* **League of Legends.** *What I've noticed over the years is that the boys, who are my friends, are generally very competitive during gameplay. Winning and achieving the next level is more important for them than to myself. That's not to say that I don't enjoy the same games, merely that I get different things out of them and have different goals. I am more interested in doing something fun together with my friends.*
>
> *Another interesting thing about playing these games with boys is that I can speak freely during gameplay and no one gets their feelings hurt. We all speak openly about each other's mistakes while playing, and all are still good friends at the end.*[23]
>
> —**Nicole Martin, graphics design student and video gamer**

Boys lean toward play that expresses power and skill. From running around the house with a cape on, imagining they have superpowers (younger ages), to beating the 100th level of a complicated game (older ages), boys are interested in icons of power and skill achievement. The desire to play with and attain power and game skills seems to be an innate attraction that shows up in many boys. Generally, boys prefer to play anything game-like, especially if it has a scoreboard or some method to show ranking. Many boys tend to favor games with some form of time pressure, games where they are forced to act or react, while some girls find this more stressful than fun over time. For boys, it helps if the game has a high-score screen where they can enter their names because ranking is important.

All kids are excited to begin playing a program, but, in general, girls and boys approach beginning new games differently.

Boys tend to jump in. They generally don't need or want to take the time to know how something works before beginning. Many boys prefer to learn through trial and error. They will get to know the gameplay, and then hunt down how-tos from outside sources as a means to increase their abilities and accumulate achievements. They begin without fear and enjoy learning how to stay alive over time and through repeated failure. Experimenting with new techniques to stay alive, they will revisit a level multiple times to obtain level mastery.

Girls prefer to know more about how an activity works before beginning. In action worlds, girls tend to approach situations carefully and methodically to avoid dying. Repeatedly starting over from the beginning of a level in a game is frustrating and nonsensical. They prefer games that can save points within a level, and fair games that balance action across players. Activities are less about success and more about process, like solving puzzles rather than obtaining the achievement.

> *Gender balance in design teams makes a difference. In general, if a team skews toward only men, there is less of a tendency to discuss ideas before they just start making. And if a team skews toward only women, there is an increase in the discussion of ideas, with some potential struggle on the start of development. Gender balance helps create a team that shares and develops ideas well together.*[24]
>
> —**Drew Davidson, Director of the Entertainment Technology Center, Carnegie Mellon University**

Talking

Young girls tend to talk more than boys do. A large number of studies have shown that girls develop their verbal skills earlier than boys do, and they use talking as a means of connection and affiliation.[25] This may be part of the reason they feel comfortable talking to characters in games to gain information. It's not that boys don't talk (they can be very chatty on favorite subjects), it is that boys tend not to talk about themselves and what they are feeling. This may be part of why boys generally prefer to jump in first and figure it out later.

Other Thoughts on Interests

Girls like to plan things. Girls like planning events, such as a birthday party or a funny skit they might perform with friends. They like to discuss, organize, and plan what they are going to do in a particular make-believe or virtual game. Sometimes they enjoy the planning and discussion *more* than they enjoy the game itself. Planning *is* the gameplay. And planning is all about talking.

The Nurture Play pattern. Caretaking and communication play express the Nurture Play pattern, sometimes called "tend and befriend." During "tea party" activities (often with dolls and stuffed animals), conversations and other tending take place. Pretend doctor or nurse scenarios, where some caretaking is needed, also display this play pattern. Apps like Sago Sago's *Sago Mini Friends*, aimed at very young users, allow for Nurture Play in a variety of ways, from feeding the characters to putting them to bed.

Sago Mini Friends app by Sago Sago Toys.

For slightly older children (eight and above), this transitions into real communication and caring about, and for, friends. The pattern is about making friends and tending the relationships. Nurture Play is also visible in programs, like *Nintendogs* or *Neko Atsume*, with digital pets that need to be fed and cared for regularly for them to prosper.

Boys love fart and burp humor. Boys find humor in bodily noises. Something about bodily, gross, and disgusting noises tickles boys at their core, and they will play them over and over to continued laughter. They also like to practice making those noises. Boys enjoy silly and outrageous physical humor, gags, pranks, stunts, and extremely goofy facial expressions. Girls may find these noises humorous and laugh at first also, but they may stop reacting before

Nintendogs by Nintendo.

the boys, who are replaying the gag in hysterics. A girl may just roll her eyes and shake her head, saying, "It was funny, but not *that* funny." But for the boys, it was funny with a capital "F."

Acknowledging gender bias. Everyone has biases based on their perspective of the world and their cultural and social conditioning. We see through the lens of our body's experiences, and that influences how we interpret what we see. Even with my sincere desire to create great products for all children, some of my own gender bias is going to come through. I imagine that even as you read this chapter you will have opinions based on your own experiences and bias. Having a viewpoint makes us individuals; the trick is always to acknowledge that others' viewpoints are not always the same as ours, and to have some awareness of what might be important to them. My goal is to help designers have some understanding of "other." Not just for guys to understand something about girls, or women to better understand something about boys, but to better support and connect with the whole spectrum of play, no matter who is playing. As designers of content for children, we need to remember to look at our own gender bias and be aware of any subliminal restrictions we might put into our products.

Gender Similarities

Considering all this discussion about the differences in how they perceive content and experience the world, here are some things that both boys and girls find appealing.

All kids love a good story. Good stories never lose their appeal. Love of a good story is a characteristic of all humans, male and female, young and old. Allowing ourselves to become part of the story and participate in the characters' experiences and world forms the basis of most media. A good story also provides memorable characters that kids can integrate into their own fantasy play.

iStock.com/Susan Chiang

All kids love to laugh. What is humorous varies by age, but there is something that tickles everyone. Laughter is contagious, so the more you have, the more you get. If you find the right interaction to get a giggle for the age group, you are off and running.

Laughter is the shortest distance between two people.[26]
— **Victor Borge, humorist and musician**

All kids like to create and build. With Creative Play, personal expression and making something from physical pieces or with digital tools (à la *Minecraft*) is satisfying for kids of all ages. This is especially true if the creations can be shared with friends and family. Imagine a family refrigerator without kid art on it! Creating is an integral part of childhood.

All kids love magic. Whether in stories, games, or their own imaginative play, all kids like playing with magical thinking and the power of "What if... ?" And why not? What better time than when we are kids?

All kids like to solve a mystery. Mysteries are often a bit scary because we are exploring the nature of the unknown, and we don't know what will happen or what we might learn (not unlike living life itself). It takes bravery, pluck, ingenuity, and luck to courageously investigate and solve a problem, especially in the face of adversity. There is usually at least one good surprise involved, too!

All kids love to be scared, at least a little. Beyond the age of five or six, kids enjoy various levels of mock danger, risk, fear, surprise, and anxiety because it gives them a rush. As kids get older, they enjoy progressively higher levels of these sources of adrenaline. The attraction is about more than a simple desire to be scared. It is about challenging childhood boundaries. Kids like to share the experience of being scared with their peers. Experiencing a scary movie or game with older kids or adults is not the same because the level of fear or risk is not an "edge" for them. Watching scary movies with friends can be a bonding experience, and amusement park rides aren't designed for the elderly. Testing bravery and exploring unknown fears seems to be part of the process of growing up.

Whatever the differences and similarities are between girls and boys, as a designer your goal is to create something beautiful, powerful, and engaging for all kids. Much of this book has focused on traits all kids share, and understanding those big ideas should serve as a foundation, even as you tailor a game to a more particular audience. The next few chapters return to less gender-specific considerations of how to make your interfaces, characters, and other game elements work with the way kids think and play.

If you want your children to bring original ideas into the world, you need to let them pursue their passions, not yours.[27]

—**Adam Grant, professor of management and psychology**

KievVictor/Shutterstock.com

PART 4

Creating Digital Playgrounds

Great interactive children's design offers an inviting "playground" with multiple opportunities for play experiences. Playgrounds are, by nature, areas of self-directed exploration where children can climb and hang and slide as their interests move them. Digital playgrounds need to offer kids the same kind of open-ended and self-directed opportunities for exploration. This section will cover the ins and outs of great interface design for children, including how to create characters, avatars, and agents that kids will connect with.

To stimulate creativity, one must develop the childlike inclination for play and the childlike desire for recognition.[1]

—attributed to Albert Einstein

Interface

We all like to be invited, to have permission, to feel welcomed, to hear the big *Yes* that means it's safe to come play. Offering intuitive interfaces and opportunities to explore and participate will create an environment that empowers, delights, and enlightens. Kids just want to have fun, and they need you to support their creative exploration by providing them with interesting environments, clear navigation, and accessible tools to empower their play.

An interface can be as simple as a signpost or as elaborate as a dashboard on steroids. It can be as impersonal as an empty room or as warm and inviting as Grandma's house during the holidays. Design magic is about knowing what's needed for the situation and creating it.

All life is an experiment. The more experiments you make the better.[2]

—**Ralph Waldo Emerson, poet**

Interface Is About the Relationship

© kikovic/Depositphotos.com

An interface has two main functions: *navigation* and *content interaction*. One gets the users to where they want to go, and the other allows users to do what they want to do once they are there. But there is a third function: to provide a quality experience. During the action–response–action cycle, all interactions have their own quality of experience, and they connect with us at different levels. We may be virtually *in* a world or game through an avatar, or *on* the surface of a screen using creativity tools to make things. Either way, the user is having a relationship with a computer-driven device *through* an interface.

Some people think design means how it looks but of course, if you dig deeper, it's really how it works.[3]

—Steve Jobs

Kids and Technology

Children born today are "digital natives" compared to many adults, who came to technology later and could be considered "digital immigrants."[4] Behavioral biologists talk about how young mammals are drawn to play at the survival skills they will need to be successful as adults—young lions practice stalking and pouncing; gazelles and zebras practice running and avoiding; young monkeys practice swinging between tree branches.[5] If this holds true for humans, then it is only natural for kids to be drawn to digital technology. It is their future.

Kids are drawn to and fearless of technology. Heliotropism is a flower's compulsion to follow the light of the sun. Kids have a kind of technotropism; they are naturally fascinated and attracted by new digital toys and personal technology devices. Take out an iPad near a group of children, and suddenly they are all interested, asking "What do you have? What's that app do?"

Kids, unlike many adults, have little fear of personal or media technology. Often, adults are more hesitant with digital devices, concerned about pushing the wrong button, whereas kids like to jump in and learn by trial and error. If a program doesn't work well, kids assume it is the program's fault, not theirs, while adults are more likely to doubt themselves.

Technology is anything that isn't around when you're born.[6]
—Alan Kay, **computer scientist and educator**

Designer's Note

When my boys were young, we gave up on our small, ancient TV, and bought a new high-tech one (high-tech for the time, anyway). I bought it on a Sunday afternoon and got it mostly set up and running that evening. When I got home Monday night, I went to check out my new TV set, and I found that my youngest son, then about five or six, had been experimenting with all the buttons on the remote control that afternoon and had set the parental lock (something he had never seen before), put in a password, and locked me out! All I saw was a blue screen asking for my personal code. He was, of course, delighted at his new power and later proceeded to show me how to get in and how it worked.

Kids are more comfortable with technology than many adults. For years, the cell phone market in Europe and Asia was driven by teenagers who got new phones every six months as the technology changed. If you want to know how to use all the latest features on any device, just ask a kid who has one: I guarantee they know how to use more functions than you knew were in there. As a designer it is also helpful to know kids who already use a new platform because they will help inform your thinking.

Designer's Note

I always say that I design my products for kids to use, and hope that adults can figure them out, too.

Technologies come and go, but some things remain constant: the way our brains work, the desire to explore, the delight we get from novel surprise, and our instinct for play. In the life of this book, several technologies might cease to exist, but the ideas behind creating intelligent, entertaining experiences will remain the same. Remember:

It's about play, not technology.

The guidelines covered in this chapter will apply to interactive design even as technologies and platforms change.

Interactive Basics

Interactive patterns in human nature can be seen every day, everywhere on the planet. A smart designer will make use of these tendencies to create accommodating designs. The following observations can be used as basic design guidelines, whether you are designing for children or adults.

Nobody Wants to Read the Manual

Our natural human pattern for dealing with computers and electronics seems to be: 1) Try something; 2) If we can't figure it out, ask someone; 3) If no one can help, look it up. Prior to developing the written word, we always learned by observing and physically interacting with our world—*we learned by doing*. It's more instinctive for us to try something first instead of reading about it. Kids are even less likely than adults to rely on text for information. They are wired to learn experientially; that is what a lot of early childhood is about. Letting this pattern inform your design will lead to programs that are as accessible and intuitive as possible. Remember, *kids in particular learn by doing*.

Toca Hair Salon 2 app by Toca Boca.

Make it easy to get started. Kids explore first and ask questions later. When they play with computers, they immediately want to see some of the possible things they can do. The best designs are those that allow them to figure things out through simple exploration and experimentation. Design programs so kids can easily get started and involved. This screenshot from Toca Boca's *Toca Hair Salon 2* shows this principle at work. Kids have no problem figuring out that they should tap on the scissors (which open to show they are active) to begin cutting the character's hair. The white dot at the bottom of the screen shows which tool set the player is looking at. They eventually understand that, by swiping left or right, they can access six more screens of tools that open up more fun activities. This dot system is a simple "map" to help kids get oriented.

Your design should allow for clearly marked navigation and some kind of animated and/or audio feedback in response to user actions. It has to be easy for kids to get involved. They learn about the rest of their world by experimenting with cause and effect, action and reaction. Why should software be any different? This may sound self-evident, but many interfaces are arcane, inconsistent, and counterintuitive to use (obviously designed by adults).

This leads us to the second observation of human nature.

Nobody Wants to Wait

Nobody wants to wait in traffic, nobody wants to wait in line, and nobody really wants to wait for programs and pages to load and start. It's human nature. We want what we want, and we want it now. We want immediate feedback in response to our actions. This is especially true for children.

Optimize interface for response time. Optimizing response time to meet the expectations of the user is a fundamental part of good interactive design. As platforms and delivery paradigms change, design must adapt in order to minimize response time on different systems. No matter how difficult it is to shorten response times on various platforms, doing so should be a design priority. A quick, crisp response *feels* right. Slow response time can make the best game feel clunky and dumb.

Optimizing response time entails a combination of maximizing your content throughput and software drivers with the limitations of your hardware or Internet connections to get the best performance possible. Some wonderful graphics and animations have killed products in the marketplace because almost no one had a machine fast enough to run them at the time they were released. When we optimize the response time, we enable the computer to respond like a person in the real world. "I communicate with you, and I get communication back"—a classic empirical definition of "interactive."

> *For a child, WAIT is a four letter word.*[7]
> —**Warren Buckleitner, Editor,** *Children's Technology Review*

The third observation of human behavior is:

Everybody Wants to Be in Control

Empowering kids with the feeling that they are in charge, at least of some aspects of a program, is key to creating engagement in activity and exploration.

Kids want to drive. Kids are fearless about new technology. They just want to drive it to see how it works and what they can do with it. They want to show you their mastery at every opportunity. They are also less worried than adults that they are going to break something. Kids' motivation to play and get feedback is what makes using computer-enhanced devices such a unique opportunity for self-driven learning.

Kids learn through exploration and discovery. A child's natural desire to "see how it works" is an inherent survival instinct that drives us to better understand the world. This instinctual curiosity is at the root of learning, and it is what pushes us, as individuals and as a species, to greater understanding. This is especially true for children. Kids want to be in control of their exploration and the pace of learning. They want to tap (trigger an action), have the program respond, and then make decisions about what they do next. They learn by doing, and this is best accomplished in an environment that lets them lead the exploration and discovery.

> *I have no special talents. I am only passionately curious.*[8]
> —Albert Einstein

Empower kids by giving them control. Whether careening a racecar through the streets of a digital city, affecting the lives of *Sims* characters, or tapping on a character to hear him laugh, a sense of control in a program is critical to the user's acceptance of a game or technology. Control is more than navigation. It can also be expressed in clear responses, whether audio or visual. Quick responses let the user know the program is listening to their actions. We hear a lot of talk about empowering kids, but when kids see a program that truly gives them control, they jump in and don't look back.

Give kids a challenge. Control by itself can be boring, but control in an interesting and challenging environment engages kids and impels them to explore. When a program can adjust to their level and push them as their skill increases, it's even better. This is why kids will stay engaged with games like *LumiKids Park*, *Winky Think Logic Puzzles* or *Off the Rails*, which offer progressive difficulty levels as players master previous puzzles. Continual challenge, just at the edge of known skills, keeps the experience fresh and interesting while also giving kids a sense of achievement and desire for further play.

The final observation of human behavior is:

Everybody Wants a Reaction

Humans want to be seen, heard, and listened to, and good feedback interaction delivers on a deeper emotional level. It's part of why favorite games get played over and over. Everyone wants a reaction to their action, and the quality of the reaction increases the amount of satisfaction from the interchange. Even if you lost the game, if the experience of playing it was enjoyable enough and you want to play again, it's a successful design.

Cause and effect. When you push a pencil, it moves. If you drop it, it makes a noise. If you talk to people, you expect them to pay attention and respond. This is the way the world works. Why shouldn't we expect the same from a computer? Everyone wants the computer to respond in ways that reflect their experiences of the real world. Kids not only *want* this, they *expect* it. If there is a doorknob in your design, tapping on it should open a door or offer a challenge to figure it out.

Everyone wants to be seen, heard, and acknowledged. Human–human interaction is the process of communication, of reciprocal actions between two (or more) people. Just as we have expectations of how physical objects should behave, we have expectations of how people should behave. When we are interacting with a computer, whether it's about communication, navigation, or manipulation, we are most comfortable when we get a reaction that resembles a response we might get from another human being. A responsive program, interface, or digital toy lets you know that the program is listening to you and is sensitive and receptive to input.

Creating Great Interfaces for Kids

Understanding the components that make up an effective interface is fundamental to designing products that are easy for children to access and use. Here are some tips on building a more typical graphic user interface (GUI) for kids. Some may seem overly simplistic, but it is surprising how often these basic rules are neglected. (For more on using sound effects in interface design, see Ch. 8, pp. 114–115.)

**The best interface is intuitively simple,
and the technology is invisible.**

Interface Design Basics

Greet the user. When kids or adults first come to your program, you don't know them and they don't know you. The goal is to get them interested, involved, and registered (if need be). Then you can begin to personalize communication.

Besides text, greetings can use direct address with audio, animation, and characters. It's important to greet players the way you would greet someone in person. Create a friendly, inviting, accessible, and engaging environment. Offer basic human communication, whether it's with audio or simple navigational links. The important thing is to involve the user quickly.

Beyond the greeting, ask the user to make a decision by creating a call to action; this gets them involved. Follow up with more calls to action and ways to participate that take the user deeper into the program.

Make it easy to use. Ease of use should be every designer's priority. During *every* step of the design and decision-making process, it is crucial to ask:

- What does the user want to do now with this software?

- How does this fit in with or affect the larger navigational and engineering system needed for delivery?

- What's the user experience going to be like?

The goal is to create an interface, toolset, and navigation paradigm that is accessible to the user. If you make navigation easy, users will pay attention to the good stuff, not your interface. To design effective navigation and interface:

- **Make it logical.** If it looks like a page-turn arrow, it should be one.

- **Be consistent.** Keep the navigational paradigm the same throughout the program. Be consistent in your use of graphic metaphors.

- **Make it work as users expect.** What makes sense to the designer who knows the program inside and out isn't necessarily naturally obvious to a new user. Kid user testing will confirm if you got it right; if not, kids will tell you. Listen to them.

- **Don't overthink things.** It is easy to imagine a variety of "What if?" situations that you might want to provide for, but this can quickly become confusing and cluttered. You probably only need one button to quit and close in each situation, and only one icon, not four with multiple options.

- **Don't have phantom buttons.** Every button should have a clear function and reaction.

Keep it simple. The best interfaces are intuitively simple, and the technology invisible. The actions of the user are as self-explanatory and obvious as possible. Navigation and participation should be obstacle-free and easily learned. Kids need to be able to guess how an interface works. Support them by making experimentation easy and by minimizing any visual confusion in the interface.

Remember, the simplest designs are often the most elegant.

Sometimes designers and programmers are so close to their own layouts and products that they can't see how ingrown their thinking has become. Kids are wonderful at pointing out that the emperor has no clothes. If you think you have an intuitive design, let some kids try it without any instruction; it can be incredibly enlightening.

Here is a great example of a simple interface from the *Nighty Night!* app by Fox and Sheep. The opening screen has many basic functions—the start icon is a well-lit large button in the center of the screen. (Many apps simply use a non-text start button shaped like a triangle pointing to the right.) The interface offers a variety of options for changing languages, adding new animals, or turning off the narration. It also shows other apps available from the publisher. This app is aimed at younger children as a bedtime story. The designers may have imagined that the app would be used as "lap-wear," with parents and children together. Either way, most kids could start the app on their own.

Nighty Night! app by Fox and Sheep.

Once in the app, there is no text. Voice-over invites kids to help put the animals to sleep. If no action is taken, a moving arrow appears, suggesting where to tap.

In children's products, the users can be readers, emerging readers, and non-readers, so interfaces need to match the target audience's abilities. By not including any text, an app will have a broader appeal. And with minimal voice-over, the product will be usable in all languages and cultures.

Give immediate positive feedback. Because kids learn best by doing, it's important to give immediate positive feedback to their actions. Positive means responsive, communicative sound effects and graphics—something that acknowledges the child's actions and achievements. Feedback lets them know how they are doing, and tells them how their actions are affecting the task at hand. It doesn't matter if they are fourteen or four, just give them a lot of immediate positive feedback, and let them go at it. Optimize the computer reaction time from click to response so that it feels instantaneous, like the real world.

There might be places where verbal feedback like, "Good job," or "That's great!" is appropriate, but in general it is better to shy away from those types of statements. Praise gets old fast, and research has shown that kids spend less time on task, rather than more, when programs constantly praise them.[9] Sound effects and small animations usually offer enough feedback reward to keep kids going as long the program itself is interesting.

Kids like BIG reactions to their actions. Kids, especially younger ones, like getting disproportionate response to their actions. Tapping on something and getting a big explosion or a fart, startling a character, can get kids laughing and repeatedly tapping for the fun of it. It's satisfying to have kid testers turn to you and say, "Look what I did!" Their sense of pride and accomplishment is a sign that your design has empowered and engaged them. Big isn't always better in terms of navigational interface, but it's helpful to remember that kids love big reactions.

Make clickability obvious. Kids are always looking for the next thing to do. Help them see their options by making it obvious what's tappable or clickable and what's not. Simple interface graphics offer clear, comprehensible visual messages. Graphics don't need to be particularly flashy. In fact, overly illustrated interface components can be confusing and distracting.

Get to the good stuff quickly. Kids have short attention spans. They will give you their attention for a while, but you must connect by delivering something early on that will capture their interest, entertain them, and deepen their involvement in your product. Avoid long lists of instructions, and make sure to deliver the good stuff before kids are three or four screens in. This is especially important with products for younger children, who have difficulty understanding delayed gratification. If the setup is too long or too difficult, or they have to wade out into the middle of a product before they can do something interesting, you may lose them before they ever get to see what's really cool. Older children are willing to learn the rules as long as *they know* it's going to let them do something really cool later, like drive a racing car or go on a quest to save the world.

Be consistent. Keep navigation and interaction functions consistent throughout the product. Users come with expectations for consistency. Interface is a tool for navigation, and kids expect it will be similar each time they visit or play a game. Honoring consistency may seem overly simplistic, but inconsistent interfaces feel Frankensteined together—kids find them frustrating and confusing.

Keep it responsive. All people hate to wait, and kids generally have shorter attention spans than adults. So design interactions with quick response times to meet kids' expectations. Kids will tolerate a fair amount of tapping around *if* the taps are meaningful—resulting in big actions or providing some form of clear feedback.

Designer's Note

In the early days of testing computer programs with younger kids, I found that if they didn't get a response within one second of clicking the mouse, they would click again, and again. They assumed the program was dead if it wasn't immediately responding. This is still true with newer technology, such as touch screens. Only now, they tap just once or twice, and if nothing happens right away, they often hit the home button.

Provide feedback for long waits. Kids expect a program to respond like a real person or like other things in the world. They touch (click on) something, and it reacts. It's that simple. If slower response times are unavoidable, a good design will let users know how long they will have to wait. Before status bars, a user was often left in a loading void, wondering if it was going to take a minute (or a year) to get to the next screen. Kids don't mind waiting (within reason) as long as

55%

Where you are in this book.

they know *how long* they have to wait. Status bars assure users that the program didn't die, that *something* is happening, and that they only need to wait as long as it takes to fill in the bar.

The most common alternative to a status bar is a simple cycle of little drawings that creates an animation at the cursor point. Cursor animation has been used since the early days of personal computers to let people know that the program is still alive and processing the user's last request. Animated cursors should only be used for very short waits. Often they are clocks or hourglasses that imply the passage of time and show that the program is thinking.

Here are some examples: Colored dots changing size in a circle are repeated and rotated to create movement. A paintbrush cursor from Ken and Karen Stillman's TypeStyler (a program for creative play with type) animates while you wait. The online world, *Poptropica,* uses both a status bar and a character Hula-Hoop animation cycle to keep kids engaged during page loads.

Poptropica by
Sandbox Networks.

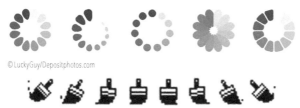

© LuckyGuy/Depositphotos.com

TypeStyler cursor, animation by Michelle Bushneff.

Designer's Note

One of the most common things we see in computer interfaces is the status animation. Beyond animating hourglasses and spinning balls, designers have created hundreds of funny or themed animations to keep us entertained. In the early days of CD-ROM games, the load between scenes was so long (7–10 seconds or more) that kids thought the computer had died. For one game, we created a little running man animation to let them know all was okay, and the game hadn't crashed. In testing, the kids would move the mouse to "run" the man all over the screen while they waited.

Keep instructions to a minimum. A good interface goes a long way toward eliminating the need for any directions. Kids want to steer their own learning, and they want to begin now! Don't make them wait, and don't give them a lot of instructions to remember. If directions are necessary, give quick, concise instructions in small portions, just at the point and moment when they are needed. Avoid providing long instructions in a big "speech" at the start of a program.

Since children's reading strengths vary greatly, from not at all to fluent, having text instructions for interface navigation may not be appropriate. If there is text, it should be in the form of short, clear sentences. If there are verbal instructions they also need to be very short and concise. Kids are ready to start the minute they begin, even while the instructions are being given, and often *only hear the last thing you say.*

Editors at the *Children's Technology Review* tell me they sometimes video record kids playing with new programs to see what the response is like. One thing they always count is how many times the child clicks or taps before they actually get to do something. On one recording, a child clicked 22 times, waiting for the instructions to be over before he could do anything. This represents a significant barrier to kid participation and acceptance.

Designer's Note

A continuing debate in children's software development is whether to make instructions interruptible or not. Generally, I think it is a good idea to make them interruptible. (How many times do you want to have to listen to the same directions?) A producer friend described his experience of watching a little girl test a new product. At one point, she leaned toward the screen and politely whispered to Dora the Explorer: "Would you please be quiet now?"

Allow tap/click-through of already heard instructions. Nobody, especially kids, wants to be held hostage by lengthy instructions or dragged through the same material in order to get to the good stuff. A sense of control is highly desired, and is what kids expect. If instructions can't be avoided, and especially if you are tracking the user, allow them to bypass the instruction via a tap or click-through, or just do it automatically for them once you know they have heard or seen it. Making a program interruptible can be tricky if the program is midway through an animation or sound file, but supporting the child's ability to steer trumps the "convenience" of forcing them to sit through something they have already absorbed

You don't have to tell kids how to do everything. Part of the fun for kids is to figure things out through exploration. Too much direction gets in the way of discovery. A well-designed game is easy to understand from just doing and experimenting. Studies have shown that kids are less interested in subjects—and stay on task for shorter periods—when concepts are completely predigested, and the do-it-yourself aspect is taken away.[10]

Make the technology invisible. When we speak of "technology," we usually mean tools that let people perform tasks faster or more efficiently. Phones, cars, computers, and microwaves are all tools. The more people you want to use a tool, the more accessible the interface needs to be. This is why **ease of use** is such a big deal. Good interface is invisible. Poorly designed interface interrupts flow, breaks concentration, and reminds you that you're using an object instead of an extension of yourself. But when the technology is invisible, you are engaged and immersed in your participation. With a great program, you become the activity itself, and the next thing you know, three hours have gone by!

Designer's Note

That zombie-like look that kids get while playing, the one that parents worry about sometimes, is usually just the child being totally immersed in the activity at hand. Imagine if that same level of interest and interaction could be consistently applied to deeper levels of traditional curriculum delivered in new ways. What kids and adults could teach themselves would (and hopefully will) jump astronomically.

Kids favor large fonts. Kids like bigger font sizes and bigger buttons because they are still developing motor skills. A study by the Software Usability Research Laboratory suggests that elementary students prefer larger 14-point font sizes and simpler fonts with clean, visible lines.[11] Remember that younger users are also beginning readers. Increased legibility means better character recognition and faster comprehension.

Provide the right tool for the job. Having full control during on-screen navigation means the interface makes sense and allows users to do what they want to do. If an interface is inconsistent in its use of navigational icons, users will get confused and frustrated, which leads to losing interest and looking for a better program. The tools should match the job, and the icons should match their functions.

Always offer a way back. A big part of learning comes through exploration and the discovery it brings. Kids are courageous, and they will navigate around just for the fun of it. To keep them from getting lost, *always* provide an easy way back. The most common practice (besides some version of a back button) is a "home" icon that is always visible to take you back to the main screen. More complex games may offer a map to help the user jump around. Also, remember to allow an easy way to quit or save a game if the game allows it.

In Wanderful's app, *Arthur's Teacher Trouble* by author Marc Brown, there are multiple modes of navigation: page turn icons in the lower corners, a *home* button to go back to the opening, a *world* icon in the upper left to instantly change languages, and a scrolling page navigator triggered by the book icon in the upper right corner. The second screen image illustrates the scrolling navigator menu, showing thumbnail pages of the storybook. (Note that some portion of the main characters have moved due to their ambient animation cycles. This subtle movement signals to the user that the scene is alive.)

Arthur's Teacher Trouble app by Wanderful.

Additionally, every item in the scene, including the characters and each individual word, is an active hotspot. If it looks tappable, it is.

Know your target user. The computer industry term "user" is almost always applied generically, but a specific user could be five or eighty-five, male or female, newbie or techie, reader or non-reader. It's critical to know *who* exactly will be using your interface. Knowing your audience is the best way to design an interface that speaks directly to them. Little kids need a "junior" interface, teens want something edgy, and parents have their own needs and expectations. This may seem obvious, but knowledge of the audience should inform every stage of design. Designers need to ask: Is the site parent- or kid-centric? What is the age range of the kid users? Are users coming for entertainment or for education? What level of expertise might they have?

Understand the input technology. Not all interactive platforms are the same, and neither are their input controllers. Each system and controller has its own special features and functions, and understanding them is the basis for creating a great interface. You are making the machine accessible, and each mode of interaction technology has its strengths, weaknesses, and quirks. Playing with competitors' input devices and understanding what you like and don't like in the experience they offer will help you build a set of interaction controls you really like. There is nothing wrong with being influenced by the good designs of others.

Touch screen interfaces. From keyboard and mouse to joy stick and console controller, humans have invented many input devices to effectively control computer interactions, but nothing is more natural to us than touch. Touch is primal to humans, and it has opened a lot of interesting interface interactions to designers. What can you let a child's finger become? A magnifying glass, knife, lawn mower, flashlight, paintbrush, laser, shovel, or anything you might imagine! In the PBS app *Martha Speaks Dog Party,* the child's finger becomes the dog's tongue as it eats up party treats.

Martha Speaks Dog Party
app by PBS Kids.

The most intuitive gestures are: tap, draw/move (finger down), swipe, drag (including slide).[12] Very young children's motor skills are still in development, and sometimes it is helpful to offer partial completion of some movements to ensure success. Also, very young children don't always get the idea of a tap and will put

their finger on the screen like they are pointing at something. Since most taps are composed of a finger-down and finger-up sequence, nothing happens when a young child parks their finger on the screen. This is not a problem unless the goal was to get a quick response, as in popping a bubble. (Please remember that ALL kids will expect bubbles and balloons on screen to be pop-able!) To accommodate very young users, allow the interaction to be triggered by only the finger-down action, thereby making it more immediate and realistic.

Less intuitive gestures include: pinch or spread (to resize), tilt/shake, flick/fling, double tap, and multitouch.[13] Multitouch is very interesting because, besides the use of multiple fingers for one child, it opens up the opportunity for two or more kids to play together simultaneously (a more natural play pattern than turn-taking for younger children). Another pattern children employ is rapid tapping. If there are satisfying consequences from the tapping, they will go at with great vigor. We used this to good effect in *Noodle Words* to shoot multiple animating words onto the screen at once.

Smart interfaces know the user. Smart interfaces include a system to track a user's actions, applying the gathered information to support the user's play preferences. A smart interface may also keep track of a user's past actions in order to tailor opportunities and options to the user's preferences. Limited tracking systems can be used for any player, and more robust systems can be developed when you have a more detailed user profile. A simple sign-in allows the design to be smarter, but signing in requires more effort on the part of the user. Some online games remember users, and sign-in is automatic, bringing users directly to their "stuff" or where they left off last time they played.

Easy to use is not always easy to make. It's easy for simple products to have simple interfaces, but often the most robust products are also perceptually simple and easy to use. An uncluttered interface allows users to focus on what they want or what they consider important. Google changed the way search sites looked by using a very simple and clean interface with kid-style primary colors on a white background as the interface for a vigorous search engine. This is a good example of a simple concept: if more people are going to use an interface, it needs to be simple and more accessible. It isn't always easy to build interfaces that are highly responsive or interruptible, but the benefits are worth the effort.

Reduce risks for accidental in-app purchases. Many apps today operate on the *freemium* model for sales and market penetration. The initial app is free, but for the complete and expanded experience, in-app purchases are required. Parents really dislike it when kids can easily incur additional expenses without their approval. To help reduce this issue, it is common practice for developers to have a separate parents' section, with any in-app purchases available there. Often, as shown in this example from Edoki Academy's *Crazy Gears* app, users solve a simple mathematical problem, and then they receive access to the parental area. Requiring the ability to read and follow a multiple finger swipe or solve a math problem are two of the most popular solutions. In some apps, parents have the ability to disable the in-app purchase feature altogether.

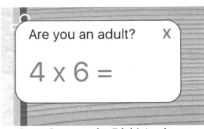

Crazy Gears app by Edoki Academy.

Tips on Designing Icons for Kids

Kids love the experience of tapping on an icon and having the interface react. It gives them a sense of power and joy. Icons are especially effective when clicking on them makes the computer do something kids expect it to do, instead of something bizarre or random. (This does not mean that kids don't like surprises. They do! They just don't like surprises from their navigation tools.) Good interface design creates clear icons that allow users to intuit where and how to do what they want to do, and to come back without getting lost in the process.

Use images that will make sense to kids. The younger the group you design for, the more literal an icon needs to be. Even though kids will construct a meaning and a link based on their experience of what happens when they tap on an icon, it's more intuitive when the image relates to something they can easily process and recognize.

Simple is better. Simpler designs are more accessible. Icons should be used mostly for navigation and jumping between functions and applications. Kids shouldn't have to work to recognize an icon or search for a place to click. In icon design, less is more.

Be consistent in style, size, and color. Create a consistent look and feel. Once kids know what one icon looks like, they will easily connect to the others. If it looks like an icon, it should be one.

Be consistent in icon placement. Once kids understand and learn the navigation rules of a place, they expect the rules to be consistent throughout that environment. This is especially true when designing for special needs children—changing the placement of navigation icons can easily throw them off.

Match the design style to the age and/or other identification of the group. Besides matching the icons to the distinctive theme of the environment, it's important to consider who will be navigating the space. Consider how your design matches who your users are or want to be. Nothing is more important than knowing your audience. For younger kids, this means matching their level of motor and other skills. Cute icons (even to the point of having eyes and faces) can be appealing to the young crowd as long as the cuteness factor doesn't obscure the function. For an older audience, be familiar with the "culture" of your target audience. Make style decisions that feel natural to the particular world, whether it is sports, nature, or fashion. If you do add a discordant element, do so purposefully. Fuzzy kittens will feel unexpected in a first-person shooter game; the player will wonder whether to save them or blow them up!

A user interface is like a joke. If you have to explain it, it's not that good.[14]

—Martin LeBlanc, CEO, Iconfinder

The User Relationship

If the interface is well designed, the computer activity becomes an extension of the user, and the child becomes deeply engaged. When this happens, the user becomes part of a *relationship* in which all the pieces, digital and human, work together. When everything is working together well, people don't notice the pieces, and nothing pulls them away from the flow. A good interface works because it meets *the player's* expectations of how it should work, and it allows them to become the activity itself.

I'll play it and tell you what it is later.[1]
—**Miles Davis, musician**

Connect with Kids

Interactivity Implies Relationship

Interactivity and play are active, not passive, endeavors. Interactivity implies an ongoing exchange, a combined or reciprocal action of two or more things that can affect each other and work together. In essence, designers create a relationship between the player and the design, whether with characters, interface, or opportunities for interaction. Beyond that, interactions create relationships with children, and the quality of these relationships affects kids' desire to listen, participate, and return for more.

> *Kids are not passive viewers, they are active users.*[2]
> —**Barbara Chase, Executive Producer, NoodleWorks Interactive**

Designer's Note

The idea of listening and partnering with kids while making a product for them may seem so obvious as to be dumb, but over and over, I meet with companies that spend hundreds of thousands of dollars on development without ever really finding out if it works for kids.

Make It Kid Friendly

The mindset of making something *for* kids is very different from the mindset of making something *with* kids. The more a design is simply a product *for* kids, the less interesting it usually is for them. This section is about the importance of the connection between you (the designer) and the kids; remember that you are designing *with* them. Can you create a relationship that invites and empowers, listens, and responds? Yes, you can. Here are a few specific tips.

Listen to and Partner with Kids

An imperative element of a real relationship is to listen. Listening to kids as you design is fundamentally important. What excites them? What are their interests? What characters, toys, and activities are they into? If you connect with them *where they are*, and honestly listen, you will be amazed at all they have to share with you. Include the input of kids in all stages of production as much as possible.

Connect with the Child's World

The world of children, especially younger children, is full of rich connections between all kinds of things. Kids haven't seen it all yet, and they are still building and imagining how they think it all fits together. In their world, there is room for magic. Their perspective is often very different than an adult's. Can you remember being that open? Can you remember wondering why things happen? Can you connect with what the world looks like for someone who's three-and-a-half feet tall? (For more discussion on children's developmental stages, see Ch. 10.)

Oversized Furniture © Ryan Somma, Flickr CC.

> *Most adults have forgotten how children are thinking.*[3]
>
> —Roald Dahl, children's author

Online "host" experts Cliff Figallo and Nancy Rhine authored several early books on building and maintaining online customer bases and communities. They offered these simple tips to creating successful online community experiences for adults:

1. Make people feel as if they are invited to a party.

2. Have others already there (at an event/chat) because no one wants to be the first one present.

3. Greet and orient people immediately as to how it works.

4. Provide some initial actions to engage guests.

5. Reward people for participating (through acknowledgment and feedback).

6. Empower users. Allow them to affect the community as a whole and share more of themselves.

> *Kids are discerning consumers, and at times are willing to tolerate a lot of bad media when they have limited choices. Companies are often too focused on the consumption of their products instead of the long-term play potential.*[4]
>
> —Scott Traylor, CEO, 360KID

Computers as Social Actors

Even though it runs counter to logic, people unconsciously accept the computer as a social actor and intuitively expect computer programs to react as humans do. The best human–computer interface mirrors good human–human interactions. As Stanford University researchers Byron Reeves and Clifford Nass point out in their book *The Media Equation: How People Treat Computers, Television, and New Media Like Real People and Places*:

> Because people have a strong positive bias toward social relationships and predictable environments, the more a media technology is consistent with social and physical rules, the more enjoyable the technology will be to use. Conforming to human expectations means that there is instant expertise just because we're human, and there are positive responses, including feelings of accomplishment, competence, and empowerment.[5]

The Media Equation theory presents the idea that people tend to respond to media as they would to another person, or to places and phenomena in the physical world, depending on prompts they receive from the media. The theory states that this type of reaction is automatic and unavoidable, and it happens more often than people realize. Reeves and Nass contend that, "Individuals' interactions with computers, television, and new media are fundamentally social and natural, just like interactions in real life."[6] That means that *being polite and cooperative* are attributes adults and children *look for* in a human–computer relationship. It also means that

The Media Equation book cover by Reeves & Nass, CSLI Publications, 1996.

we attribute personality characteristics (such as expertise, aggressiveness, humor, and even gender) to programs we interact with.

This is not abnormal behavior; this is universal, natural human social behavior. People know that computer-driven devices are made from wires, circuit boards, batteries, and glass in plastic cases, but they can still easily and unknowingly assign personality attributes to them. The computer is not doing it; people assign the human behaviors all on their own, and do it automatically and without conscious

Designer's Note

I believe that, ultimately, as we saw on *Star Trek*, computer–human interfaces in the future will use more verbal commands and interactions. With hand gestures showing up in a variety of games, and with fingers replacing the stylus, mouse, and keyboard, we are closer to the most basic ways humans have interacted with the natural world for millennia. I think we won't be satisfied until computer interface controls match our innate modes of communication and interaction.

effort. People are experts in relating to people, and *The Media Equation* maintains that designers should consider using basic human social interaction skills when designing new media for children or adults. It is human nature to create relationships with other "living" things.

What we are looking for in a human–computer interface is a human–human interface!

Understanding what adults and kids want in a satisfying human interaction is an important concept to keep in mind as you begin the design process.

Invitation by Agent

One of the best ways to invite participation is with an interface agent, a game-related character who talks directly to the user. An interface agent is usually a key character who helps kids navigate interface options and supports gameplay. Sometimes an agent is the person players play against. Agents are especially helpful for programs focused on prereaders and emerging readers since text instructions are lost on them. Interface agents look at the players and speak directly to them, usually using voice (and gesture) to elicit a response. Kids—especially young kids—respond enthusiastically to animated characters and are ready at the drop of a hat to imbue characters with human qualities.

Curious About Shapes and Colors app by Houghton Mifflin Harcourt.

In the Curious George app, *Curious About Shapes and Colors*, there are two agents: the Man in the Yellow Hat and George. The Man in the Yellow Hat offers instructions at the beginning of a screen or when tapped. George doesn't speak but reacts positively with different animations to the user's actions and inactions.

Interface Agents

Here are some tips about using agents as interface support and as active participants:

- **Agents facilitate action.** Beyond inviting participation, an agent supports kids in focusing on what to do. An agent is there to facilitate engagement in the program, not to draw a lot of attention to itself (unless the character *is* the game).

- **Social rules apply.** Interface agents are usually friendly and helpful. They are the "host," and they will normally introduce themselves and welcome kids to the program or activity. The agent might offer an action the kids can take to get started, or explain a little about how things work (e.g., "Click here to do this" or "Click over here to do that"). When the child makes a choice, the agent usually offers support by saying, "Okay," or, more collaboratively, "Yes, let's go!" If they are in a game that supports quitting, the agent might be a good host and wave good-bye, saying, "Good-bye, see you next time," or something similar.

- **Keep instructions short.** Since kids often only hear the last instruction given them, it's important for agents to keep instructions to a minimum. If more instructions are to come, share them as needed. Some programs offer a *help* button that calls the agent, who can then ask or answer questions related to the specific place in the game where the child is stuck. It's generally not good to have overly chatty agents. The agent should support what the child wants to do and help make it happen quickly.

- **Allow click-through instructions.** Instructions become boring and repetitive if they're given over and over. Designers have used a variety of tricks to alleviate this issue. One trick is to track the internal calendar or clock, and if the game has been run repeatedly for several days, the instructions can be truncated or dropped altogether. The most common trick is to allow kids to click out of or click through the instructions, and then have the character agree immediately with the course of action. (It's more fun for kids when the design fosters the illusion that the character is listening to them and supporting their choices.)

- **Give known users more personal attention.** Many children's programs these days don't have personal sign-ins or game names, but when they do (more likely in a paid virtual world), it is much easier for the agent to provide personal attention. Think of these agents as *smart* agents. A smart agent will

Designer's Note

Some years ago, longtime game designer Ernest Adams gave a lecture titled "Putting the Ghost in the Machine" to attendees at the 1998 Computer Game Developers Conference. Adams asked the audience to consider that, if poetry is the art of language, interactive entertainment is the art of artificial intelligence. Not to be confused with Artificial Intelligence (AI) of the kind imagined in science fiction movies and books, the **illusion** of artificial intelligence is the perceptual experience that someone on the other side of the screen is playing against or with you, which relies on the player's suspension of disbelief. In other words, the art of computer game design is to create the sense that someone is paying attention to your actions, reacting, or provoking a response from you. *It is the illusion that someone is there.* Over the years, this definition for the art form of interactive design has seeped more and more into my work.

know, for instance, if a child hasn't played a game for a while. When the child comes back to the game, the agent might say, "Hi, haven't seen you in two weeks, what'cha been doin'?" or "You were playing *Baby Battle Droids* last time I saw you—do you want to pick up where you left off?" The agent may even admire a painting the child did during the last visit. Knowing a specific user allows designers to track preferences, create specific responses as games progress, and invent other ways to enhance the illusion that the program is *paying attention* to the child.

- **Proactive agents set pacing.** A proactive agent is different from an interface agent, whose job is to facilitate the child getting somewhere and doing something. A proactive agent will do more than just respond to the user's actions. It may also drive the interaction forward and prompt the user to respond, or go on without them to facilitate a quick response. The agent creates a sense of pacing, and it lets the user know that someone (the game) is expecting a reaction; it challenges the player to interact. As computer interfaces strive to become more human in their response, creating believable, proactive agents is more and more important.

   Proactive pacing fosters the illusion that the character is paying attention to the kid's decisions and will respond the way a friend might. Proactive agents are especially good as someone to play against (as in a card game), or in learning environments where the simulation of a tutor may be advantageous.

Designer's Note

The game *YOU DON'T KNOW JACK* is a great example of a very proactive agent/ interface. It is all done in voice-over, as if you, the players, are contestants on a radio show. I set up one of my sons and a friend of his to play one day. As the program started, you could hear backstage noise, and the announcer said, "Welcome to *YOU DON'T KNOW JACK*: Contestant One, please sign in." The boys looked at each other, trying to decide who would go first, but before they could move, the announcer said something like, "Contestant One, you're taking too long. I will just put in 'Urinal Cakes' for your name." Then he said, "Contestant Two, please sign in." At this, my son's friend dived for the keyboard and put in his name, making my son "Urinal Cakes." The game itself hadn't even started yet, and already the proactive agent had created calls to action and a sense of pacing that couldn't be ignored! The whole game is designed so there are only a few limited choices or decisions to make at any time, and the pace is kept quick, lively, and as you can tell, humorous.

YOU DON'T KNOW JACK
by jackbox games.

Considering Special Needs Children

Good design is good design, and if the interface is clear and straightforward, most children with special needs will find it relatively accessible. There is no program that can replace a good teacher or loving parent, but well-designed computer programs can mirror and support some of the aspects of how a special education teacher might work with students. Here are some design qualities that computers can use to good effect:

- **Consistency.** Computer programs can be consistent in their response, making the same response hundreds of times in exactly the same way, reinforcing the experience and information. (This can be especially motivating if the response is delightful and entertaining to begin with.)

- **Individualized pacing.** Computer programs can allow the child to move at his or her own pace.

- **User control.** Computer programs can support a deeper sense of being in control by making something happen in response to the child's action.

Different abilities require different design considerations. When working with programs for the visually impaired, consider allowing adjustable font size or spoken commands and instructions. With motor skills impairments, design factors may include the size and placement of buttons or modes of input. In some cases, designers need to employ a combination of special considerations to empower users.

If you are asked to design products for special needs children, take a look at what they like already and what other kids with similar challenges enjoy. Also be sure to include these kids in your testing and development cycle.

Kris Moser, long time children's content designer and producer, knows first hand what works and doesn't with special needs children. She has graciously shared a few tips from her personal experience.

iStock.com/Christopher Futcher

iStock.com/Kim Gunkel

iStock.com/Susan Chiang

by Kris Moser

Considering Autism and Special Needs Kids

I am a children's software designer and the mother of a special needs child. I've been working with my daughter Anna on her iPad and evaluating various iPad apps, including games, interactive storybooks, and communication programs for kids with special needs. What I have learned with my daughter is that the most successful apps, games, and programs for special needs individuals have simple, clear and consistent interfaces.

How a special needs child accesses an interface is an important issue, and keeping the access simple is paramount. As an example, my daughter is interested in two interactive storybooks. Both storybooks allow the reader to turn pages with the iPad swipe movement, but one of them also has arrows at the bottom of the page that my daughter can touch to turn the page. The page swipe feature of the iPad is hard for my daughter to use because kids with special needs often have impaired fine motor skills. It took my daughter years of work with her occupational therapist to develop the ability to point and to use her index finger with enough force to use a touch screen. Touching an icon is far simpler and easier than understanding how to swipe a page, especially when there is no visual cue for page-turning and learning how to swipe the page. Designers forget who they may be excluding when they choose to implement features like the finger-swipe page-turning without including another option that allows access for special needs individuals.

Designers with a desire to create inclusive applications should consider adding visual cues. One game we tested has an animated hand outline demonstrating the swipe movement the first time the player needs to turn a page. This is very helpful. Adding page turn icons in addition would be a big plus for those with limited fine motor skills.

Accessibility is improving with the introduction of the iPad and other tablets. Old touch screens sometimes needed frequent recalibrations and were not as sensitive to touch as the iPad. Games and educational and communication software for the iPad are improving the lives of many special needs children. Many children with special needs cannot speak, and they rely on various communication devices by companies like Tobii DynaVox, Prentke Romich, and Saltillo. While these

---

About the Contributor

Kris Moser is a project director and producer of four award-winning interactive children's books, and producer of more than a dozen children's games and an educational theme park attraction. She has a twenty-six-year-old daughter with a rare neurological disorder who has been using touch screens since she was two.

companies have been working hard to serve the needs of kids who cannot speak, the devices are very expensive and have been difficult for parents and teachers to deal with. They are heavy, bulky, and often break down, requiring school districts or parents to repeatedly send the devices in for repairs. The iPad is much less expensive and offers Apple tech support. There are also a number of communication programs available for the iPad. At this time, many kids are using *Proloquo2go*, but there are several less expensive programs as well, including *TouchChat*, *OneVoice*, *iConverse* and *Voice4u*.

If you are looking for information about iPad or iPod touch apps that are good for special needs children, check the *Apps for Children with Special Needs* website (http://a4cwsn.com). The iPad is a magnet for typical kids. A child with special needs and an iPad has more opportunities to use her communication software to engage and connect with typical children. Accessible games that she can play with her typical friends can offer great new socialization opportunities.

A few interface tips. The ideal game provides customization options to fit the needs of the individual. While games and programs with limited scope and budget cannot realistically offer a lot of customization, some key issues can improve accessibility. Size, spacing, and placement of buttons, in particular, are critical.

- **Make it easy to press the right button.** Big, well-spaced buttons work best.

- **Make buttons easy to distinguish.** Make sure buttons or key elements have enough contrast and can be seen clearly.

- **Move frequently used buttons to the bottom of the screen.** Locate frequently used buttons where they can be reached easily. Typically, if the child will be pressing a button a lot, it's best to place it at the bottom of the screen. This is a real plus for those who are movement impaired.

- **Provide additional modes of help.** Offering additional audio and visual support, when possible, can be very helpful, especially if there have been multiple misses in a game. If there is a feature you know will be inaccessible to impaired kids, consider adding a button or cheat with an icon that may provide a similar experience for them. As an example, in a number of new iPad storybooks, there are pages where the child can tip the iPad to scatter leaves, cupcakes, candies, or other objects. Since severely impaired kids cannot do this, a button that scatters the objects in a burst effect would be a good addition. Then the child would be able to scatter the objects with one finger press. Design so these children can feel powerful!

When you create a successful interface design for a disabilities product, you don't simply create a solution that benefits users with disabilities, you create a solution that benefits everyone.[7]
—**Scott Traylor, CEO, 360KID**

Designer's Note

Computer games might not be the most obvious tool to consider using with special needs kids, but good design can help all kids to free their creative and emotional potential. Computers are good at being patient; they can wait almost endlessly for you to click or tap. Computers give consistent responses to actions, no matter how many times the action is repeated. In this respect, computers can mimic special education teachers and parents, who are well versed in giving patient, consistent positive reinforcement of actions performed at the child's own pace.

For designers of children's software, some of the best moments come when we receive feedback from parents about how their children benefit from our programs. Here is a story that taught me more about what my team and I had created.

Not long after Living Books had entered the marketplace, we began getting feedback from parents and teachers telling us about the effect of our titles on their children and students. At trade shows, we met parents who made a point to share their stories. One mother told us the story of her autistic daughter. One of three children, her daughter's impairment was severe enough that, at age ten, she didn't speak, although she had learned some sign language. The daughter was uncomfortable in crowded stores and malls because she had difficulty handling the social interaction and stimuli input of so many people.

Her parents tried to get her interested in the computer because they knew it was a great tool, but nothing seemed to work until she played with one of our early titles. As her parents tried to demonstrate its exploration environment, the child pushed her parents out of the way and began to click on what SHE wanted. They were amazed. She then spent hours every day, working her way through the pages of the interactive story, sometimes clicking on the same button over and over and over again.

After several weeks of independent play, she came to the breakfast table one morning and said, "I'm sorry," which was a line spoken by one of the characters in the story. Her parents nearly fell out of their chairs! She had been teaching herself to speak. Even her special education teachers noticed a change in her, remarking that she seemed to be "blossoming."

After some discussion they began to understand, in a general sense, that she was empowered to CONTROL something for the first time in her life. The ability of control to engage and empower is especially noticeable when you are working with disabled children. For kids who feel they don't have control of anything in their lives, not even their bodies or their emotions, having an environment where they can move at their own pace and click on things a hundred times if they want to is very empowering. THEY can steer. THEY can be in control. It can be healing.

It also seemed that this child was taking her experience of self-empowerment from the computer environment and mapping it onto the real world around her. She felt more in charge of her own experience, and so she was. The pressure to respond "appropriately" in social situations, something that is often hard for autistic kids to grasp, was lessened, and so was her own sense of being overwhelmed by circumstances from outside herself.

This story underscores, in an extreme case, how important that sense of being in control is for all kids. The word "empowering" is often used to describe kids' software, but when a program actually delivers empowerment, everyone is amazed by the creativity of the kids who use it and make it their own.

Characters, Avatars, and Agents

It's no secret that kids love animated characters, but designing great characters for interactive environments and apps comes with its own set of tricks and considerations. Knowing how and where characters will be used is critical in the initial design phases. This chapter looks at why and how we relate to characters, and it provides tips on designing characters children will love.

Animation can explain whatever the mind of man can conceive.[1]
— Walt Disney

Character Development

Animated characters are important players in most interactive products for children. What makes children care about characters? As a designer, how can you create characters that are both memorable and easy for kids to identify with? To better understand character design, it helps to look at how humans communicate with each other.

Our first language is body language; we all use non-verbal communication. Long before humans developed the mental capacity for verbal language, they communicated primarily in the form of expressive movements. The interesting thing is that we still do, often without realizing it. We can guess how a cartoon character is feeling based on the same visual cues we have learned from people, and sometimes from other animals.

We respond to gestures with ... an elaborate secret code that is written nowhere, known by none, and understood by all.[2]
—**Edward Sapir, anthropologist and linguist**

Animators Are Actors

To *animate* is to bring to life, and to be a good animator is to understand how an actor moves in order to bring the illusion of life to characters. Understanding body language is fundamental to being a good communicator, actor, dancer, or character creator. Our bodies speak a language of internal states that our conscious mind does not completely comprehend but that our unconscious mind does. Many gestures are understood across cultures because they speak to the universal dialect of our shared human nature.

Deafness has left me acutely aware of both the duplicity that language is capable of and the many expressions the body cannot hide.[3]
—**Terry Galloway, actress, writer, and performance artist**

Body Language Shows the Mental/ Emotional State of a Character

Body language tells us a lot about both the physical states and the internal emotional and mental dialogues of characters. Are they happy, sad, proud, frightened, confident, energized, or tired? Are they trying to pretend they are something other than what they are? Are they hiding their feelings? Part of the basic training of animators is to learn to draw characters in such a way that others can interpret and project emotional states *onto* the characters.

> *As the tongue speaketh to the eares, so doeth the gesture speake to the eyes.*[4]
>
> —**King James I, from** *Basilikon Doron*

A classic animation training exercise is to imagine human movement and emotion in a drawing of a sack of flour. The exercise keeps the same volume or size in different poses, but it is also a wonderful way of looking at how we project meaning onto a character or object guided only by subtle changes in form and expression.

Did you interpret those shapes as emotional states and human-like actions? You are not alone. It is very human to look for ourselves, even in objects. We create stories and interpretations based on archetypal body postures we have learned from watching each other. We are all naturally students of human movement. When we see human postures echoed by inanimate objects, we easily suspend reason and jump into enjoying the fantasy of a talking teapot or a lovesick robot. Children, especially younger children, are ready and willing to believe animated characters are breathing, feeling beings that can have human interactions. They are even willing to believe that these characters "see" the kids themselves through the screen!

I speak two languages, Body and English.[5]

—**Mae West, actress**

About face. If humans are good at reading body language, we are *spectacular* at reading other human faces, especially the eyes. We study faces from birth, and soon become experts in the nuances of expression. We can learn incredible amounts of information from watching faces.

The eyes of men converse as much as their tongues, with the advantage that the ocular dialect needs no dictionary, but is understood the world over.[6]
—**Ralph Waldo Emerson, poet**

Photo by Jessica Pyska.

Making faces. In creating characters, we distill real emotions into a set of expressions that are used like shorthand to let us know the essence of what the characters are feeling. Body language supports what the face communicates.

Cartoon characters' faces and body positions (if visible), are usually exaggerated in order to show the changing moods and reactions clearly. (Sometimes this is pushed to extremes for comic effect.)

Enculescu Marian Vladut/Shutterstock.com

We Identify More with Simple Characters

Not only is it easier to "read" the state of simply drawn characters, it is also more likely that we will use imagination to project our own emotions onto them. Cartoonist Scott McCloud offers a brilliant explanation of the phenomenon in his book *Understanding Comics: The Invisible Art*, a book every student of interactive design should read.

Thanks to Scott for explaining this concept in such an entertaining way. This same idea is used regularly in Japanese anime character design. The lead characters' faces (the ones you identify with) are drawn simply, and villains have more detail (less easy to identify with). This information comes into play when designing engaging characters, especially avatars, which become extensions of the users and players of a game or interface.

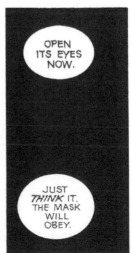

ALL SET? GOOD.

NOW, *SMILE.*

C'MON, NOBODY'S LOOKING.

GOOD. NOW, WHAT *CHANGED* WHEN YOU SMILED? WHAT DID YOU SEE?

NOTHING, RIGHT.

YET, YOU *KNOW* YOU SMILED! NOT JUST BECAUSE YOU FELT YOUR CHEEKS COMPRESS OR THE CRINKLING AROUND YOUR EYES!

YOU *KNOW* YOU SMILED BECAUSE YOU TRUSTED THIS MASK CALLED YOUR FACE TO *RESPOND!*

BUT THE FACE YOU SEE IN YOUR *MIND* IS NOT THE SAME AS *OTHERS* SEE!

WHEN TWO PEOPLE INTERACT, THEY USUALLY LOOK DIRECTLY *AT* ONE ANOTHER, SEEING THEIR PARTNER'S FEATURES IN *VIVID DETAIL.*

EACH ONE *ALSO* SUSTAINS A CONSTANT AWARENESS OF HIS OR HER *OWN* FACE, BUT *THIS* MIND-PICTURE IS NOT NEARLY SO VIVID; JUST A SKETCHY ARRANGEMENT...A SENSE OF SHAPE... A SENSE OF *GENERAL PLACEMENT.*

SOMETHING AS *SIMPLE* AND AS *BASIC*--

--AS A *CARTOON.*

THUS, WHEN YOU LOOK AT A PHOTO OR REALISTIC DRAWING OF A FACE--

--YOU SEE IT AS THE FACE OF *ANOTHER.*

BUT WHEN YOU ENTER THE WORLD OF THE *CARTOON*--

-- YOU SEE *YOURSELF.*

I BELIEVE THIS IS THE *PRIMARY CAUSE* OF OUR CHILDHOOD FASCINATION WITH *CARTOONS,* THOUGH OTHER FACTORS SUCH AS *UNIVERSAL IDENTIFICATION, SIMPLICITY* AND THE *CHILDLIKE FEATURES* OF MANY CARTOON CHARACTERS ALSO PLAY A PART.

THE CARTOON IS A *VACUUM* INTO WHICH OUR *IDENTITY* AND *AWARENESS* ARE PULLED...

...AN *EMPTY SHELL* THAT WE INHABIT WHICH *ENABLES* US TO TRAVEL IN *ANOTHER REALM.*

WE DON'T JUST *OBSERVE* THE CARTOON, WE *BECOME* IT!

THAT'S WHY I DECIDED TO *DRAW* MYSELF IN SUCH A SIMPLE *STYLE.*

WOULD YOU HAVE *LISTENED* TO ME IF I LOOKED LIKE *THIS* ??

I *DOUBT* IT! YOU WOULD HAVE BEEN FAR TOO AWARE OF THE *MESSENGER* TO FULLY RECEIVE THE *MESSAGE!*

APART FROM WHAT LITTLE I TOLD YOU ABOUT MYSELF IN *CHAPTER ONE,* I'M PRACTICALLY A *BLANK SLATE!*

IT WOULD NEVER EVEN *OCCUR* TO YOU TO WONDER WHAT MY *POLITICS* ARE, OR WHAT I HAD FOR *LUNCH* OR WHERE I GOT THIS *SILLY OUTFIT!*

I'M JUST A LITTLE VOICE INSIDE YOUR *HEAD.*

A *CONCEPT.*

YOU GIVE ME LIFE BY READING THIS BOOK AND BY *"FILLING UP"* THIS VERY *ICONIC* (CARTOONY) *FORM.*

WHO I AM IS IRRELEVANT. I'M JUST A LITTLE PIECE OF *YOU.*

BUT IF WHO I AM MATTERS *LESS,* MAYBE WHAT I *SAY* WILL MATTER *MORE.*

THAT'S THE *THEORY,* ANYWAY.

SO FAR, WE'VE ONLY DISCUSSED *FACES,* BUT THE PHENOMENON OF *NON-VISUAL SELF-AWARENESS* CAN, TO A *LESSER DEGREE,* STILL APPLY TO OUR *WHOLE BODIES.* AFTER ALL, DO WE NEED TO *SEE* OUR HANDS TO KNOW WHAT THEY'RE DOING?

THERE'S *MORE,* TOO!

Character Design

Agents and Avatars

Two of the most important character types in children's software are agents and avatars. What exactly are these, and why are they so important?

Agents. Animated agents are present in most children's programs. They might be highly branded characters from a TV show or children's book, or they could be original characters designed to complement a title's theme (like underwater or outer space). Either way, agents offer the child an active personality to connect with and guide them. An agent's function is to support navigation, gameplay, and story line, and to offer instructions, hints, and directions to keep the player on-track and involved. When an agent is also interesting or funny, it's an added bonus.

In StoryToys' *Leonardo's Cat* the agent is Leonardo da Vinci himself. In the beginning, he sets up the story line for the game, and thereafter advises the user from a window in the corner, always available for advice, pointers, and some humor. The team at StoryToys, led by designer Emmet O'Neill, decided to go for star power in the voice-over, and they were lucky enough to get actor Patrick Stewart for the voice of Leonardo.

Leonardo's Cat app by StoryToys.

Agents can be hosts who welcome newbies and show them around, or they can add a deeper level of role-playing to an adventure. In virtual worlds, the role of agents is often to populate the world with possibilities for interaction. In adventure and massively multiplayer online role-playing games (MMORPGs), an important part of the quest is talking to characters you meet along the way; this is how you learn things, get advice, and move forward. Agents stay in character and react differently than avatars might.

Avatars. One of the most crucial features of a virtual world for kids is the design of the avatars, the characters who represent the child within the world. An avatar is an extension of the child in the virtual space. A well-designed avatar facilitates kids' participation by letting them easily create, craft, and personalize an identity through character options, clothing, and props.

Here are some tips on creating great agent and avatar characters for kids.

Character Considerations

Some questions to ask before you begin the design process are: How is your character going to be used? Is it going to be an agent who talks directly to the child, or a helper who communicates with the child's avatar? Does it need a lot of full body animation as an avatar might, or will it merely peek its head into the scene from offscreen to communicate with the user?

The characters you design will have a relationship with the user, either directly through the screen or as participants in a story line. As children age, the kinds of characters they choose (and the actions of the characters) change along with them. As you design, it's important to focus test with the target audience to get their impression of the characters' attributes and personalities. Obviously, you want characters your audience understands and wants to have a relationship with.

Calvin, of Bill Watterson's *Calvin and Hobbes* comic strip, is one of my favorite characters. Although Calvin was never animated (Bill prefers to keep *Calvin and Hobbes* in pure comic form), he is a well designed character for storytelling. Calvin is two heads tall, a proportion we consider cute. Having a large head also focuses our attention on facial expressions. Hobbes, not shown here, is three heads tall or more, since he is slightly older and more worldly than Calvin. This cartoon is also a perfect example of a well told joke because the punchline in frame four shows Calvin using the umbrella to play in an unexpected way. The strip is also done without text, allowing it to be universally understood.

Designer's Note

While working for several companies building products for five- to nine-year-olds, I had to perform focus tests of potential logos. During testing, the kids overwhelmingly responded positively to *any* logo that had a character. Kids in the five to nine age group have a strong fascination with characters. Tweens still like characters, but they are getting more and more interested in other kids their age.

Characters come in families. If you are designing for a world with multiple avatars, you will need to develop "families" of characters: characters that exhibit a similar look and feel even when they are drawn with different proportions and details. The more characters in a world, the greater the opportunity for a wide range of personalities and interactions. Multiple personalities facilitate opportunities for drama and storytelling. (Keep in mind that multiple characters can also add *dramatically* to animation costs and possibly production time.)

Agents must appeal to the target age. Know your audience. You need the right characters to engage kids' interest. All kids can like cute characters, but as children get older (at around eight years of age, kids sometimes feel the need to distance themselves from "little kid" stuff), the appeal of edgier, taller, more angular, and weird characters starts to grow.

Main agents tend to be "normal" characters. Main interface agents, or the "host" agents, tend to be relatively normal characters without a lot of emotional baggage. A "normal" persona makes the character stable, accessible, and safe. This is more important for younger audiences than older, but an agent's function is to help the user play the game and move forward. The agent should be on the player's side in terms of playing successfully and winning. *Normal* sometimes translates as *boring*. Don't make your main characters too perfect. They need a few personality flaws to feel real.

An example of a good "normal" character is Mickey Mouse, who is friendly and accepting—an ideal host and guide. In contrast, Donald Duck loses his temper, is often triggered emotionally, and gets offended easily. Donald's personality, in general, would make a terrible guide for young children, but he's an entertaining and dramatic character for other purposes.

Designer's Note

Donald Duck was the main host in Disney's Academy Award–nominated featurette *Donald in Mathmagic Land* in 1959. This was one of the best educational uses for animation I have ever seen, and I learned a lot from it as a kid. Donald was (for him) relatively well behaved in this film.

Where else might this character go? When designing a new character (or world of characters), it never hurts to consider other venues the character might migrate to. Besides being designed for efficient interactive production, might they ever go to TV, appear in children's books, or get made into a plush toy at a later date? Considering possible migrations to other media, or designing for transmedia at the beginning, may inform or influence design decisions. (For more on transmedia, see Ch. 17, pp. 285–289.)

What makes successful agents. Agents need to give very simple instructions. Guides work best when they give kids small bursts of information as needed to help children make action decisions: "Tap over here if you want the story read to you," "Tap over *here* if you want to play inside the story." Directions must be simple and straightforward. Kids often only hear the last thing said to them. A long string of instructions is just laziness and wishful thinking on the part of designers.

Agents also need to have a consistent level of presence. Kids feel tricked when a highly animated character welcomes them into the game and then that same character never shows up again or is wooden (cheaply animated) and not as charming later in the program. The kids end up feeling baited into playing by an agent who didn't really show up to interact with them.

Does the character fit within technological constraints? Creating a character that looks cool is great, but if it can't dance or move about easily (and economically), this could limit the character to behaving like an on-screen zombie (which might be your goal in a zombie game, but otherwise looks terrible). Be clear on what

1985   1988   1990   1991   1996   2002   2007   2013

Mario character shown over time, Nintendo.

you want your characters to be able to do, and be sure that the programming staff agrees that your ideas are viable. More than a few companies have had to revamp the size and style of their characters after they ran a load test on a low-end target system and watched the characters struggle to animate in slow jerky motions. You can see in this image how Nintendo's Mario character progressively changed as the hardware advanced.

Characters have personality. What about characters makes them characters? Perfectly behaved characters, although pleasant, are usually boring. They have no vices, fears, quirks, issues, or overwhelming interests. They never get in trouble, they never get upset, they never do the wrong thing, and they don't feel very real to kids. Perfect equals predictable. Kids like characters that, like themselves, aren't perfect. They like characters who are motivated by desire or interest, or whose simple goal they can easily understand. George of *Curious George* is curious (a favorite trait with kids); SpongeBob SquarePants is fun-loving, quirky, and hyperactive; Super Mario is an active protagonist who relies on jumping, stomping, and other kinetic powers. Good characters draw kids in; boring, perfectly behaved characters don't hold their interest for long.

SpongeBob SquarePants, Nickelodeon.

How Many Heads Tall?

Avatars and agents, like all illustrated characters, are measured in "heads." A head is not a fixed size, but rather a module used for determining proportion. The average man or woman is about 7 heads tall, a proportion noted by Greek sculptor Polykleitos, who was sculpting circa 450–420 B.C.[7] Sculptors and artists kept adding a little bit of height to natural proportions because it made their figures look more impressive. By the time of Michelangelo (1475–1564), the "perfect" proportion had reached 8.5–9 heads tall.[8] Because of how this proportion was regularly used, it became known as the heroic proportion. It is the basis for most comic book heroes today, from Superman to Batman.

Human proportions. Children change proportions rapidly as they grow. Newborn babies are approximately 4 heads long, which means that their heads are a quarter of the length of their bodies. By the time children reach age four, they will be about 5 heads tall. At eight years old, they will be close to 6 heads, and by twelve years old they will be approximately 7.5 heads tall, the head-to-height ratio they will be through most of their lives. What this means is that our heads grow smaller in proportion to our bodies as we age.

Animated characters are shorter. Animated and cartoon characters tend to be more compressed than real people, meaning they are seldom drawn with the 7.5 heads proportion. Baby characters (and *everything cute*), are usually 2–3 heads tall. Dora, the Minions, the characters from *Peanuts*, SpongeBob SquarePants, Mario, and Bart and Lisa Simpson are all 2–3 heads tall (or bananas, if you're a Minion).

Dora the Explorer by Nickelodeon.

The Minions, from *Despicable Me* franchise, Universal Pictures.

When creating avatars, agents, and kid characters in general, the smaller the body in relation to the head, the younger the character will seem. As characters develop more adult proportions (smaller head in relation to body), they seem older.

Simple is best. As we learned from Scott McCloud's comic, simply drawn characters tend to work best for a variety of reasons. The first reason is emotional: it's easier to project onto a simple character than a detailed one. A detailed character is *defined* by its details, but the simple character is defined by what the user puts into it via imagination. This is a real case of *less* can be *more*. The second reason is economic: simpler and smaller characters are easier and cheaper to animate than larger and more detailed ones.

Designer's Note

For a consummate example of simple and cute, look at what Sanrio Company, Ltd. did to create their appealingly cute character, Hello Kitty®:

- Big head (√)

- Two to three heads tall (√)

- Baby animal references—kitten ears, whiskers (√)

- Dressed in core colors with bow (√)

- Simple design (√)

Hello Kitty has two small ovals for eyes (which seldom change), another small oval for a nose, and no visible mouth or expressions. This character is a blank slate whose *personality is projected onto it by the viewer*. Seemingly, there is not much there, and yet Sanrio has created a huge international merchandising brand, including restaurants and electronics, all based on the simplest and cutest of designs. I am not suggesting that all avatars and characters for young kids should look like this; Sanrio used character and color preferences that young girls like, and they distilled those qualities down to something at the most basic level. This concept works because it speaks to the interest of the target age and gender, but also leaves a lot of room for the kids to create their own connection and meaning.

Size matters. Kids have some preferences in size. In general, younger kids tend to favor shorter (which often means "cuter") characters. Most kids live in a world where everyone older is taller, and they perceive taller characters as being older. Following their natural affinity for people their own age, kids will often initially pick avatars that are kid-sized like them. Short and cute can hold kids' interest until they get close to their tweens. Older kids and teens gravitate toward taller, more adult-looking characters as they begin to see themselves as older, but this is true only if the character has got the moves they want. Kids value the functionality of their characters more than height.

Size matters from the animation perspective as well. Smaller (and therefore often simpler) characters are easier and cheaper to animate than larger, more detailed ones. They also use less computing power, allowing a community to have more active citizens on screen at once.

Sameness creates equality. Although most adult virtual worlds offer a wide variety of character shapes and sizes, in most kids' worlds, there is a sameness of size and proportion. This is not a bad thing to kids. In many popular children's worlds, like *Club Penguin* and *Pixie Hollow*, the kid is either a penguin or a pixie, and that's it. Every character is about the same size. This is done in large part for animation reusability, but it also creates equality for everyone entering the world. Being mostly the same helps to level the social environment and immediately integrates kids with the world's other players. Even so, expressing uniqueness is important to kids of all ages, and differentiation created through colorization, clothing, props, and names adds a lot to a child's ownership of their avatar.

© Disney

Cuteness matters. Kids, especially younger ones, have a fondness for cute, and the attraction to cute tends to last longer for girls. Puppies are cuter than dogs, kittens are cuter than cats, and a baby *anything* is cuter than teenagers because of compressed body size. Cute is why plush animals are popular with young kids, and it works for avatars as well, at least until kids get older. With some characters, it may also activate caregiving instincts.

Design characters for action and interaction. Consider right from the beginning what kinds of interactions and actions you want your characters to be able to perform. Are they simple intro hosts, or do they participate in the games as well? Will you see their bodies or just their heads peeking in to give advice and support? Will they be able to dance, run, jump, or sit? What makes your characters special? Do they spend a lot of time in direct address with the user? Understanding the possible actions your agents or avatars may need to perform will have a major influence on how you design them.

Cut the Rope app by ZeptoLab.

Om Nom is the main character in the *Cut the Rope* app series by ZeptoLab. He was designed to not take up a lot of room on a phone screen, to be cute (inviting), to be expressive so everyone would want to feed him, and to be easy to animate. He doesn't walk or run much; he mostly eats. He is basically 1 head tall and all mouth. I asked kids about Om Nom when the character first came out, and they all liked him. At this point, ZeptoLab has a series of apps, cartoons, and merchandise using Om Nom. This is a reminder that it's good to consider what other transmedia platforms your character might end up on.

Cut the Rope app by ZeptoLab.

A great example of simple but effective animation, Om Nom is always moving. This is good because the rest of the screen is completely still until the user acts. When waiting in ambient mode he stretches up and down (middle frame), simulating breathing, occasionally wiggling his left and right foot for variety.

In order to get your attention, Om Nom occasionally waves to the user (first frame). From time to time he reminds us to feed him. If the candy food gets close but misses, we get the sad face (third frame).

When food is close, the open mouth is ready to receive it. If the food is well placed, it is swallowed, and there is a chew and swallow sequence (second and third frames). As this demonstrates, Om Nom is a perfect level of character design for his function inside the product. Not too much and not too little, with a lot of personality and a simple but satisfying payoff.

Design avatars with their outfits and props in mind. Clothes, hairstyles, and props are the main visual differentiators between many avatars. Design your avatar characters with all the assorted props, outfits, and fashion extensions you think they might ever need. Consider how clothing looks from the side, back, or 3/4 view, or from above. How does your animation playback software track and use the different props and pieces? It saves a lot of effort to have some idea of how new props might be used over time instead of having to make fixes after you discover issues well into the process.

Defining a Character's Personality

It is important to consider who your characters are, so you understand how they might react in a given situation. How do they feel about themselves? What are they good at? What are they afraid of? How old, big, or smart are they? What are the most important aspects of their personalities? You have to know the answers to these questions in order to know what it is you want from your actors during production.

Stereotyping. It is a natural fact, although sometimes unfair, that humans tend to stereotype people and/or anything we can anthropomorphically project as having human traits. We instinctually stereotype animal voices in cartoons based on some set of qualities we believe that critter has. Cows and sheep are intellectually slow, owls are wise, crabs are crabby, rats and weasels are untrustworthy, dogs are friendly, and so on.

We have natural expectations about what we think a character should sound like. Should the Tortoise talk s-s-s-s-l-l-l-l-o-o-o-o-w-w-w-w and the Hare talk *fast!*? In our minds, probably yes. Stereotypes are a kind of shorthand that tells the audience a lot about a character quickly. Preconceived expectations and prejudices are often applied automatically. The fun then can come from playing personality traits against the stereotype. Imagine a big powerful gorilla who freaks out at a little spider, or has a high squeaky voice.

CHAPTER

15

Supporting Play Patterns

Understanding and supporting children's natural play patterns is at the heart of creating award-winning games and activities for children. They are the glue that makes interactions magical. This chapter takes a further look at how to find and recognize play patterns, and it also provides tips on supporting them to create magical and engaging experiences.

It is a happy talent to know how to play.[1]
—**Ralph Waldo Emerson, poet**

Chapter 1 defined *play* and listed categories of play, including Active Body, Mastery, Social, Object, Creative, and Make-Believe. All play patterns fall into these groups, and sometimes into several at once. Chapter 2 talked about how to create invitations for play, and it described seven play pattern examples. Now that we are deeper into the book, let's revisit that information and talk more about recognizing and using patterns when you see them.

Play Patterns

Play patterns are so natural, they are almost invisible. We make games out of what we do, how we speak, even how we walk, and in the course of a day, we constantly slide in and out of different forms of play (whether we notice it or not). For children, play is the quintessential engine for learning about their world, and they go for it with great gusto and enthusiasm. They don't need to be taught how to play; they simply engage in it effortlessly and naturally whenever the opportunity arises.

You can interpret play patterns in many ways, and it's easy to break them down into finer subcategories depending on one's viewpoint (educator, toy designer, marketer, parent, etc.). But for a children's designer, the most important skill to develop and practice is learning to follow your own experience and discover play patterns yourself.

How to Find Play Patterns

When you begin a new project, how do you identify what play patterns you want to include in your design goals? Here are some ideas for doing just that:

Visit Toy Stores

Games and toys in stores come already segregated into good working play pattern categories, and many products have been around since before you were born. Go to any large or small toy store and look at the different areas and genres of games and activities available—all with age range suggestions. You'll see products catering to Active Body Play (physical skill with all manner of sports equipment), Role-Play (costumes, dolls, and action figures), Social Play (strategy, board, and card games, among others), Creative Play, and everything in-between.

Review Favorite Popular Games

What games do you like? Can you identify why you like them? What are the most engaging parts for you? What sparks your curiosity or gets your attention, and *why*? Understanding what is truly engaging in a game or activity is not always obvious. You might think it is the particular challenge of the game, but it might only be fun when you play it with friends, making it more social. Deconstructing classic legacy games with known audience appeal can lead you to new insights about why they have survived the test of time.

Watch Kids Play

This is the surefire best way to have some insight into play patterns. Whether they are using a touch screen, playing on a sandy beach, or just messing with an empty cardboard box, watch what children do as they explore, create, and invent. This will inform your understanding more than almost anything else you could do. It is especially instructive if you are watching them play with one of your prototypes! (For more on the value of testing with kids, see Ch. 20.)

Keep in mind that play isn't always just about games. Play includes creative exploration and simple skill attainment. It only needs to be interesting enough to pique a desire for investigation or challenging enough to inspire further engagement and exploration.

Designer's Note

When I was about eleven, my father helped me build a little duck cage for some ducklings we were given. A five-year-old boy who lived across the street saw us with tools and was immediately hovering around us wanting to do something to help. After a while my father took a 2" × 4" block of wood, a hammer, and a big nail. He started it with a whack or two, then told the kid, "Put this [the nail] in there [the wood]." The boy was delighted, and he started to work on trying to get that big nail into the wood for the next hour. He was totally engaged and focused in the **game** of hitting the nail with the goal of driving it into the wood. When he was finished (a couple of bent nails later), so were we, and we thanked him for his  help. He was delighted (and later went on to become a builder). The level of appropriate physical challenge with a clear goal was perfect for his stage, and it matched his desire to be helpful.

Children's software designers often get into this business because they were inspired by their own children's emerging interests and interactions with the world as they learned. A child's amazing curiosity and thirst for understanding is palpable, and they want to try everything. They remind adults about the magic way the world looked when we were young, and it's that perspective that reopens our adult view of all the creative possibilities we have been missing.

©AsierRomeroCarballo/Depositphotos.com

"It's not a bug, it's a feature!" Sometimes in the process of software development, the programmer's code follows its own logic and produces an unexpected result. If it is something that hangs up the program, slows response time down, or is otherwise a hassle, we call it a "bug." Occasionally, the code will do something serendipitous and unexpected that leads to new functionality and play patterns. Sometimes, this new "functionality" isn't hideously bad, just interestingly weird, and the kids like playing with it. When this happens, keep—and even enhance—the "bug." (The programmers like to claim, often with bravado, "It's not a bug, it's a feature!" Or, as Pee-wee Herman famously said after a show-off bicycle trick went terribly awry in the movie *Pee-wee's Big Adventure,* "I meant to do that!!!")

Designer's Note

In the early days of interactive content, our programming team had just implemented our first audio features that allowed kids to click on individual words in a storybook and get a highlighted word with a quick audio response. Even though the words were short, we noticed that if you clicked again really quickly, it started the word over again (i.e., clicking rapidly on the word "baby" sounded like "ba-ba-ba-baby"). The programmers and consulting educators were concerned that the word wasn't played out fully, and hence learning wasn't served. But when we watched how the kids really used the program, we saw that clicking quickly allowed them to "rap" and be more playful with the words in the sentence. It gave the kids more control, not less, and allowed them to hear the first syllable clearly. So we kept it as a feature, not a "bug." We even used the "rap" feature during product demos; it always got a laugh. Kids will play with things you never expect, and their curiosity is a gift they offer about intuitive play patterns—if you pay attention.

iStock.com/Courtney Weittenhiller

Using Play Patterns

Integrating, supporting, and enhancing play patterns will make any product better. When you are clear about the goal, it's easy to let go of things that aren't necessary and instead focus on the good stuff. It also helps to keep your project on budget and on schedule.

If frogs were digital buttons, what kind of reaction could you create to be as delightful and surprising as the frog? Keep in mind that, in looking to use a play pattern, you are supporting these three questions a child asks once their curiosity and attention are engaged:

1. **What's that?**

2. **What does it do?**

3. **What can I do with it?**

"What can I do with it?" is just the starting point. If you scaffold the learning and consecutively add more things to do as the challenge increases, kids will grow with the title as far as you can take them. They will continue to ask the question. "*Now*, what can I do with it?"

Deliver answers to these questions with play patterns that support further inquiry, give quick, positive feedback, and deepen skill development; then you will create products that children of all ages love to use (no matter what the topic).

The journey is the reward.[2]

—Steve Jobs

Games

What Is a Game?

Games have many properties, but in general games are a structured form of play in which there are rules and goals. Clear rules are very important because games are defined by their rule sets. Rules determine the order of turns and when each player can be active. Rules outline the responsibilities, roles, and rights of each player, including the meta-goal for the game. All games, by their nature, come with specific challenges and strategies for winning.

Challenge

Challenge, a main property of games, comes from following the rules in pursuit of the goal. Chapter 1 explains how curiosity leads to exploration and greater play as a child gains confidence. The key takeaway for children's activity designers is that a toy or game *must* offer rewards for curiosity and opportunities for deeper exploration.

This desire to get better and to achieve new levels of skilled play seems to be ingrained in the human spirit, and we love the deep sense of engagement that comes from a good (and perceived as doable) challenge. It is not the drive to attain that motivates us, but rather that sense of a doable challenge and immersion in the experience of executing it.

Challenge and mastery are key components in most games. Think of any game you enjoy playing, and I'll bet there is a healthy level of challenge involved. Finding the right level of challenge and control is fundamental to user engagement. If it's too easy, they get bored. If it's too hard, they get frustrated and go do something else. Remember that Chapter 9 described Mihaly Csikszentmihalyi's theory of flow? (You did read all that theory, didn't you?) It comes into play here, too. An optimum flow experience can be achieved by raising the level of challenge once the player has a comfortable skill level and feels in control of gameplay. Control without challenge is boring; challenge without some control is frustrating. (For more on creating optimum engagement, see Ch. 9, pp. 140–141.)

Chance, an unknown or random factor that may arbitrarily be inserted into a game, adds a level of enhanced challenge to gameplay. It causes players to continually review and generate new play strategies. It has the ability to reverse fortunes and take games in unexpected directions. Common devices for chance are: specialty cards, dice rolls, spinners, random acts of nature (*SimCity*), and the action of other players (including interactive agents and the game itself in digital environments).

In games like *Uno* or *Othello*, a big part of the fun is how a player's actions significantly change the situation, move by move, fostering new consideration of possible outcomes, risks, and strategies.

Designer's Note

In *Uno* the goal is to get rid of all your cards. The ability to mess with other players, who may be close to winning, comes in the form of randomly drawn (chance) cards that can seriously effect their gameplay and ability to win. The dreaded "Draw Four" allows the player to change the color in play and make the next player draw four cards.

Strategy

Strategy is a Problem Solving Play pattern that uses available resources to achieve the goal within the constraints of the rules. Challenge stimulates what I call the human strategy response system. People naturally like solving problems. We have been evolving our problem-solving skills for millennia, and those competitive skills are probably a big part of why we are the dominant (for better or worse) species on the planet. When a player is challenged, whether in life or in a game, they begin an internal simulation using the specifics of the situation and decision-tree thinking to create a hypothesis for multiple possible solutions. This pattern happens so instinctively we barely notice it, whether we are looking for a parking place or dreaming up the next move to beat someone at *Go Fish*. Good games present us with problems to solve, and we do so via strategy. Without a goal or problem to solve, it is not a game: it is an activity.

Two main modes of Strategy Play are real-time and turn-based. Turn-based strategy games proceed one player at a time in turn. Real-time strategy games are based on ongoing continuous gameplay where all players' actions (including the computer's) drive in-the-moment strategic decisions. Both are valid, but turn-based leaves more time for planning.

Good questions for designers to ask in terms of challenge and problem solving are:

- What problems am I asking players to solve?

- Are the goals clear?

- Do I offer more than one way to solve a problem?

- Do new problems arise out of solving previous ones?

- What is the right level of challenge?

- What can I do to stimulate thinking and curiosity?

- Do the gains of solving a level apply to solving bigger problems later?

Challenge and subsequent strategies for winning change depending on the game genre and play pattern, but they *are partners in every game played*.

Educational Games

Any game genre can be considered educational, but the degree of learning depends on the level of educational content the game contains *and* whether information was actually imparted and absorbed. One of the wonderful things about interactive content is that kids are drawn to it as long as the gameplay is inviting and fun. The trick is to offer some real content inside, or even as a by-product of, engaging play. A game is no longer play if the child is made to do it; then it is work.

Educational games that combine intrinsic motivation with real content are the true winners. Games like Scot Osterweil and Chris Hancock's original *Zoombinis* series, and any of Daren Carstens' titles (such as *Sums Stacker* or *Attributes*) are great examples. One of my favorite examples of intrinsic motivation is found in Daren's *Splat Go Round* game in his *Math Doodles* app, where you must determine the proper percentage of the circle in relation to the fly in order to "splat!" the fly. The game moves fast, and kids are motivated to learn quickly which angular position of the swatter will swat the fly. It's fun and educational.

Math Doodles app by Carstens Studios.

Reader Bee and the Story Tree app by Learning Circle Kids.

Sometimes it's helpful to approach educational material from a new point of view. Ann McCormick, Ph.D., a founder of The Learning Company (maker of *Reader Rabbit* and other learning titles) has spent years helping children and adults learn how to read. Over time, she realized that the use of an innovative new keyboard might help foster exploration and learning in new ways. Her recent app series, *Reader Bee*, uses this new interface which allows children to quickly and easily select related letter/sound combinations to form simple common words.

More Examples of Play Patterns

Identify, Collect, Sort, and Match

Although the roots of this may come from our hunter-gatherer ancestors, there is still a simple pleasure in identifying, collecting, sorting, and matching things—or Classification Play. Kids like to collect and sort, and the level of discrimination and detailed categorization deepens as they age. Additionally, visual challenges like the "Hidden Pictures" puzzles in *Highlights* magazine, *Where's Waldo?* and *I Spy*, along with classic jigsaw puzzles, speak to our love of searching for special or matching pieces. Classic card games (*Go Fish*, *Old Maid*, *Crazy Eights*, *Solitaire*, *Uno*) take the Collecting Play and Sorting Play patterns and add Strategy Play (How will I use my cards?) and Social Play (What will the other player do?) to increase the variables of play (including chance) to add challenge and fun.

Collecting takes many forms. It may be collecting "moves" for your avatar, finding hidden interactive "Easter egg" buttons in a scene, or collecting special items in order to complete a quest in an adventure game. If there is something to collect (and hopefully a place to keep the collection), children will do it.

Designer's Note

Some years ago, I was testing the puzzle area in MarcoPolo Learning's *MarcoPolo Ocean* app with my four-year-old grandson. The app incorporates a classic shape

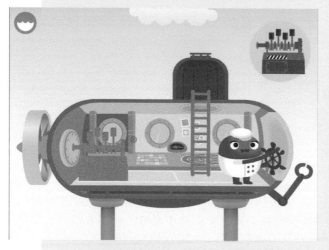

recognition activity where you are given only one piece at a time and, having been given several places it might go, must figure out where to place it. In this puzzle game, you are building things, like an orca or a submarine. As you place each piece, its name is spoken, and the piece then comes alive with a small animation. The Puzzle Play pattern is easy enough that my grandson could figure it out quickly, and interesting enough that he wanted to keep placing more pieces. It worked better than I expected, and, after finishing several—sometimes long—puzzles, he turned to me and said invitingly, "Well, what shall we build now?" He was totally engaged. It wasn't just a puzzle to him; there was also the endgame of creating something, and he was the builder. This is a great example of how compelling a game can be when multiple play patterns are engaged at once.

Kids like visual recognition games because they are very easy to get started. Players don't need to have prior knowledge, math skills, or special vocabulary. As a result, there is a prevalence of visual games. This leaves an opportunity for designers to create games that address language and math skills that do require some prior knowledge. The trick is to identify where the child's skills are when they begin, and then offer just the right level of challenge. Next, you need a path for expanding skills or vocabulary that is as entertaining as it is educational. The best games have a mildly addictive nature and are fast, fun, and challenging as well as easy to begin playing. (For tips on creating fast-moving simple games, see Ch. 3, pp. 44–47.)

What-If Play

During mental problem solving, we ask and experiment with "What if?" statements. Problem solving is something humans do naturally, so it makes good sense that we create games that allow us to solve a wide variety of engaging problems. Creating strategics and solving problems are a major part of skill advancement and are found in every game. What-If Play, because of its reliance on reasoning skills, becomes more noticeably used and important as children get older, especially over seven years of age. This popular play pattern has led to the *strategy games* genre.

Social Play

Although many games can be played against the computer, playing with others is a big part of the fun of many games. The banter, the trading, the unexpected rise and fall of fortunes—and especially how everyone reacts—makes it engaging. To enhance a card or board game played against a computer program, you can spice up the play experience dramatically by adding animated characters with jovial and reactive personalities for the kids to play against. (See Cards with Tutter example, Ch 3, p. 36.)

Character skins in *Minecraft* by Mojang.

Designer's Note

Over the years, every children's designer/producer has felt compelled (or been compelled!) to do at least one version of the most over-used game for kids, *Concentration*. When companies come to me all excited about the "fun" things they have at their site for kids, and then show me some version of *Concentration*, I know they haven't put enough effort into the design of their activities.

> ### Designer's Note
>
> There is a huge difference in many games developed after the Internet became widely available. Before the Internet, all computer games involved the user playing against the program (or a friend playing on the same console). But after the Internet, opportunities arose to play against real people anywhere in the world. *The Sims* is a good example of a game that was designed (originally as a CD-ROM-delivered app) as a single-player game, and *Minecraft* is an example of person-to-person Internet-enabled play. Because of safety issues, Internet-enabled play is not the best for younger children. But considering where we are headed with the ability to play with anyone anywhere, I think all designers should consider how their designs might be enhanced or played with Internet connectivity.

Hunting and Shooting

Based on our human instinct to search, hunt, and gather is the **Seek-and-Find Play** pattern. Once a survival skill, this pattern continues in a variety of forms in everything from simple arcade-style games to major adult first-person shooter games like *Halo* or *Call of Duty*. There is something powerful about getting a big reaction on the screen from a small action by the user, and if that bigger action creates further reactions, all the better. The skill in this form of Challenge Play is to find and hit targets without being hit yourself. This pattern is so powerful a draw that even educational game companies have used it in learning activities to keep kids involved.

> ### Designer's Note
>
> The shooting pattern is ubiquitous, especially for males. Gene Portwood and Lauren Elliot, the creators of the original *Where in the World is Carmen San Diego?* game, knew this: they once created a trigger-happy game titled *If It Moves, Shoot It!*
>
> Davidson & Associates—an educationally focused company—also found themselves with a surprise hit when they created *Math Blaster*, an arcade-style math game. Besides being a shooting-alien-ships game, it had a high scores ranking—and this drove the competition in the classroom even further.

Action Games

Hunting and shooting falls under a larger category of action games, which includes vehicle racing, two-person combat, sports, and platform titles like Nintendo's Mario franchise. These games are mostly about hand–eye skill development (sometimes called "twitch-games") in fast-paced environments with running, jumping, climbing, and avoiding (or blowing away) the bad guys. The fast-paced action and need to continually act and react creates a sense of immediacy and engagement that is popular with certain segments of kids (primarily tweens and teens).

Quests and Adventure Games

Involving multiple play patterns at once, adventure games and quests are popular with many kids. Adventure games take the player on a journey through an explorative environment of connected rooms, territories, and levels. Usually, there is a goal-based, linear story line, and you (as the on-screen protagonist) travel through the game world, interact with characters, and collect an inventory of objects needed to solve various puzzles along the way. The concept of players keeping a persistent earned inventory (a collection of all the items they've gathered along the way) began in adventure games, and is now also widely used in virtual worlds.

Adventure games are not one-way, leveled games, where players seldom go backwards. Instead, they allow players to continuously explore (even areas previously examined) where they might find new items or where they now have "keys" to unlock doors they couldn't open before. The idea that someone thinks you (the child/player) are just the person to solve the puzzle and *save the world* is a very empowering and engaging premise. (For more on inventories, see Ch. 16, p. 266.)

Virtual and Augmented Reality

Virtual reality is an immersive experience in a totally different world, time, or place with the aid of a headset. In contrast, augmented reality brings a view of an alternate world into the real world via a headset with goggles or a camera on a tablet/phone. Items, characters, and events from the game experience are overlaid onto the view screen.

In the world of digital gameplay, there is always new technology just around the corner; some technologies are more disruptive to the marketplace than others. As designers, it is always important to keep an eye out for emerging markets and new opportunities to create innovative children's products. As I write this book, waves of opportunity in the form of virtual and augmented reality are on the horizon.

A recent great example of augmented reality for both children and adults is the *Pokémon GO* app by The Pokémon Company and Niantic. Whether players are at home or on vacation, this game encourages them to go outside on quests to catch Pokémon in the wild, something *Pokémon* players have dreamed of doing for years. Nearby real-world landmarks are mapped onto gyms and Pokéstops, and rare legendaries are located in special locations around the world, such as Kyoto and Vatican City. These unique gameplay features help create new ways to explore outside and get some exercise. But, as the game says, be careful of traffic, and watch where you are going!

Barbara Chase catching a Squirtle, photo taken with *Pokémon GO* by Niantic.

Role-Play

Although role-playing games (RPGs) emerged in popular culture as board games with the *Dungeons & Dragons* craze of the late 1970s, they have evolved online to become massively multiplayer online role-playing games (MMORPGs). Role-Play is part of Make-Believe Play, and it is an opportunity for kids to try on archetypes and explore different worldviews. It happens with dolls and action figures, in virtual worlds with avatars, and any time there is an opportunity for kids to express themselves and pretend to be what they are not.

Sims and God Games

Simulations, or "sims" for short, are computer games that try to emulate an experience in the real world. For instance, flight simulators let you fly a virtual plane and thereby teach you something about how to fly. One of the first big sim titles for kids was *SimCity*, where the player becomes the city manager/planner. It was designed by Will Wright, who has gone on to develop many other sim titles, including the hugely popular *The Sims*.

Simulations are sometimes called "God games" because the users control, and often build, the world in which animate and inanimate things come to life. There are sims that mimic everything from an ant colony (*SimAnt*) or life with a pet (*Nintendogs + Cats*, *The Sims 3: Pets*) to towns (*SimTown*), planets (*SimEarth*), and alien evolution (*Spore*). Will Wright, the designer of Sims, considers his games "toys" that teach through play. Eight- and nine-year-olds have amazing discussions about what factors they have been dealing with while running their own city. How many adults consider issues of city asset management and the benefits and pitfalls of raising taxes?

These games are a great example of What-If Play, where the play pattern is all about exploration and experimentation: "If I do this, what will happen?" If the result is

surprising, or at least interesting, then users feel empowered and want to explore further. Because sims have built-in systems that keep them evolving or changing in relationship to parameters set up by the user, they are like wonderful science experiments; the user doesn't know with certainty what will happen, and must stay tuned to see the outcome.

SimCity Social online game by Electronic Arts.

Storytelling by itself is a play pattern. Children and adults alike spontaneously make up stories all the time to make sense of our lives and the world around us. Little children can tell impromptu stories to themselves at the drop of a hat. It's a kind of self-entertainment, and it extemporaneously appears. Jason Krogh and the team at Sago Sago created *Doodlecast*, a charming program for young children that allows them to record their voice as they draw. The stories they tell are often adorable, and the results can be shared with family members.

Maker–Builder–Creator Play

Kids love to make things, from sandcastles to sandwiches, from drawings to dwellings in *Minecraft*. They love the inventive and creative process of putting things together to make something new. This play pattern shows up spontaneously in adults as well as children; all anyone needs is the opportunity. If there is a pile of dominoes and a flat surface, people will begin fiddling, arranging, and building with them while waiting or talking. Our human hands gravitate to Object Play, and this holds true in all digital experiences as well. Here are some tips to support Maker-Builder-Creator Play:

Always Have Plenty of "Stuff"

This is true of all creativity and building programs. Whether the tools are digital blocks, stickers, parts, or paint effects, always give kids enough interesting pieces to work with so they are motivated to begin experimentation and exploration.

Faces iMake app by iMagine Machine Israel.

> *To invent, you need a good imagination and a pile of junk.*[3]
>
> —Thomas Edison

Whimsical stamps and magic brushes, as shown in this example from the app *Faces iMake*, can add delight to paint programs. Decorating artwork is as much fun and as important as making it, so include hearts, sparkles, stars, and more for kids to play with. A wide variety of stamp/sticker options allows for greater expression. If you have libraries of character and object stamps, along with a few backgrounds, kids will tell stories and create "parties" of characters by collage.

Kids also use object libraries/collections to decorate their virtual rooms and create outfits for their avatars. Provide lots of choices; the outcome from recombining existing graphical props can feel very unique. Keep in mind that not all sets of stickers or blocks need to be available at first; more can be added over time to bring renewed interest or reflect seasonal themes.

The iPad—touch tablets and mobile phones in general—ushered in a new generation of tools with easily accessible cameras, allowing children to become authors, stop-motion animators, and movie producers like never before. But kids often need a nudge to get started, some sort of challenge to get them solving problems. Using the device camera to collect a set of colors in the world around them (Curious Hat's *Color Vacuum*) or patterns to apply to outfits they are designing (Toca Boca's *Toca Tailor*), gives them a reason to begin hunting with the camera.

Toca Tailor app by Toca Boca.

Offer a Clear Path to Begin

Story starters are always a good idea. Whether writing, drawing, or building, a blank screen can leave anyone hesitant about how to begin. So, to help give kids' creativity a push, offer them a point of departure. In other words, give kids a "starter" to get them playing, and they will jump in and add their own creativity. A textual example is *Mad Libs*, where the user fills in blanks in already-created sentences. The resulting stories can be quite silly. In a paint program, offer part of a picture and ask them to create the rest. Place a character in a car, waving, but only draw the top half of the character and the wheels and then invite the kids to draw the car any way they wish. Or invite them to draw their favorite animal or food.

Designer's Note

Apps that support the Maker-Builder-Creator Play pattern come in all sizes. An example of a small app we made while I was at JuniorNet is *Pizza Maker*, which we

made using a paint program engine underneath. Kids were given the basic "pie" with sauce, and then they could add (via pictured food stamps and special condiment brushes) various items to build a pizza. Besides the traditional toppings, we included worms and other strange things. The whipped cream (brush) was a favorite because of the sound effect it made while decorating your pizza. The incorrect and unusual toppings were a big hit with kids, but we also found that many adults in our company made pizzas and posted them in their work areas. This game was for a children's online network, and we easily changed it so that, during some months, it was *Sundae Maker*, *Sandwich Maker*, or whatever, all with some rather quirky ingredients added for fun.

Allow Kids to Expressively Delete Their Work

One of the most well-liked and copied inventions of the Kid Pix painting program, besides the fact that the drawing tools all had cool sound effects, was the ability to "explode" and otherwise creatively delete a picture with dramatic visual and sound effects. This has been very popular with kids.

Kid Pix by Software MacKiev.

Allow Kids to Save, Print, and Share Their Masterpieces

There is a sense of accomplishment and ownership from creating something. Kids can generate tons of content while they are playing, and they like to share it with friends and family. Today, the opportunities to share creative expressions are more numerous than ever before. Printing creates a physical reminder of this moment in time, and the results often end up on the family art gallery, the refrigerator.

Fridge Art

Play patterns show up spontaneously, and often unexpectedly, and it is critically important to notice when they do. In testing, you know you have found one when the kids forget you are there and play repeatedly with whatever has caught their attention. Follow the kids' lead. Observe their play preferences. That is what matters. If you are not learning from the kids, then anything you build is likely to miss its true play potential.

When we play, we are engaged in the purest expression of our humanity, the truest expression of our individuality. Is it any wonder that often the times we feel most alive, those that make up our best memories, are moments of play?[4]

—**Stuart Brown, founder, National Institute for Play**

Community and Virtual Worlds

Building communities and virtual worlds for kids is like building and stocking a bird feeder. As a designer, you are creating something kids want, but also making sure the environment is inviting, nourishing, and safe. You want kids to discover new things during each visit so they will want to come back to play more. If the kids have a good time, they will tell their friends. If they learn something, and stay safe, their parents will support their participation. This chapter takes a closer look at all the components needed to bring everything together to create a cohesive and sustainably enjoyable experience.

Never doubt that a small group of thoughtful committed citizens can change the world; indeed, it's the only thing that ever has.[1]
—Margaret Mead, cultural anthropologist

Creating Community for Kids

What is the difference between a community and a virtual world, and why are these two things so important to designing for kids? Although a virtual world may have aspects of community, not all communities are virtual worlds. Virtual worlds have avatars, environments to explore, and the ability to see other children's avatars active in the space. Communities gather around common interests (often creative activities) and offer kids ways to see and share each other's creations. Communities and virtual worlds go beyond the simple human–computer interaction and become interactive playgrounds that involve other users. Because there have been many books on community and virtual worlds, the focus of this chapter is on kid-specific considerations.

Community is about connecting. Community, to children, means *other kids are there.* Kids want to connect with and hang out with other kids. Communities and virtual worlds offer playgrounds where kids can be with their peers, and they can choose to connect or not in a shared and open environment. When designing a community environment or a virtual world, designers and producers should start by reviewing similar services. This may provide ideas for improving on a site or better understanding what works well already. Design should focus on the best ways for kids to safely interact, share, communicate, and connect with each other.

Community-oriented virtual worlds have several distinctly different features from most traditional games. First, they have various levels of social space where kids can meet and play kid-to-kid rather than kid-to-computer. And because there is a visual place to meet, kids need a visual presence, an avatar, to explore the world, and to be seen. As they interact in the world they earn, win, collect, barter for, and create virtual things—and then bring them all back to their "room." Kids breathe life into their virtual personas and become invested in their collections, their virtual decorating, and being with and being seen by their friends. This combination of personalization, persistent identity, personal place, and the ability to connect, share and play with friends from afar are some of the hallmarks of great virtual worlds and communities for kids.

The goal of community. Community offers opportunities to be seen and heard. It offers a public space as well as a personal space. A good creative community has a variety of ways for kids to participate: various levels of chat, games, voting, posting artwork, poems, or stories, and sharing items they have made.

Socialization and self-expression are critical goals in community design. For designers, the goal isn't to get kids to stay online as much as possible, but to enrich their lives while they interact with others. Kids will stay of their own accord if their social, creative, and emotional needs are met.

Chat for Kids

Chat rooms or chat-ability features are very popular with kids because they can connect with other kids. It's hard to call a virtual space a "community" if you can't talk or communicate with anyone else.

Chat needs differ by age group. The younger the group, the less chat matters; the older the group, the more it matters. Since the youngest kids are pre- and emerging readers, their language and social skills are limited. As they ascend the age and developmental ladder, communicating peer-to-peer, along with the quality of what is communicated, becomes much more important. By the time kids hit the tweens, they have begun to care about and use chat-related services and features. By the time they are teens, chatting and texting are an integral part of their lives.

Child safety. Child safety equals parental confidence. Keeping your community world safe and open at the same time is a balancing act that designers and producers are always tweaking to keep appropriate. A great virtual world provides a safe environment without revealing anything about kids' real-world selves. This is where community begins. Specific legal language for online child safety is spelled out in the Children's Online Privacy Protection Act, or COPPA, at www.coppa.org.

Chat is moving toward voice. For many kids, the desire to communicate with known friends while playing online has driven them to become independent of in-service text chats. Kids simply communicate by voice over telephone, Skype, Ventrillo, Zoom, TeamSpeak, and other technologies while they play. Navigating, negotiating, playing games, and even battling evil is more fun when done collaboratively in real time. Kids often play online with friends they see regularly. Instead of trying to find an opportunity to get together physically, they can play virtually from home any time they are free. Adult games like *World of Warcraft*, where co-operative team play is the only way to overcome certain monsters and challenges, broke ground for this kind of play, which has distinct psychological and sociological characteristics.

Varieties of Chat

Despite the move toward voice chat, text chat is still the predominant form of communication in online games and communities for children. When designing a community for kids, it's essential to know the pros and cons of different types of chat and to choose what is best suited to—and most safe for—your target demographic. Whatever the drawbacks or technical hassles of chat interfaces, they are a necessary part of communities and an integral part of the growth and development of socialization in kids as they play.

Text chat falls into four main categories: canned, filtered, monitored, and selected open chat (chat with an approved buddy list). In the effort to find a balance between communicative function and safety, there has been a lot of mixing, matching, and borrowing of features from each of the groups below. *All* versions of chat require some monitoring; the more open chat is, the more monitoring is required. (During a conversation in 2007, *Club Penguin's* CEO estimated that seventy of their one hundred staff were involved in monitoring.[2])

Canned chat. Canned chat, or closed chat, means that all dialogue is preset by the service, and kids are not allowed to type in their own words. The sets of preselected words and phrases are usually available from a pull-down menu. For example, in the online world *Animal Jam* by National Geographic Kids, there are two chat menus. The first is a collection of emoticons, and the second a list of several phrases.

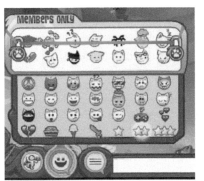

Chat icons, *Animal Jam* by WildWorks.

Chat text, *Animal Jam.*

One of the benefits of canned chat is it can be pretranslated into other languages so the same communication, limited though it may be, can be global. Canned chat also needs less monitoring than the other forms. Another benefit is that pre-readers can more easily memorize what canned chat phrases mean, and then use them without any reading assistance. The downside of closed or canned chat systems is the communication limitations. Older kids will quickly migrate to another game site where they can connect more spontaneously and meaningfully with their friends.

Some virtual world creators, knowing kids want more communication, allow them to "earn" or buy additional words. For instance, in Disney's early virtual world *Toontown Online*, a player could only use the limited number of phrases and words in the approved *Toontown* dictionary. But players could add additional phrases to their menu by purchasing them from the in-game "Cattlelog" (*Toontown Online* was a world of animated animals). This same strategy is used in other worlds, where kids earn or buy extra moves, pets, or clothes for their avatar character, thereby allowing them to be more expressive, communicative, and cool.

Filtered chat. Filtered chat is constructed from canned chat phrases and additional purchased words, or it is made up of words directly typed into a chat text box. The "filter" means all typed words are run through something like a spell-check program that searches for inappropriate words and phrases. When the filter finds something inappropriate, it may let the user know a word is not valid by highlighting it in red (meaning it won't be allowed and must be replaced with something more suitable before sending). Chat filtering programs also look for invented spellings, word–number combinations, and phonetic words—all created by kids over the years to get around the rules. (The list is often quite extensive.)

Some kids (especially boys) are relentless in their efforts to swear or be acknowledged for their language. One site that recognized this issue automatically substituted sweeter words into the "tough" kid sentences, e.g., "What the *flower* is going on here?" This completely changed the intended effect. In *Club Penguin*, when a comment is blocked, the user who made the comment sees it, but other users are unaware it was ever made.

Another benefit of filtered chat is that it allows for a much greater level of connection and socialization while also doing its best to keep communication "clean" and civilized. Filtered chat is sometimes used in conjunction with a canned word and phrase list, which helps the poor spellers and may speed up communication. The downside is that it tends to need monitoring, and the filtering program needs to be maintained, updated, and adjusted.

It is also common for a service to offer several levels of chat and to allow parents to determine safety settings and what is appropriate for their child.

Monitoring Chat

All chat has some degree of monitoring. Shortly after the phenomenon of chat rooms arose, monitored chat developed as a way of keeping some level of civility and fairness. Monitored chat used to mean that a moderator was present or at least nearby. Now it means multiple levels of monitoring are occurring.

"Foreground" monitoring is when monitors have a visual presence. Like a room monitor or hall monitor in school, they make themselves available to anyone needing assistance. Foreground monitors tend to hang out in high traffic areas and are available to answer questions and help maintain a pleasant chat environment.

"Background" monitoring is when monitors are not noticeably present, but are tracking multiple ongoing discussions. Background monitoring tends to be more fun for the kids because they feel they are alone with their friends and can be themselves. Background monitoring is successful at catching problem users who let their guard down because they have forgotten there are adults in the background monitoring their actions.

"Filtering" (described previously) is a form of monitoring. Monitors cannot be everywhere at once and, with the high-volume popularity of chat, filter software can monitor all conversations at once and automatically "censor" or replace words before they are broadcast. Filtering is not, however, good at actually connecting with problem kids and resolving situations.

Buddy lists (selected open chat). Buddy lists developed out of kids' desire to connect with their real best friends while playing online. Since "buddies" are other children that parents already know, it's easier for parents to agree to open chat with them. Some services offer direct parental control on the selection and approval of buddies. Buddy lists are called a variety of names inside sites, including "Real Friends," "True Friends," or simply "Buds." Sharing an interactive experience is always better with friends, and some kids will run multiple conversations at once while exploring, and playing.

Features to Consider for Chat Interface

Buddy list. There are a variety of ways to track friends, and sometimes it's beneficial to have multiple lists because some "buddies" are casual acquaintances (communicated with through canned chat), and some are real friends. There might also be other affiliated groups (clans, tribes, teams, etc.) kids want to track inside a world. Buddy lists are usually kept in an easily accessed place. The most successful services let kids know when their real friends are online, and sometimes even what they are doing at the moment.

Image	Description	Code
	Chocolate Ice Cream Cone	E+W
	Strawberry Ice Cream Cone	E+1
	Pizza	E+Z
	Cake	E+K
	Popcorn	E+O
	Coffee	E+C

© Disney

Emoticons. Emoticons have become a regular part of communication. Having emoticons (animated or not) adds a level of expression and fun to any level of chat. A unique set of emoticons linked to the style and characters can add a lot of charm to your site. *Club Penguin* even has a wiki page showing all of them.[3]

Image	Description	Code
	Laughing Face	E+1
	Happy Face	E+2
	Indifferent Face	E+3
	Sad Face	E+4
	Surprised Face	E+5
	Poking Out Tongue Face	E+6
	Winking Face	E+7
	Sick Face	E+8
	Mad Face	E+9
	Upset Face	E+0
	Meh Face	E+U

© Disney

Avatar moves. Being able to make an avatar gesture might not be considered a piece of classic chat interface, but in a virtual world,

Move options, *Animal Jam.*

avatars face each other, and conversations may take place in a speech bubble above their heads. Allowing and planning for a variety of avatar moves, such as those shown on the left from *Animal Jam*, adds a fun level of creativity to communication. Most avatars have at least a hand wave and some basic dance moves. In some services, acquiring new moves is one of the perks of gathering points and winning games. This area of development has a lot of room for growth, humor, and expression.

Chat rules. Many of the rules that kids (and parents) agree to when joining a kids' online world have to do with the rules for chat. Kids are at all different levels of socialization and have very mixed training in terms of social etiquette. (How to communicate with another person via chat in courteous and respectful ways is not something that is always taught in school.) But agreement on rules is crucial because an infraction or violation could result in anything from a simple warning to possible termination or suspension of services.

Basic rules. Basic rules are those rules that kids must, in theory, agree to *before* they can use the service. Some basic rules (with an *Animal Jam* example) are:

- No exchanging of personal information.

- No profanity or otherwise "bad" language.

- No bullying.

- You agree to follow the rules.

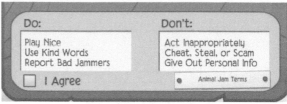

Animal Jam's basic rules.

Animal Jam's report button.

Report button. Kids can be quite good at policing themselves, and giving them an accessible way to report bullying or other issues is an important feature (for them and their parents). Since all transactions between characters are in the history database, all interactions are available for review by site staff. The report button may offer more than one option depending on whether the child wants to ask a question, report an incident, report a particular user, or bring up some other problem. Here is *Animal Jam's* example of a report button.

Ignore or block button. One way to help kids deal with someone who bugs them is to give them an ignore button, which makes the person who has been bugging them invisible and incapable of interacting with them.

Parental controls. Parental controls are not part of the chat interface, but they are an important part of any service. Parents want to have a say in the experience, to be able to affect what content and level of chat their children are exposed to. Sometimes parents have two or more children on one service, and they need to be able to set independent levels of interaction for each.

Designer's Note

In focus tests for a children's service some years ago, I found that parents who had the most objections to chat had never taken part in an online chat. They knew chat rooms only by reputation. The parents who knew and used chat themselves were considerably more relaxed about it. In several cases, they had discussed safety issues with their children, had a good sense of how monitoring worked, and felt their children would be okay and enjoy it.

The Power of Personalization, Customization, and Ownership

Personalization Creates Ownership

Kids' ability to personalize things and express themselves through customization fosters ownership and retention. The first thing most virtual worlds do is to let kids create an avatar. Virtual worlds also give kids a place—or way—to collect and keep things they earn, gather, or make while in the world. This creates an instant sense of ownership.

Avatar creation. Ownership doesn't get much more personal than having an avatar. From naming it to tweaking its physical attributes, adding outfits and collecting accessories, kids have the opportunity to create their own character identity to inhabit a world. It is a new kind of Role-Play that allows for a wide range of creative expression. It also creates a reason to collect and assemble a large closet full of virtual accessories, including animated dance and action moves. (For more on avatar creation, see Ch. 14.)

Here are examples of three different user-decorated avatars. A *Club Penguin* penguin decked out in geisha garb (from the player's card), one of the pets from *Webkinz World*, and a rainbow-decorated avatar from *Minecraft*.

There are various ways to customize an avatar, and a quick web search will bring up many avatar builders that you can consult for reference. This example comes from Pocoyo's avatar creator, *Pocoyize*. Each image to the immediate right and below the character brings up a set of feature options. These include skin color, hair color/style, facial features, gender and non-gender clothing, as well as clothing-based role-play. This avatar is for a younger age group (three- to seven-year-olds). When creating for an older group, characters are usually taller and look more like tweens.

Pocoyo's online avatar creator, *Pocoyize*.

Naming characters. Naming a character is a simple way for a child to have input into *any* game or activity. For instance, naming a character or car in a race game means that the child's name (whatever "handle" they create for themselves) will show up on the scoreboards and leader-boards, and will appear under their avatar in crowd scenes in the virtual world.

© Disney

Room decoration. Being gifted a room (bedroom, igloo, cave, condo, or hollow tree trunk) of their own when they enter a world immediately gives kids a sense of ownership and belonging. They now have a private space that is all theirs. It's a natural place to keep their pets, awards, outfits, amazing creations, and anything else they might gather.

The functions available in a personal room can vary, but basically it is a space that can be decorated, furnished, and customized to fit how kids may be feeling on a given day. It is also their personal storeroom for items, games, and programs they may have earned, won, or traded for. The rooms are *their* places, where *their* avatars come to chill out. A room is a digital dollhouse that allows for Expressive Play. Having control over their own area gives them a sense of larger ownership in the world. It is a place they may use with friends, showing and sharing what choices they have made and why. From *Club Penguin* to *The Sims*, having a personal character—and a place for that character to live—is a winning combination that supports user retention.

The magic backpack. In some virtual worlds (and in most adventure games), users are offered a "backpack" or other device for storing and carrying all the things they acquire and need while out on a quest or adventure. Since they may not easily be able to return home, the backpack allows immediate access to everything they

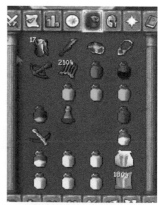

have in their inventory. It operates a bit like Mary Poppins's magic bag, which can include all items, tiny or giant. For example, in *Putt-Putt Saves the Zoo*, the player needs to find and gather items in the car's glove compartment that will be used later to save the lost animals. In *RuneScape*, the player can carry 28 various items at a time in their backpack to help them with their quests.

Putt-Putt Saves the Zoo app by Tommo.

RuneScape by Jagex.

Role-Play. Another engaging aspect of virtual worlds for children is the ability to explore different aspects of personality through role-playing. Kids will do it without props, but if you add a place (e.g., a themed room), virtual props, and clothing, kids will organically invent role-playing scenarios to match the environment. Various situations allow for different kinds of Role-Play exploration. Role-Play might follow professional aspiration, where the roles are workers and customers/clients, such as with games formed around a hospital, airport, school, restaurant, or day care center. Role-Play may also spring from a disaster situation involving victims and saviors. Scenarios can involve medieval royalty, current shows kids watch, or some form of battle. Including a place and props creates the opportunity for kid-created role-play adventures.

Regularly offer new items. Since outfitting their avatars and decorating their spaces is a big deal for most kids, one good way to keep a digital world fresh is to regularly offer new tools, props, accessories, and outfits (usually attainable after some interaction in the world). One easy way to do this is to offer seasonal and pop-culture-related items that are available for a limited time. Sites will often build up buzz about upcoming offerings or events. For example, on the eve of Halloween, an entire site might get decorated, and specialty items (witch hats, masks, cauldrons, bats, black cats, etc.) might become available. Special events and items create a reason to be at or return to a particular site or world because it promises new things to see and do. Mentioning "coming attractions" before they arrive helps to build excitement, anticipation, and a reason to return regularly.

Tips on Games (in Virtual Worlds)

Games are the mainstay of any kid product or service. Games offer variety and something to do that appeals to the different genders and ages. Games offer an opportunity to extend a service's look and feel while adding skills that have a purpose in the world beyond playing. Here are some tips on games for online worlds.

Have a good mix, and keep it fresh. A good mix of games with varying skill levels, challenges, and genres makes the environment more fun. Games need to work for girls as well as boys, and for the bottom of your target age range as well as the top. Always have new games in production. Rolling new games out regularly, with much fanfare and prelaunch buzz, keeps things fresh and lively.

Create connection opportunities. Most games for young players are designed for solo play because they are safer than multiplayer games, where it isn't always clear to parents how their kids will be connecting or with whom. But situations that allow kids to play against and with each other foster a greater sense of community. These may take the form of a racing game where members race whoever else shows up at the starting gate or a quest that requires multiplayer cooperation in order to be successful. The design goal is to provide children with the opportunity to play together easily, and to support creative, cooperative problem solving.

Play means points. In virtual worlds, games are often the main way players earn points (or the currency of the realm) in order to partake in the economy of the world. Playing games is a kid's "job" in many virtual worlds. Variety with increased challenge levels is an important path to higher rewards.

Designer's Note

I have watched kids play a game that they are bored with over and over because it was an easy way to earn points. When a game becomes only a means to an end (and it is no longer enjoyable or educational), it is time to offer something more challenging. It's possible to track all games played in a virtual world, which creates an opportunity to proactively offer something new that might stretch kids' skills. One of the values of leveling in games is that there is always somewhere new to go.

Virtual worlds need a map. Since most virtual worlds have many areas in which to gather and explore, it's standard to have a map available at all times in the interface. A map not only lets the player know what is available, it serves as a mode of transportation to get somewhere quickly. This map from *Kung Fu Panda World* follows the artistic theme, and not only shows you (via the panda image) where you are but which areas include power, speed, and cleverness games.

Map from *Kung-Fu Panda World* by DreamWorks Animation.

Creating Participation Opportunities

Personalization and customization foster ownership. When your product includes opportunities for creative expression, personalization, and recognition, it fosters a sense of ownership that can't come from just playing games. Having one's participation recognized in a way that is visible to all is a big hit with kids. Kids like to see that they got the high score or that the online, in-community daily newspaper accepted their poem or drawing. They like to be thanked for something they shared. All these efforts will make a child feel seen and appreciated. Find ways to support and enhance kid contribution recognition; it's an important goal for any designer who wants to inspire kid involvement and partnership.

Sharing. Kids like to share. Whether it is passing friendship jewels to their best friends or passing on tips for how to achieve a new level in a game, they enjoy sharing what they have and what they know. They also like to trade, have virtual yard sales, recycle, and do things for others. Some sites allow kids to donate in-game currency to real world organizations that help children or the environment, and then the company makes a matching real-world financial contribution. Kids enjoy performing meaningful actions for others, and it adds a certain value to their playtime. Create openings for them to share, trade, and do things for others, and they will get busy doing so.

The power of sharing creative output. As is plain from the huge popularity of social networks, sharing your thoughts, photos, artwork, and more creates a sense of participation and expression that fosters user retention. The same is true for kids. Another plus to supporting kids' creativity in game design is that their original art often ends up on the family refrigerator (with your site logo or character associated with it). Since parents are the ones paying for a service, they like seeing the visible benefits of their investment.

Designer's Note

One of the first successful online communities for kids was *Blackberry Creek* on AOL, created by Joanne Taeuffer. Kids are big consumers of content, and Joanne knew she couldn't compete with the highly funded software companies' many programmers and animators. What she knew she could do was to inspire kids to participate by having them create their own content. One tool she built was the first comic-making program for kids, which included tips on how to begin.

Each day she had themes and projects for the kids to participate in. One day, she might offer a partial drawing of a couple (heads and feet), leaving it up to users to draw the prom dress and tux, Halloween costumes, or other fantasy outfits, depending on the theme. Kids would download the "starter" art and do the work on their own home computer's paint program, then upload their finished drawings when they were done. Even though the kids were no longer on her site while drawing, they still felt connected.

Each child had a place to store their files, and although the larger group never saw most of the posts, the kids knew they were there and available for all to see. This created a strong bond to the site (and the community), which lasted for years. Each day, some of the many creations posted were chosen and shown in a common area.

The audience is important. Having an audience motivates people to be creative. It's not necessarily the fact that people will really look at the stuff you make, it's the idea that they might. This potential is what has the impact on the creator. So, you will be a much better creator when you create for an audience or when you imagine a wonderful audience involved with you. One of the important things the online worlds do for kids is give them a potential audience. Because of this, they get excited about what they are doing; they are excited about sharing it with that audience. The truth is, it doesn't matter if there really is an audience or if anyone ever really looks at their creation. The very notion that there might be an audience is very exciting and motivating for kids.[4]

—**Dr. Amy Bruckman, founder of Electronic Learning Communities**

Leave room for user-generated phenomena. Many virtual world sites focus their assets on specific activities they want kids to do, but interesting phenomena have appeared on *Club Penguin* and a few other sites: the kids themselves spontaneously create activities and impromptu role-playing. Something like this only happens when the world has interesting open-ended places for kids to play. (For more examples of user-generated social activities, see Ch. 21, p. 338.)

Designer's Note

Reusing a child's creative output can surprise and delight them. Some years before Rand and Robyn Miller created *Myst,* they created a small black and white game called *Cosmic Osmo.* Players explored Osmo's unusual world as they looked for

him. In one room, there was a blank easel and some drawing tools. Everyone who came through would doodle for a while before moving on. Much later in the game, you would finally find Osmo sitting in an easy chair, reading a paper in front of the fireplace. After a moment, you'd realize that the painting hanging over his fireplace was that doodle YOU had made way back in that room. It was a delightful surprise, and it was amazing to see how something simple could be so charming. The use of your drawing made you feel connected and, in a funny way, appreciated.

Interpersonal Game Structures and Economic Models

Virtual Worlds (and sometimes communities) need "economic models" in order for the participants to share, exchange, and build on the efforts of their activities. Economies are not necessarily about currency. They are more about how one's achievements and actions can be measured against others, and hence create a value that can be used as "coin-of-the-realm." The design of economies is particularly important in virtual worlds and communities for children because kids change as they age, developing different ways of interacting and feeling a sense of accomplishment. Economic models for massively multiplayer online games (MMOGs) such as *World of Warcraft* have evolved into several general categories, some of which work well in children's content.

Leveling. In traditional adult MMOGs, there is almost always some form of leveling. Special powers are the benefits of ascending multiple levels and challenges through repetitive long-term play and participation. For most parents, the idea of their kids doing a lot of repetitive, long-term gameplay to get a "power-up" is the antithesis of what they want out of their child's time on the computer. They generally want their kids, and the service they pay for, to offer more for their children, but that doesn't diminish the sense of accomplishment *kids* get from attaining new levels.

In educational products, leveling is used as a form of scaffolding to support the child's acquisition of progressive skills. Just as you learn your ABCs before you learn full words, or basic counting before multiplication and division, leveling allows for the sequentially appropriate learning course.

Helping. Even though kids' worlds offer quests, and kids enjoy them, they are usually less about levels and power-ups than adult virtual worlds. It is difficult to create a world that doesn't have some form of elitism, as longtime players begin to isolate themselves from new players. Just the difference between what a free and a paid member can do creates a society with haves and have-nots. Think of ways to create solutions that empower and invite experienced users to help the new users, and design your virtual world with opportunities for free and paid members to have some common ground.

Honoring achievement. Everyone likes to be noticed and to have their efforts appreciated, especially kids. Through a system of badges, ribbons, and awards, kids can be acknowledged for their efforts and participation. Lack of accomplishments shouldn't prevent one from having interactions with the other players. A sharing system lets accomplishments be known, and when a player's friends acknowledge his or her awards and achievements, they get a bonus. Everybody gets something out of the deal.

Some game designers think that kids will play anything just to get points or badges, but this isn't true, and this kind of thinking has killed many a game. Kids like the extrinsic benefit of awards and acknowledgment, but the game *must be* interesting in itself in order to earn their full participation.

Trading. Trading is a traditional and very basic part of in-game economics: you earn stuff and have more than you need, so you trade it to get other stuff. Kids enjoy the fun of trading, and it creates a user-to-user connection. Trading is also something that may need to be monitored because newbies can be taken advantage of. Again, it is all about the flavor of the world you are trying to create.

Designer's Note

Secret Paths, one of the first kids' online communities to incorporate gifting, did so in some truly unique ways. Users collected and shared items called Secret Stones. The community's co-creator, Brenda Laurel of Purple Moon, wrote:

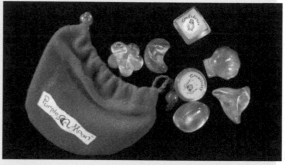

© Brenda Laurel

The Secret Stones existed in both virtual and physical form. They were "collected" by players of the *Secret Paths* CD-ROM series. Each stone had a special power or message associated with it (e.g., imagination, courage). In the *Secret Paths* games, a player would choose a character who had a particular problem (e.g., an absent father, a fight with a friend, a death in the family) and undertake a journey to help that character. During the journey, the player would solve puzzles embedded in the landscape in order to collect stones for her character/ friend. If the player successfully collected all the stones on a path, she would be able to view an animation of an appropriate folk tale (some of these were really swell; girls would take the journeys over and over in order to see particular stories again). The stones would form themselves into a necklace that the player could place around the character's neck. Each game came with a packet of three (more or less) random stones and materials for making your own necklace. On the web, Secret Stones morphed into 'gifts' that girls could collect and trade or gift. I think we beat Facebook and others by a mile on this sort of interaction.[5]

The key to the success of this method of gifting was that it used a form (jewelry) that appealed to the specific target audience. Beyond collecting, it encouraged and created opportunities for connecting and doing something for and with other players. Contrast this with a community like Twitter, which employs generic means of interacting: favorites, replies, followers. When designing for kids, specific audience and demographic are far more important to keep in mind.

Gifting. Gifting allows friends the opportunity to express appreciation. Gifting fosters generosity and opens up a flow between friends that is quite sweet. It is hard for kids to give their real toys to friends, but it's quite easy to give virtual gifts. Kids do this naturally when they play; they collect things not just for themselves, but also for their friends, because they know their friends will like it.

Hoarding versus collecting. Hoarding is common practice in many adult MMORPGs. Since it's the player against the world, it is important to have a large private stash of everything, and to acquire exclusive and scarce objects. Hoarding is not a practice generally fostered in children's programs.

Children do, however, love to collect things, and given the opportunity they will create large collections. Gathering is fun, and the activity of gathering widely scattered items together is intrinsically enjoyable. Kids are fond of arranging, sorting, and presenting their collections. Collected items often become the basis for trade economies. One design goal is to create ways to help kids get value from sharing and utilizing what they have gathered, rather than just hoarding for stockpiling's sake. Designers should consider how kids' collections can contribute to the group.

Solo quests and group goals. Quests are a popular activity with kids, and they are great for designers. You can easily invent new quests using background scenes and locations you already have. Many console games are quests done alone or with just one or two other players. As tribe and group quests become more available to kids' environments, designers have interesting opportunities to create and facilitate group goals—goals where others gain from your actions, and where activities contribute to group ends.

Creating appealing community in virtual worlds will always rely on the give-and-take between openness and control. For kids, it's especially important to foster a gentle environment that draws new players in and recognizes the contributions of players over time, environments where kids can explore new skills and experiences and build relationships. Luckily, we have many great examples from the early days of virtual worlds to look back on and learn from.

PART 5

Enhancing the Design Process

The designer's process covers a wide range of tasks, from the first bud of an idea to the nitty-gritty of testing and ironing out the wrinkles in how a game or app performs on a given platform. The process involves many more people than the designer: it includes the designer's team members, the client, parents, and, most importantly, kids. This section will walk you through the myriad stages and considerations that are part of creating a final product kids will love.

This is the real secret of life—to be completely engaged with what you are doing in the here and now. And instead of calling it work, realize that it is play.[1]

—**Alan W. Watts, philosopher**

Predesign Considerations

Designing for children involves many of the same demands that are part of any game or app design: balancing the desires of the client and the technical needs of the platform, working with existing intellectual property, dealing with budgets and bugs, and creating an environment for strong teamwork. Children's design requires something further: taking into account the needs and wants of parents or educators while also knowing everything you possibly can about the needs and wants of the kids you're working for. Truly engaging interactive content for children is a blend of technology and psychology that listens to and responds to the kids. This chapter encompasses good practices and processes to keep your design on target, tips on what parents want, fatal design decisions to avoid, and designing for transmedia properties.

The creation of something new is not accomplished by the intellect, but by the play instinct acting from inner necessity. The creative mind plays with the object it loves.[2]

—**Carl Jung, psychotherapist**

Companies, Clients, and 12 Fatal Design Assumptions

Before you begin the design process, it's helpful to consider paths you absolutely do not want to take. Eliminating fatal design assumptions before you begin your development process will mean a smoother path with fewer hurdles arising late in the game. Many common assumptions about producing products for children are ultimately costly at best, and fatal to the projects at worst. These assumptions arise over and over again as companies new to children's software attempt to enter the market. Even experienced companies may struggle with them. These ideas are often highly seductive and seemingly logical to adults, but they don't end up connecting with kids at all.

Designer's Note

Even though some of these are briefly mentioned in other places in this book, I thought it might be helpful to put them all in one place for easier reference. They are listed as fatal assumptions so that when someone comes to you and lays one of these on you, you can hold up the book and say, "Oh, that's one of the classic fatal assumptions of children's design." Your client may not be dissuaded, but at least it's not you alone who thinks their idea might be problematic.

Fatal Assumption #1:
"We can easily offer something for all ages."

This assumption could also be called "All kids are created equal" or "One size fits all." In fact, the opposite is true: one size fits none. Offering something for all kids ("ages three to fifteen" is a common grouping heard) sounds great to adults. In theory, it helps a company reach an entire kid market with one product. This type of broad category is especially inaccurate in children's products because emotional needs, emerging interests, and developmental levels vary dramatically over time. What is appealing or appropriate for preschoolers (up to age six) is viewed as "baby-stuff" by kids seven and above, who actively reject the younger stuff in an effort to show how much they have matured and grown. This distancing effect is true of every age group, because they each feel they are no longer the "little kids" they were just a few years before.

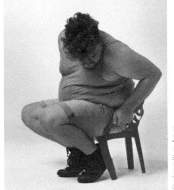

In the end, a product based on this one-size-fits-all approach means that no one group of kids feels the offering is especially for them, leaving them feeling not seen or heard, and therefore not interested. There is plenty of competition for a child's attention, and if you don't connect with them they will go elsewhere, quickly.

Solution: Launch a product or service that clearly addresses a specific age market, and then expand the appeal by rolling out "like products" or services in a modular form. First, get to know one audience well. Members of each new audience/market need to feel they have their own separate and distinct place with content just for them. Any branded service for kids under seven is usually called the "junior" version of the older kid service because the older kids don't want to be grouped in the same category as the "little kids." Most children's television networks deal with this by developing a brand for an older group, and then offering a junior version for the little kids, as in Disney Junior and Nick Jr.

Fatal Assumption #2:
"It's going to be easy to repurpose our company's existing content."

Repurposing content always sounds like a good way to further monetize existing assets by selling them in a different medium. It may seem that certain content is perfect for interactive media. But, in general, linear media (e.g., books and movies) are less interesting in an interactive environment unless you take the time and money to correctly repurpose them. In addition, other issues often arise: the source content is not in a digital format, no one knows where the originals are, the author's original contract didn't include digital media, etc.

Another aspect of this fatal assumption is thinking it will be easy to access all the content a company owns. In many cases, each of the separate divisions, groups, and subsidiaries (even if they are all owned by one parent company) tend to view their hard-earned assets as their own. Groups are often territorial and uncooperative about sharing content assets, and they first want to know what they get out of the deal.

A related common assumption, a favorite of marketing departments, is: "We need a highly branded character to sell this." While it is true that branded characters are easily recognized by kids, it does not automatically mean the brand will translate into a successful product. Success depends on how much effort and ingenuity is applied during design and production.

Solution: Repurposing content is effective if the project is led by experienced interactive designers and producers who know how to assess the existing content and deliver it in a new format. Before you begin to develop a concept based on any existing content or properties, evaluate all the assets and investigate the rights. Talk to the various owners of the content and understand their issues about using it. It often costs much more than expected to move assets to an interactive environment. However, repurposing content is an effective way to breathe new life into older content and give your audience something they can't get anywhere else, like one of their favorite branded characters.

Fatal Assumption #3:
"We are going to make a ton of money on this!"

You and your company (or client) can make money with a great kids' product, but if the first motivation to create something for kids is profit, building your studio, or being famous, your product will most likely fall short of your (and your investors') expectations. If you are thinking about your ego, it is hard to think about the kids you want to connect with; making a product for yourself may create something that isn't very interesting for them.

> *So many people think that kids are an easy mark, that making something for young people might be a really easy way to make money. They think we can just give kids the same old thing because of the theory that kids love repetition, or because it's been done before, and kids loved it then, so we can just put some new artwork on it, and we are done. Don't do what's been done before. If you really think about how a child's mind interprets data from the world, then your own creative possibilities are endless.*[3]
> —Bridget Erdmann, Creative Director, Gizmo6

Solution: Listen and read between the lines when clients come to you with a "great idea for a kid's product." Are they really connected to kids, or is it a get rich scheme for them? Often, it is some of both. Enthusiasm is great, and it's fun to work with clients who are excited about their ideas and the potential of a product. The trick is to work with the enthusiasm and excitement while you creatively sort out what will truly work for kids and what is a fatal assumption.

Fatal Assumption #4:
"This new technology will make it way better."

Software developers often get swept up in the excitement of new technologies with their accompanying promises of all new capabilities and features. But products designed solely around a new technology can lose their appeal quickly once the novelty wears off, and you run the risk of designing for a small market. In the worst-case scenario, kids may never really take to the technology at all, and your product will have no platform of users. Too often, companies and engineers add functions simply because the new technology is cool, and they can do it, not because anyone wanted it. As a result, the interface gets overly cluttered, extra time is spent in QA (quality assurance and compatibility testing), more time is spent with customer support, and valuable resources are wasted.

Solution: Great interactivity holds up over time. Early in the production, it is important to review new features or functions to determine if your average user will actually value them. Watch a few kids use a product, and you can quickly tell if it's working for them or not. New technologies can be very empowering and fun, but they need to connect with kids. Kids will often use products in ways the adult designers never imagined. When you see kids adapting and applying their creativity to a new technology, then you know you have something you can expand on.

Fatal Assumption #5: "Let's make a product just like that."

A copycat product strategy based on following the success of a current market leader is not a recipe for automatic success. There are two main problems with this strategy. First, if a new product is truly a standout, then a lot of time and money went into the technology and production to make it that good. Most copycats are risk averse to begin with, and they seldom want to invest what it takes to make great kids' products. Second, something that is selling well is often a highly leveraged brand that had a 3D movie and multilevel marketing campaign to promote the characters, world, and story line. It may not be selling because it is well-designed software but because it is well marketed and recognizable.

Solution: Don't mimic what's hot at the moment. Understand what it is that makes a product popular. What did the design team do right? What did they do wrong? Build on what you learn from that product to take your design to the next level.

Fatal Assumption #6: "We know what learning is."

Some clients do know what learning is, but the problem arises when the statement is translated to mean, "We know how interactive learning should work and what's best." With educational titles, companies often think a linear path must be rigidly followed, because that is "what learning is." Even though kids will put up with almost anything on a computer in a school setting, they might not go anywhere near the same product in their free time unless it delivers something they are really interested in.

Solution: Learning is instinctive to kids, and finding a way for them to "play" with the concepts you want to teach is considerably more powerful than coaxing them with something that doesn't really speak to them.

I dislike it when companies say, "We make learning fun!" Learning is fun! Our job [as software designers] is not to wreck it![i]
— **Daren Carstens, game designer**

Fatal Assumption #7:
"Because it's interactive, kids will love it."

To rely on interactivity alone is a fatal assumption behind many "educational" product concepts. Some companies interested in creating educational products follow a medicinal approach, offering kids only what they believe is good for them, and lots of it. These companies think a product works for kids because it allows them to click to go to the next card. Kids know when they are being fed chocolate-covered broccoli. Just because kids *can* click on something, adults assume kids *will* want to click on it. Having grown up with emerging technologies, kids are more sophisticated about interactivity than adults comprehend. Kids need a level of interactivity that empowers and inspires them to go further because they want to, not because they have to.

Solution: Good interactive content invites and inspires interaction by offering an intrinsically fun way of doing something. If you are trying to teach angle percentages (90°, 180°, 360°) you can show flash cards with the right and wrong answers for learning the correct percentage (boring) or you can include those angles as part of gameplay to make something happen. This takes the learning from conceptual to experiential.

Fatal Assumption #8:
"We already know exactly what kids want."

Assumptions by business executives, educators new to digital content, and folks with a cute idea can lead to thinking kid products are easy to produce successfully. Their ideas can be developmentally off base, and not up-to-date with kids' evolving interests and expectations. Even many child developmental psychologists, who know a lot about children, know little to nothing about interactive play and the motivating factors that can cause a child to spend hours with a digital game.

To assume you know who kids are, and then to build products based on those assumptions is risky in such a competitive marketplace, but it happens all the time. Even with the best intentions, a product may end up talking down to kids or ignoring their interests. This category of assumption includes comments like:

- **"It has to be safe, safe, safe."** It is important to stay away from violence and inappropriate content in children's design, but that does not mean there should never be conflict. Kids, especially age seven and above, are increasing drawn to stories and games that have conflict and battles between light and dark. They act out these conflicts spontaneously in their fantasy play. Besides the action inherent in conflict stories, kids are interested in overcoming adversity, witnessing struggle, and generally becoming empowered through their actions. Overly "safe" products are perceived as boring and only for "little kids." The digital arena is where kids explore their power, especially by wrestling with confrontation.

- **"They'll buy anything sweet."** This is true on the surface, but it is a flawed plan for kids above seven. Some sweetness is okay, but too much becomes junk food that doesn't nourish the imagination. Like overly safe and perfectly behaved characters, sweetness ends up being seen as boring, bland, childish, and false. Kids know that overly saccharine characters and situations do not reflect the real world, and they end up feeling talked down to. Kids hate being lied to, and they know when they are not being respected.

- **"The characters need to be wholesome role models."** This assumption is to some extent true for the youngest kids (six and under), who don't like a lot of discord and who want characters to be friendly. But even the youngest ages want slapstick humor, silly characters, and some action. "Perfect" characters are boring, flat, dull, and unrealistic. Flaws (like being overly curious), weird habits, and fear-based behaviors help make characters interesting, vulnerable, and accessible to kids.

Designer's Note

I consulted with a company whose handheld learning device featured their own branded characters, all of whom were good-natured, "perfect" kids. But the products featuring these characters didn't sell that well because kids didn't relate to them. Then the same company introduced a SpongeBob SquarePants title, and the kids ate it up. SpongeBob is silly and full of personality, and it helped immensely that the kids knew him from television.

Solution: Research needs to be an integral part of the product design and development cycle. Talk to your audience; involve kids in the creative process. After all, you are making the products for them. Listen firsthand for what parents and kids need, fear, and want. Never underestimate or talk down to kids. In a perfect world, all content should be parent- and kid-tested and approved before you launch. Companies that implement a thorough research strategy and test products with target users throughout development are more successful in delivering the experience their customers want.

Fatal Assumption #9: "We can easily supply enough content for kids."

A large number of hits used to be the standard by which website popularity was judged. For children's sites, what's more important is retention: getting kids to come back regularly. You can never create enough content. Companies who build kid sites often underestimate how much new, updateable content they need in order to meet kids' insatiable demand for something NEW. Kids will voraciously explore every game and activity, thirsting for more.

Solution: In addition to consumables, offer kids tools to create their own content and ways to participate at a deeper level in a service or game. Creative tools give kids a sense of ownership. Kids love making something they can share, and when they make their own content, it saves on expensive multimedia development. Instead of premaking everything, create activities that are "constructivist" by design, allowing kids to participate in their own learning through exploration, play, and personal expression.

> *Making good interactive content for kids costs money. That's why there is so much schlock out there in the children's market. You can only re-skin* Concentration *so many ways and expect kids will have any joy playing with it.*[5]

—Scott Traylor, CEO, 360KID

Fatal Assumption #10: "If we build it, they will come."

Assuming every kid is just waiting for you to deliver your product is risky in a world where there is a lot of other content available. Companies need to make prototypes and test to make sure they have content kids are drawn to. Even with good market research—and good marketing—it may still take a while to iron out the wrinkles and build market awareness and acceptance. Basing your sales figures on the assumption that hordes of kids will come immediately—and stay—is perilous.

© Kobyakov/Depositphotos.com

This and similar scenarios have happened occasionally in online environments when the business development and marketing departments generate revenue guesstimates based on market analysis of how many parents or kids are ready to join up. (These companies did raise a lot venture capital with those numbers, but they later had to scramble to salvage their business plans.) It takes time to get kids and parents to be aware of your company, to like what you offer, and to agree to join. It also takes time to fix the technical bugs and other unforeseen issues that always arise. Assuming you can do all those things, it still may take six months to a year (or longer) to reach good numbers.

Solution: Assuming you have a product kids want, you might consider rolling out the product in key test markets, creating a "pilot program." Handled this way, the product is not tied to a short-term revenue window; instead the business plan should accommodate a controlled growth window during which the development team has time to work out all the kinks before expanding nationally or internationally with a coordinated marketing and public relations campaign. Good public relations and word of mouth are the most effective forms of advertising.

Fatal Assumption #11: "This product can easily run on everything."

Much like defining your target audience, it is equally important to specifically define your target playback machine/platform. This is especially true for products that run on home and school computers and across various mobile platforms. Screen resolution, programming quirks, chip speed, RAM, plug-ins, browser type, and more can vary wildly between computers and devices.

Solution: Clearly define all target machines the client is interested in developing for *before* production begins. It's best to understand and manage a client's expectations at the beginning of a project rather than learn about them at the end. Doing this also helps you to come to mutual conclusions about an appropriate budget for production. Just because it is a product for kids doesn't mean it's going to be cheaper. In fact, great kids' products often require more than a client might think to make them magical.

Fatal Assumption #12: "The market needs one of these."

This is also called the "pants first, *then* shoes" mistake. In software, this kind of product is called "vaporware" because there is nothing solid there. Marketing departments are salespeople, and they want something to sell. Many companies find themselves at a strange disadvantage when their marketing department has sold a preliminary "rough concept" (including features and price points) as a near-finished product. Of course, this frequently happens before the company really knows what the product is or what it will cost (in time and money) to produce.

Too often, a business plan is developed separately or prior to the product design. When this happens, a cascade of issues may occur: unreal expectations about the product, underestimation of the technical difficulty, lack of connection to the target market, and higher overall costs of execution. It is almost guaranteed that the product will change substantially from the initial rough design, which then means the marketing department must "resell" the product to the distributor and/or senior management.

Designer's Note

Over the years, I've noticed that there are times in the life cycle of a platform where new and unbranded titles can be breakaway hits. This happens at the beginning of a new technology wave before a market matures around it. You can tell this is the case when small, low-budget "garage band" developers play with the new technology and ship innovative titles and products. A few years later, the market is dominated by larger companies pushing only branded characters. I have seen this cycle happen about six times since the early days of interactive technology. It's always amazing to see the playing field leveled, allowing for some bursts of new creativity.

Solution: Even from a rough draft of a design, you can create an initial brand strategy, a content acquisition and production estimate, and a rough technology evaluation. Your projections are never going to be exact, but including realistic input from all the groups that will ultimately be responsible for the delivery makes a smart company.

Working with Transmedia

Transmedia is a term used to describe the process when designers recreate a known brand or title in a different medium. As a designer, you may never take on a transmedia project, but in the event that you do, it's important to be aware of the issues you may encounter and the specifics you should consider as you migrate the intellectual property to a new medium.

Designer's Note

When we created Living Books (early animated interactive storybooks), we were very careful to respectfully recreate the paper book's art, look and feel, the personalities of its characters, and the relationships between characters. Our goal was to bring alive the pages of the storybooks, keeping all of the original charm and wit intact. We were the first to give Marc Brown's Arthur and D.W. voices (years before the TV series) and to write additional Dr. Seuss interactive dialogue. We felt a huge responsibility to keep these properties (and all our titles) consistent with the charm and personality that attracted us to the books in the first place. We wanted kids to feel like they were playing inside the storybooks they already knew and loved.

Interactive environments allow for interaction with the characters in new ways. It isn't just that people can play with the characters, but that they can play actively *inside the character's world*. In any interactive transmedia environment, the *world* and its special attributes set the conditions for imaginative play there.

While developing transmedia content is a fun challenge, it comes with certain responsibilities. If you bring a branded character to a new medium, you are playing with somebody else's baby. The creators carefully built a brand, an archetype, a world. How you treat their property is critical. If done properly, the new product can enhance the brand and give it new life. Before production development begins, get to know the various existing transmedia properties and what each has added to the experience.

One of the most interesting discussions of transmedia comes from Jesse Schell, game designer, CEO of Schell Games, and author of *The Art of Game Design: A Book of Lenses*. Jesse has graciously allowed me to share some of his thinking on transmedia in the following section:[6]

by Jesse Schell
Transmedia Worlds

I would like you to come along with me to a long time ago and a galaxy far, far away—and when I say a long time ago, I mean 1977—to the release of *Star Wars*. It turned out to be an unexpectedly tremendous hit, and the action figures turned out to be quite popular. One of the interesting things about these characters was that adults assumed that kids would act out scenes from the movie, but that wasn't what was happening. What they learned was that kids would make up their own stories and adventures, sometimes creating new names for the characters.

Why were these toys so insanely popular if it wasn't the story line, and it wasn't the characters that kids were responding to? The only conclusion that I've been able to make is that what kids were responding to was the *world* of *Star Wars*, and that was the magic part of it. They wanted to visit and play in that world again.

When you're talking about creating a transmedia world, you're not talking about creating a product. We all get so wrapped up in our products, in our games, in our books, in our movies, in our TV shows—we're focused on product, product, product, when in many cases the thing we're creating isn't a product at all but a world that doesn't actually exist—you can't put it on a shelf, you can't download it for 99 cents. It's this imaginary place that *you* are creating, but what you're selling are the gateways to that world.

They Exist Apart
Transmedia worlds are not enmeshed in the products you make. They exist separately. And that's why, when you go to throw away a magazine or newspaper, it's easy, but when you go to throw away a comic book, you hesitate a little because there is a world in there, and you're not sure you should be throwing away that world so trivially.

If you've created a story line with characters, you have also created a world, whether you know it not. New worlds appear simultaneously with the beings who live there. We created *Toontown Online*, and when we were doing our homework and looking at the history of Toontown, what we had was the *Roger Rabbit* movie, and then a theme park land that was in a Roger Rabbit theme, but, really, we didn't have very much. So we had to ask, "What is Toontown? What does it consist of?"

About the Contributor
Jesse Schell is CEO of Schell Games, a Distinguished Professor of the Practice of Entertainment Technology at Carnegie Mellon University, and the author of *The Art of Game Design: A Book of Lenses*. He is also a juggler, comedian, and someone who still knows how to play.

The movie tells us very little. So we went out asking, "Well what do you think Toontown is?" Everyone had similar answers. They said, "Well, it's where all those Toon characters live." And I realized that, when the *Roger Rabbit* movie came out, people *already* knew about Toontown. You didn't need to tell them because they had been watching cartoons their whole life and already knew intuitively that all the cartoon characters lived off somewhere by themselves. That Daffy Duck and Donald Duck could hang out, it was just obvious to everyone. And when you find a world that's intuitive that way, you have found something powerful. It's a place that existed before anyone decided it existed. The world was created by the characters, by virtue of them living there.

Successful transmedia worlds have many gateways. You can come in through games, TV, board games, and a book. Why not a plush toy and a card game? To think of them as separate products is a mistake. They are all just gateways into one solid world with excellent solid rules and interesting things happening. They exert a real influence over people because they end up sort of being people's utopias. If they're well constructed, they're the place you wish you could go, the place the world should be like.

Evolve over Time

These worlds change; they evolve over time. Most worlds begin as the brainstorm and passion of one individual, but these worlds live in the minds of those who love to go there, and, if successful, are passed along to new generations and may outlive their creator. Over time, others may try to add to the world's mythology. No one person makes the decision. Pieces get added along the way, and if everyone who likes the world agrees, then it becomes part of the history and physics of the world.

A great example is what I tend to think of as the patron saint of transmedia worlds, Santa Claus. His beginnings are a little murky, with lots of various stories about him as St. Nick, but there are some key points in his evolution as Santa Claus. First was the poem, "A Visit from St. Nicolas" (or "'Twas the Night Before Christmas," as we know it today), published in 1823. In that poem, a lot of the magic and story of Santa were clearly defined for the first time. All of a sudden, things like a sleigh pulled by flying reindeer and coming down the chimney helped to congeal Santa Claus into a more consistent story. A hundred years later, someone writes a kid's book and a song that connects with everyone, and BAM! "Yes," everyone agrees, there is a ninth reindeer, Rudolph, with the shiny nose. Does this just mean that you can throw anything at the lore of a world, and it all sticks? No. Many attempts have been made (and continue to be made) to glue things onto the Santa story. No less than L. Frank Baum, author of *The Wizard of Oz*, took a whack at it with a book, *The Life and Adventures of Santa Claus*, trying to write about Santa's origin, but it was kind of strange, and people just rejected it saying, "Sorry, no, this is not part of the story." It seems that, after a time, we collectively define what works in these worlds.

Santa's world lives today. Consider that here is an imaginary character, and you and your kids can go sit on his lap and have your picture taken with him. That he gets millions of letters to him every year. That you might leave cookies and milk for him on Christmas Eve, and that this imaginary character might come to your house and eat your food! And then he actually shows up and delivers the goods under the tree. Think of the amount of work we all go through, and are willing to do, to make this seem real. Consider the amount of deceit and deception and lies in order to allow our kids to play in this world for a little while. And we do this because we think it's a really important concept to support the idea of a figure who considers *your* fondest wish and decides whether or not to bring it to you, and that maybe he *will* because you deserve it. It is something we feel is important somehow, and so we do it, and by supporting that world, we get to play in it, too.

Tips on What Makes a Good Transmedia World

In looking at many of the most enduring, successful, and sustainable transmedia worlds, they all have some attributes in common. These shared attributes I believe are key to making any good transmedia world.

- **Rooted in a single medium.** It seems that one thing we know is they always tend to be rooted in a single medium. The ones that really succeed didn't start as some global mega-net system plan to make ten things for ten different types of media. They started as one successful thing. Once they had success there, they grew to other places.

Shoppers visit the Siam Paragon mall in Thailand during the Pokémon Festival.

- **Have a single creator.** Not only were they rooted in a single medium, they each had a single creator. Almost every really successful transmedia world that you can look at has one person behind it: Walt Disney (*Mickey Mouse*), J.K. Rowling (*Harry Potter*), Satoshi Tajiri (*Pokémon*), Nobuyuki Okude (*Transformers*), Jim Henson (*Muppets*). This is probably the case because, in order to survive the pressure of these many gateways, there needs to be a creative unity that is difficult to sustain when a committee designs something. When one person has a vision of how it should be, the thing is able to withstand the pressure that is exerted by all those gateways.

- **Consistent worlds that make sense across media.** It's important in transmedia worlds that they make sense through all of their gateways. A great example of this is *Pokémon*. You can come in anywhere, and *Pokémon* consistently makes sense. You can read a book, play a game, or pick up a toy, and the rules are clear. Compare that to the world of *The Matrix*, where they made video games and comic books and weird animations and all these things, and a lot of times you watch it and think, "What's this? I don't get this." And you ask someone else, and they're, like, "Oh yeah, to know that, you have to play the game and watch all three movies, and you have to read this story, and *then* you get it." Well, that doesn't work, and *The Matrix* franchise naturally has collapsed as a result.

- **Facilitates the telling of many stories.** Another thing about transmedia worlds is that they facilitate the telling of many stories. There are some worlds with one story, and when the story is over, there's not much more to do. The long-surviving transmedia worlds are places where many, many, many stories can happen. So you think about a world like *Star Trek* as a great example. It's designed to be very episodic—many, many stories can happen there for an infinite period of time.

I love the story that J.R.R. Tolkien used to tell. Someone at a conference once said to him, "You know, I love your stories, but one thing that really frustrates me— you always talk about the distant mountains, these things off in the distance, and you tell a little bit about the history of this village that lived over the mountain, and what was out there—you only tell a little, and I want to hear so much more about these distant lands at the periphery of things." And he said, "Well, yeah, I could tell you all about the distant mountains, but then I'd have to make more distant mountains." In order to feel like a world, there needs to be a scope and a scale and a grandeur to it that is bigger than the story you're telling. And you can see in *Star Wars*, for example, it's very obvious. There's a universe of worlds and planets and people that we don't know much or anything about. That's part of what makes it feel so real, the distant mountains.

These Worlds Can Have Long Lives If Done Right

If we, as designers and world builders, respect a consistent vision of a world across media and platforms, the different gateways will all support each other, and the franchise and magical world that is created will be strong and prosper.

What Parents Want

So far, we've talked about the needs of people involved before a product reaches the market, but just as important are the people who buy and use what you design. In order to create successful services and products, addressing not only the target audience but also their parents, is important. Without the support of mom, dad, and other caregivers, it's harder for children's content to survive, because parents are the ones who most often purchase games and software for their kids. So what is it that parents really want?

> *The truth is that we and our children ultimately want parallel things from technology. We want to be informed and entertained, not lulled. To be engaged, not bored. To be connected, not disconnected. To consume and to create. We seek joy, not just the completion of tasks or momentary distraction from the unbearable, mundane, and day-to-day.*[7]
> —Anya Kamenetz, parent and lead education reporter for NPR

"Teach our kids something positive."

Especially for the parents of younger children (who are already in the social skill acquisition mode), promoting positive values is a plus. Over and over again in children's books and movies, we see the reinforcement of positive values like sharing, kindness, communication, self-esteem, self-discipline, and honesty.

In addition to considering what parents want, it's important for designers to consider ways to help parents participate and stay connected with their children's technology use. Some research has shown that children are better prepared to appropriately utilize the Internet and technology when parents embrace technology and act as mentors for their children.[8]

"Give us a brand we can believe in."

Parents, like all of us, are quite brand-savvy, and they tend to migrate toward brands they know, especially when it comes to services for their children. A "brand" is defined as a company or product that offers a consistent experience. Parents have a preference for brands they can trust, and trust is based on the perceived and real promises certain brands offer. Parents may not have the time to investigate a new brand, so they go with what they know. Marketers believe that children are also becoming brand aware at younger ages than in the past.[9]

"It's got to be right for our kids."

Parents understand that their younger kids have different needs than their older ones, and they want products that cater to different developmental levels. It is critical for a family channel or service to address these different developmental needs by creating a depth and breadth of content appropriate for each age group.

"It's got to be safe."

Parents will demand that a service be safe. They expect that nothing about the product will hurt their children, either emotionally or physically, nor will it expose them to inappropriate material. With the youngest children, that means content is generally nonviolent, not scary, and not sexual. Because Internet communication can be two-way in nature, there are safety issues related to creating content where kids can "escape" the program and end up on the web. Designers need to consider all of these factors.

"We want to see what our kids are doing."

Parents like to see tangible results from their kids. What are the kids sharing about their digital device time? Are they delighted, excited, engaged? Are they happy? This might also include awards and artwork that come off of the computer (through the printer) and end up on the refrigerator. Think of classroom teachers who send home the latest class projects or printouts so parents can keep up with what their kids are doing. It is a measurable result that the whole family can share.

"We have different priorities than you do."

What parents want and are willing to pay for varies by country and culture. In Asian markets, English language learning (as a second language) is the highest revenue-generating category for educational apps. In contrast, the top revenue categories in the U.S. are brain training and knowledge-based learning apps.[10] It's very likely these revenue differences reflect how parents in Asia and the U.S. have different learning priorities for their children. Additionally, parents are more willing to pay for a serious learning environment for their children, especially if the child will be engaged for some time and the app will grow with the child.[11]

"We want to get more for our money."

Parents don't want to buy something they can get for free, but they are willing to invest in an app or program if they know it will be worthwhile (i.e., their children will enjoy it and get something from it).[12] They are also willing to pay a monthly fee for a virtual world membership if it offers replay-ability, many hours of ongoing use, and multiple child users.

Parents may buy individual DVDs, books, or apps that may be appropriate only for one child in their family, but when it comes to committing to a subscription service, parents want something for more than one of their children. If you're thinking of using the subscription model for your product, look to the successful magazines (from companies like Cricket Media or Highlights for Children) that offer a subscription product with content that appeals to multiple ages and that can grow with the child.

"Sometimes we need a babysitter."

Parents are very busy people, and sometimes they are happy to have something that entertains and engages their kids when they can't, like when they need to drive or fix dinner. Parents prefer it when the digital fare their children are consuming is good for them, rather than being junk food for the mind.

Designer's Note

I have known many families who shied away from Game Boy, Nintendo DS, and iPod touch for years until they had to sit through a cross-country airplane flight. Then they bought one device for each child, hoping that, for those hours, it might act as a "child immobilization device." Usually, it helped quite a bit. These days, parents regularly hand their phones to their young children for mobile entertainment.

"Our kids know more about the computer than we do."

Many parents aren't as computer/app literate as their children, and the prospect of having to read a lot of on-screen directions about a service in order to get their child online can be daunting, especially when they have a young child eagerly tugging at their sleeve. Some parents are intimidated by technology, and they may not be inclined to complete a complicated installation or registration process. A successful, well-designed subscription service or app store makes the sign-up and purchase process as simple as possible.

"We don't want to be the learning police."

Many working parents feel guilty about the limited amount of time they spend with their kids. They want their time together to be enjoyable. Although parents are concerned with helping their kids be successful, many don't like to force their kids to do extracurricular learning. They would rather spend their limited family time doing enriching and engaging activities that are fun for everyone.

Several (U.S.-based) companies offer after-school enrichment centers. Parents can drop their kids off, and the center staff then drives the kids through hard-learning exercises (focused, linear, rote learning with little gameplay) on the computer. Interestingly, in one such program I encountered, even though parents asked for an online version of the service so they wouldn't have to drive their children to the centers, they admitted later in focus groups that they would not make their kids use a learning program at home if the kids didn't enjoy using it.

"We want the best for our kids."

It seems fair to assume that most parents are concerned about getting the best possible education (and educational advantages) for their children. If their kids are having trouble with a subject, or if their schooling seems less than perfect, parents will be motivated to supplement that education by other means, if they have the resources to do so. In the U.S., many families cite "educational enhancement" as the main reason they purchase a home computer or tablet device.

© Darren Baker | Dreamstime.com

"We don't have time for this, but we want to be involved."

Because parents feel they don't have enough time to do all they want for their children and themselves, they want quick and easy solutions to help them. Parents may get frustrated if they have to spend precious time in front of the computer, trying to make a program work. On the other hand, parents want to be involved with

Saklakova/Shutterstock.com

something as important as their child's education, and they respond positively to good progress reports and updates on their child's efforts. Some learning programs track what children are good at, and where they need improvement. When asked, parents say they are interested in receiving information about their child's performance, but, in my experience from talking with parents, a learning program's reports are seldom read or acted upon. This may be due to the fact that no one likes to hear someone—especially a faceless computer program—criticize or critique their children.

The Most Important Clients—Kids

While this entire book is about designing for kids, it's worth taking a moment to discuss kids as your *clients*, clients whose needs and wants are your priority when you're designing. At the end of the day, they are the reason you're doing what you're doing. Imagining, empathizing, listening, and watching a child soak up experiences is a wonderful practice for designers.

We Are the Children

An important part of designing for kids is to take time to play yourself. What toys, games, or TV inspire you now? What inspired you when you were a kid? Try to remember those old favorite games and activities, or get some and play with them again. Why do they resonate with you? What makes those toys special? When we can connect with our own inner child, and see the world through that lens, it inspires us to be better designers, and it supports deeper intuition about the children we design for.

> *Understanding kids is an inside job.*[13]
>
> —**Rob Seidenspinner, life coach**

Our childhood memories and programming remain with us in adulthood, and those experiences affect our adult viewpoint on the world. If our goal is to offer wonderful experiences to the next generation of children, it helps to understand ourselves—our motivations, joys, and fears—as we begin creating content.

What Is Your Motive?

Many of the best children's interactive designers came into their line of work because of the sheer joy of doing it. The opportunity to make a difference for kids and the pleasure of creating something fun each day are what inspired them in the beginning, and those qualities have sustained them through the sometimes grueling process of launching multiple products. Being a children's designer is one of those rare jobs where you get to make a difference in the world and see the results of your efforts on behalf of others.

Intent, Attitude, and Altitude

In practical magic, to know your intent is everything because it so deeply influences what you end up with. What is the cause for what you are about to do? ("I am doing it because...") The same principles and questions hold true when designing children's content. Your product intent (hopefully in line with your heart's intent) guides you through the whole creative process as you make design decisions.

> *Attitude is the difference between an ordeal and an adventure.*[14]
> —Dr. Larry Hazen, sailor

If your intent is to "just get something out," then your decisions will be all about expediency and time to market. Even though the realities of production must include decisions about time and delivery, setting a higher intent at the beginning facilitates the creation of a product that you feel good about, that your company feels good about, and that kids and their parents enjoy.

> *No pessimist ever discovered the secrets of the stars, or sailed to an uncharted land, or opened a new heaven to the human spirit.*[15]
> —Helen Keller, author

Designer's Note

Over the years, I have met and heard from many kids who have enjoyed my titles. Some have learned a second language from them; others share a love of surprise and the joy of exploration; and some autistic children have learned to speak. It is always a delight to hear how a title has touched a child. For a designer, there is no greater satisfaction than to have one of your end users come back and tell you, often years later, what a difference your creation made to them.

Consider the airplane wing. The shape/angle of the wing that gives it lift and altitude is called the *attitude*. It is the same for us. Your attitude *while you are creating* has a significant effect on *what* you create. The state of your consciousness—and your team's—will come through in what you build together. *Joy is infectious.* Even though it is not always easy to shift from *grind* to *groove*, to make the effort is worth it. You and your team will have more fun, and so will the kids who use your product.

Be a Child Play Advocate

Play is how children naturally learn about the world. We have a responsibility to offer kids the best and most honest play experience we can. The more we can connect with them through the power of play, the more they feel seen, heard, and empowered to explore and discover. Come to your design with a child's point of view.

Remember to listen, to ask questions, and to be curious. Look at things you already understand as though seeing them for the first time. Let yourself be *child-led*. In other words, follow children's interests, and look for their motivations. There is a difference between things with intrinsic value (from within) and things with a value imposed from the outside. Sometimes products with good intentions will impose so much structure and process that the games are no longer enjoyable and *alive* for the kids. As a result, kids interact with the game only due to coercion rather than joy and freedom of choice. Be the child play advocate you wish someone had been for you.

> *We all talk about making experiences that are interactive.*
> *I try to make them 'inneractive' because they promote*
> *internal problem solving.*[16]
>
> —**Daren Carstens, game designer**

Listen and Partner with Kids

As designers, you create relationships with the kids you design for. The quality of the relationship affects the quality of the product and the kids' desire to listen, participate, and return for more. An imperative element of a relationship is to listen. It is critical to have a clear understanding of the kids your hard work is headed toward. What excites them? What are their interests? What characters, toys, and activities are they into? If you connect with them *where they are*, and honestly listen, you will be surprised by all they have to share with you. Include the input of kids in all stages of production as much as possible.

There is a distinction between making something *for* kids and making something *with* kids. The more a product is *for* kids, the less interesting it is for them. Adults often form opinions and assumptions about kids before kids are done talking or communicating what's on their minds. Consequently, kids don't feel heard or seen. A few tips to facilitate listening to kids include:

- **Slow down.** We producers and designers live in an adult world focused on deadlines and fueled by caffeine. Often our minds are so full and so busy that it may take some effort to slow down and tune in to the viewpoint and vibrational frequency of a child. Taking a few deep breaths always helps.

- **Pay attention to them.** Kids are teaching you about themselves and what they want. Don't assume anything. Let the conversation unfold. The goal is to see things from their point of view. It might help if you are talking eye-to-eye, and not eye-to-belt-buckle. Sit down on the floor or set yourself up so they don't have to look up at you when they talk. Small things like this can help equalize the conversation.

- **Notice your own thought patterns.** Watch your own thinking to make sure you are not filling up with your own words, ideas, and biases. Leave room for what the kids are saying. Be careful to not overlay your agenda and goals onto their communication. They are teaching you. If you want authentic communication, you need to be available for it.

- **Ask questions in response to what kids are saying.** Are you really hearing them? Do you understand the details of their stories and why they matter? Kids can't always find the right words to tell you what they are feeling. Don't just listen to their words, pay attention to their body language. In what way are they expressing their opinions and emotions without their words?

Designer's Note

My children were my inspiration for getting into children's design. I wanted to create great things for them, things they wanted to use. It was my children who helped me remember the joy of my own inner child and my own love of play. Playing with them gave me permission to let that part of me come forward again. I believe that inner child is in all of us, just waiting for an opportunity to come out and play. When you connect with your playful self, you will be able to better connect with the kids you design for. Many of the things that you would have loved to do, that would have turned you on creatively as a kid, are the same things that will spark a fire in kids today. The best design comes from a meeting of your child and theirs. Play nicely

One of the most difficult tasks men can perform . . . is the invention of good games. And it cannot be done by men out of touch with their instinctive selves.[17]

—Carl Jung, psychotherapist

The Design Process

How, as a children's designer, do you come up with a great new idea? And how do you nurture that idea to bring it from concept into being? The process can be quite messy, as great art often is, but with some solid guidelines to follow during the different stages, a playful and engaging result can always be reached. This chapter explores how to help ignite the personal creative spark in the beginning and keep it alive all the way through production.

Good design is clear thinking made visible.[1]
—Edward R. Tufte, author, statistician, and artist

The design process is so called because creativity needs continual tweaking and attention to grow from concept to reality. Design development has its own organic path as new concepts, information, and ideas reveal themselves. We never know exactly how it is going to turn out, but with practice and some trust in the process, great games, apps and toys can be consistently invented. In a market where creativity and innovation are the keys to success, learning to trust yourself and the process is essential. Let's begin by talking about how different creative viewpoints can bring different results.

Balancing Creative Modalities

People don't often think about the ways creativity works, or when they should apply different kinds of creativity. Two main creative styles in production design are Blue Sky Creativity and Problem Solver Creativity. A great production sequence needs both, a balance of the two working together at different parts of the process.

Blue Sky Creativity

This is used when you want to come up with something totally new and original—outside the box. Big ideas that might create whole new product categories come from thinking big. In large companies, the Blue Sky group is often called research and development (R&D) and is responsible for product innovation. Blue Sky thinking is characterized by open-ended mental play that allows new combinations and connections to be made. It often requires:

- **A place free of distraction.** It's easiest to get into Blue Sky Creativity when you can step away from email, smartphones, and the numerous details of daily life (at least for a little while). The goal is to open some space for new ideas, change the brain waves to a playful setting, and invite the essence of imagination to inspire you.

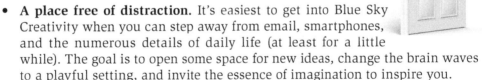

Almost all creativity involves purposeful play.[2]
—**Abraham Maslow, psychologist**

- **Stretches of uninterrupted time.** You need time to think and to explore something long enough that you can see and understand it in new ways. It's important to gain new perspectives. Blue Sky Creativity is all about expansive play with new ideas, not about getting from point A to point B in the most efficient way. It is about creating something fresh, novel, and innovative. Creativity and invention need a certain freedom and support for experimentation. This is a time to take off the "critic hat" and just play.

The problem is never how to get new, innovative thoughts into your mind, but how to get old ones out. Every mind is a room packed with archaic furniture. . . . Make an empty space in any corner of your mind, and creativity will instantly fill it.[3]
—**Dee Hock, founder and original CEO of Visa**

Designer's Note

A teacher told me many years ago that if I could think sixteen consecutive new thoughts about the same thing (object or concept), without going off on a tangent, at the end of those 16 thoughts, I would understand the object or concept better and actually be in a different consciousness in relationship to it. I have used this exercise many times over the years, and for me, he was right.

Blue Sky Creativity is an *additive process*. The approach may be a great way to come up with something new and fantastic, but on the downside it can make it more difficult to lock down a finished design because new ideas keep coming. Designs that are constantly "improved" (read: changed) become very expensive, and the end product may have trouble being born.

Problem Solver Creativity

This is just what it sounds like: an approach used to find creative solutions to design production problems. It may sound similar to Blue Sky, but Blue Sky is additive and expansive, while Problem Solver Creativity is a subtractive and practical creative process. Problem Solver Creativity is all about making things happen, getting from point A to point B in an efficient manner, and producing an end product. Most producers are very good at this kind of creativity because it is what helps them get products to launch on time. Being reductive by nature, this kind of creativity tends not to generate wildly new concepts; instead, it uses a critical process to make decisions. Criticism has a tendency to kill creativity (this is especially true for children), but at certain stages of product development, it can be useful. We all use problem solver creativity in aspects of our lives, especially when we are playing games or solving puzzles.

Wearing Both Hats

If we want to deliver imaginative content for kids, we need both ingenious innovation and the ability to take our insights into reality and completion. Creators of children's content frequently balance these two creative modalities at once because we act as designer/producers or producer/designers, wearing both hats at the same time. It's a juggling act, but it's very satisfying when true innovation leads us into exciting new places.

It helps to know when in your process to use each creative style. And, though it can be easy to go from Blue Sky to Problem Solving, it is not often as easy to go the other way. True creative innovation does not just switch on and off. It is a process that takes time and nurturing. **Be sure to leave enough room at the beginning of a new project for inventive Blue Sky dreaming in connection with the needs of the kids.** When there is an opportunity for new things to grow through play and connection, you will be able to produce titles that delight and are loved.

> *Real artists ship.*[4]
> —Steve Jobs

Design Stage One: Developing a Product Vision

Sometimes there is a resistance to actually spending much time on the preliminary design, especially in medium to large companies. When production timetables drive the schedule, the part that tends to get shortchanged in development is the new design and ideation process. This is not a good idea because it often ends up costing more in either production changes or the quality of the final product. At the beginning of the design process, it is critical to carve out some time to just play with new ideas. With that creative space ensured, there are some well-worn steps that help create the conditions for innovation.

> *One must still have chaos in oneself to be able to give birth to a dancing star.*[5]
> —Friedrich Nietzsche, philosopher

Phases of the Creative Process

Here is a basic overview of the process I use. Everyone will have their own stages, but I think an example is helpful.

Larger Goals Preparation

As you begin a new project, it is important to gather all the information available in order to understand the current landscape of the target market. Information about competitive products, what defines your audience, budget and time limits, technical capabilities, and the expectations of your client or company are all important to understand. The first stage of product design is all about defining the parameters of those components in order to give you a canvas and a palette of tools to develop a product vision.

©smithore/Depositphotos.com

Define your goals and objectives. A good place to start is by sketching out some rough ideas about what you think might be a good content area to explore. If you are working with clients, do they allow you a lot of creative freedom, needing only a quick approval of a concept in order to move ahead into the design phase, or are their ideas very specific and concrete? It's important to know your clients. Meet and discuss the project with them to get a clear idea of what they want and what they hope to build for kids. Understanding and managing your client's expectations is part of the job. Just like they might hire an architect to design a building for them, they hired you to design a digital playground or plaything for kids. Get clear on what they want, what their budget is, and what they expect from you.

Help your client figure out what they want. More often than you might think, a company or group will arrive with a basic concept of what they want, usually based on something they have seen somewhere else. They come to you for your expertise in children's content, and to find out about the marketplace. They have some ideas, but they're probably unaware of how much they don't know yet. Your job is to help them figure it out.

This is not an unusual situation. Your first job may be to educate them enough so that they can make informed decisions. Support them while they figure out what they want. This preprocess can take up a chunk of time before you have a contract. One of the best ways to deal with this stage is to write up a short contract for exploratory work (sometimes called the discovery process). An exploratory contract gives you and the client a chance to work together to see if there is a good fit before committing to something larger, and it doesn't cost either of you too much time or money. At the end of the discovery stage, based on your mutual conversations and brainstorming, you can deliver a few concepts, choose directions in which to move forward, and ballpark a more realistic budget for production.

Without this initial commitment, you risk spending a lot of time trying to help the client figure out what they want without a contract or guarantee that the time you spend now will be paid for.

Get to know your target technology. Before you begin to design, you need to know what your technological platform can do. The key to pushing your design as far as it will go is to play with the technology, follow your own feelings in the play process, and get to know the strengths and weaknesses of your platform. The design process is the most inventive when we understand what the technology has trouble doing, because this takes us into problem-solving mode to enhance performance and experience. That often leads to great new insights and ideas.

Outline a rough product size and budget. At this stage, it is too early to define the real scope for your project, but it is important to have some idea about how big the app is going to be and generally what resources may be available. Having a ballpark budget as a starting place will inform your creative thinking and, if you come up with a brilliant game-changer concept, you can always revise accordingly.

Determine your audience's developmental sweet spot. Children have relatively distinct ages and stages of development (sometimes called "age banding"), in which a group will have similar interests, needs, desires, and play patterns. Since kids are always growing, leaving one stage and migrating toward the next, it is helpful if you can determine the "sweet spot" for your product design. Put another way, who is the most likely subset of the target audience who will want the product, really love it, and act as an advocate to other potential players? (For more about kids' ages and stages, see Ch. 10.)

Designer's Note

Being a former kid doesn't make you an expert. More than once I have seen a company waste a year's production and a lot of money only to realize that their art director has created a world or characters that he or she thinks are way cool and edgy, and look good in their portfolio, but which the five-year-old target market can't relate to. In one reading product I consulted on, most of the animated characters were tall and looked like teenagers or young adults (big kids). There was only one small peripheral character that was "cute," and that was the *only* one the target-age kids connected with.

Making Information Soup

Part of intelligent design is having enough information and knowledge about the subject you are interested in exploring. This does not mean you have to follow what others have done, or review everything that has ever been done in this area, but it is a wonderful opportunity to gather resources to help stimulate innovation and the creative process. Here are a few things I like to do to stimulate my thinking.

Play with some legacy titles. There are some wonderful older legacy titles and great newer (but little-seen) apps that can be very inspirational. Most titles have redeeming features, and I like to collect the parts that work. Truthfully, there is a lot of junk out there, but I love looking at some of the older titles and solving the problems they didn't know how or didn't have the technological tools to solve. Legacy apps are like prototypes you didn't have to build. The little bit of money and time invested is way cheaper than building it yourself.

> *[Old products] are basically free prototypes. You can learn tremendous amounts ... [doing] game archeology.*[6]
> —**Will Wright**, creator of *The Sims*

Look at what's on the market now. Gathering some understanding of the current marketplace gives your invention some context, validity, and hopefully a clearer relation to the market landscape and opportunities. What's missing?

One invaluable resource for research on current and legacy children's products is Children's Technology Review Exchange (CTREX), developed by Warren Buckleitner. This database has over 12,000 reviews dating back to 1993. The information is well organized, with powerful search tools, and the reviews can teach you a lot about what works and what doesn't.

Gather idea fragments to stimulate invention. In the course of coming up with a final idea I usually have a little pile of good ideas left over that I keep handy and bring out to play with when I start a new project. They include things I'm interested in, things I know my target audience likes, and things that made me laugh, surprised me, or otherwise got my attention. Sometimes combining ideas creates new perspectives. Like when you mix a name for something warm and friendly (say, *kitchen*) with something active and fun (say, *cha cha*), and get the Cha Cha Kitchen! Just a whimsical name can stimulate a dozen more ideas.

Characters or not? If characters are going to be an important part of an app or game I like to start inviting them in early, because they often become one of kids' favorite places to look for interaction. I begin collecting characters' models and personalities as soon I think there may be a place for them.

Know your intellectual property (IP). If you are working with licensed characters, it's critical to get very familiar with them at the beginning of your design process. If you are about to use a licensed property, the first thing you have to do is learn everything about the character. Major licensed characters often come with a design bible or style guide, and a list of dos and don'ts.

Designer's Note

I have heard horror stories from other producers who have missed small details on a character model sheet. In one case, a large section of animation had to be redone because the famous children's character appeared to have a "crotch" due to the accidental addition of one small line that wasn't in the model sheets. On a more positive note, I was fortunate enough to be the first licensee to convert Dr. Seuss into an interactive format. Since we were taking a beloved book property into a new medium, we followed very close guidelines for how the characters looked, acted, and sounded. With Dr. Seuss, the correct meter and rhyme for any newly created interactive dialogue is essential, so we worked with Random House's Seuss expert at the time, Sharon Lerner, to make sure that every piece of dialogue was appropriate and in sync with license guidelines. A fun side effect of that project was that everyone in the office talked in rhymes and alliteration for months!

© zahradnik/Depositphotos.com

Immersion Play: Blue Sky Creativity

Now that the innovation soup has been made, and there are general guidelines and edges to your sandbox, it's time to actually play.

Let go of preconceived restrictions. For now, forget all the above considerations except a few sparks to inspire a starting place. If there is anything you need to remember, *it* will remind you. Once you have some working ideas you are excited about, you can review your basic goals to see how they align.

Freely borrow ideas you like. I am not suggesting co-opting anyone's idea, but when something is done well, and it tickles you, borrow it. Play with it. **Connect it** with other ideas to see what happens. Take it someplace new. Borrow from the best.

> *It's not where you take things from—it's where you take them to.*[7]
> —Jean-Luc Godard, filmmaker

Freely combine contrasting elements. Mix it up—make a mess—take risks! Look at things from different perspectives, especially the point-of-view of your target-age child. Get playful. Now is the time! Make new relationships and connections.

> *Creativity is just connecting things. When you ask creative people how they did something . . . they just saw something. . . . That's because they were able to connect experiences they've had and synthesize new things.*[8]
> —Steve Jobs

© carballo; mmaxer; Provectors; lapotnik; Raysay; inides/Depositphotos.com

Follow your intuition. Let your intuition drive your play and see what shows up. Ask lots of "What if?" questions. "What if?" questions support new perspectives and recombining. If need be, go tell the (internal) critic to go hang out on the couch while you play. Let your excitement guide your awareness.

**If we walked on our hands instead of our feet,
would we wiggle our toes to say "Hi!" when we meet?**

Scribble down or draw the good ideas. You don't need to go into great detail. Stay with the big picture, but start getting your basic insights down on paper. Inspiration can pass by in an instant; it's important to capture it while it's fresh.

> *Inspiration exists, but it has to find us working.*[9]
> —Pablo Picasso

Sorting and Selecting: Letting the Cream Rise to the Top

Now it's time to begin the gentle shift from Blue Sky to Problem Solver Creativity.

- **Gather up the three juiciest ideas.** Hopefully, you have come up with several award-winning concepts, and now it's time to begin picking the best ones.

- **Compare them to your original goals.** How do they compare? Do they support or enhance your goals? Do you need to revise your goals based on your ideas? How extendable are the concepts into additional titles in a line? Do any show promise as intellectual properties that might work in other media (books, board games, toys, television, etc.)?

- **Make a list of benefits and possible drawbacks for each.** Making a list of strengths and weaknesses can offer insight into a concept's larger viability.

- **Loop in some appropriate-age kids for feedback.** It's not a make-it-or-break-it moment when you share your concept with kids because they may or may not get your idea. It's still very early. But it is important that you begin including kids in your design as early as possible to make sure you haven't come up a with a great idea for adults instead of for the right age of kids.

- **Pick the strongest product concept.** It can be hard to pick one over the others, but usually by this time one idea is standing out and has you the most creatively excited. Go for it.

Design Stage Two: Docs, Prototypes, and Planning

The next stage is about taking your favorite idea and building it out further. Each stage teaches you new things, and related ideas and improvements will continue to bubble up. That's how it's supposed to be. The point is not to get overly distracted by something completely new (you can always write it down for later if it's *that great*). Keep your focus on enhancing the concept you are creating.

Put Your Vision into Words

This is a good place to start thinking about communicating your vision to others. Having a product *vision* implies seeing something new (such as characters, a setting that allows for extended story lines, a gimmick or special power that creates dynamic tension, etc.).

What do you want to call your product and why? How might you communicate the invitation to play to your users?

Further, can you define your product vision in one or two simple sentences? What is your "elevator pitch" (the way you would describe your product concept on a one-minute elevator ride)? Imagine that you and the company president are suddenly stuck between floors. What is the differentiator, the coolness factor that makes this project a must-have for the company?

Refine the design. Revisions and additions come into play as the concept gets fleshed out and a production path becomes clearer. Creating a product is like building a house: it's good to have plans! You can't begin until you know where the foundation will be, where the doors and windows go, or where the wiring and plumbing run. The design document takes in all the pertinent information and creates an integrated plan to work with.

Not all designers work the same way. Some designers find it best to work through the concept stage of new designs on their own. Others like to take the initial seed of an idea and then gather a small group of "creatives" they can jam with to expand the design. You have to do what works best for you.

The Documentation Process

You've had the creative spark, and made notes; now it's time write it all down in one place. Something with a beginning, middle, and an end. Design documents are made to change, but writing your concepts down forces you to think in more detail and to explore how the pieces might connect together. Good design documentation keeps track of details and can be a map that helps you (and others) remember where you are going. Here are the basic design documents:

- **The design treatment.** The first document is often called a *design treatment*. It is a quick, one-page, bullet-point discussion of your product's unique features and its intended audience. It's a quick pitch to generate interest and market your idea.

- **The preliminary design document.** After treatment approval, if you are working with a client, you move on to a preliminary design document that discusses the main content, interactivity, character behaviors, and uses of the technical platform. It expands the ideas of the treatment and fleshes out the initial look and feel. If it's going to be a large project, this is a good time to share the preliminary design with other potential team members and begin to get input on programming, animation, and audio needs. Brainstorming helps you consider other points of view and assemble bullet-point feature lists to help qualify or disqualify ideas before time is wasted writing long descriptions.

Somewhere near the end of this preliminary stage, enough of the concept is worked out that a decision can be made about going forward. So far, the process hasn't cost too much because the production team hasn't begun. It's a great time to agree if the concept has what it takes to go further. If there is budget for it, it is also a good time to put together quick prototypes for preliminary (or "proof-of-concept") testing with kids.

- **The working design.** The working design document becomes the blueprint used to bid, plan, and organize for production. It continues to be a refinement of the preliminary design doc with much more added detail. It often includes new information learned from testing prototypes, and it reflects a more-than-conceptual attitude about how things will work.

- **The final design doc.** The final design document has locked down any changes, and it reflects complete production goals and objectives. (Of course, in real life, things always change some, but the final doc is something the team can refer to if they forget things along the way.)

The final design doc is particularly critical when dealing with dispersed teams. This document is the map for other departments to use while they do their more specialized work. For example, using the final design doc, the art director should be able to break out an art asset list, the lead engineer should be able to do the technical specification, and marketing should be able to begin generating ideas that will help the game at launch.

- **Time lines, schedules, and milestones.** Now that there is some idea of how big the project is, it's time to assemble schedules, time lines, and concrete milestones. Get real estimates and delivery commitments from your team members. Figure out what your most critical pieces are and how they align. Will any one of them delay all the others? Is there an optimum time to release the title? Set priorities accordingly. Schedules and delivery estimates may change based on a variety of unseen issues. If possible, leave yourself a little bit of room in each portion of the time line to allow for unexpected delays or hurdles. Remember, *things almost always take a little longer than we think they will!*

The Production Process

The production process often involves many people and specific sequential steps to assemble, build, and launch a project. The most important aspect of production is not the production stages themselves, but how to navigate those stages in a way that supports team building, buy-in, and the delivery of something everyone feels good about, including the end users—kids. The designer is important not only at the beginning of the production process but also throughout production because his or her continued involvement helps to keep the product vision alive, which means an end result that is cohesive and consistent—magic instead of mud.

Quality is the best business plan of all.[1]
—John Lasseter, CCO, Pixar and Disney

Design Stage Three: Produce and Assemble the Pieces

Production of everything begins. This is where Problem Solver creativity rules, and Blue Sky listens and occasionally adds insight. The design may still need some new pieces to adjust for unforeseen things learned in testing, but your (mostly) complete design plans are now becoming production plans. Changes beyond this stage get *a lot more expensive*, so it's important to have the design pretty much resolved and agreed upon. It's a lot easier and less expensive to change the look of your avatar in planning stages than it is after hundreds or thousands of frames of animation have been generated.

Production is a solid, not a gas. In the design stage, the entire project is held in the imagination of just a few people. To make changes, you rewrite a few lines in the design document; it is relatively easy. The time spent in the design stage is flexible depending on how complete the concept needs to be. It can be easily shortened or compressed, like a gas. But when production begins in earnest, budgets are set, team members have been hired or allocated, and the time line clock starts ticking. The production stage is like a solid. It is not easily shortened or lengthened without changing one of the big three: time-to-completion, budget, or quality. If you start adding changes to the design at this point, the old saying applies, "Of fast, cheap, and well done, you can have any two out of three."

Designer's Note

Because they often don't understand the technical issues involved in software production, clients are sometimes surprised that their "little changes" are greeted with looks of horror. To change the color of an avatar's shirt in the last few weeks of production may be easy, or it may trigger big changes affecting the budget and time-to-launch. It all depends on the development environment and the code. Where code is involved, you can't just throw bodies at it and expect it to change quickly. It may be so deeply interwoven with everything else that changing one thing breaks many others. That, in turn, affects the overall testing cycle. It can be a mind-blowing experience for clients when you explain the possible cascade of effects from their late-stage change suggestions.

Use quick prototypes to check the main functionality. At this stage, prototypes are still valuable as a way to continue testing your assumptions about functionality and interaction. Prototypes are relatively inexpensive, and even very small ones can quickly tell you if you are on track or not. They don't have to be fancy; they just have to allow for interaction. But remember, at this point, even your prototypes need to focus on problem solving rather than inventing new features. Plan prototypes carefully, and stay focused on using them to answer specific questions about usability and interface design.

Try out prototypes with kids. Ultimately, kids are your clients. Make sure they are part of your prototype testing cycle. To watch kids play with even a simple prototype can be amazing, and it will teach you a great deal. *Thinking* about how children might interact with your design is different than experiencing what they *actually* do. (For more about how to talk with kids during testing, see Ch. 20.)

Designer's Note

Watching kids play with prototypes has saved us tons of money over the years because we were able to change course without it being a big deal. Kids have found programming bugs in minutes that no adult on the team had seen in weeks or months of working on the program. Kids will also begin to play spontaneous games and assign causal relationships to objects and characters, causal relationships we never intended to create. Frequently, we have modified our designs based on what the kids **expected** to see happen.

© Syda_Productions/Depositphotos.com

Stay connected to your team. Things start to move at this stage, and as working prototypes emerge, you will learn things you didn't think of in the early stages of design. This is a critical time because the design may need to change based on information gleaned from testing. Keep the team updated on how the design may be evolving, what you are learning, and how that might impact *their* production responsibilities.

Leave room for the unexpected. No matter how well you prepare, unexpected "stuff" (good and bad) happens mid-production. Inevitably, you will need to redo or create new portions that weren't included in the original design plan. This will impact and possibly stress the production schedule. Knowing this, it is always smart to include some extra money and time in advance to cover unforeseen karmic entanglements during production. If you need the time and money, you are covered; if you don't, you can potentially be a superstar by delivering your product ahead of time and under budget.

Alpha, beta, and final testing. Quite often, the ability to deliver on time is ensured by well-defined alpha, beta, and final testing phases in the schedule. To avoid any train wrecks, build these phases into your production time line from the start. **Alpha** software needs to be entirely playable, but only one element of each feature needs to be present. You can have crash bugs and placeholder art, but you need to have functional work-arounds to judge the totality of the experience. Once you can see it, you can get a grip on any major problems.

By the time you get to **beta**, there should be little or no placeholder art and no crash bugs. You should be ready for a content lockdown. If any of this is missing, you aren't ready for beta.

Design Stage Four: Implementation and Sweetening

Nothing is more exciting than when all the pieces come together to create a new living (as in interactive) experience. At this point, you will have already learned some things from your active prototypes, and now you get to see how it all fits together. Congratulations to you and your team! (Remember to thank them and show your appreciation for their efforts—you want them to enjoy this stage too.) This is a very exciting time because you get to see what works and what doesn't!

The whole is greater than the sum of its parts. As it all starts to come together,

something new begins to emerge: the experience you have of the project as a whole. There is a moment when it stops being the pieces, and it becomes an interactive entity. That entity has its own look and feel. As you interact with it, you begin to understand more about it. You are having an interactive experience. Interactive design is ultimately all about creating just this experience, one that entertains and engages the users, and then leaves them with a feeling that inspires them to come back for more.

Keep your design goal focus. As projects evolve, they have a tendency to collect a lot of other bells and whistles. It's important to remember what your main design goal is. For example, if your game is about meeting people, everything in the game should support doing so. At this stage of production, it's a good practice to do a "check-in" to make sure your focus is still intact. Great games are great because they do what they say they will do, and they do it well.

Not all bugs are equal. Prioritize. Sometimes you get to the end of a product, and you still have some persistent technical bugs that are hard to get rid of without breaking something else. Ultimately, most software products go into release with some bugs, but not all bugs are equal. Some bugs are showstoppers, and you just have to bite the bullet and fix those. It's good to prioritize your bugs and know which ones you are willing to live with.

Sweetening at the end greatly enhances the experience. When you first bring an application to life, it probably functions at only a percentage of the end result. In the final stage, it is something that can be played with and examined for how it feels. This is a time of learning. The application isn't just a concept anymore; it's alive and responsive. The iterative process of tweaking, massaging, and completing the experience moves your title to the next level, and it is a very important part of the design process because this is where you finesse the final experience the user will have. Just like in the construction of a house, all the detailed trim work at the end is what provides character. This stage can take longer than expected, but it is worth it in the end. The final tweaking and tuning of the interactive experience based on real usage by kids is what turns an okay experience into a compelling and satisfying one.

> *It's that last ten percent on a project that brings it alive. Even if you get it all in there, and it doesn't crash, the difference between good and great is that last ten percent.*[2]
> —**Bridget Erdmann, Creative Director, Gizmo6**

Plan and leave time for this massaging; it will *really* help to bring your application alive and to its full potential. Over the years, every designer has seen this same result: the time you spend tweaking the last portion of your project is what helps it come into focus and resemble the vision of what you hoped for way back in the beginning. Many years ago, animated film director John Lasseter (Pixar/Disney) was nice enough to visit my company and speak with

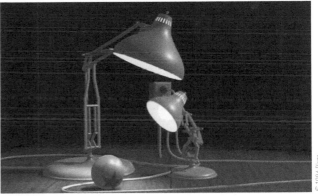

© 1986 Pixar

the animators (he had just won his first Oscar for *Tin Toy*). One of the main things he shared was this same point: the nuances added at the end of the process are what really bring forward the pathos and charm in his animated characters.

Tips on Working with Teams

Everyone is creative, but not in the same way. This is one of the values of working with teams. Having teams is a benefit because everyone brings their own particular styles, viewpoints, experiences, and talents to the table. Whether you have an idea of your own, or you have been handed a project, you are probably going to need a team to help you produce it.

Designer's Note

You might ask why understanding team dynamics matters in children's design. Over and over, it has become obvious that a team that works together well creates an enjoyable experience for everyone, and the end product is something to be proud of. One company I worked with for some years had such a bond that, even though the company itself has been gone for more than a decade, everyone still gathers semi-annually to stay connected. This is the kind of work situation I would choose again and again over companies that have structure but no collaborative cohesion and purpose.

Create a Shared Vision

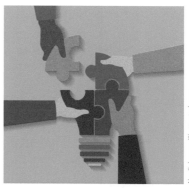

It's human nature to join together to do things with a common purpose or goal. One of the best ways to create cohesion for your team is to develop a positive shared vision about what you are trying to accomplish. Once engaged, your team will feel energized and excited, which makes the entire process more enjoyable and ultimately creates a better product. The following tips for engaging and working with creative members can help you create successful team cohesion regardless of company culture.

Have a worthwhile goal. There is a difference between having a job that just pays your bills, and having work that excites and impassions you when you wake up each morning. When you're inspired and excited about getting to work, it's a sign that your work is feeding your soul (as well as your bank account). People get energized when their work and group/company is accomplishing something truly worthwhile.

Each day, as a children's designer, you have the opportunity to build something wonderful and amazing for kids, something that may change their lives in ways you can't even imagine. Find a way to connect with this higher purpose to inspire your team to cooperative action on behalf of those kids. People want to support a vision of the world working right, and the development of truly engaging kids' content is a great way to promote that positive future. When teams are truly engaged in something they feel will make a difference in the world, they will go beyond what was asked of them and become advocates for the shared vision.

Be inclusive. No one likes to be excluded, and inclusion fosters ownership. As you actively become the lead salesperson for the product vision, engage others' participation in that vision. It can be useful to include and connect with people beyond your team, such as the marketing and sales department, administrative assistants, and others. They too can become your advocates and support your vision in ways you might never have expected.

Connect with everyone. Just like when you were a kid on the playground, it's easier to play together when you already know somebody. Make it a point to connect with each team member individually. *You* are the glue that initially connects everyone. Once you get to know everyone, and they feel seen, it can greatly influence their level of participation, care, and ownership in the final product. People are inspired when they can see a personal role for themselves in bringing a vision to life.

Designer's Note

When I began work at one software company, I came in as an animator, but I was really there because I had an idea for a line of children's products. Being an unknown designer, I thought it would be easier to sell my idea from the inside. After three months of pushing the idea, I got enough agreement from management that I was allowed to begin a small prototype of my concept.

Things became a bit awkward with my co-workers because they were still doing all the assigned work and I, along with a hot new computer and a couple of monitors, got to work on my own project. I decided to figure out how to involve them so that they felt more included in what I was doing. At one point, when I needed voices and sound effects, I invited my co-workers to be some of those voices. That way, every time I played the prototype, tweaked it, or demoed it (and that was often), they were a part of it. Even when their voice or noise was highly altered from being tweaked up or down, they still identified with it. In the midst of a demo from two cubicles away, I would hear someone say, "That's me!" It turned out to be so much fun that I invited my boss—and my boss's boss—to be voices, too. Everyone ended up with ownership in the project. We were part of a shared vision. We wanted to see it succeed, and it did.

Follow your vision. To bring something to fruition takes more than an idea; it takes ongoing passion. You must be the advocate at the center of the circle who keeps the project alive. If the project is going well, and others participate, the vision will evolve and become more of a group vision. Incorporate new ideas that support, enhance, and expand the developing shared vision. Honor others' activities and participation in the overall goal, but remember that **it is still *your* vision, and it's your passion that drives everyone forward.**

iStock.com/shylendrahoode; © belchonock/Depositphotos.com

Team Dynamics

Communication skills are a big plus. If you don't have any, get some! To be a good designer/producer, you need to be good at communication (unless you are a one-man-band kind of studio, and, even then, being a good communicator helps to sell your product after production). Working well with your clients is what keeps you in business, but they may not always know much about kids; you need strong communication skills to convey what kids really want. When you have clear and supportive communication with the production team, it saves time, money, and a lot of frustration.

No designer is an island. Engage your team. No children's designer is an island, and most of us end up working with larger teams. Proactively engage your programmers, sound designers, artists, writers, and kid advisors early in the production process to help avoid pitfalls later. Don't make *assumptions* about their ideas, strategies, preferences, or passions. Ask them questions. Have conversations with them. Remember to involve your team at each stage of your design process. They are fundamental to the creation of an integrated design that will actually work when it's built. Remember that you don't know everything and that each team member brings expertise to the table. Your job is to find a way to let their specific talents shine through in the overall design.

Foster a safe environment for team share. Google has investigated what makes great teams in order to improve their own team efficiencies. They found that it wasn't just putting all the smartest or most organized people together. No special combination of experience, technical skill, or personality seemed to make a difference. As they said, "The 'who' part of the equation didn't seem to matter."[3]

It turns out that to raise a group's collective intelligence they needed groups who were fair about talk time, meaning that everyone got about the same amount of time to speak. This is also called "conversational turn-taking". The best groups also had participants who where good at "intuiting how others felt based on their tone of voice, their expressions and other nonverbal cues."[4] Psychologists call this *social sensitivity*, and the best teams were high or above average in this ability.

A group environment that supports empathy and conversational turn-taking creates a safe place for team members to connect and express themselves. Freedom from fear of rejection, punishment, or embarrassment when sharing ideas allows for greater interpersonal risk-taking and creativity. Harvard Business School professor Amy Edmondson says team safety "describes a team climate characterized by interpersonal trust and mutual respect in which people are comfortable in being themselves."[5] What could be better than a team that feels seen and heard at work?

Don't design by committee. You need a leader. It is important to connect with, listen to, and consider the many creative ideas that team members bring to product development, but don't let a committee take over the driver's seat. The problem with design by committee is that it is all about compromise, and it tends to end up being bland and overly complex. What's needed is one clear, strong, passionate vision of what the product should be. Someone needs to spearhead that innovation, drive the look-and-feel, and then shepherd the project all the way to launch (and sometimes beyond). If it's your design, that person should be you!

Small creative teams work best. Small creative teams can move fast, more easily come to agreement, and give each person a real contributive voice. The creative energy of small teams can be quite exhilarating and hilarious, and there's a good chance that energy will show in the final product. Find a creative mix of people that works for you; it's important. Some of the most groundbreaking ideas seem accidental, but they actually occur because of the unique chemistry within teams.

Nurture creative opportunities. Whether you have a brown bag lunch with your team (outside of the office, hopefully), see the latest kids' movie together, play with new toys, or invite other "creatives" to come talk, it's important to find ways to stimulate your team's creative juices. This makes for a smarter and more enjoyable work environment.

Navigating production stages with your team so that everyone feels involved, connected, and integral to the product will pay off in all sorts of ways, from increased creativity and good morale to better QA and final product. As well as providing the creative and interpersonal glue for the team, you as the designer/producer need to make sure they get the feedback they need about how the product is working for its most important audience—kids. The next chapter will discuss various aspects of play testing and user testing and how to deliver valuable formative evaluation of the product at every stage along the way.

Designer's Note

While attending the first Dust or Magic AppCamp, I had a chance to talk with colleagues about the future of children's application development. Daren Carstens, a veteran award-winning graphic artist and software designer, shared the following: "We need to be passionate about what we are creating. If you are given a project and only feel so-so about it, you need to find someone who is excited by that subject. It doesn't matter what it is, there is someone out there who thinks that it is just the coolest thing. You need to find out who that person is and get their help."[6]

I like open office arrangements, despite the interruptions to programmers. I'd rather have everyone working 60% efficiently in the right direction rather than 90% efficiently in the wrong one.[7]

—**Rob Martyn, game production executive**

Testing with Kids

Testing! The word has inspired dread since childhood. Testing is not only an incredibly important part of developing an interactive game or interface, but it can also be the most fun. This is the stage of development where you as the designer have a chance to interact with your target audience—kids. It may sound intimidating to show your work to the people who will eventually be using it, but this chapter is meant to simplify what seems complicated, and it will also give you the support you need in order to put together a positive testing experience for both you and the kids who are offering their feedback.

Program testing can be used to show the presence of bugs, but never to show their absence![1]

—**Edsger Dijkstra, Dutch computer scientist**

User-Centered Design

Much of the discussion in this book shows you how to go from a designer's viewpoint to a viewpoint centered on kids. What's it like for them? How is their perspective different than yours? How do they experience the product? What are they interested in? What needs does it fulfill for them? Ideally, you are making sure the software works for the users at the other end of the design process. This practice is called *usability*, the degree to which something is easy to use and a good fit for the people who use it, in our case kids. Is it efficient, effective, and satisfying?

User-centered design (also referred to as UX, for user experience) is an approach that aims to create high levels of usability for a target audience. It is a philosophy and multistage design process that optimizes the interface for how people *want* to use a product. This process enables designers to adapt to the user's behavior, instead of users adapting to the designer's decisions. One of the key factors with this approach is that it requires testing user behavior in the real world, using real members of the target audience. This process puts pressure on assumptions about user behavior, giving the designer more information about the validity of those assumptions.

Most user-centered design philosophies focus on a four-step process:

1. **Understand your real end users.** Identify your target group and what makes them special. What similar products already work for them? What will they use your product for, and under what conditions? Begin to specify their context for use.

2. **Define your goals.** Identify user goals (what you hope kids will get from your product) that must be met for your title to be successful. One of the trickiest tasks is to transfer one's perception of a user to an interface design that actually works for them. Be clear about what you want, and it will be easier to get there. Testing is where you will find out how well you are reaching your goals.

3. **Design, prototype, and test iteratively.** Create design solutions, but don't get locked into a single solution too quickly. The prototyping at this stage might be broken into low- and high-fidelity versions.

   - *Low-fidelity prototyping* allows for greater experimentation, swift evaluation, and design evolution. It occurs early in the testing process to validate a basic concept. It is not detailed, but rather uses rough audiovisual assets to simulate key interactivity.

   - *High-fidelity prototyping* uses semi-final audiovisuals to simulate the real look and feel of the experience. It comes later in the process as assets become available, and it provides better data on exact user behavior, likes, and dislikes. It may be a little more in-depth than the low-fidelity testing, including a few more "bells and whistles." All prototypes should be designed to be developed as quickly and as economically as possible. The goal with prototypes is to learn about any problems in the design *before* you have spent the time and money to get to a beta version.

4. **Evaluate the design throughout production.** Products tend to morph a bit as they go through the production process. Things that worked for kids in the prototype may have lost some of their magic when the design was refined. Reevaluate with usability testing along the way to ensure an end product that truly delivers that great experience kids were expecting—and the great sales you were hoping for.

When you practice good user-centered design, you get a product that kids will use. It's alive for them, and it does what they want and expect. It may seem more expensive in the beginning, but it is always cheaper than building a large product on inaccurate assumptions that lead to a beautiful site or activity that kids aren't interested in.

Prototype Testing with Kids

Working with kid testers. Getting authentic feedback isn't always as easy as one might think. Here are some tips for successful testing.

- **Use small test groups.** You don't always need a large sample group of children to get a feel for how things are going interaction-wise. Just a few kids in the target age group and gender will give you plenty of helpful feedback. Kids are experts in play, and in what they like, and they are not afraid to share their interests with you. Have children in to play-test in groups of one and two, and allow different team members to moderate (with your supervision and help). Make sure to include kids from all the socio-economic groups you hope to reach within your age range.

- **Share only the minimum amount they need to get started.** Don't tell kids too much about how your prototype is *supposed* to work. Just let them play, and see if it's obvious to them.

- **Don't hover or act like you care too much.** Get out of the way and be relatively invisible so the kids can have an authentic experience. You want to minimize their feeling of being watched—too strong a presence from you can be distracting. This is especially true if they think you have a vested interest in them liking the product. Kids will skew their responses to match your expectations if you ask leading questions, or if you let your desire for a specific response show. You really want the most authentic response you can get; accept whatever they say as a valid response in a positive tone, and be careful about asking for clarifications.

- **Actions speak louder than words.** The real learning happens as you watch kids navigate and interact, rather than from asking them what they liked. Kids want to please, and they may not offer much critical feedback when asked. The best feedback happens while they are engaged in playing. This is where real interaction problems will show up and also where real moments of delight might spontaneously erupt. Could they figure out how to play the game on their own? Did they do some things over and over just because it was fun? If they got stuck, what was unclear for them? What were their expectations for the interaction?

iStock.com/Susan Chiang

- **Test in different environments.** In an effort to reach different social strata and groups of kids, test drive the prototypes in a variety of settings, such as schools, clubs, and organizations. Send prototypes home, and ask the parents to give you feedback about how the kids played with the product in their most comfortable environment. You can learn from each of these settings.

Older testing models used to require that kids not know each other for the sake of "objectivity." These techniques have been disproved, but linger in the public mindset. If social media tells us anything, it is that kids learn about games from their friends. So in my opinion, it's great if the kids are real life friends and talk about it. For heaven's sake, let's all be a little subjective![2]

—Gano Haine, game designer

- **In-school testing.** Kids are generally very excited to play on the computer when they're at school. This may be due in part to the level of control and engagement they get from the activity compared to their regular classroom activities. Even if your product is well received in a school setting, your overall assessment needs to take into account that computer access may be unique and special in this environment, and your results might be skewed.

- **In-office testing.** Some kids can be overwhelmed by the "cool factor" of being in an adult environment, and they might have an initial tendency to want to please you. Invite small groups of children (and parents) into your office on a regular basis; this helps everyone relax and offers you some consistent knowledge of each child's individual personality. It also helps you connect to the parents, who can give you their feedback about the value your product offers their children. They may even tell you things that happened after they left your office.

- **In-home testing.** In a home setting, you can't watch the kid–game interaction in the same way, but you do get to go beyond the novelty effect of playing in a special situation. This allows you to see how popular the prototype is when played in the final destination. How does it hold up against all the usual distractions of home? Parents are more than happy to share what seemed to work, where their child spent his or her time, and what didn't interest them. Beta prototypes—those that have most of the functionality but are not very refined—are good choices for home testing because the beta version of the product gives more of a complete experience, and you don't have to watch as closely to see what works.

Naive and expert kid testers. These days, many kids have been so immersed in interactive media that it is not always easy to find a truly naive tester, but it's easy to find kids who are new to a genre. The value of naive testers is that they will show you problems with the interface and the process of getting started. The naive, or new, user doesn't already have a mindset about what is supposed to happen; they just react naturally to what is happening. Expert kid testers have usually spent more hours with the platform or genre than anyone on your adult team. They have played and experimented with tons of apps and environments, and they are able to critique your design or prototype in comparison with other things they have played. This can be enormously informative and, occasionally, embarrassing. Better to be embarrassed while you can still do something about it.

iStock.com/Imgorthand

Designer's Note

At one point, two members of my design team argued about a piece of animated interface, and they both thought they were right. We invited two brothers to come in, ages five and eight, to play with the game and give us feedback. Their mom was a computer artist with our company, so they were used to having adults around while they played. The older one was definitely an expert user. They played together for a while, and then the older one turned to us and proceeded to give an honest critique while his brother continued to play. He was brutally straightforward about his likes and dislikes. It was especially interesting for the arguing team members because our tester ripped one of the ideas to shreds, calling it "lame," unaware its creator was standing there. He resolved the argument in a way no one could disagree with, and he gave us some great insights to make the interface even better.

Prototypes are powerful. Prototypes are where you, as the designer, really get to see if your concepts work. Was your intuition correct? Does the prototype connect with kids? Do they know what to do? Do they do what you expected them to do? Do you see delight, enchantment, and engagement when they play with it? If a picture is worth a thousand words, a prototype is worth a hundred thousand. Even very small interactive prototypes provide surprises and insights that you can't get any other way, because you've added kids to the equation. Through their play, they create new games and uses you never dreamed of. They will assume expectations of functionality that you might have missed, and they will take the game to a whole new level.

Designer's Note

After years of experience with development and testing, I've learned that prototypes are supposed to be something you assemble quickly, learn from, and then set aside. Too often, companies start with a prototype, and then continue to build on it. Major problems can arise when you invest time and money in something that wasn't necessarily designed to become a full product. Don't make the prototype too fancy. It's a test, not a hot rod. Learn from your prototype, and then move on with a more robust architecture to support your real product goals.

Paper testing and small prototypes. Some games and activities lend themselves to paper testing. Lay cutouts of the proposed game on a table, explain the rules to kids, and then let them play and experiment. It is infinitely cheaper than building prototypes for everything, and it allows for quick, iterative changes and retesting.

Sometimes, when testing a concept for interactivity, the only good method is to build a small prototype. If you have built activities for a while, you may have similar code, already-animated characters, etc. that you can reuse to keep expenses down. If you need to create all new content, it is a good idea to use character sizes and pieces that you might be able to use later in the final product. Production costs go up quickly once a team is engaged. Therefore, interactive designers always try to get the most from any preliminary tests and borrowed content.

Prototypes as sales vehicles. A simple prototype can really help you sell a concept when you look for funding. It is sometimes hard for someone to imagine a game when you're talking about it, but using a prototype provides direct experience that hours of talking can't provide. Prototypes allow investors to imagine the larger potential of a product.

The Advantages of a Testing Lab

Many of the aforementioned testing strategies work for small companies testing a limited number of projects, but if you do ongoing testing, one of the best ways to get reliable results is to set up a testing lab.

Barbara Chamberlin, Director of the Learning Games Lab at New Mexico State University, has been developing interactive media and games for over twenty years. She has graciously provided her insights about building a testing lab and communicating with her "game consultants." It is important to note that, even though Barbara is talking about a testing lab for multiple games and interfaces, her suggestions can be applied to small-scale testing as well. The bottom line is to develop positive and effective ways of communicating with the kids who are providing feedback on your designs.

by Barbara Chamberlin, Ph.D.

Trying Hard to Make Games That Don't Stink
User Testing at the NMSU Learning Games Lab

Traditionally, getting reliable information from product testing with kids can be hard. In addition to all the hassles of scheduling, consent forms, and kid continuity, you only get the kids for short periods of time, and you have a lot of testing territory to cover. Testers often need some kind of preparation in order to give valuable feedback, even if it is just some practice in expressing their thoughts in a way that is clear to others. At New Mexico State University (NMSU), we sought a solution that would give us more frequent access to testers, an environment and structure that would help testers give us the best feedback possible, and ways we could test our products with kids while also developing our intuition in making better games from the start.

Youth working together on character design.

We established the Learning Games Lab, a dedicated space designed specifically for getting feedback, with areas that allowed us to interact with the kids in different ways. We equipped it with a bank of various computers and consoles, as well as mobile devices, for on-site testing. In addition to the games and computers, the space includes a couch and chair area for relaxed conversations; tables and bean bags where kids can be creative and comfortable; and specific areas dedicated to generating individual feedback, such as the Video Closet and Blogging Area.

Strategies We Enacted:

Increase access. To solve the problems of having consistent and continual contact with kids during a testing cycle, we began by bringing kids in over the summer for a series of two-week sessions—a sort of kid think tank. They came in for half days, every day for two weeks. This allowed us to get to know them better, and it gave the kids a chance to relax in the environment. We had continual access to our target audience during the summer, and once we trained the kids, we built a team of "experts" we could call on to test games whenever we needed to during the school year. Changing the group every two weeks creates a flexible environment for testing, where testers can bring in middle school kids for one session, then high school

---

About the Contributor

Dr. Barbara Chamberlin develops games and directs learning research at the Learning Games Lab at New Mexico State University. She's also a math and science nerd, museum fan, and a mom to two boys.

kids when testing a game for older audiences. The two-week schedule also gives a window in which to identify a problem in a game, fix it, and test it with a fresh set of users. The strategy has helped to improve our consistency and continuity over a product cycle, has dramatically increased how much testing we do, and is fun for us because we have an ongoing relationship with our team of consultants.

"Game consultants," not kid testers. We reframed how we involve the kids by calling them "game consultants." We don't call them "kids," "users," or "gamers." This re-naming makes clear that we listen to and honor their input as consultants who are helping us refine the products we are working on. We found that when we *emphasize their role to them*, they take their role more seriously. At the beginning of our time together, we tell them, "I need you as an advisor. I'm not a twelve-year-old; help me understand what twelve-year-old kids are thinking." When you give them this role, it becomes real for them. More than a focus group, it's an invitation to join the team and really help to build something great. This ability to do something real can be incredibly empowering for kids. It improves the quality of the feedback as well. Instead of simply asking consultants about their own views on a game, they are encouraged to advise our development team based on how they feel their peers would view the game. This encourages more thoughtful reflection among the kids.

Train consultants for communication. The Games Lab consultants go through a training procedure so they can learn some basic things about game dynamics and a common vocabulary for talking about them. Our training program includes activities where consultants learn about the different types or genres of games. They come to understand *challenge* or *flow* in a game. This builds their vocabulary and helps them articulate their preferences. For example, rather than saying the game just didn't seem "fun," they may recognize that it didn't keep up the level of challenge appropriately throughout the game. We give them practice by letting them warm up on somebody else's game that is similar, so they have some context before the game we really care about is in front of them.

NMSU Games Lab consultant talking with a tester.

The benefit of all this is that if, at any moment, we hit a snag and need to know *Are these graphics too juvenile? Is this level too difficult, or is it about right for what they should be learning?* we can take the game immediately to the kids to test and see what happens. We don't have to guess whether something works or not. We know. Better still, we don't have to prepare for a longer test session: when we want a simple answer on graphics or character design that may only take ten minutes, we can do it almost immediately. This improves our productivity during development.

Tips on Getting Real Answers and Information

At the heart of all testing, what developers really want to know is *Does the user like it?* And not just that, but also specifics related to their likes or dislikes, such as *Why?* or *Why not? Is it too hard or too easy? How could we improve it?*

Unfortunately, while these questions seem straightforward enough, it has been our experience that we can't just come out and ask these questions. Generally speaking, *people are not very good at saying* why *they like something.* This may seem counterintuitive because kids often seem eager to render an opinion. Many kids don't seem shy at all about telling you *what* they like about something. They are so forthright that you might think there would be no problem with getting a straight answer, but it doesn't quite work that way. Here is why:

Imagine *you* are my tester. For you to be able to tell me *why* you like something, several things have to happen. You have to:

1. **Know you like it.** Though it seems obvious, what you *like* is influenced by different things at different times. Are you just in a really good mood, and you like everything today? Do you generally *like* something, or do you just not *dislike* it? It is actually a complex question to get a straight answer to. You may feel neutral toward something, but when put on the spot, you can't think of why you *don't like it*, so you say you like it.

Testing on iPads in the NMSU Learning Games Lab.

2. **Know *why* you like it.** This may be even more complex because you may not fully understand why you like something. We aren't always good at identifying our own motivations for liking something. Often our likes and dislikes can come from cultural conditioning or something that happened a long time ago, and we may not be consciously aware enough to express a clear answer. You may like something simply because the color appeals to you, or because it reminds you of a childhood game, not because it actually has appeal to you as an individual product or game.

3. **Move beyond noticing.** Noticing is what we are good at, and the things we notice are where we go for a quick answer. With someone waiting for an answer, testers might just pick the first thing they notice. This is why, when you ask kids about a game, they almost always comment first about the graphics because that is what's most noticeable. But as you go deeper into it, gameplay may be what's important. If the kids get engaging gameplay, bad graphics are totally forgivable. This happens in everyday events. If you compliment me on my appearance, and I ask, "How so?" you may just mention

the first thing you notice: "That color looks good on you." Chances are it isn't the color specifically, but rather the cut of the shirt or the pattern in the jacket, and you would need some training to understand these finer points of wardrobe design. Game design is the same way.

4. **Overcome influences.** Testers often want to please the interviewer or agree with what other kids have said to feel part of the group. Maybe they just saw a movie that influenced their interest in a particular subject or characters, but those interests may be just a passing thing and not on their radar in two months. Understanding possible social reaction patterns helps to keep answers authentic.

5. **Communicate clearly.** Finally, testers need to be able to communicate and accurately express what they are feeling. This is extremely difficult, particularly in an environment in which children feel pressure from interviewers or their peers. Additionally, the interviewer has to be able to communicate clearly and be free of subtle expressions of their personal biases.

We can't completely overcome these challenges, but we try to recognize their influence in the feedback we receive. Here are some of the best strategies we have learned in our research.

Ask the Right Questions

Practice asking questions which can't be answered with a *Yes* or *No*. While this seems obvious, it's harder than you might think because most natural questions fall into the *Yes* or *No* category. When casually asking questions as they come to you in an interview or focus group, or when following up, we've found we easily slip into *Yes* or *No* questions, but we don't realize it until after we've reached the end of the question. Here are some tips we found helpful:

- **Don't begin any sentence with "Do..." or "Is..."** They always lead to Y/N answers.

- **Instead, start with "Tell me..." or "How..."** If you can rephrase your question to begin with "Tell me..." or "How...," you have already gone a long way in the battle against Y/N questions. It opens the conversation for more descriptive answers.

- **Write your questions down first.** This is a good way to keep from asking Y/N questions. It helps you stay on task and not forget to ask something important. Even if you don't ask the questions exactly as you've written them, this list gives you good phrases and formats to use in avoiding questions that lead to Y/N responses.

- **Allow for pauses that give room for more thought.** When you have questions on a clipboard, you can insert important pauses in the dialogue. You might say, "Let me look through these questions," and then add, "Is there anything else you want to tell me about that while I am looking?" This gives kids time to consider what you have been asking them. It's amazing how that pause, while you are engaged in reviewing your questions, will prompt kids to say something more thoughtful.

- **Treat consultants as advisors, not subjects.** Change the questions to be less about them personally and more about what their friends and siblings might think. It frees them up to be able to speak as "others," rather than focusing on their own likes and dislikes. Sample questions might be, "What age is this game for? Think of your friends, who will like this? Which of your friends would you recommend this for? What kinds of games do kids in your class like?" This really helps your kids take on the role of advisor and to be more reflective in how they respond.

- **Practice asking your question in different ways.** It's not that your consultants didn't answer it well the first time, but by the time it comes around again, they will have had time to reflect on it. They will possibly have a new idea or information to give you. This method leaves time for more answers to percolate to the surface.

Using Multiple Ways of Getting Feedback

At the NMSU Learning Games Lab, we found that, to get the best and most complete answers to questions, we had to be a little more clever and ask the questions in a variety of different formats. Each user is going to have their own best way of giving us feedback. Here are some of the different modalities we use:

- **Observation.** Direct observation has always been one of the most reliable ways of understanding interactivity because you actually get to see *what kids do* rather than hearing what they say. Direct observation is one of the best ways to see if there are interface problems or to see how a particular on-screen interaction might tickle kids. Which interactions do they do over and over for the joy of it? Watching engaged interactivity can be very telling and straightforward about what is and what is not working. Because our consultants spend so much time in the lab with adults, they are used to having observers throughout their time. This lessens the impact of feeling *watched*.

Games Lab consultant playing
Gate, a numeracy game.

- **Focus groups.** Focus groups allow peers to compare notes and experiences, often reminding each other what they liked about a product. But because social dynamics come into play, it can also give you "group think"—skewed results based on each group's social structure and particular mix of participants. However, it has its benefits as well. For example, the dynamics of a group may release taboos, or generate a strand of discussion. In research regarding the perception of characters in fitness games, we found that, when questioned individually, kids were hesitant to talk about overweight characters on-screen, and they generally avoided it. However, once they were in a group setting, and several people were commenting on it, they were more at ease in discussing how they felt.

- **Direct interviews.** Usually conducted one-on-one, interviews offer the opportunity to ask your kid advisors direct questions about their impressions of a product and its place in the market. Try to get kids to feel that their comments are important, and get them to delve into how the game is designed instead of just offering their first impressions.

- **The Video Closet.** The Video Closet has been one of our more successful review techniques. It is just a private space set aside with a video camera  on a wall. There is a place to sit and a white board with one or more questions on it. (This, of course, implies you are working with kids who can read.) The kid consultant goes in, reads the question, and can sit, reflect, and they think about it. When ready, he or she turns the camera on and talks. This has been amazing in controlling "group think." It has also helped kids who are a little reticent in group discussions or kids who like to think and reflect before answering. A nice feature of it is that you have it all on videotape and can review it later if needed.

Games Lab Video Closet.

- **Blogging Area.** We ask our kids to write down their questions and comments. (We found that most didn't like using pencil and paper, but were fine on the computer.) Writing is not the favorite of all of our kids, but some really prefer it, and we think it is good to support their efforts in literacy and giving feedback. Every day during their two weeks, they practice blogging and Video Closeting so that they gain proficiency in those modalities and in expressing their ideas, even if they are just blogging/writing about an existing commercially developed game. Though we use blogging software and share their feedback on a password-protected site that our developers can access, this is essentially journaling. By creating a specific area with barstools and high counters, and making clear that this written feedback will be read by the game developers, we encourage our consultants to take feedback more seriously.

- **Creative development (as assessment tool and way of getting feedback).** Throughout each two-week session, consultants design a game and, on the last day, give the development team a presentation that includes the name and description of the game, character sketches, and a description of gameplay. Though we will likely not build the game they propose, we hear them describing the characters, game characteristics, or artwork, and we get better intuition into the lives of our users. We hear what they like and enjoy, and that makes us better developers on future projects.

We also use creative activities as a way of getting feedback on our own games. For example, rather than just designing pirates for an upcoming science game, we asked consultants to draw pirates on a ship, explain who they are, and describe how they relate to each other. We asked consultants to draw a picture of a pirate captain, cabin boy or cabin girl, and the first mate. They named them and wrote a description about each character. This gave us ideas about what they would like to see in future characters. Similarly, when creating ninjas for a cooking game, we showed consultants several sample drawings of characters we were considering, then asked them to draw their own. We didn't have to ask what they liked or disliked about *our* characters; we could see what they liked when they included it in their own drawings.

Hands-on supplemental activities help engage the imagination.

Most importantly, using multiple ways of getting feedback works to give a well-rounded picture. We rarely depend on just one strategy. Instead, we might conduct a focus group, ask kids to answer similar questions in the Video Closet, then have them blog about a more general question. Each opportunity to talk with kids generates new ideas and thoughts regarding the game. Some kids are good at expressing thoughts verbally, whereas others want to write their thoughts and reflect on them. We have received seemingly contradictory answers from the same kid, who might say one thing in focus group, and another in the video closet. By giving consultants the ability to express things in different ways and answer similar questions in different formats, we are able to understand more of the *why* or *why not* behind their answers.

Additional Thoughts on Testing

- **Have the developers be part of the testing process.** Have your developers come in so they can ask questions directly. Through questions and direct observation, they get to see the problems firsthand, and this can save time when it comes to fixing existing issues. It also makes them better developers on the next project.

- **Use multiple reviewers.** We always have at least two reviewers, so that one can take notes while the other asks questions. We don't designate these roles ahead of time, and we encourage all reviewers to take notes and participate in asking questions. While one developer is asking questions or listening to one consultant, another reviewer may notice facial expressions or concern on another consultant's face. In addition, when we recognize a problem in a game, it is tempting for us to take notes on how we think a problem should be fixed, rather than really understanding the nature of the problem. Multiple reviewers bring different perspectives on what kids really mean to say.

Animator getting feedback from consultants on a paper prototype.

- **Involve stakeholders, producers, or anyone who might block development or distribution if they are not on board.** In addition to testing with kids, we also bring in stakeholders, such as teachers or parents. Even if kids like our product, if the gatekeeper to the classroom thinks kids *wouldn't* like it, it still won't get used.

The goal of testing is to remove the barriers to enjoyment and increase the levels of engagement and involvement. You'll know when a game is working because the kids will *ask you* if they can play it.

The proof of the pudding is in the eating!
—Traditional proverb

PART 6

Case Studies

Sometimes taking a closer look at an app can help to illustrate what makes it work or not work. Here are two simple case studies that pinpoint specific features, design considerations, and techniques that made the apps charming and engaging for children. These examples also discuss how designers worked around technical limitations.

The secret of genius is to carry the spirit of childhood into maturity.[1]
—T. H. Huxley, biologist

Case Study:
Club Penguin

Club Penguin was introduced in 2005 as an ad-free virtual community for kids age six through fourteen. The game has won numerous awards, and by 2013, over 200 million accounts had been created,[2] with players in every country in the world. Registering to play is free, which makes the game very inclusive, but paid accounts offer additional privileges. *Club Penguin's* success makes it a great case study for designing a virtual community for kids.

If it doesn't matter to a kid ... it doesn't matter.[3]
—Lane Merrifield, *Club Penguin* co-creator

Deceptively Simple

Beyond being accessible and easy to play, *Club Penguin* appears simpler than it is. Competitive design teams hoping to copy its success may look at it and say, "We can do better than that," "We can make lots of different characters," and so forth. They may accomplish these goals, but in the process they often lose some of the simple magic that kids really like about *Club Penguin*.

Good design often appears to be simple; that is part of its magic.

Why Penguins?

One animation moves all. *Club Penguin* was designed to be very economical in both animation costs and on-screen redraw computational power, which works on a wide range of systems (a good strategy, considering that kids often have their parents' older hand-me-down devices). The characters, even with clothing adornments, still read well when small, and they allow for a good-sized crowd of penguins to be together on screen at one time. Since everyone is an identical penguin shape, an animation of *any movement* can be reused across millions of penguin avatars. It also means that clothing, wigs, or other props work for *all* characters. There is no fancy walk cycle—it's just a simple two-frame waddle—but the simple animation still gives the characters believable mobility on a budget because one animation cycle works for *all* the avatars. The waddle also adds to the penguins' cuteness. (For tricks on inexpensive animation, see Ch. 6, pp. 89–95.)

Designer's Note

If it works, enjoy it; don't try to fix it. This is a deceptively simple truth of animation design. An animation director might say, "Look at these simple little characters. We can make them much more interesting and varied, and give them better animation." But the fact that the penguins work for kids just the way they are begs the question, "Will greater resolution and quantity of characters really improve the child's experience?" The answer is, "Maybe, but maybe not." Don't just assume that because you can do it, or you would have fun doing it, that it will be all that much better for the kids.

> *One of the first things Lane [Merrifield] ever said to me is "Club Penguin is not cool. It's the opposite of cool. The only thing that is cool is who you are." Everything about the Penguin encourages silly and goofy and different, not conformity and elitism. And that is ingrained throughout everything we do.*[4]
>
> —**Chris Heatherly, SVP/GM, Disney Mobile Games**

Penguins are small, cute animals. Kids like cute, and kids like animals. Penguins are also friendly, a little silly, and don't have a reputation for being violent or dangerous. Therefore, picking penguins as a universal avatar touches on several kid

favorites. What makes a character cute, as discussed earlier, is that it is often only 2 or 3 heads tall. Penguins can be cute and cuddly, and they are short, like kids. In most of the scenes in *Club Penguin*, whether on purpose or not, the background buildings are drawn as if they were designed for adult-sized humans, even though much shorter penguins inhabit the world. Big furniture is how kids see the world. In the *Club Penguin* world, with its adult-sized environment, kids can easily identify with their flippered friends.

> *We have seen that [having penguins as avatars] gives kids permission to go beyond traditional gender roles. We commonly see girls playing "boy" games like* Card-jitsu *or making mash-ups like* Princess Captain America. *Boys feel they have permission to care and nurture their Puffles instead of battle with them.*[5]
>
> —**Chris Heatherly, SVP/GM, Disney Mobile Games**

See it big, imagine it small (the binocular effect). One of the things kids love to do is to dress their avatars in outfits that express who they want to be on a given day. Sometimes just dressing the avatar is its own activity. But in order to have 20 or more characters animating live and interacting on-screen at the same

time, those characters need to be relatively small. Small means that much of the detail goes away. For example, a red scarf might end up being only a few red smudges when the character is small. That is not a problem because when kids dress their penguin on the Player Card (a personal profile each penguin owns), the penguin is quite large, and kids can see and appreciate all the detail. A player can form a mental model of the avatar with the detailed red scarf around the neck, knows it is there, and only needs those few red dots to acknowledge its presence when the avatar is smaller.

Equality is *very* appealing. When all your characters are basically the same, it is a major social leveler, much like everybody wearing the same camp T-shirt. Looking the same fosters a sense of equality. This is a really important point and one of the deceptively simple design elements that makes *Club Penguin* stand out. Every kid starts *Club Penguin* the same (except for color and name). There is no inherent race or gender, and everyone is the same size. Because characters and clothing are universally the same, when something new shows up, everyone notices. When someone got a wizard hat, it stood out, and then everyone else wanted to know how to get one.

Designer's Note

Using a single penguin model to create a whole world of characters with no race or gender was a really important design decision. If you have multiple races, genders, ages, classes, and species as avatars, then the animation time and development costs go up astronomically, especially if you want to offer each character a full range of movement and clothing options.

Simple avatars are easier to identify with. It's easier to listen to and project imagination onto avatars with simple faces. (Remember Scott McCloud's cartoon pages in Ch. 14, pp. 229-232?) An avatar is a representation of oneself. If there is a lot of detail in the face, then more is known about the character, and there is less room for you to imagine who it is. The penguins in *Club Penguin* are pleasantly bland. They are easy to map onto, and their accessories stand out.

Leave room for kids to co-create the experience. *Club Penguin* is a complex world, with fourteen unique sections (such as the Plaza, the Dojo, or the Dock). At last count, there were over 100 different rooms within this world, many designed for specific activities. Some of these spaces leave room for kids to invent and co-create group and role-playing activities, which kids do.

Sometimes just the items we create inspire kids to role-play. We see kids creating "flash mobs" with big flashy items, where they all gather together and dance in a huge congested group and chat and encourage others to join.[6]

—**Nikki Zak, Sr. Research Analyst, Disney Interactive**

Designer's Note

Club Penguin's design team also applied their accessibility standards to their delivery platform decisions. Chris Heatherly of The Walt Disney Company said, "Part of *Club Penguin's* success is that instead of aiming for the higher-end PCs and the latest technology, as many other virtual world designers did, Lane [Merrifield] and Lance [Priebe] were maniacal about getting *CP* to work on the widest range of devices available, and they consciously tailored it to this goal every step of the way. The result was global reach, with players in every country. In some places, *Club Penguin* was only one of a few programs available for kids when their region got the Internet.

"Nearly a decade later, the same tricks were required for mobile because it also is an environment with constraints on CPU, GPU, network, etc. The most common mistake is to focus on what the developers want to play with instead of what the audience has. But *CP* focused on making an experience that feels right and charming in a constrained environment."[7]

Leave room for user-generated phenomena. Many sites are so focused on what they want kids to do that all assets are channeled toward specific activities, leaving no room for kids to go off in their own direction. Interesting phenomena have appeared in *Club Penguin*: the kids themselves spontaneously create activities and engage in impromptu role-playing. Something like this only happens when the world has interesting, open-ended places for kids to play, *and* the designers are listening to the kids. Here are just three examples out of hundreds of games and role-playing experiences kids have invented during their time in *Club Penguin*.

1. **Tipping the iceberg:** This game is based on the myth that if you can get enough penguins gathered on one end of an iceberg, then you can collectively tip it. On any given day, there may be a gathering of newbies trying to tip the iceberg, a phenomenon that has been going on for years.

2. **Role-playing pizza maker and customers:** In the pizza shop, one penguin pretends to be the manager, one is a server, and the rest are hungry patrons. The built-in chat offers a pizza emote for ordering.

© Disney

3. **Adoption game:** It is unclear how this one got started, but it takes place in the Pet Shop. One penguin offers itself as a young child looking to be adopted, and other players pretend to be parents looking to adopt. Sometimes friends will go together as siblings. To be a baby penguin, you change your looks, often wearing a headpiece and no wig. Or you are a toddler, and you wear the pigtails wig. The participating penguins add each other as friends, then go to the parents' igloo. From there, they figure out the rest of the gameplay by themselves.

The *Club Penguin* design team created an environment where kids can feel safe trying on different roles and inventing their own themes. Over time, *Club Penguin* has become home to a variety of role-playing communities that have emerged organically as kids play. The design lets the members explore and create, and in turn, the designers follow the social trends and build new experiences that expand on those interests. This helps keep the environment fresh and alive, and the design team tuned in to their members' evolving passions.

Case Study:
Noodle Words

While writing this book, I began design on my first tablet/phone app. I was inspired to create it using the principles espoused in this book as a kind of theory and practice exercise. If I followed my own advice, could I create an original product that would be well received by children, parents, and educators? As a true test, I decided to invent something by letting the process of the theory guide the design. Here is a short study in how we (myself and a small, talented team) created the *Noodle Words–Actions* app.

It furthers one to undertake something.[1]
— The I Ching

Begin at the Beginning

Even though I had been creating interactive games and activities for decades, that didn't mean that I had a clue or knew where I was headed—only that I wanted to create something fun for children, and it wouldn't hurt if it had some educational value. It was a step out into the unknown. A step I believe many game designers identify with. I have faith in the creative process, faith that something wonderful or weird will make itself known to me once I get underway. And so I jumped in.

Apply the Blue Sky Creative Process

At the beginning, the creative options are limitless, and it's helpful to define a few boundaries in order to have a sandbox to play in. I began with a few preliminary questions:

- **What:** What ideas have tickled me lately? What would be fun to build? What genre of activity interests me right now? Is there an obvious need for something in the marketplace?

- **Who:** Who is it for? If for children, what age and developmental stage? Who would be the primary person driving the purchase? (Something for a three-year-old must appeal to the values of the parent as much the child, but a product for a twelve-year-old is primarily designed for the kid—parents may still be involved, but they are not driving the decision.)

- **Where:** What is the distribution platform? Is it digital or physical (toy, cartridge, CD-ROM, DVD, book, etc.)? What are the benefits, drawbacks, and limitations of each? Are there opportunities for transmedia migration? (Can a book be an app? Can a game character become a plush toy or action figure?)

In many projects, some of these questions already have answers. In this case, I knew I wanted to build an app for children, and the initial distribution platform was the Apple iOS, specifically the iPad, since Apple had the largest market share of apps for families at that moment. The real dilemma was what to build. Having answered the question of platform, it was time to better understand the Apple iOS and see what was being created for it already.

Here was my process:

Review my creative notebooks: I keep a notebook of anything that comes to me that sounds like fun, makes an unusual/surprising connection between concepts, stirs up my creative juices, or looks like a real opportunity to do something new. I started looking through my notebooks with the iPad interface in mind.

Look at the competitive landscape: When I am casting about for a new idea, I like to look at a variety of new products to see what's being done, examine why things are popular, and review older, award-winning titles to see if I can connect with the combination of components that made them work for kids (and adults). The multi-touch and multifunction iPad was already inspiring a tsunami of original apps, and it was easy to look at the competitive space. It was a great opportunity to make notes on what pieces of apps appealed to me; what I wanted more of, and might incorporate or expand on; and what good ideas were executed poorly. I didn't want to build something that someone else had already done a great job on.

As I replay and review new interactive titles, I track my internal experience to see if anything tickles, challenges, entertains, or engages me enough that I want more of it. In other words: How does it make me feel? I take notes on the things I find myself doing over and over because I like them. For further confirmation, I always check with kids I know to see what they like about these games. Their answers often confirm my own experience—but sometimes surprise me.

What did I learn from these games?

- The iPad/iPhone was a good platform for (skill/puzzle) games using physics simulators.

- I liked the direct interaction that my finger movements could have, affecting things on-screen.

- The emotional state of any characters (which I could influence) made the experience more fun for me.

- The platform only seemed to support very tiny or limited animation of characters (except as movie clips, which are not interactive). I wanted more animation than what I was seeing.

This last observation took me further into looking at other apps to see who, if anyone, was able to animate characters in a more expansive way. After exploring animation tools for iOS games, I found that, at the time, it was not easy to do full animation of characters (other than as movies). Knowing that I wanted to have more animated characters than what was then available (a market opportunity), I had to begin the process of trying to learn what animation tools a small developer could use.

Look for opportunity: Simultaneously, I decided to better understand the children's app market and what looked like the best opportunity to get seen (on a small marketing budget). In a new and emerging market, almost anything halfway good will be seen and sell well, but in a mature market, it's much harder to break in—mindshare tends to go toward bigger companies that can afford more expensive production values and highly branded characters.

At that moment in time, there were tons of new games every week, but not many in education. Following that observation further, I began reviewing existing educational apps. Many had cute graphics, but the apps were often more focused on what parents wanted, rather than what kids might enjoy.

Make preliminary decisions. Based on the information I had gathered, I decided to focus on a fun-to-play app for the educational category, but I still had other decisions to make: What age and developmental range? What subject? Openly asking those questions helped to center my Blue Sky thinking further.

Next, I considered my knowledge of child development so that I could home in on a target age group, even though I knew everything might change once a great idea came to me. I enjoy the four- to seven-year-old age group, who are eagerly consuming new concepts and beginning to master many basic skills. They are also still in "The Magic Years" (ages three to six), and are open to being surprised and engaged in simple ways.

What I knew about the market helped shape my vision of what I wanted to create:

- American parents prioritize reading and then math.

- Four- to seven-year-olds are emerging and beginning readers.

I already knew a lot about how kids use interactive highlighted text, and I had also explored text that changed to objects in several of my Living Books apps. This led me to think more about words themselves. Words have power, and it interested me to think about how I might reveal the secret meaning behind them.

The Innovation Process

When starting a project, there are, of course, many considerations: technical limitations of a platform, needs of the target age group, product mixes, and production costs. But when it comes to being innovative, all those constraints are only the edges of the sandbox. They need to be set aside to let the interactive "Muse of Play" talk with you about something fun. If one is overly concerned about the restrictions, it's harder to Blue Sky (which, remember, is additive) and play with all the possibilities.

Think Like a Kid

Where do new ideas come from? Often they come from having a fresh perspective. My youngest grandson was, at the time, thirteen months old, and I had been watching him hop through developmental levels, including language acquisition. He understood more than he could communicate verbally, and his parents had been using some sign language with him. I began thinking from the point of view of a child about how we acquire language, how we first learn the names for things.

When kids are playing with something, they are involved in an explorative relationship. At a certain point with reading, black and white shapes become letters and words to them, words they hear in their heads. This is an amazing moment for a child, when the word changes from something incomprehensible to something meaningful.

This led me to wonder: **If words were toys, how could we play with them?** What would they do? Each word has meaning, some object or action associated with it, so what is it that could be fun about words that come alive? Living Words! Words with personality! Words that could DO *what they are!*

The idea was that these *Noodle Words*, words you could play with, would animate as they were tapped, swiped, dragged, and generally poked at. We thought verbs would be perfect because they are already about action. POP could pop, SPIN could spin, STRETCH could stretch, and DANCE could dance all over! They could build on the concept of onomatopoeia, words that sound like what they describe, only these would animate—onomatopoeiamations! Now I was excited. I had a basic concept which met my criteria for learning and play! And words were something we could build on incrementally over time, creating libraries and app extensions.

Creating Characters

We knew we wanted characters. Even though the words themselves are *like* characters, we wanted agents that could further express and act out the actions of the verbs in other ways. This would extend the play with the word concepts (time on task, as educators call it), and it would also provide something kids this age like: characters.

We did a casting call for bugs, and we had quite a crew show up for auditions. Some were too big, some were too small, some were too weird, but we looked at and worked with them until our stars, Stretch and Squish, showed up. And then we got down to the hard work of developing their personalities and getting good performances out of them. As we went further along into development and testing, it became apparent that we needed a talking character for a tutorial, so we created Bitsy Bee.

Making It Work on the Platform (Pushing the Platform)

We looked at a lot of products to see what folks were doing. There really wasn't a lot of character animation going on, unless it was in a non-interactive movie. We checked out different development programs, but they all had drawbacks for what we wanted to do and could afford. Finally, we just kept pushing our wonderful programming partner, Yadong Liu of KwiqApps, until we came up with a path to get the words moving and the bugs grooving. Our main animator, Dave Magliocco of Driscal Designs, helped to bring the Noodle Bugs to life and further develop their personas, along with Michael Barrett of Barrett Tone Audio Productions, who did our music and sound effects.

As it worked out, trying to keep the overall app file size moderate (so it would work in schools and on older iPads) we had to use small characters and keep them mostly in the lower left-hand corner. In order to considerably expand the animation of the characters, this was a small design constraint price to pay.

We tried to include many of the new interface features available on touch devices. Kids could blow on the microphone to blow the word BLOW across the screen. Swiping the word BUMP left and right made it bump against the edge of the screen. Shaking the screen during DANCE changed the music and the dances of the characters. Holding a finger down on a word made it animate under your finger (like SPIN), after which dragging the still animating word near the characters caused them to react in response. One favorite response with kids was dragging BUMP near the bugs, who then were surprised to find themselves forced to bump butts while the word was near. We listed all of these special hidden features and more in the "Tips for Parents" section of the app. Kids enjoyed discovering hidden features, and parents enjoyed being able to show their children something cool.

Most animation was driven by a tap (down and up), but we found that some words called for faster and more immediate reactions, like popping bubbles on BUBBLE. Those where optimized to happen immediately and on the down tap. That way, kids could tap all over the screen quickly popping bubbles. (There is an unwritten rule in kids' software design that, if there are balloons or bubbles on-screen, they should be poppable because every child tries to pop them. Crisp reactions and a satisfying sound complete the experience.)

Prototype Testing

I am a big believer in testing early prototypes with kids to see how they actually use what we've built (in contrast to how *we think* they will use it). When we saw that kids could use our interface, were laughing (our hidden surprises were working), repeating touch sequences where words were spoken as the meaning played out (associative learning via time on task), and generally having a good time, we knew we were on the right track. We also saw, through their own expression of words, that kids were absorbing and recognizing meanings.

Although we didn't have a lot of problems with things not working, we did see play patterns that were unexpected and that caused us to modify parts of the program.

For instance, with the word STRETCH, kids could pull out one side or the other, stretching the word like a rubber band and then letting it go. What we saw over and over was that kids would try to shoot the word at the Noodle Bugs in the corner. So we had to go back in and add special instance animation so that could happen.

One tester, a boy of about eight or nine, had the idea that, while swiping the word BUMP to make it bump the edges of the screen, a little red ball could be randomly floating around. When the ball was in front of a bumpable zone, the word could hit the ball and make it go crazy on-screen. This was a great idea, and we thanked him for it. But, in thinking more about it, we realized he was several years older than our target age and could already read all the words. He was looking for more gameplay. When we asked kids in the target age range what they wanted, the answer was "MORE BUGS!" So we passed on the red ball idea, and instead added *a lot more* animation of the characters to the product.

Kid-Informed Design: Changes We Made

We believe that what we make is for kids, not for us, and their feedback and input is essential. In testing, we watched as they played, and their actions took us places we never thought we'd go. Based on the kids' reactions, we emphasized the following in our design:

- We made a toy, not a game. There was no winning, no scoring, and no losing. There was only reward for exploring and experimenting.

- We made *everything* instantly interruptible in order to better empower kids' actions and encourage exploration (no waiting for animations to finish).

- We made all the animations have crisp reactions in order to make everything feel alive.

- We emphasized humor and surprise in the interactions to support engagement.

- We pushed to take advantage of and integrate as many of the iOS's tricks as we could.

- When we saw a play pattern that kids kept trying to enact, we figured out a way to let them do it. For instance, we saw that when kids realized they could tap on the box of words to get another word, they began rapidly tapping the box to make words shoot out. Each word had an opening animation, which lasted several seconds. With rapid tapping, the screen soon became filled with piles of competing animations until it crashed. Our programmer offered to make it so the kids couldn't do that. But what was happening was a kid-invented game feature! So we asked our programmer to find a way to let kids rapidly tap the box without crashing the program. And he did.

The Result

Noodle Words went on to be a hit with young children, parents, and teachers. It won the 2012 KAPi Award for Best Educational Product, Editor's Choice award from *Children's Technology Review*, and a Gold Award from Parents' Choice Foundation, among others. It was mentioned in *The New York Times* and *USA Today* and was featured by Apple. It also is widely used by educators, especially speech pathologists.

I didn't know when I began the app what would happen, or exactly where we were headed. But I trusted the creative design process at every step along the way, and I trusted that kids would help me figure everything out. I was, nonetheless, greatly relieved for the app to be so well received. I have been following the same practices in the process of writing this book. I hope you have enjoyed it.

Conclusion

Like no other generation before, our children have been born in a world of instant access to information, and they have been weaned on digital media and entertainment. They are digital kids. They are comfortable using technology, and they expect to access the same content through animated interactive interfaces that former generations accessed primarily through textbooks. The question is not if children will use digital media, it is whether the content they access is beneficial and substantial. Our job as designers of interactive media is to offer enlightened content opportunities that support strong, smart, confident, independent, and creative children.

Children are our future. Children want people to get along, to share, to have care for the world, and to play together nicely. Adults forget this view of the world, and they easily become overwhelmed with how badly we treat each other and take care of our planet. A vision of the world *working right* is often what's missing for adults.

I believe it's critically important for us to embrace the child's vision of a cooperative and inclusive view of mankind working together in a sustainable world for the good of all. This view, and its positive effect on our inspiration, will spark us to design products that encourage and enlighten the children of our future.

> *How did the rose ever open its heart and give to this world all its*
> *beauty? It felt the encouragement of light against its being.*[1]
> —Hafiz, 14th-century Persian poet

Like the rose, we all need to feel the encouragement of light against our being. To understand kids is also to deeply understand ourselves. What feeds our souls and empowers us to bravely live our lives with joy and wonder are the same gifts we want to offer children through our work in the world.

In fact, the things that make *great* children's products are the same things that make our own lives more complete, satisfying, and filled with magic and wonder. To feel empowered, to be heard and seen, to have a sense of choice in our lives, to contribute to the whole, and to have multiple opportunities for play—everyday— are ingredients for a contented and engaged life.

I humbly wish all these gifts and more for the children of the world, and for us all.

Afterword

Sometimes, when you set out on a path, you don't know where you will end up.

When I first came to software design in the late 1980s, there where no road maps, no schools, and no books that taught about interactivity and children. There were only a few inventive products, gatherings of devoted early adopters, and enthusiastic designers passionate about sharing what we were learning. We learned a lot about what worked and what didn't, and we were developing a good set of ground rules about connecting with children and understanding what they liked in an interactive experience.

By the late 1990s, I noticed that, every time a new technology emerged, the market was flush with offerings for children, but it seemed that those new designers were just guessing about what worked for children, and were starting from scratch, as we had done. I thought it might be a good idea to create a guide for the next generation of designers by writing down lessons we early interactive designers had already collectively learned.

Around that same time, I was invited to attend a Native American Sun Dance ceremony, a very sacred gathering of fasting and prayer on behalf of others. It was a "non-Indian people by invitation only" event, and I felt like I might never get the opportunity again, so I went with a friend to help support dancers we knew. The event lasted most of the week, with the dancers in the center and supporters under a great arbor in a circle around them.

One day, in the midst of the drumming and dancing, I heard a voice in my head. The deep male voice simply said, "Do the book!" Immediately, I heard my own voice reply, "I can't do a book! I've got kids in college, I'm not a writer, I don't have time, etc., etc." At the end of my internal rant of excuses, the voice answered, "We got you covered."

Later, during a break, I turned to my friend Rob and said, "Hey, I think I had a vision." He laughed and said, "Duh, dude! This is vision central. If you are gonna have a vision, you'll have it here." I thought it was an interesting experience and left it at that.

A few weeks later, a publisher came to me out of the blue and said, "We heard you would be a good person to write a book on kids and interactivity." I was dumbfounded. I believe that when something comes to you like this, it's a good idea to acknowledge it. I didn't think about it for long, I just said, "Yes." That was over 16 years ago.

Even though I ended up publishing this book myself so I could really take the time to do it right, the initial shove from the Universe got me moving. And in the process of writing the book, I learned so much more than I could have ever imagined.

Although I may have been the vehicle through which this book came into the world, I very much feel that it was guided and supported by the collective hearts and spirits of all those who want to promote a vision of the world working harmoniously, and by the desire to offer beautiful things to future generations.

Acknowledgments

This book has been inspired by the many wonderful people who have taught me and shared their passion with me over the years. It is a soup of their great wisdom, love of learning, and joy of life. I am very grateful for their influence and participation.

First, I have to bow down in gratitude to my beloved partner, Barbara Chase, for her willingness to dive in and help me bring this book into the world. It was a huge effort, and I deeply appreciate her belief in my vision.

I want to thank my sons, Jerome, Jesse, and Aaron, for being the inspiration that took me into children's design in the first place; my grandsons, Roman, Ryven, and Cayden, for continuing to help me learn; and my stepdaughter, Nicole Martin, for all she has shared with me, and for teaching me more about the way girls view the world.

I am very grateful to my content contributors, Jesse Schell, Kris Moser, and Barbara Chamberlin, Ph.D., for allowing me to share their insights. I want to deeply thank my editors, J.D. Ho and Amy Smith Muise, for helping me sound so much better. Thank you to Carol Daly, Angie Dean-Schlichting, and Jessica Pyska for allowing me use their photos, and to educators and advisers, Warren Buckleitner, Ph.D., Scot Osterweil, Valerie Landau, and Michael Barrett, who helped me by reviewing early versions of the manuscript.

A special thanks to all the designers who have inspired me along the way and shared their thoughts and insights into children's design. Although there isn't room to thank everyone, I would like to especially thank Daren Carstens, Scott Traylor, Bridget Erdmann, Keli Winters, Kate Wilson, Ann McCormick, Ph.D., Michael Dashow, Gano Haine, Drew Davidson, Ph.D., Brenda Laurel, Chris Heatherly, Joyce Hakansson, Joanne Taeuffer, Emmet O'Neill, Jens Peter de Pedro, Dan Russell-Pinson, Jason Krogh, Margo Nanny, Scott Kim, Aleen Stein, Annie Fox, Amy Bruckman, Ph.D., Jeff Essex, and Dave Magliocco.

And those that have offered advice and support along the way: Teri Rousseau, Stevie Sturla, Bill Hensley, Mickey Mantle, Rob Seidenspinner, Judy Balint, Paul Mandelstein, Nancy Rhine, Cliff Figallo, Rob Martyn, and Florian Brody.

And, finally, I sincerely appreciate all the children who tolerated my presence during product testing, and who shared all of their joy and honest feedback with me.

Credits

The main fonts used in this book

Main body text:	ITC Slimbach® Std by Linotype
Titles:	Nueva Std by Adobe
Headers:	Hiragino Sans GB by JIYUKOBO Ltd.
Cover:	Shag Lounge™ by House Industries, Sanchez Slab by Linotype, and ITC Slimbach® Std by Linotype

Book Cover

Cover photo   Girl: copyright Asia Images Group Pte Ltd / Alamy Stock Photo
Back photos   Group of kids: copyright © serrnovik/Depositphotos.com
Mark Schlichting photo: copyright Kaare Christian. Used with permission.

All Part pages

Character silhouette by Mark Schlichting. Original concept sketch created by Will Guy.

Chapter 01

p. 1   Photo by Angie Dean-Schlichting. Used with permission.

Chapter 02

p. 22   The characters Squash and Stretch, Noodle Bugs from the *Noodle Words* app, designed by Mark Schlichting and animated by Dave Magliocco of Driscal Designs, http://www.driscal.com/

Chapter 03

p. 36   Photo of Peter Linz reprinted by permission of Paul Lundahl.

p. 37   The characters Squash, Stretch, and Bitsy from the *Noodle Words* app, designed by Mark Schlichting and animated by Dave Magliocco of Driscal Designs, http://www.driscal.com

Photo of surprised girl reprinted by permission of David Notowitz. Notowitz Productions, http://www.notowitz.com

p. 40   Poem reprinted by permission of Rolf Nelson, http://www.designbyproxy.com

Bizarro cartoon reprinted by permission of Dan Piraro, http://www.Bizarro.com

p. 41   The characters Squash and Stretch designed by Mark Schlichting and animated by Dave Magliocco of Driscal Designs, http://www.driscal.com

Chapter 05

p. 65   Highlights illustration copyright © Highlights for Children, Inc., Columbus, Ohio. All rights reserved. Used by permission.

p. 76   My Very Hungry Caterpillar © 2016 StoryToys. The Very Hungry Caterpillar © 2016 Eric Carle LLC.

Chapter 06

p. 79   Kids swimming photo reprinted by permission of Carole Daly, https://www.CaroleDalyPhotography.com

p. 84   Camp Bewajee prototype, reprinted by permission of Alex Levitch.

The characters Squash and Stretch designed by Mark Schlichting and animated by Dave Magliocco of Driscal Designs, http://www.driscal.com

p. 86   The characters Squash and Stretch designed by Mark Schlichting and animated by Dave Magliocco of Driscal Designs, http://www.driscal.com

pp. 88–89 The characters Squash and Stretch designed by Mark Schlichting and animated by Dave Magliocco of Driscal Designs, http://www.driscal.com

p. 90   Walk cycle reprinted by permission of Dermot O'Connor, http://www.angryanimator.com

p. 92   Eadweard Muybridge. Animal locomotion: an electro-photographic investigation of consecutive phases of animal movements. 1872-1885. USC Digital Library, 2010. http://digitallibrary.usc.edu/cdm/ref/collection/p15799coll58/id/6264

Chapter 07

p. 107   Mister Rogers' Neighborhood photo © The Fred Rogers Company. Used with permission.

Chapter 08

p. 111   Photo of the WGY "Noise makers" courtesy John Schneider, http://www.theradiohistorian.org

Chapter 09

p. 134   B.F. Skinner photo: Msanders nti [screen name] (Author). (2015, May). *B.F. Skinner* [digital image]. Image used under Creative Commons Attribution-Share Alike 4.0 International license (https://creativecommons.org/licenses/by-sa/4.0/). Retrieved from https://commons.wikimedia.org/wiki/File:B.F._Skinner.jpg

p. 135   Jean Piaget photo: Meylan, Y. (Photographer). (n.d.). *Jean Piaget in his garden Pinchat* [photograph]. We are grateful to the Jean Piaget Foundation for graciously allowing us to reprint photo #131, *Jean Piaget in his garden Pinchat*, by Yves Meylan.

p. 135   Maria Montessori photo: We are grateful to the Association Montessori Internationale for graciously allowing us to reprint the photo. http://www.ami-global.org

p. 139   Albert Bandura photo: Bandura, A. (Source). (2005, October). *Albert Bandura Psychologist* [digital image]. Creative Commons Attribution-Share Alike 4.0 International license (https://creativecommons.org/licenses/by-sa/4.0/). Retrieved from https://commons.wikimedia.org/wiki/File:Albert_Bandura_Psychologist.jpg

p. 139   Kids with bike photo reprinted by permission of Carole Daly, https://www.CaroleDalyPhotography.com

p. 140   Mihaly Csikszentmihalyi photo courtesy of Mihaly Csikszentmihalyi. Used with permission.

Chapter 10

p. 143   Jean Piaget photo: Photographer unidentified. *Jean Piaget in Ann Arbor*, ca. 1967–1968, published in 1968 in Michiganensian without a copyright notice. Retrieved from https://commons.wikimedia.org/wiki/File:Jean_Piaget_in_Ann_Arbor.png

p. 146   Erik Erikson photo: Sharnya G Raj [screen name] (Author). (2015, November). Erik Erikson [digital image]. Image used under Creative Commons Attribution-Share Alike 4.0 International license (https://creativecommons.org/licenses/by-sa/4.0/). Retrieved from https://commons.wikimedia.org/wiki/File:Erik_Erikson.jpg

p. 148   Mother and baby photo reprinted by permission of Carole Daly, https://www.CaroleDalyPhotography.com

p. 153   Boy in boots photo reprinted by permission of Carole Daly, https://www.CaroleDalyPhotography.com

p. 156   Hyman, Z. (Photographer). (2016). Sesame Street, Season 46 [digital image]. Sesame Workshop.

p. 164   Williams, B. (Photographer). (2009, January). *He's so focused* [digital image]. Image used under Creative Commons Attribution License 3.0 (https://creativecommons.org/licenses/by/3.0/). Retrieved from https://www.flickr.com/photos/limedivine/3296498540

p. 172   Millan, J. (Photographer). (2007, November). *Teenage Angst Has Paid Off Well* [digital image]. Image used under Creative Commons Attribution License 3.0 (https://creativecommons.org/licenses/by/3.0/). Retrieved from https://www.flickr.com/photos/stopdown/2044566016/

Chapter 11

p. 183   Watercolor reprinted by permission of Michael Dashow, https://www.michaeldashow.com

Chapter 12

p. 198   Bizarro cartoon reprinted by permission of Dan Piraro, http://www.Bizarro.com

Chapter 13

p. 215   Somma, R. (Photographer). (1980, January). Oversized Furniture [digital image]. Image used under Creative Commons Attribution License 3.0 (https://creativecommons.org/licenses/by/3.0/). Retrieved from https://www.flickr.com/photos/ideonex-us/5970457301/in/faves-42289762@N00/

pp. 221–222 A special thanks to Kris Moser for sharing her article, "Considering Autism and Special Needs Kids". Used with permission.

Chapter 14

pp. 229-232 Scott McCloud images are from pp. 34, 35, 36, 37 of UNDERSTANDING COMICS by SCOTT MCCLOUD. Copyright (c) 1993, 1994 by Scott McCloud. Reprinted by permission of HarperCollins Publishers. Mickey Mouse © Disney.

p. 237   Minions. (September 15, 2015). In *Facebook* [Group page]. Retrieved from https://www.facebook.com/minions/

Chapter 16

p. 272   Photo of Purple Moon's The Secret Stones courtesy of Brenda Laurel. Used with permission.

Chapter 17

pp. 286–289 A special thanks to Jesse Schell for sharing his article, "Transmedia Worlds". Used with permission.

p. 294   Group of kids photo reprinted by permission of Carole Daly, https://www.CaroleDalyPhotography.com

Chapter 20

pp. 325–332 A special thanks to Barbara Chamberlin for sharing her article, "Trying Hard to Make Games That Don't Stink: User Testing at the NMSU Learning Games Lab", and for providing us with a great set of photos. Used with permission.

Chapter 21

pp. 335–339 A special thanks to Chris Heatherly at Disney Mobile Games for helping us obtain screenshot images of *Club Penguin*.

Chapter 22

pp. 342–347 The characters Squash and Stretch designed by Mark Schlichting and animated by Dave Magliocco of Driscal Designs, http://www.driscal.com

Endnotes

Introduction
1. Postman (1994), p. xi.
2. Legge (1861), Vol. II, p. 198.

Chapter 1: The Power of Play
1. Pearce (1977), p. 160.
2. King (1997), pp. 65–76.
3. Rogers (n.d.).
4. Brown (2009); Gray (2013), pp. 130–131.
5. Goldstein (2013).
6. Yelland (1999), pp. 217–220.
7. Emfinger (2009), pp. 326–334.
8. Christie & Stone (1999), pp. 109–31.
9. Elkind (2007).
10. Gray (2013), pp. 130–131.
11. Lengel & Kuczala (2010).
12. Stafford (2006).
13. Buchsbaum, Gopnik, Griffiths, & Shafto (2011), pp. 331–340.
14. Bonawitz et al. (2011), pp. 322–330.
15. Goldstein (2013).
16. Bonawitz et al. (2011).
17. McLuhan quote reproduced by Editorial Board of the *International Journal of McLuhan Studies*.
18. Gray (2013), p. 112.
19. Johnson (1998); Pellegrini (2008), pp. 181–191.
20. Parker (2013).
21. Herz (1999).
22. Gray (2013).
23. Lepper & Greene (1975), pp. 479–486.
24. Johnson, Adams, & Cummins (2012).
25. Gray (2013), p. 120.
26. Gray (2014).
27. The complete set of categories is a mix from my own years of game design, Mattel's list of play patterns (http://shop.mattel.com/category/index.jsp?categoryId=3719988), Stuart Brown's book (*Play: How it shapes the brain, opens the imagination, and invigorates the soul*), and the National Institute for Play's website (http://nifplay.org).
28. Montessori (1972), p. 97.
29. Gray (2013), p. 122.
30. National Institute for Play (n.d.).
31. Elkind (2007), p. 113.
32. W. Wright, personal communication, ca. 1994.
33. Acuff (1997), pp. 15–16, 72, 85.
34. Wilson (1998); Brown (2009), pp. 85–86.
35. Stafford (2006).
36. Gray (2013), pp. 134–139.
37. Bonawitz et al. (2011).
38. Gray (2014).
39. Living In Digital Times Videos (2016).
40. Woll (2012).

41. Key properties of play are included as defined by Stuart Brown. Adapted, with permission, from "What is Play, and Why Do We Do It?", from PLAY: HOW IT SHAPES THE BRAIN, OPENS THE IMAGINATION, AND INVIGORATES THE SOUL by Stuart Brown with Christopher Vaughn, copyright © 2009 by Stuart Brown. Used by permission of Avery, an imprint of Penguin Publishing Group, a division of Penguin Random House LLC.
42. Brown (2009), p. 17.
43. Ratcliffe (2001), p. 73.
44. Brown (2009), p. 17.
45. Gray (2013), p. 141.
46. Brown (2009), p. 17.
47. Ibid.
48. Keycs (2006), p. 50. Additionally, an interesting history of this quote can be found here: http://quoteinvestigator.com/2014/11/24/hot-stove/#note-10163-1
49. Ginsburg (2007), pp. 182–191.
50. Brown (2009), p. 17.
51. Csikszentmihalyi (1990).
52. Brown (2009), p. 18.
53. Ibid.
54. Buckleitner (2015b).
55. Freeman (1997).

Chapter 2: Creating Invitations to Play

1. This quote is often attributed to Plato, although there doesn't appear to be any evidence that it's from his written texts. For an interesting history of this quote's origins see: http://quoteinvestigator.com/2016/06/26/shape/
2. MarcoPolo Learning, Inc. (2014).
3. Reeves & Nass (1996).

Chapter 3: Maintaining Engagement

1. Applewhite, Evans, & Frothingham (2003), p. 323.
2. Buckleitner (2015b).
3. J. Hakansson, personal communication, April 11, 2000.
4. Buckleitner (2004).
5. Oxford University (n.d.), "Surprise."
6. Berns, McClure, Pagnoni, & Montague (2001), pp. 2793–2798.
7. Piaget & Garcia (1991), pp. 128–130.
8. Gray & Bjorklund (2014), p. 424.
9. Skinner (1965), p. 99.
10. McGonigal (2010).
11. Used with permission. http://www.designbyproxy.com
12. Hagood et al. (2012).
13. J. Hakansson, personal communication, April 11, 2000.
14. A. Fox, personal communication, August 13, 2010.
15. Gottlieb (2002).

Chapter 4: Old Brains in a Modern World

1. Wolf (1996).
2. Lewis, Amini, & Lannon (2000), p. 21.
3. Ibid., pp. 20–31.
4. MacLean (1990), p. 9.
5. Beerda (2015).
6. Lewis et al. (2000), pp. 22–23; Dubuc (n.d.); Greenfield (1996), pp. 116–117.
7. Lewis et al. (2000), p. 22–23; Greenfield (1996), p. 116.
8. Lewis et al. (2000), p. 25.
9. Ibid., p. 24; Dubuc (n.d.).

10. Lewis et al. (2000), p. 26.
11. Ibid., p. 228.
12. Field (1995); Goleman (1988).
13. Hrdy (2009).
14. Taylor (2002), pp. 36–37.
15. Ginsburg (2007); Dewar (2014).
16. Lewis et al. (2000), p. 26.
17. Ibid., p. 27.
18. Dubuc (n.d.).
19. Lewis et al. (2000), p. 27.
20. Inspired by Isaac Shapiro during a lecture on 2/10/2005 at the North Berkeley Senior Center where he said, "What we don't want to feel is what drives us."
21. Taylor (2002), p. 12.
22. Lewis et al. (2000), pp. 62–65.
23. Ibid., pp. 62–63.
24. Ibid., p. 64.
25. Ibid.
26. Reeves & Nass (1996).
27. Lerner, Li, Valdesolo, & Kassam (2015), pp. 799-823.
28. Del (1997), pp. 203–205.
29. Colbert (2005).
30. This quote is often attributed to John Lennon, but there is no definitive evidence to support this. For an interesting discussion of the history behind this quote and similar sentiments, see: http://quoteinvestigator.com/2013/05/29/grow-up-happy/

Chapter 5: Seeing is Believing: Visual Perception

1. Toliver (2004), p. 240.
2. Medina (2008), p. 240.
3. Martinez-Conde, MacKnik, & Hubel (2004), pp. 229–240.
4. Schell (2008), p. 302.
5. McCloud (1994), p. 49.
6. Ibid., pp. 63–67.
7. Medina (2008), p. 223.
8. McCloud (1994), p. 62.
9. This doesn't appear to have come from an actual study at Cambridge University. However, there have been some studies done on this subject. You can learn more at http://www.mrc-cbu.cam.ac.uk/people/matt.davis/Cmabrigde/.
10. Oxford University (2005), pg. 61.
11. Raymo (2004).

Chapter 6: Seeing is Believing: Art and Animation

1. This quote is often attributed to Marshall McLuhan, and is even documented as such by Lewis H. Lapham on pg. xxi of his Introduction to the MIT Press Edition of Marshall McLuhan's book *Understanding Media: The Extensions of Man*. However, it's not clear whether Marshall McLuhan coined the exact phrase or not; it doesn't appear to be in any of his written texts. For an interesting discussion of this quote see: http://quoteinvestigator.com/2016/06/26/shape/
2. "Colorblind Population," 2006.
3. B. Laurel, personal communication, May 1999.

Chapter 7: The Magic of Audio: How We Hear

1. Gordon & Willmarth (1997), p. 31.
2. Reeves & Nass (1996), p. 210.
3. Owen (2009).
4. Than (2008).
5. Owen (2009).

6. Cooper (2013).
7. Storr (1993), p. 1.
8. Lord (2008), p. 38.
9. Plato (2004), p. 84, 401d:4–6.
10. Bantjes (2008).
11. Angelou (2002), p. 95.
12. Nass, Steuer, & Tauber (1994), pp. 72–78.
13. Rogers (2003).

Chapter 8: The Magic of Audio: Designing Soundscapes for Kids

1. Holman (2005), p. 161.
2. J. Essex, personal communication, August 2000.
3. M. Barrett, personal communication, March 16, 2001.
4. J. Essex, personal communication, August 2000.
5. M. Barrett, personal communication, March 16, 2001.

Chapter 9: How Kids Learn

1. Reader's Digest Association. (1997), p. 57.
2. Holt (1995), p. 293.
3. Leonard (2002), p. 16; Gould (2012), p. 19; Gray & Bjorklund (2014), p. 106; Carlton (2012a); McLeod (2007a).
4. Leonard (2002). pp. 29-30; Gould (2012), p. 54; Gray & Bjorklund (2014), p. 16–17; Carlton (2012b); McLeod (2007b).
5. Leonard (2002), pp. 37–39; Gould (2012), pp. 47–50; Carlton (2012c); Chamberlin (2014).
6. Leonard (2002), pp. 86–87; Gould (2012), p. 91; McLeod (2007d)
7. Rogers (1969), p. 104.
8. Gray & Bjorklund (2014), p. 116; McLeod (2007c); Hammond, Austin, Orcutt, & Rosso (2001), p. 5.
9. Leonard (2002), p. 142; Skinner (1965), p. 183; Gray & Bjorklund (2014), pp. 116–117; 120-121; O'Donohue & Ferguson (2001), p. 150.
10. Giovanni (2011).
11. Piaget & Garcia (1991), pp. 128–130; Buckleitner (2015a), p. 9; McLeod (2009).
12. "Introduction to Montessori Method"; "Maria Montessori Biography"; Seldin (n.d.); Hammond et al. (2001), p. 8.
13. Lillard (1972), p. 118.
14. Vygotsky (1978), pp. 86–88; Gray & Bjorklund (2014), pp. 430–433; Carlton (2012d); McLeod (2007e); Hammond et al. (2001), p. 7.
15. Vygotsky (1978), p. 102.
16. Gray & Bjorklund (2014), p. 131–132; McLeod (2011).
17. Csikszentmihalyi (1990), p. 4.
18. These four elements of flow are adapted from Csikszentmihalyi (1990), pp. 48–67.
19. Montessori (1995), p. 283.

Chapter 10: Ages and Stages: Why Kids Do What They Do

1. Kennedy-Moore & Lowenthal (2011), p. 3.
2. Gray & Bjorklund (2014), pp. 425–426, 430; McLeod (2009).
3. Good lecture video of Piaget's stages of development at: http://premedhq.com/cognitive-development
4. Buckleitner (2015a), p. 7.
5. Gray & Bjorklund (2014), p. 428; Buckleitner (2015a), p. 7; McLeod (2010d).
6. Gray & Bjorklund (2014), p.428; Buckleitner (2015a), pp. 7–8; Acuff (1997), pp. 72–73; McLeod (2010c).
7. Gray & Bjorklund (2014), p.429; Buckleitner (2015a), p. 8; McLeod (2010a).
8. "Play quotes."
9. Gray & Bjorklund (2014), p.429; Buckleitner (2015a), p. 8; McLeod (2010b).
10. Crandell, Crandell, & Vander Zanden (2012), pp. 35–37; Papalia, Olds, & Feldman (2009), pp. 28.

11. This and each of the next three sections is drawn from, and named after, Erikson's stages of the development of children; Crandell et al. (2012), pp. 35–37; Papalia et al (2009), pp. 188–189, 198, 256, 323; McLeod (2013).

12. Erikson (1993), p. 269.

13. Russ (2004), p. 8.

14. "Research Brief," 2016.

15. Robbins (1976), p. 115.

16. National Association for the Education of Young Children and the Fred Rogers Center for Early Learning and Children's Media at Saint Vincent College (2012).

17. Lemish (2013), p. 175–176.

18. Kuhl (2010); Kuhl, Tsao, & Liu (2003).

19. Kuhl (2010).

20. Brooks & Kempe, (2012), p. 77.

21. Sears, Sears, Sears, & Sears (2013), p. 532.

22. Reader's Digest Association. (2013), p. 123.

23. Acuff (1997), p. 61.

24. McLeod (2010c).

25. Acuff (1997), p. 78.

26. Ibid., p. 83.

27. McLeod (2010a); Acuff (1997), pp. 83–84.

28. Acuff (1997), p. 100.

29. Yates (2009), p. 145.

30. Acuff (1997), pp. 15–16, 72.

31. G. Haine, personal communication, February 21, 2011.

32. Hafen, Laursen, & DeLay (2012), pp. 69–70.

33. Abraham-Hicks Sessions (2015).

Chapter 11: Gender: Understanding the Play Patterns of Girls and Boys

1. Angelou (2015).

2. B. Chase, personal communication, March 14, 2015.

3. Thoreau (2009), p. 65.

4. "Sexual health," 2015.

5. Kosfeld, Heinrichs, Zak, Fischbacher, & Fehr (2005).

6. Paoletti (2012), pp. 85–92; Maglaty (2011).

7. Kirkman & Scott (1999), p. 74.

8. "Timeline 1940–1949."

9. Hansegard (2015).

10. Madrid (2015); Hains (2015).

11. Wieners (2011).

12. Beato (1997).

13. Sweet (2014).

14. Gray & Bjorklund (2014), p. 482.

15. G. Haine, personal communication, February 24, 2011.

16. Gray & Bjorklund (2014), p. 482.

17. Laurel (1999), p. 125.

18. Ibid., p. 124.

19. Acuff (1997), p. 142.

20. Delaney (2014), p. 190.

21. Acuff (1997), p. 142.

22. Ibid., p. 68.

23. N. Martin, personal communication, March 27, 2016.

24. D. Davidson, personal communication, February 24, 2015; Drew Davidson discussed this topic in more depth in a lecture he gave at Dust or Magic, November 4, 2014.

25. Brooks & Kempe (2012), p. 158–160.

26. Barber (2003), p. 64.

27. Grant (2016).

Chapter 12: Interface
1. Honoré (2008).
2. Emerson (1982), p. 245.
3. Jobs (1996).
4. Prensky (2001), pp. 1–6.
5. Gray (2013), pp. 120–122.
6. Frand (2000), pp. 15–24.
7. Buckleitner (2010).
8. Einstein (2011), p. 20.
9. Buckleitner (2004).
10. Bonawitz et al. (2009).
11. Bernard, Mills, Frank, & McKown (2001).
12. Sesame Workshop (2013), p. 6.
13. Ibid., p. 7.
14. LeBlanc (2014).

Chapter 13: The User Relationship
1. Szwed (2004), p. 134.
2. B. Chase, personal communication, September 16, 2010.
3. Inskeep (2009).
4. S. Traylor, personal communication, August 30, 2010.
5. Reeves & Nass (1996), pp. 8–9.
6. Ibid., p. 5.
7. S. Traylor, personal communication, August 30, 2010.

Chapter 14: Characters, Avatars, and Agents
1. Smith & Clark (1999), p. 19.
2. Sapir (1985), p. 556.
3. Galloway (1981), pp. 182–186.
4. James I (1616/2002), p. 46.
5. Leider (2000), p. 39.
6. Packer, Slater, & Wilson (2003), p. 95.
7. Thomas (2006), p. 35.
8. Bradley (2003), p. 35.

Chapter 15: Supporting Play Patterns
1. Emerson (1982), p. 138.
2. Steve Jobs deployed this aphorism, which may be a proverb of Chinese or other Asian origin, as one of the themes during the September 1982 Macintosh team retreat. More information about the Macintosh team retreats here: http://www.folklore.com/StoryView.py?project=Macintosh&story=Credit_Where_Due.txt
3. "Famous Quotations from Thomas Edison."
4. Brown (2009), p. 5.

Chapter 16: Community and Virtual Worlds
1. Lutkehaus (2008), p. 261.
2. L. Merrifield, personal communication, November, 2007.
3. The complete list of *Club Penguin* emoticons can be found on the *Club Penguin Wiki* page at http://clubpenguin.wikia.com/wiki/List_of_Emoticons
4. A. Bruckman, personal communication, November 9, 2015.
5. B. Laurel, personal communication, August 15, 2010.

Chapter 17: Predesign Considerations
1. Watts (1975), p. 31.
2. Jung & Read (2014), Vol. 6, p. 123.
3. B. Erdmann, personal communication, June 15, 2010.

4. Carstens (2010).
5. S. Traylor, personal communication, November 16, 2013.
6. The section "Transmedia Worlds," by Jesse Schell, is based on his talk at the 2010 Dust or Magic conference. Included here, with permission. Traylor, S. [straylor]. (2010, November 11). Dust or Magic 2010 - Jesse Schell, CEO of Schell Games [Video file]. (J. Ho, Ed.). Retrieved from https://www.youtube.com/watch?v=XmktkUCAFPs
7. Kamenetz (n.d.).
8. Samual (2015).
9. Comiteau (2003).
10. Adkins (2015a), p. 19; Adkins (2015b), p. 17.
11. McCarthy et al. (2012), pp. 16–17.
12. Ibid.
13. R. Seidenspinner, personal communication, January 5, 2012.
14. Bitchin (2006), p. 99.
15. Keller (1903), p. 56.
16. Carstens (2016).
17. van der Post (1975), p. 411.

Chapter 18: The Design Process
1. Corcoran (2000).
2. "Play quotes."
3. Waldrop (1996).
4. Isaacson (2011), p. 144.
5. Nietzsche (1977), p. 129.
6. Wright (2006).
7. Handley (2014).
8. Wolf (1996).
9. "Words of art," 2013.

Chapter 19: The Production Process
1. Goldenstein (2008).
2. B. Erdmann, personal communication, September 2, 2010.
3. Duhigg (2016).
4. Ibid.
5. Edmondson (1999), p. 354.
6. D. Carstens, personal communication, May 3, 2010.
7. R. Martyn, personal communication, February 10, 2011.

Chapter 20: Testing with Kids
1. Dijkstra (1970).
2. G. Haine, personal communication, September 12, 2010.

Chapter 21: Case Study: *Club Penguin*
1. Applewhite et al. (2003), p. 146.
2. Graser (2013).
3. Merrifield (2008).
4. C. Heatherly, personal communication, November 30, 2014.
5. C. Heatherly, personal communication, November 30, 2014.
6. N. Zak, personal communication, February 2, 2015.
7. C. Heatherly, personal communication, November 30, 2014.

Chapter 22: Case Study: *Noodle Words*
1. Wilhelm & Baynes (1967), p. 166.

Conclusion
1. Hafiz (1999), p. 121.

Bibliography

Abraham-Hicks Sessions. (2015, July 18). Abraham Hicks 2015: These kids are cable ready 2015-05-09 B Philadelphia, PA [Video file]. Retrieved from https://www.youtube.com/watch?v=oiLVA_5FZNw

Acuff, D. S. (1997). *What kids buy and why: The psychology of marketing to kids*. New York, NY: The Free Press.

Adkins, S. S. (2015a, January). *The 2014–2019 China Mobile Learning Market*. Retrieved from http://www.ambientinsight.com/Resources/Documents/AmbientInsight-2014-2019-China-Mobile-Learning-Market-Abstract.pdf

Adkins, S. S. (2015b, July 21). *The 2014–2019 global edugame market*. Session presented at the Serious Play Conference, Pittsburgh, PA. Retrieved from http://www.seriousplayconference.com/wp-content/uploads/2015/07/Ambient2015GlobalMarketReport.pdf

Ames, L. B., & Haber, C. C. (1985). *Your seven-year-old: Life in a minor key*. New York, NY: Dell.

Ames, L. B., & Haber, C. C. (1989). *Your eight-year-old: Lively and outgoing*. New York, NY: Dell.

Ames, L. B., & Haber, C. C. (1990). *Your nine-year-old: Thoughtful and mysterious*. New York, NY: Dell.

Ames, L. B., & Ilg, F. L. (1976). *Your four-year-old: Wild and wonderful*. New York, NY: Dell.

Ames, L. B., & Ilg, F. L. (1979). *Your five-year-old: Sunny and serene*. New York, NY: Dell.

Ames, L. B., & Ilg, F. L. (1979). *Your six-year-old: Living and defiant*. New York, NY: Dell.

Ames, L. B., & Ilg, F. L. (1980). *Your three-year-old: Friend or enemy*. New York, NY: Dell.

Ames, L. B., Ilg, F. L., & Baker, S. M. (1988). *Your ten- to fourteen-year-old*. New York, NY: Dell.

Angelou, M. (2002). *I know why the caged bird sings*. New York, NY: Random House.

Angelou, M. [Maya Angelou]. (2015, August 21). *How important it is for us to recognize and celebrate our heroes and she-roes* [Facebook status update]. Retrieved from https://www.facebook.com/MayaAngelou/posts/10153772078394796:0

Applewhite, A., Evans, T., & Frothingham, A. (2003). *And I quote: The definitive collection of quotes, sayings, and jokes for the contemporary speechmaker* (Rev. ed.). New York, NY: Thomas Dunne Books.

Arntson, A. E. (1998). *Graphic design basics*. Fort Worth, TX: Harcourt Brace College Publishers.

Bantjes, M. (2008). 3 smart things about music. *Wired Magazine, 16*(6). Retrieved from http://archive.wired.com/entertainment/music/magazine/16-06/st_3smartthings

Barber, D. (2003). *The music lover's quotation book*. Toronto, ON:Sound and Vision.

Beato, G. (1997, April 1). Computer games for girls is no longer an oxymoron. *Wired Magazine*. Retrieved from http://www.wired.com/1997/04/es-girlgames/

Beerda, J. (2015, May 14). *Octalysis gamification: How to un(b)lock your reptilian brain* [Blog post]. Retrieved from http://octalysisgroup.com/gamification-knowledge/octalysis-gamification-how-to-unblock-your-reptilian-brain-2/

Bernard, M., Mills, M., Frank, T., & McKown J. (2001). Which font do children prefer to read online? Usability News 3.1 [Online]. Retrieved from http://usabilitynews.org/which-fonts-do-children-prefer-to-read-online/

Berns, G. S., McClure, S. M., Pagnoni, G., & Montague, P. R. (2001). Predictability modulates human brain response to reward. *The Journal of Neuroscience, 21*(8). Retrieved from http://www.ccnl.emory.edu/greg/Koolaid_JN_Print.pdf

Bitchin, B. (2006). *Sailing life*. Dobbs Ferry, NY: Sheridan House Inc.

Bonawitz, E. B., Shafto, P., Gweon, H., Chang, I., Katz, S., & Schulz, L. (2009). The double-edged sword of pedagogy: Modeling the effect of pedagogical contexts on preschoolers' exploratory play. Retrieved from https://cocosci.berkeley.edu/Liz/BonawitzShaftoetalRevised.pdf

Bonawitz, E. B., Shafto, P., Gweon, H., Goodman, N. D., Spelke, E., & Schulz, L. (2011, September 8). The double-edged sword of pedagogy: Instruction limits spontaneous exploration and discovery. *Cognition, 120*(3). doi:10.1016/j.cognition.2010.12.001

Bradley, B. (2003) *Drawing people: How to portray the clothed figure.* Cincinnati, OH: North Light Books.

Bronson, M. (1995). *The right stuff for children birth to 8: Selecting play materials to support development.* Washington, DC: NAEYC.

Brooks, P., & Kempe, V. (2012). *Language Development.* Chichester, UK: BPS Blackwell.

Brown, S. L., & Vaughan, C. C. (2009). *Play: How it shapes the brain, opens the imagination, and invigorates the soul.* New York, NY: Avery.

Buchsbaum, D., Gopnik, A., Griffiths, T. L., & Shafto, P. (2011, September 8). Children's imitation of causal action sequences is influenced by statistical and pedagogical evidence. *Cognition, 120*(3). doi:10.1016/j.cognition.2010.12.001

Buckleitner, W. (2004). *The relationship between software interface instructional style and the engagement of young children* (Doctoral dissertation, Michigan State University). Retrieved from http://citeseerx.ist.psu.edu/viewdoc/download?doi=10.1.1.115.176&rep=rep1&type=pdf

Buckleitner, W. (2010, November 7–9). Comment during Dust or Magic Institute sponsored by *Children's Technology Review*, Lambertville, NJ.

Buckleitner, W. (2015a). *Child development 101 for interactive media designers: An overview of influential theories, applied to practice* [iBook]. Retrieved from https://itunes.apple.com/us/book/child-development-101-for/id978468921

Buckleitner, W. (2015b, May 31–June 2). Comment during Dust or Magic AppCamp sponsored by *Children's Technology Review*, Monterey, CA.

Buckleitner, W. (2016). *Buckleitner's guide to using tablets with young children.* Lewisville, NC: Gryphon House Inc.

Carlton. (2012a, January 6). *Behaviourism and games.* Retrieved from http://playwithlearning.com/2012/01/06/behaviourism-and-games/

Carlton. (2012b, January 11). *Cognitivism and games.* Retrieved from http://playwithlearning.com/2012/01/11/cognitivism-and-games/

Carlton. (2012c, January 20). *Constructivism and games.* Retrieved from http://playwithlearning.com/2012/01/20/constructivism-and-games/

Carlton. (2012d, February 8). *Social learning and games.* Retrieved from http://playwithlearning.com/2012/02/08/social-learning-and-games/

Carstens, D. (2010, May 2–4). Comment during Dust or Magic AppCamp sponsored by *Children's Technology Review*, Monterey, CA.

Carstens, D. (2016, May 21). Comment during Dust or Magic AppFest sponsored by *Children's Technology Review*, San Francisco, CA.

Carter, R., Aldridge, S., Page, M., & Parker, S. (2009). *The human brain book.* London: Dorling Kindersley Limited.

Cassell, J., & Jenkins, H. (1999). *From Barbie to Mortal Kombat: Gender and computer games.* Cambridge, MA: The MIT Press.

Chamberlin, B. (2014, June 9). How to design for how children learn. Presentation at Dust or Magic AppCamp sponsored by *Children's Technology Review*, Marshall, CA.

Christie, J. F., & Stone, S. J. (1999, June 01,). Collaborative Literacy Activity in Print-Enriched Play Centers: Exploring the "Zone" in Same-Age and Multi-Age Groupings. *Journal of Literacy Research, 31*(2).

Cohen, L. J. (2001). *Playful parenting.* New York, NY: The Ballantine Publishing Group.

Colbert, G. (Producer), Colbert, G. (Director). (2005). Ashes and Snow [Motion Picture]. Canada.

Colorblind Population (2006, April 28). Retrieved from http://www.color-blindness.com/2006/04/28/colorblind-population/

Comiteau, J. (2003, March 24). When does brand loyalty start? *Adweek.* Retrieved from http://www.adweek.com/news/advertising/when-does-brand-loyalty-start-62841

Cooper, B. B. (2013, November 20). *8 surprising ways music affects and benefits our brains.* [Web log post]. Retrieved from https://blog.bufferapp.com/music-and-the-brain

Corcoran, D. (2000, February 6). Talking numbers with: Edward T. Tufte; Campaigning for the charts that teach. *The New York Times*. Retrieved from http://www.nytimes.com/2000/02/06/business/talking-numbers-with-edward-r-tufte-campaigning-for-the-charts-that-teach.html?pagewanted=all

Crandell, T. L., Crandell, C. H., & Vander Zanden, J. W. (2012). *Human development* (Tenth edition). New York, NY: McGraw-Hill.

Csikszentmihalyi, M. (1990). *Flow: The psychology of optimal experience*. New York, NY: Harper & Row.

Davidson, D. [dustormagic]. (2014, November 4). *Who makes the magic? A look at the teams behind the products* [Video file]. Presentation at Dust or Magic Institute sponsored by *Children's Technology Review*. Retrieved from https://www.youtube.com/watch?v=Gdplt10BvMU

Del Vecchio, G. (1997). *Creating ever-cool: A marketer's guide to a kid's heart*. Gretna, La: Pelican Pub. Co.

Delaney, B. (2014). *Sex, drugs and tessellation: The truth about virtual reality, as revealed in the pages of CyberEdge Journal*. CyberEdge Information Services.

Dewar, G. (2014). *The cognitive benefits of play: Effects on the learning brain*. Retrieved from http://www.parentingscience.com/benefits-of-play.html

Dijkstra, E. W. (1970). Notes on structured programming (T.H. Report 70-WSK-03). The Netherlands: Technological University Eindhoven. Retrieved from https://www.cs.utexas.edu/users/EWD/ewd02xx/EWD249.PDF

Donohue, C. (2015). *Technology and digital media in the early years: Tools for teaching and learning*. New York, NY: Routledge.

Dubuc, B. (n.d.). *The brain from top to bottom*. (A. Daigen, Trans.). Retrieved from http://thebrain.mcgill.ca/flash/d/d_05/d_05_cr/d_05_cr_her/d_05_cr_her.html

Duhigg, C. (2016, February 25). What Google learned from its quest to build the perfect team. *The New York Times*. Retrieved from http://www.nytimes.com/2016/02/28/magazine/what-google-learned-from-its-quest-to-build-the-perfect-team.html?_r=1

Editorial Board. (2012, April 17). Pattern recognition. Probes and ideas. [Blog post]. *International Journal of McLuhan Studies*. Retrieved from http://www.mcluhanstudies.com/index.php?option=com_content&view=article&id=489:patternrecognition&catid=98:mcluhan&Itemid=585

Edmondson, A. (1999). Psychological safety and learning behavior in work teams. *Administrative Science Quarterly, 44*(2). doi:10.2307/2666999

Einstein, A. (2011). *The ultimate quotable Einstein*. A. Calaprice (Ed.). Princeton, NJ: Princeton University Press.

Elkind, D. (2007). *The power of play: How spontaneous, imaginative activities lead to happier, healthier children*. Cambridge, MA: Da Capo Press.

Emerson, R. W. (1982). *Emerson in his journals* (J. Porte, Ed.). Cambridge, MA: The Belknap Press.

Emfinger, K. (2009, December 01,). Numerical Conceptions Reflected during Multiage Child-Initiated Pretend Play. *Journal of Instructional Psychology, 36*(4).

Erikson, E. H. (1993). *Childhood and society*. New York, NY: W. W. Norton & Company, Inc.

Essex, J. (1996). *Multimedia sound and music studio*. New York, NY: Random House.

Famous Quotations from Thomas Edison. (n.d.). Retrieved from http://www.thomasedison.org/index.php/education/edison-quotes/

Field, T. M. (1995). *Touch in early development*. Mahwah, NJ: Lawrence Erlbaum Associates.

Figallo, C., & Rhine, N. (2002). *Building the knowledge management network: Best practices, tools, and techniques for putting conversation to work*. New York, NY: John Wiley & Sons, Inc.

Fisher, C. (2015). *Designing games for children: Developmental, usability, and design considerations for making games for kids*. Burlington, MA: Focal Press.

Fox, A. (2000). *Can you relate?: Real-world advice for teens on guys, girls, growing up, and getting along*. Minneapolis, MN: Free Spirit Publishing.

Fox, B. (2005). *Game interface design*. Boston, MA: Thomson Course Technology PTR.

Frand, J. (2000). The information age mindset. *EDUCAUSE Review, 35*(5). Retrieved from http://er.edu-cause.edu/~/media/files/article-downloads/erm0051.pdf

Freeman, T. (1997, Sept. 29). Powers to the kids! Retrieved from http://www.gamasutra.com/view/feature/131639/power_to_the_kids.php

Gardner, H. (1991). *The unschooled mind: How children think and how schools should teach.* New York, NY: Basic Books.

Galloway, T. (1981, April). I'm listening as hard as I can. *Texas Monthly, 9*(4).

Gelman, D. L. (2014). *Design for kids: Digital products for playing and learning.* Brooklyn, NY: Rosenfeld Media.

Gilliam, T., & Cowell, L. (1978). *Animations of mortality.* London: Eyre Methuen.

Ginsburg, K. R. (2007). The importance of play in promoting healthy child development and maintaining strong parent-child bonds. *Pediatrics, 119*(1), 1820191. doi: 10.1542/peds.2006-2697

Giovanni Bonaiuti. (2011, December 20). B.F. Skinner. Teaching machine and programmed learning [Video file]. Retrieved from https://www.youtube.com/watch?v=jTH3ob1IRFo

Gladwell, M. (2002). *The tipping point: How little things can make a big difference.* New York, NY: Little, Brown and Company.

Gladwell, M. (2005). *Blink: The power of thinking without thinking.* New York, NY: Little, Brown and Company.

Goldenstein, P. (2008, July 1). Pixar's secret ingredient? Quality. *The Los Angeles Times.* Retrieved from http://www.latimes.com/

Goldsmith, T. H. (1991). *The biological roots of human nature: Forging links between evolution and behavior.* New York, NY: Oxford University Press.

Goldstein, J. (2013, January 01). Technology and Play. *Scholarpedia, 8*(2), 30434.

Goleman, D. (1988, February 2). The experience of touch: Research points to a critical role. *The New York Times.* Retrieved from http://www.nytimes.com/1988/02/02/science/the-experience-of-touch-research-points-to-a-critical-role.html?pagewanted=all

Gonick, L. (1993). *The cartoon guide to (non)communication: The use and misuse of information in the modern world.* New York, NY: HarperCollins Publishers.

Gordon, W. T., & Willmarth, S. (1997). *McLuhan for beginners.* New York, NY: Writers and Readers Pub.

Gottlieb, H. (2002). *The jack principles of the interactive conversation interface.* Retrieved from http://demos.jellyvisionlab.com/downloads/The_Jack_Principles.pdf

Gould, J. (2012). *Learning theories and classroom practice in the lifelong learning sector.* Thousand Oaks, CA: SAGE Publications Inc.

Grant, A. (2016, January 30). How to raise a creative child. Step one: Back off. *The New York Times.* Retrieved from http://www.nytimes.com/2016/01/31/opinion/sunday/how-to-raise-a-creative-child-step-one-back-off.html

Graser, M. (2013, July 11). 'Star Wars' takes over Disney's Club Penguin. *Variety.* Retrieved from http://variety.com/2013/digital/news/star-wars-takes-over-disneys-club-penguin-1200561084/

Gray, P. (2013). *Free to learn: Why unleashing the instinct to play will make our children happier, more self-reliant, and better students for life.* New York, NY: Basic Books.

Gray, P. (2014, May 10). *The decline of play and rise of mental disorders: Peter Gray at TEDxNavesink* [Video file]. Retrieved from http://tedxtalks.ted.com/video/The-Decline-of-Play-and-Rise-of

Gray, P., & Bjorklund, D. F. (2014). *Psychology.* New York, NY: Worth Publishers.

Greenfield, S. (1996). *The human mind explained: An owner's guide to the mysteries of the mind.* New York, NY: Henry Holt.

Guernsey, L. (2007). *Into the minds of babes: How screen time affects children from birth to age five.* New York, NY: Basic Books.

Gurian, M., Henley, P., & Trueman, T. (2001). *Boys and girls learn differently: A guide for teachers and parents.* San Francisco: Jossey-Bass.

Hafen, C. A., Laursen, B., & DeLay, D. (2012). Transformations in friend relationships across the transition into adolescence. In B. Laursen & W. A. Collins (Eds.), *Relationship pathways: From adolescence to young adulthood*. Thousand Oaks, CA: SAGE Publications.

Hafiz. (1999). *The gift: Poems by the great Sufi master*. (D. Ladinsky, Trans.). London: Penguin Books

Hagood, D. E., Batchelder, H. M., Dent, K. M., Goymer, P. D., Lee, H. J., & Bainum, C. K. (2012, April). *Joke's on you! Preschool boy's preference for aggressive humor*. Poster session presented at the annual meeting of the Western Psychological Association, San Francisco, CA. Retrieved from https://www.puc.edu/__data/assets/pdf_file/0020/99200/Jokes-On-You-Final-WPA-Poster.pdf

Hains, R. (2015, February 12). The problem with separate toys for girls and boys: What started our obsession with assigning gender to playthings, and how can parents combat it? *Boston Globe*. Retrieved from https://www.bostonglobe.com/magazine/2015/02/27/the-problem-with-separate-toys-for-girls-and-boys/2uI7Qp0d3oYrTNj3cGkiEM/story.html

Hall, R. (1997). *The cartoonist's workbook*. New York, NY: Sterling Publishing Company.

Hammond, L., Austin, K., Orcutt, S., & Rosso, J. (2001, December 27). *How people learn: Introduction to learning theories*. Retrieved from http://web.stanford.edu/class/ed269/hplintrochapter.pdf

Handley, D. (2014, April 24). Three reasons to steal, not copy: Here's how and why. *Huffington Post*. Retrieved from http://www.huffingtonpost.com/derek-handley/three-reasons-to-steal-no_b_5176290.html

Hansegard, J. (2015, December 29). Lego builds stronger ties to girls. *The Wall Street Journal*. Retrieved from http://www.wsj.com/articles/lego-builds-stronger-ties-to-girls-1451420979

Haykin, R. (Ed.). (1993). *Demystifying multimedia: A guide for Macintosh developers from Apple Computer, Inc.* Cupertino, CA: Apple Computer, Inc.

Herz, J. C. (1999, January). Let us play: Tinder to fuel musical sparks. *The New York Times*. Retrieved from http://partners.nytimes.com/library/tech/99/01/circuits/articles/28game.html

Holman, T. (2005). Sound for digital video. Amsterdam: Elsevier Focal.

Holt, J. C. (1995). *How children learn*. Cambridge, MA: De Capo Press.

Honoré, C. (2008). *Under pressure: Rescuing our children from the culture of hyper parenting*. New York, NY: HarperOne.

Hourcade, J. P. (2015). *Child-computer interaction*. (self-published).

Hrdy, S. B. (2009, April). Meet the alloparents: Share child care may be the secret of human evolutionary success. *Natural History Magazine*. Retrieved from http://www.naturalhistorymag.com/htmlsite/0409/0409_feature.pdf

Inskeep, S. (Host). (2009, November 13). For would-be Dahl movie adapters, a critical test. [Radio broadcast episode]. In *Morning Edition*. Washington, DC: National Public Radio. Retrieved from http://www.npr.org/templates/story/story.php?storyId=120375896

Introduction to Montessori Method (n.d.). Retrieved from http://amshq.org/Montessori-Education/Introduction-to-Montessori

Isaacson, W. (2011). *Steve Jobs*. New York, NY: Simon & Schuster.

James I, McIlwain, C. H. (1616/2002). *The political works of James I*. Cambridge, MA: Clark, NJ: The Lawbook Exchange, Ltd.

Jobs, S. (1996, Feb). Steve Jobs: The next insanely great thing / Interviewer: Wolf, G. *Wired Magazine*. Retrieved from http://archive.wired.com/wired/archive/4.02/jobs_pr.html

Johnson, D. (1998, April 07). Many schools putting an end to child's play. *The New York Times*. Retrieved from http://www.nytimes.com/1998/04/07/us/many-schools-putting-an-end-to-child-s-play.html?pagewanted=all

Johnson, L., Adams, S., & Cummins, M. (2012). *The NMC horizon report: 2012 higher education edition*. Austin, Texas: The New Media Consortium.

Jung, C., & Read, H. (Ed.). (2014). *Psychological types*. In *The collected works of C. G. Jung*. (Vol. 6). (H. G. Baynes, R. F. C. Hull, Trans.). New York, NY: Routledge.

Kamenetz, A. (n.d.). You tell me: When kids + screens = happiness. Retrieved from https://medium.com/@anya1anya/b7f2a1738a7b#.6i5eo9ejc

Katz, L. G. (2015, April). *Lively minds: Distinctions between academic versus intellectual goals for young children*. Retrieved from https://deyproject.files.wordpress.com/2015/04/dey-lively-minds-4-8-15.pdf

Keller, H. (1903) *Optimism: An essay*. New York, NY: T. Y. Crowell and Company.

Kennedy-Moore, E., & Lowenthal, M. S. (2011). *Smart parenting for smart kids: Nurturing your child's true potential*. San Francisco, CA: Jossey-Bass.

Keyes, R. (2006). *The quote verifier: Who said what, where, and when*. New York, NY: St. Martin's Griffin

King, N. R. (1997, December 07). Play and Community in the Classroom. *School Community Journal, 7*(2).

Kirkman, R., & Scott, J. (1999). *Ten years and still in diapers: A Baby Blues treasury*. Kansas City, MO: Andrews McMeel Publishing.

Kirkman, R., & Scott, J. (2001). *Butt-naked Baby Blues: A Baby Blues treasury*. Kansas City, MO: Andrews McMeel Publishing.

Kirkman, R., & Scott, J. (2006). *Framed!: A Baby Blues treasury*. Kansas City, MO: Andrews McMeel Publishing.

Kirkman, R., & Scott, J. (2008). *X-treme parenting: A Baby Blues treasury*. Kansas City, MO: Andrews McMeel Publishing.

Kondo, H (Ed.). (2005). *Character design collection*. Tokyo: PIE Books.

Kosfeld, M., Heinrichs, M., Zak, P. J., Fischbacher, U., & Fehr, E. (2005). Oxytocin increases trust in humans. *Nature, 435*, 673–676. Doi:10.1038/nature03701

Krug, S. (2014). *Don't make me think, revisited: A common sense approach to web usability*. San Francisco, CA: New Riders.

Kuhl, P. K., Tsao, F., & Liu, H. (2003). Foreign-language experience in infancy: Effects of short-term exposure and social interaction on phonetic learning. *Proceedings of the National Academy of Sciences, 100*(15). doi: 10.1073/pnas.1532872100

Kuhl, P. K. (2010, October). *The linguistic genius of babies* [Video file]. Retrieved from https://www.ted.com/talks/patricia_kuhl_the_linguistic_genius_of_babies/transcript?language=en

Labinowicz, E. (1980). *The Piaget primer: Thinking, learning, teaching*. Parsippany, NJ: Dale Seymour Publications.

Laurel, B. (Ed.). (1990). *The Art of human–computer interface design*. Reading, MA: Addison-Wesley Publishing Company.

Laurel, B. (1999). An interview with Brenda Laurel (Purple Moon). In J. Cassell & H. Jenkins (Eds.), *From Barbie to mortal kombat: Gender and computer games*. Cambridge, MA: The MIT Press.

Laurel, B. (2001). *Utopian Entrepreneur*. Cambridge, MA: The MIT Press.

LeBlanc, M. [leblancstartup]. (2014, May 14). A user interface is like a joke. If you have to explain it, it's not that good. [Tweet]. Retrieved from https://twitter.com/leblancstartup/status/466638260195041280

Legge, J. (1861). *The Chinese classics: The works of Mencius*. Hong Kong: The London Missionary Society.

Leider, E. W. (2000). *Becoming Mae West*. New York, NY: Da Capo Press.

Lemish, D. (Ed.). (2013). *The Routledge international handbook of children, adolescents and media*. New York, NY: Routledge.

Lengel, T. L., & Kuczala, M. S. (2010). *The Kinesthetic Classroom: Teaching and Learning Through Movement*. Thousand Oaks, CA: Corwin.

Leonard, D. C. (2002). *Learning theories: A to Z*. Westport, CT: Greenwood Press.

Lepper, M. R., & Greene, D. (1975, January 01). Turning play into work: Effects of adult surveillance and extrinsic rewards on children's intrinsic motivation. *Journal of Personality and Social Psychology, 31*(3).

Lerner, J. S., Li, Y., Valdesolo, P., & Kassam, K. S. (2015). Emotion and Decision Making. *Annual Review of Psychology, 66*. doi: 10.1146/annurev-psych-010213-115043. Also retrieved from http://scholar.harvard.edu/files/jenniferlerner/files/annual_review_manuscript_june_16_final.final_.pdf

Lewis, T., Amini, F., & Lannon, R. (2000). *A general theory of love*. New York, NY: Random House.

Lillard, P. P. (1972). *Montessori: A modern approach*. New York, NY: Schocken Books Inc.

Lipton, B. H. (2008). *The biology of belief: Unleashing the power of consciousness, matter & miracles*. Carlsbad, CA: Hay House.

Lipton, B. H., & Bhaerman, S. (2009). *Spontaneous evolution: Our positive future (and a way to get there from here)*. Carlsbad, CA: Hay House.

Living In Digital Times Videos. (2016, January 27). *Shigeru Miyamoto accepts the Lifetime Pioneer Award at the KAPi Awards* [Video file]. Retrieved from https://www.youtube.com/watch?v=IgSqOb-9JvU

Logan, R. K. (2010). *Understanding new media: Extending Marshall McLuhan*. New York, NY: Peter Lang Publishing.

Lord, Suzanne. (2008). *Music in the Middle Ages: A Reference Guide*. Westport, CT: Greenwood Press.

Lutkehaus, N. (2008). *Margaret Mead: The making of an American icon*. Princeton, NJ: Princeton University Press.

MacLean, P. D. (1990) *The triune brain in evolution: Role in paleocerebral functions*. NY: Plenum Press.

Madrid, I. (2015, July 2). From gender neutral beginnings to pink princess themes and today's female STEM minifigs: LEGO's messy history of marketing to girls. *PRI's The World*. Retrieved from http://www.pri.org/stories/2015-07-02/gender-neutral-beginnings-pink-princess-themes-and-todays-female-stem-minifigs

Maglaty, J. (2011, April 7). When did girls start wearing pink? *Smithsonian*. Retrieved from http://www.smithsonianmag.com/arts-culture/when-did-girls-start-wearing-pink-1370097/?no-ist

Malone, T. W. (1981). Toward a theory of intrinsically motivating instruction. *Cognitive Science, 5*(4), pp. 333–369. doi:10.1207/s15516709cog0504_2. Also retrieved from http://citeseerx.ist.psu.edu/viewdoc/download?doi=10.1.1.455.9328&rep=rep1&type=pdf

MarcoPolo Learning, Inc. (2014). *MarcoPolo Ocean* (Version 2.0.2) [Mobile application software]. Retrieved from https://itunes.apple.com/us/app/marcopolo-ocean/id797157312?mt=8

Maria Montessori Biography (n.d.). Retrieved from http://amshq.org/Montessori-Education/History-of-Montessori-Education/Biography-of-Maria-Montessori

Martinez-Conde, S., Macknik, S. L., & Hubel, D. H. (2004). The role of fixational eye movements in visual perception. *Neuroscience, 5*. Retrieved from http://hubel.med.harvard.edu/papers/HubelMartinez-condeetal2004NationReviewNeuroscience.pdf

McCarthy, B., Atienza, S., Yumol, D., Silberglitt, M., Li, L., & Kuhns, K. (2012, August). *Mobile devices and mobile applications in pre–K to grade 3 families: Report body. A report to the CPB–PBS ready to learn initiative*. Retrieved from http://www-tc.pbskids.org/lab/media/pdfs/research/Y2-WestEd-PBS-MobileAppsReport_ReportBody.pdf

McCloud, S. (1994). *Understanding comics: The invisible art*. New York, NY: HarperPerennial.

McGonigal, J. (2010, February). *TED2010: Gaming can make a better world* [Video file]. Retrieved from http://www.ted.com/talks/jane_mcgonigal_gaming_can_make_a_better_world

McGonigal, J. (2011). *Reality is broken: Why games make us better and how they can change the world*. New York, NY: Penguin Books.

McLeod, S. (2007a). *Behaviorist approach*. Retrieved from http://www.simplypsychology.org/behaviorism.html

McLeod, S. (2007b). *Cognitive psychology*. Retrieved from http://www.simplypsychology.org/cognitive.html

McLeod, S. (2007c). *Edward Thorndike*. Retrieved from http://www.simplypsychology.org/edward-thorndike.html

McLeod, S. (2007d). *Humanism*. Retrieved from http://www.simplypsychology.org/humanistic.html

McLeod, S. (2007e). *Lev Vygotsky*. Retrieved from http://www.simplypsychology.org/vygotsky.html

McLeod, S. (2009). *Jean Piaget*. Retrieved from http://www.simplypsychology.org/piaget.html

McLeod, S. (2010a). *Concrete operational stage*. Retrieved from http://www.simplypsychology.org/concrete-operational.html

McLeod, S. (2010b). *Formal operational stage*. Retrieved from http://www.simplypsychology.org/formal-operational.html

McLeod, S. (2010c). *Preoperational stage*. Retrieved from http://www.simplypsychology.org/preoperational.html

McLeod, S. (2010d). *Sensorimotor stage*. Retrieved from http://www.simplypsychology.org/sensorimotor.html

McLeod, S. (2011). *Bandura - Social learning theory*. Retrieved from http://www.simplypsychology.org/bandura.html

McLeod, S. (2013). *Erik Erikson*. Retrieved from http://www.simplypsychology.org/Erik-Erikson.html

McLuhan, M. (1994). *Understanding media: The extensions of man*. Cambridge, MA: MIT Press.

McLuhan, M., Fiore, Q., & Agel, J. (1996). *The medium is the massage: An inventory of effects*. San Francisco, CA: HardWired.

Medina, J. (2008). *Brain rules: 12 principles for surviving and thriving at work, home, and school*. Seattle, WA: Pear Press.

Merrifield, L. (2008, February 18-22). *At their service: Making a difference by putting players first* [Video file]. Presented at the Austin Game Developers Conference, Austin, TX.. Retrieved from http://www.gdcvault.com/play/168/At-Their-Service-Making-a

Montessori, M. (1972). *The secret of childhood* (M. J. Costelloe, Trans.) New York, NY: Ballantine Books.

Montessori, M. (1995). *The absorbent mind*. New York, NY: Henry Holt and Company.

Muybridge, E. (1955). *The human figure in motion*. New York, NY: Dover Publications.

Muybridge, E. (1957). *Animals in motion*. New York, NY: Dover Publications.

Nass, C., Steuer, J., & Tauber, E. R. (1994) Computers are social actors. In *CHI '94 Proceedings of the SIGCHI Conference on Human Factors in Computing Systems*. New York, NY: ACM.

Nass, C. I., & Yen, C. (2010). *The man who lied to his laptop: What machines teach us about human relationships*. New York, NY: Penguin Group.

National Association for the Education of Young Children and the Fred Rogers Center for Early Learning and Children's Media at Saint Vincent College (2012, January). Technology and interactive media as tools in early childhood programs serving children from birth through age 8. Retrieved from http://www.naeyc.org/files/naeyc/file/positions/PS_technology_WEB2.pdf

National Institute for Play. (n.d.) *Pattern of Play* [Website]. Retrieved from http://www.nifplay.org/science/pattern-play/

Negroponte, N. (1995). *Being digital*. New York, NY: Alfred A. Knopf, Inc.

Nietzsche, F. W. (1977). *The portable Nietzsche* (W. Kaufmann, Trans.). New York, NY: Penguin Books.

Norman, D. A. (1990). *The design of everyday things*. New York, NY: Doubleday.

O'Donohue, W., & Ferguson, K. E. (2001) *The psychology of B. F. Skinner*. Thousand Oaks, CA: SAGE Publications Inc.

Orenstein, P. (2011). *Cinderella ate my daughter: Dispatches from the front lines of the new girlie-girl culture*. New York, NY: HarperCollins Publishers.

Owen, J. (2009, June 24). *Bone flute is oldest instrument, study says*. Retrieved from http://news.nationalgeographic.com/news/2009/06/090624-bone-flute-oldest-instrument.html

Oxford University. (2005) *New Oxford American Dictionary, 2nd edition*. NY: Oxford University Press.

Packer, B. L., Slater, J., & Wilson, D. E. (Eds.). (2003). *Collected works of Ralph Waldo Emerson, Volume VI: The conduct of life*. Cambridge, MA: Belknap Press.

Panskeep, J. (1998). *Affective neuroscience: The foundations of human and animal emotions*. New York, NY: Oxford University Press.

Paoletti, J. B. (2012). *Pink and blue: Telling the boys from the girls in America.* Bloomington, IN: Indiana University Press.

Papalia, D. E., Olds, S. W., & Feldman, R. D. (2009). *Human development.* New York, NY: McGraw-Hill.

Parker, I. (2013, January 29). *Mapping the future of digital learning games.* Retrieved from http://www.instituteofplay.org

Pearce, J. C. (1977). *Magical child: Rediscovering nature's plan for our children.* New York, NY: Dutton.

Pearce, J. C. (1992). *Evolution's end: Claiming the potential of our intelligence.* New York, NY: HarperCollins Publishers.

Pellegrini, A. D. (2008). *The recess debate. A disjuncture between educational policy and scientific research. American Journal of Play,* 1(2).

Piaget, J., & Garcia, R. (1991) *Toward a logic of meanings.* P. M. Davidson (Ed.). Hillsdale, NJ: Lawrence Erlbaum Associates, Inc.

Pijpers, R., & Bosch, N. V. (Eds.). (2014). *Positive digital content for kids: Experts reveal their secrets.* Ludwigshafen: POSCON & Mijn Kind Online.

Piraro, D. (1992). *The best of Bizarro.* San Francisco, CA: Chronicle Books.

Piraro, D. (1994). *The best of Bizarro: Volume II.* San Francisco, CA: Chronicle Books.

Plato. (2004) *Republic* (C. D. C. Reeve, Trans.). Indianapolis: Hackett Pub. Co.

Play quotes (n.d.). Retrieved from http://www.museumofplay.org/education/education-and-play-resources/play-quotes

Postman, N. (1994). *The disappearance of childhood.* New York, NY: Vintage Books.

Prensky, M. (September 01, 2001). Digital Natives, Digital Immigrants Part 1. *On the Horizon,* 9(5). doi: 10.1108/10748120110424816

Pritchard, A. (2009). *Ways of learning: Learning theories and learning styles in the classroom.* New York, NY: Routledge.

Ratcliffe, S. (2011). *Oxford Treasury of Sayings and Quotations.* Oxford: Oxford University Press.

Raymo, C. (2004, July 11). *Smiling faces, orbs of fire.* [Web log post]. Retrieved from http://www.sciencemusings.com/2004/07/smiling-faces-orbs-of-fire.html

Reader's Digest Association. (1997). *Quotable Quotes: Wit & wisdom for every occasion.* Pleasantville, NY: Reader's Digest Association.

Reader's Digest Association. (2013). *Quotable quotes: All new wit & wisdom from the greatest minds of our time.* White Plains, NY: Reader's Digest Association.

Reeves, B., & Nass, C. I. (1996). *The media equation: How people treat computers, television, and new media like real people and places.* Stanford, CA: CSLI Publications.

Research Brief: Parenting and child development. (2016, March). Retrieved from http://www.kronkosky.org/Research/Foundation-Research/DownloadReasearch?f=678

Richardson, J. A. (1977). *The complete book of cartooning.* Englewood Cliffs, NJ: Prentice-Hall.

Robbins, T. (1976). *Even cowgirls get the blues.* New York, NY: Bantam Books.

Rogers, C. R. (1969) *Freedom to learn.* Colombus, OH: Charles E. Merrill Publishing Company.

Rogers, F. (2003) The world according to Mister Rogers: Important things to remember. New York, NY: Hyperion Books.

Rogers, F. (n.d.). *Fred Rogers & Us*: Children's Museum of Pittsburgh. Retrieved from https://pittsburghkids.org/exhibits/fred-rogers-us

Russ, S. W. (2004). *Play in child development and psychotherapy: Toward empirically supported practice.* New York, NY: Routledge.

Saltzman, M. (1999). *Game design: Secrets of the sages.* Indianapolis, IN: Brady Publishing.

Samual, A. (2015, November 4). Parents: Reject technology shame. *The Atlantic.* Retrieved from http://www.theatlantic.com/technology/archive/2015/11/why-parents-shouldnt-feel-technology-shame/414163/

Sapir, E. (1985). *Selected writings in language, culture and personality.* D. G. Mandelbaum (Ed.). Berkeley, CA: University of California Press.

Schell, J. (2008). *The art of game design: A book of lenses.* Amsterdam: Elsevier/Morgan Kaufmann.

Scott, J., & Borgman, J. (2000). *Humongous Zits: A Zits treasury.* Kansas City, MO: Andrews McMeel Publishing.

Scott, J., & Borgman, J. (2001). *Big honkin' Zits: A Zits treasury.* Kansas City, MO: Andrews McMeel Publishing.

Scott, J., & Borgman, J. (2003). *Zits Supersized: A Zits treasury.* Kansas City, MO: Andrews McMeel Publishing.

Scott, J., & Borgman, J. (2004). *Random Zits.* Kansas City, MO: Andrews McMeel Publishing.

Scott, J., & Borgman, J. (2006). Crack of noon: A Zits treasury. Kansas City, MO: Andrews McMeel Publishing.

Sears, W., Sears, M., Sears, R., & Sears, J. (2013). *The baby book, revised edition: Everything you need to know about your baby from birth to age two.* New York, NY: Little, Brown and Company.

Seldin, T. (n.d.). *Montessori 101: Some basic information that every Montessori parent should know.* Retrieved from https://issuu.com/timseldin/docs/montessori_101___guided_tour?e=1891855/1937928

Seligman, M. E., Reivich, K., Jaycox, L., & Gillham, J. (1996). *The optimistic child.* New York, NY: HarperCollins Publishers.

Sesame Workshop. (2013). Best practices: Designing touch tablet experiences for preschoolers. Retrieved from http://www.sesameworkshop.org/wp_install/wp-content/uploads/2013/04/Best-Practices-Document-11-26-12.pdf

Sexual health: Considering testosterone therapy to help you feel younger and more vigorous as you age? Know the risks before you make your decision. (2015, April 1). Retrieved from http://www.mayoclinic.org/testosterone-therapy/ART-20045728

Shepard, R. N. (1990). *Mind sights: Original visual illusions, ambiguities, and other anomalies, with a commentary on the play of mind in perception and art.* New York, NY: W. H. Freeman and Company.

Shulevitz, U. (1985). *Writing with pictures: How to write and illustrate children's books.* New York, NY: Watson-Guptill Publications.

Skinner, B. F. (1965). *Science and human behavior.* New York, NY: The Free Press.

Smith, D., & Clark, S. (1999). *Disney: The first 100 years.* New York, NY: Disney Editions.

Springer, S. P., & Deutsch, G. (1997). *Left brain, right brain: Perspectives from cognitive neuroscience.* New York, NY: W. H. Freeman and Company.

Stafford, S. H. (2006, November 20,). *MI: District gets physical with reading.* Retrieved from http://www.centerforpubliceducation.org/Main-Menu/Success-stories/Urban-success-stories-/MI-District-gets-physical-with-reading.html

Storr, A. (1993). *Music and the mind.* New York, NY: Ballantine Books.

Surprise. (n.d.). In Oxford dictionaries. Retrieved from http://www.oxforddictionaries.com/us/definition/american_english/surprise

Swann, A. (1990). *How to understand and use design and layout.* Cincinnati, OH: North Light Books.

Sweet, E. M. (2014, December 22). Should toy marketing be gender neutral? *The New York Times.* Retrieved from http://www.nytimes.com/roomfordebate/2014/12/22/why-should-toys-come-in-pink-and-blue/how-did-toys-get-stereotyped-by-sex

Szwed, J. (2004). *So what: The life of Miles Davis.* New York, NY: Simon & Schuster Paperbacks.

Taylor, S. E. (2002). *The tending instinct: How nurturing is essential for who we are and how we live.* New York, NY: Times Books.

Than, K. (2008. July 2). *Stone age art caves may have been concert halls.* Retrieved from http://news.nationalgeographic.com/news/2008/07/080702-cave-paintings.html

Thomas, F., & Johnston, O. (1981). *Disney animation: The illusion of life.* New York, NY: Abbeville Press.

Thomas, F., & Johnston, O. (1987). *Too funny for words: Disney's greatest sight gags.* New York, NY: Abbeville Press.

Thomas, J. (2006) *The art of portrait drawing: Learn the essential techniques of the masters.* Cincinnati, OH: North Light Books.

Thoreau, H. D. (2009). *The journal of Henry David Thoreau, 1837–1861.* New York, NY: The New York Review Book.

Timeline 1940–1949: The LEGO Group History. (n.d.). Retrieved from http://www.lego.com/en-us/aboutus/lego-group/the_lego_history/1940

Toliver, W. (2004). *The little giant encyclopedia of inspirational quotes.* New York, NY: Sterling Pub. Co.

van der Post, L. (1975). *Jung and the story of our time.* New York, NY: Pantheon Books.

Vygotsky, L. S. (1978). *Mind in society: The development of higher psychological processes.* M. Cole, (Ed.). Cambridge, MA: Harvard University Press.

Waldrop, M. M. (1996, October 31). Dee Hock on management: Dee Hock's management principles, in his own words. *Fast Company.* Retrieved from http://www.fastcompany.com/27454/dee-hock-management

Watterson, B. (1988). *The essential Calvin and Hobbes: A Calvin and Hobbes treasury.* Kansas City, MO: Andrews and McMeel.

Watterson, B. (1990). *The authoritative Calvin and Hobbes: A Calvin and Hobbes treasury.* Kansas City, MO: Andrews and McMeel.

Watterson, B. (1992). *The indispensable Calvin and Hobbes: A Calvin and Hobbes treasury.* Kansas City, MO: Andrews and McMeel.

Watts, A. H. (1975). *The nature of man: The essence of Alan Watts.* Berkeley, CA: Celestial Arts.

Wieners, B. (2011, December 15). Lego is for girls: Inside the world's most admired toy company's effort to finally click with girls. *Bloomberg Businessweek.* Retrieved from http://www.bloomberg.com/news/articles/2011-12-14/lego-is-for-girls

Wilhelm, R., & Baynes, C. F. (1967). *The I Ching or book of changes.* Princeton, NJ: Princeton University Press.

Williams, R. [Richard]. (2009). *The animator's survival kit.* London: Faber and Faber Limited.

Williams, R. [Robin]. (2015). *The non-designer's design book: Design and typographic principles for the visual novice.* San Francisco, CA: Peachpit Press. Wilson, F. R. (1998). *The hand: How its use shapes the brain, language, and human culture.* New York, NY: Pantheon Books.

Wolf, G. (1996, February 1). Steve Jobs: The next insanely great thing. *Wired Magazine.* Retrieved from http://www.wired.com/1996/02/jobs-2/

Wolf, M. (Ed.). (2014). *LEGO studies: Examining the building blocks of a transmedial phenomenon.* New York, NY: Routledge.

Woll, C. (2012, September 17). *The Role of story in mobile games.* Session presented at Game Design Conference, San Francisco, CA.

Words of art: Inspiring quotes from the masters. (2013). Avon, MA: Adams Media.

Wright, W. (2006). *What's next in game design?* Keynote presentation at 2006 Game Developers Conference [Video file]. Retrieved from http://www.gdcvault.com/play/1014845/Will-Wright-Keynote-What-s

Yates, K. A. (2009). When "keeping it real" goes right. In K. A. Wisniewski (Ed.), *The comedy of Dave Chappelle: Critical essays.* Jefferson, NC: McFarland & Company.

Yelland, N. (1999, June 01,). Technology as Play. *Early Childhood Education Journal, 26*(4).

Index

Specific ages are indexed under the following entries: babies (0–1); toddlers (2); young children (3–6); children (7–9); tweens (10–12); teens (13–17).

S